Archetype

Anthony Stevens

Archetype

A natural history of the self

Routledge
Taylor & Francis Group
LONDON AND NEW YORK

First published in 1982
by Routledge & Kegan Paul Ltd

Published 2016 by Routledge
4 Park Square, Milton Park, Abingdon, Oxon OX14 4RN
605 Third Avenue, New York, NY 10017

First issued in hardback 2016

Routledge is an imprint of the Taylor & Francis Group, an informa business

British Library Cataloguing in Publication Data
A catalogue record for this book is available from the British Library

ISBN 13: 978-1-138-17710-9 (hbk)
ISBN 13: 978-0-415-05220-7 (pbk)

This book is dedicated to PETER FRANCIS SCOTT
and is in loving memory of HONOR IRENE CHAMPERNOWNE

Contents

Acknowledgments

I would like to express my thanks to the following: to Basic Books Inc., New York, and the Hogarth Press, London, for permission to quote from *Attachment and Loss: Volume 1, Attachment* by John Bowlby; to Harcourt Brace Jovanovich Inc., New York, and Methuen & Co., London, for permission to quote from *Behind the Mirror* by Konrad Lorenz; to the Princeton University Press, Princeton, NJ, and Routledge & Kegan Paul Ltd, London, for permission to quote from the *Collected Works of C. G. Jung*; and to Random House Inc., New York, and Routledge & Kegan Paul Ltd, London, for permission to quote from *Memories, Dreams, Reflections* edited by Aniela Jaffe.

I am also indebted to Dr Edward F. Edinger, the C. G. Jung Foundation for Analytical Psychology, New York, and G. P. Putnam's Sons, New York, for permission to use the diagram on page 93; and to Dr Paul MacLean and the Toronto University Press, Toronto, for permission to reproduce figure 13.4 which appears on page 263.

I am extremely grateful to Dr Spyros Doxiadis of the Institute of Child Health, Athens, to the children and staff of the Metera Babies' Centre, to Dr John Bowlby and fellow members of the London Attachment Seminars, and to my patients in London and Devon for providing me with the rich experiences out of which this book has grown. My special thanks are due to Cliff, Colin, Tancred and Hamish.

A note to the reader

In order to reach a wide audience I have done my best to eschew jargon. Of course, it has not been possible to avoid special terms altogether, but where I have felt compelled to use them I have defined them in the text where they first occur. Should your memory prove fallible, you can rediscover their meaning by referring to the Glossary at the end of the book.

If you are deterred by theories, you may like to skip Part I and pass straight from the Personal introduction to the archetype of the family, though I naturally hope you will resist the temptation to do so since the material contained between pages 21 and 76 is, I believe, itself fascinating and important; it is, moreover, crucial to an understanding of how the microhistory of the individual is grafted on to the macrohistory of our species, and it provides the foundation on which my whole argument stands (or falls).

Personal introduction

On the slopes of Mount Parnis just outside Athens there is an unusual institution for unwanted children called the Metera Babies' Centre. The name 'Metera' ('mother' in modern Greek) was chosen carefully, for it expresses the conviction of those who work there that a residential centre for the care of infants can only succeed if it performs the functions of a mother. From the time that the Metera opened in the mid-1950s, its declared policy has been to provide every child, for as long as the Metera is its home, with a substitute mother with whom he might share that warm, intimate, continuous relationship which is now known to be indispensable to normal human development.

When I went to Greece in 1966 to study the formation of attachment bonds in infancy, there were as many nurses in residence at the Metera as there were children: approximately 100 infants were being looked after by a staff of 36 qualified and 60 student nurses, all products of the Centre's own School of Nursing. But despite these fairly large numbers, it was a friendly, intimate place. The soulless anonymity of traditional institutions was avoided by splitting up the community of nurses and children into small, relatively autonomous groups, each centred on one of eight separate pavilions. Each pavilion contained twelve children. Their cots were arranged in four compartments, which were divided from one another by partitions about three feet high. To each compartment was allocated one of the four graduate nurses who lived in the pavilion with the children. A graduate was known as a mother-nurse, and she was expected to devote herself exclusively to the three children in her compartment or 'box', as the nurses preferred to call it, using the English word.

At that time, the Metera had an English matron, who was a firm believer in the box system. Not only did she appoint a mother-nurse to each box, but she also allocated two student nurses to assist the mother-nurse specifically in the care of her three children. A brisk, upright lady with aquiline features, quick bird-like movements and sharp, twinkling eyes, the matron resembled a vigilant, though not unkindly, eagle: on her daily rounds, she would swoop down on each pavilion, checking that it was working to her satisfaction, and administering sharp pecks to any nurse she found attending to children other than those from her own box. As a result, I noted, both medical and senior nursing staff appeared satisfied that each child was receiving intensive care from a small number of women – much as a normal family-reared Greek child might be looked after by its mother, grandmother and eldest sister. It seemed an admirable arrangement.

However, within days of beginning my research it became clear to me that the only occasion on which the box system seemed to work satisfactorily was when the matron made her rounds. As soon as she took off from a pavilion, her neat theoretical arrangement invariably dissolved into a general free-for-all. Nurses and children became interchangeable to an extraordinary degree, so that during the course of a few hours – provided that the matron remained in the fastness of her eyrie – each nurse came into contact with practically every child in the pavilion. A form of maternal Marxism reigned in which caretaking was shared – from each according to her ability, to each according to his need. If a child had to be fed, comforted or have its nose wiped, as often as not it was the nearest nurse with her hands free who coped with the situation, and not the nurse officially designated as 'mother'.

I decided to keep a careful check on what was happening, and found that in one month every child at the Metera, irrespective of the pavilion he was in, had been fed, on average, by fifteen different nurses, bathed by seven nurses, changed by fifteen nurses, put to bed in the evening by ten nurses, and lifted again in the morning by ten different nurses. It was evident that these infants were receiving multiple mothering on a scale which was possibly unprecedented in the existence of our species. Never in the whole history of mothering had so few received so much from so many.

This discovery excited me. For I realized that I had fallen into a situation which was perfectly set up to test two rival theories which were then the subject of heated and unresolved controversy. It was a stroke of good fortune such as seldom occurs in the life-time of a researcher, and when I went to the Metera I had no inkling that it was about to happen to me. Let me explain.

The theories in dispute related to the manner in which children may be supposed to become attached to those who look after them. Right up to the end of the 1950s, it had been accepted that infant attachment behaviour, like practically all other forms of human behaviour, was learned through a form of 'operant conditioning' associated with natural rewards and punishments, the caretaker's presence and nurturant behaviour being experienced as rewarding, and her absence or lack of maternal attention being experienced as punishing. As with most theories espoused by academic psychologists at that time, the primary reward held to be responsible for eliciting infant attachment behaviour was food, and, as a consequence, it came to be known as the 'cupboard love' theory. Practically all psychologists, psychiatrists and psychoanalysts accepted the cupboard love theory as accounting for the facts, and it went unquestioned for decades.

Then, in 1958, an English psychiatrist called Dr John Bowlby published a now famous paper entitled 'The nature of the child's tie to his mother', in which he attacked the cupboard love theory and suggested instead that infants become attached to their mothers, and mothers to their infants, not so much through learning as by *instinct*. Mothers and infants had no need to learn to love one another: they were innately *programmed* to do so from birth. The formation of mother-infant attachment bonds is a direct expression of the genetic heritage of our species.

It would be inaccurate to describe the academic reaction to Bowlby's paper as one of critical interest; fury would be closer to the mark. His theory outraged too many cherished assumptions for it to be received with equanimity. In the first place, the term 'instinct' had become unacceptable to academic psychologists, who insisted that innate factors played little or no part in the behaviour of human beings. And secondly, in advancing his theory, Bowlby drew parallels between human attachment behaviour and that observed among mammals and birds. Such comparisons, many argued, were unwarranted, since human behaviour is too plastic, and too susceptible to environmental factors, to bear any resemblance to the behaviour of lesser breeds.

It was the second factor that most upset the academics, who objected to the readiness with which Bowlby borrowed concepts from the relatively new science of *ethology* (the study of behaviour patterns in organisms living in their natural environments) and applied them to human psychology. But Bowlby was adamant that such comparisons between different species were biologically justifiable; and in attacking the cupboard love theory he was able to cite many examples from the ethological literature of the existence of strong infant-mother bonds which had been formed through mechanisms bearing no relation to feeding gratification and which developed in the absence of any conventional rewards such as those postulated by the learning theorists.

By the time I took up my research appointment at the Metera, however, several workers had published findings which were in line with Bowlby's theory. For example, Dr Mary Ainsworth (1963) of Virginia University and Dr Rudolf Schaffer and Dr P. E. Emerson (1964) of Glasgow independently described the formation of strong attachments by human infants to familiar persons who played no part in feeding them. But, on the whole, the denizens of University Departments of

Psychology throughout the world remained resistant to Bowlby's ideas, preferring to believe with Freud's eminent daughter, Anna, that a human child *learns* to display attachment to his mother because she is his primary source of oral satisfaction: 'When its powers of perception permit the child to form a conception of the person through whose agency it is fed,' she wrote (1946), 'its love is transferred to the provider of the food.' This view had been fully endorsed by the American psychiatrists, Dollard and Miller, who wrote (1950):

> In the first year of life, the human infant has cues from its mother associated with the primary reward of feeding on more than 2,000 occasions. Meanwhile the mother and other people are ministering to many other needs. In general there is a correlation between the absence of people and the prolongation of suffering from hunger, cold, pain and other drives; the appearance of a person is associated with a reinforcing reduction of the drive. Therefore the proper conditions are present for the infant to learn to attach strong reinforcement value to a variety of cues from the nearness of mother and other adults. . . . [It] seems reasonable to advance the hypothesis that the human motives of sociability, dependence, need to receive and show affection, and desire for approval from others are learned.

This view was still extremely influential.

These, then, were the rival theories prevailing at the time. Although Bowlby's 'ethological' theory was gaining ground, the cupboard love theory still had the greater number of adherents. It was against the background of this controversy that I recognized my luck in arriving at the Metera Babies' Centre at that particular time. I saw at once that the richly polymatric (=many-mothered) environment prevailing at the Metera would provide me with a unique opportunity to test the relative validity of the two theories.

My reasoning ran like this: if the cupboard love theory were valid it must follow that multiply-mothered children would form multiple attachments. A Metera child would become attached to all the nurses who regularly cared for him. Moreover, the nurses to whom a child attached himself would necessarily be arranged in a hierarchy of preference, the nurses at the top of the hierarchy being those who fed him the most.

If, on the other hand, Bowlby's theory were valid, the outcome would be very different. In the circumstances in which our species evolved (what ethologists call 'the environment of evolutionary adaptedness') the women responsible for an infant's care would be few in number (usually the mother and perhaps a close relative) and the innate mechanism controlling the development of attachment would tend to focus on only one or two figures. The tendency for an innately determined behavioural system to take as its goal a particular individual or a small group of individuals Bowlby believed to be a biological characteristic of our species, and he gave it a name: he called it *monotropy*. If Bowlby was right, therefore, a Metera child would not become attached to the great majority of his caretakers as the cupboard love theory would predict, but would come to demonstrate a clear preference for one nurse above all the rest.

It was wonderfully straightforward. All I had to do was select a group of infants and make regular observations of their social progress. Quickly I chose twenty-four unattached children, aged three months and above, and began recording their interactions with their nurses. Within six months I had collected enough data to establish beyond doubt that far from becoming attached to all their nurses, three-quarters of the children became specifically attached to one nurse, who was preferred way above all the rest. Even by the strictest statistical criteria (allowing for the small size of the sample) Bowlby's monotropic principle was confirmed.

Most children established their preference by eight or nine months of age (i.e. at about the same age that family-reared children show unequivocal signs of specific attachment to, and conscious recognition of, their mothers). Six of the children did not become specifically attached, it is true, but this was probably because most of them left the Metera for adoption before they reached the age at which specific attachment becomes obvious.

Worse still for the cupboard love theory was my finding that no less than a third of the children became attached to nurses who had done little or nothing in the way of routine caretaking of the child before the attachment bond had been formed. Thereafter, the nurse invariably did a lot more for the child – usually because she came to reciprocate the attachment, but also because the child would often refuse to be tended by any other nurse when 'his' nurse was in the pavilion. The crucial factors leading up to the pairing off of a particular nurse with a particular child were not so much linked with routine feeding as with play, physical contact and social interaction; the whole process was more akin to falling in love through mutual delight and attraction than to 'operant conditioning'. I was also fascinated to discover that in few cases did a child become primarily attached to the nurse whom the matron had officially designated as his 'mother-nurse'. Attachments, it seems, cannot be made to order. One cannot legislate in matters of the heart.

The intellectual consequences of this research were for me far more important than any contribution that my work may have made to the sum of human knowledge. It convinced me that human psychology, like animal psychology, is dependent on genetic as well as environmental factors. We are programmed from birth to form attachments; and, as I shall suggest in chapter 6, I believe that the programme operates on the *a priori* assumption that when our birth takes place it will be into the bosom of a family, where the primary caretaker and principal object of attachment will be mother.

Far from wishing to lend my voice to the chorus raised in protest against the application of ethological concepts to the study of human behaviour, I began to see the ethological approach as the means by which psychology might liberate itself from the behaviourists and neobehaviourists in whose thraldom it had languished for over half a century, and it made me want to cheer.

In my twenties, I had spent four precious years of my life in the mainly dispiriting study of academic ('experimental') psychology. Like many idealistic young people, I had gone to the university believing that 'the proper study of mankind is man' and that the modern science of psychology must hold some of the keys; and like most of them, I suspect, I was disappointed. Psychology, we discovered, possessed few keys, and the doors which they opened led into dismal chambers. Despite more than 70 years of effort, psychology had still fallen short of its ambition to become a respectable science, largely because it lacked any sound foundation on which to base itself, but also because it attempted to emulate the wrong models, conceiving of itself more as an offshoot of physics than as an integral part of biology. Consequently, decades of experiment had yielded a wealth of disparate findings, but, as yet, there existed no coherent thread to tie them all together.

Possessing no solid basis in biology, psychology could only lend itself the semblance of coherence by adopting the quasi-theological subterfuge of establishing dogmas that it became heresy for the faithful to deny. In the psychology laboratories and lecture rooms of university departments throughout the Western world a form of neobehaviourist fundamentalism prevailed which it was academic suicide to question. Thus, it was an article of faith that organisms should be studied as 'blank slates' (i.e. unstructured, unprogrammed, owing little to heredity and practically everything to experience) and that no determining principles existed in life apart from a handful of 'drives' and the famous 'laws of learning'.

As a student, first at Reading University and later at Oxford, where I went to study medicine as well as psychology, I found all this wearying. Because of the obsession with physics – a model only appropriate to the study of material phenomena devoid of consciousness, feeling or volition – we were discouraged by our tutors from the use of taboo words like 'mind' and 'psyche', and taught to eschew all talk of 'inner' or 'mental' processes as the correlates of observable behaviour. Nor were we allowed to attribute 'purpose' to behavioural responses: instead we must repeat the ritually prescribed texts which said that responses were 'emitted' purely as a means of gaining gastronomic or sexual rewards, or for the avoidance of pain. Moreover, the use of introspection as a research tool was scorned, since it was held that little value could be placed on anything that people 'said' about their 'experiences'. Behaviour was what counted – especially behaviour that could be quantified and analysed statistically; and the laws governing the acquisition and 'emission' of learned responses, with scant regard for *the nature of the organism* emitting them, were the Nicene Creed of psychology. Indeed, the very idea that anything so structured as human or animal *nature* could exist, with inherent laws of its own, was anathema, and in many quarters it still is.

As I completed my research project at the Metera, therefore, I felt greatly encouraged. The thought that the ethologists could help one to throw off the ideological straitjacket in which the behaviourists had bound us gave me cause to rejoice. And, as I was soon to discover, I was not alone in this. As the 1960s drew to a close, ethology achieved a tremendous popular success, which persisted throughout the 1970s. Books by Konrad Lorenz, the father of modern ethology, went to the top of the bestseller lists, while the works of such writers as Desmond Morris and Robert Ardrey brought an appetizing blend of ethological fact and speculation to a vast and appreciative audience. There was, apparently, no shortage of people who were intrigued by the thought that human nature and animal nature were linked through a common ancestry and that many features of contemporary human behaviour might be understood in terms of their evolutionary origins.

It was clear that the application of ethology to human psychology need not be restricted to the development of intimacy between mothers and children. There were equally good reasons for examining the possibility that we are innately territorial, inclined to mate for life, potentially co-operative with allies and hostile to foes, prone to congregate in hierarchically organized communities, and so on, much in the same way as many other mammalian and primate species. To many this seemed a highly original attempt to understand the extraordinary ways in which human beings conduct their affairs. It was both stimulating and amusing to stand back and view ourselves as one animal among many with a repertoire of behaviours which are at once characteristic of our species and at the same time traceable to earlier evolutionary forms.

Easily the most important contribution of ethology was the brilliant demonstration that behaviour can be studied *comparatively* – in precisely the same way as anatomy. Just as two bones, the radius and ulna, have been shown by anatomists to be homologous in the wing of the bird, the foreleg of the mammal, and the forearm of man, so ethologists began to trace the evolution of patterns of behaviour by describing homologous behaviour patterns in different animal species of ascending phylogenetic (i.e. evolutionary) complexity. This crucial insight – that all species have behavioural characteristics which, if we have eyes to see them, are as distinctive and as classifiable as their physical characteristics – has placed us in an exciting position: it becomes possible at last to trace the evolutionary history and describe the essential parameters of human nature. If this can be achieved, then psychology as a science will indeed have arrived. Moreover, such an achievement would inevitably be of profound significance for all branches and applications of the human sciences, not least for psychiatry, where it would permit us to approach a precise definition (which has eluded us until now) of what is 'normal'.

Hitherto, psychiatry, no less than psychology, has lacked a biological foundation: its obsession with ontogeny (individual development) and individual psychopathology has in the past tended to blind psychiatrists to the truth that mental disturbance can be properly understood only against a background of phylogeny (the development of the species). Increasingly, it has seemed to me entirely appropriate to find new hope for the future of my profession (and of our species) in the unifying perspective which the phylogenetic dimension can offer. Ever since the second half of the nineteenth century, when psychology left its parent philosophy to start an independent life of its own, its progress had been hampered by the same territorial, political, and hierarchical feuds which afflict all human attempts at co-operative endeavour. As, over the last hundred years, their separate disciplines grew up, academic psychologists, psychiatrists, analysts of various schools, sociologists, anthropologists, and so on, all went their several ways, staking out territories of their own choosing (since human beings can be territorial about *ideas* as well as property and land) which they proceeded to defend with a tenacity which would shame a tank of cichlid fish. In contrast to this militant disarray, what more hopeful prospect could there be than the inauguration of a unified science of humanity?

Unfortunately, few psychologists, psychiatrists or sociologists appeared ready to share this idealistic vision. When they addressed their attention to the ethological movement, their utterances varied from polite scepticism to frank hostility. I tended at first to put this down to sour grapes, especially in the case of the psychologists. It was, after all, too galling for them to admit that, having devoted decades to the systematic study of behaviour, their efforts were being brilliantly surpassed by an upstart group of zoologists who enjoyed themselves observing the carryings on of creatures *living in the wild*: not students watching tachistoscopes and pressing electric buttons in psychology laboratories; not rats learning mazes under strictly controlled conditions; but birds and mammals defending territories, courting partners, and rearing young, without any controls whatsoever. It wasn't fair. But much later I realized that their resistance was essentially *doctrinal*. For, like the nineteenth-century theologians whom they in some ways resembled, twentieth-century psychologists clung doggedly to their assertion that the differences between animals and men were so fundamental as to invalidate any inferences which might be drawn from the behaviour of one to the psychology of the other (though an exception was made, for some reason, in the case of the unfortunate Norway rat, where the 'laws of learning' derived from the endlessly repeated maze performances of that sorely tried creature were applied enthusiastically to students by educational psychologists in our schools and universities). Alone among contemporary scientists, psychologists still argued as if they believed in the 'special creation' of our species – that at the moment of our emergence from the forests a *fulguratio* occurred, whereby the *Ruah Elohim* (the Breath of God) inflated us, producing a complete transformation which eradicated forever all but a mere anatomical continuity between ourselves and the rest of the animal kingdom. It was as if Charles Darwin had never existed.

However, Bowlby remained undaunted by the 'flat-earthers' who ignored or denigrated his work. Together with his colleagues (who came to be known collectively as *attachment theorists*), he persevered with his efforts to elucidate the innate response patterns which he held to be responsible for mediating the formation of attachment between mothers and infants. He conceived of the growth of attachment as being dependent on a series of goal-directed behavioural systems which operate cybernetically (like electronic systems, through positive and negative feedback) in both mother and child. Thus, response patterns in the child, such as staring, smiling, crying, babbling and laughing, release parental feelings in the mother together with maternal behaviour which is both appropriate and adjusted to the baby's needs. The universal occurrence of such responses left Bowlby in no doubt that they were innate and that they had evolved as a result of their survival value for the species. To those who found it inconceivable that innate behavioural mechanisms could exist in human beings, Bowlby countered that one need have no greater difficulty in accepting the existence of these than in accepting the existence of innately determined physiological or anatomical systems of comparable complexity.

> Just as within the ordinary expectable environment of a species genetic action ensures that a cardiovascular system comes to develop, with its amazingly sensitive and versatile components for controlling blood supply to the tissues in constantly changing conditions of organism and environment, so can we suppose that genetic action ensures that a behavioural system develops, with components of equal or greater sensitivity and versatility for controlling a particular sort of behaviour in conditions that also con-

> stantly change. If instinctive behaviour is regarded as the result of integrated control systems operating within a certain kind of enivironment, therefore, the means whereby they come into being present no special problems – that is, problems no greater than those in respect of physiological systems. (1969)

By making use of the ethological discovery that patterns of behaviour are as much the product of natural selection as anatomical and physiological structures, Bowlby was, in fact, doing no more than affirm and apply an insight originally advanced by Charles Darwin, who wrote: 'Instincts are as important as corporeal structures for the welfare of each species.' A major obstacle to the acceptance of this view had been the difficulty of imagining by what possible means the detailed instructions, or 'programme', required for the organization and expression of instinctive behaviour patterns could be encoded in the genome (the genetic constitution of the individual) and then made available for use in the appropriate circumstances at the right time and place. However, this conceptual problem has become less of an obstacle since the invention of the computer.

The advantage of Bowlby's attachment theory is that it provides simpler and more consistent explanations of the data of human attachment formation than the psychoanalytic and learning theories which preceded it. That attachment theory has subsequently gained many converts and has stood the test of time is due to Bowlby's wisdom in linking it directly to observable phenomena, which has thus rendered the theory susceptible to test and verification. This, together with its basis in control theory and evolution theory has been responsible for drawing developmental psychology into the mainstream of biology, where it rightly belongs.

In 1967 I returned to England to complete my training as a psychiatrist and to write up the results of my research at the Metera for a doctorate at Oxford University. Between admitting patients to hospital, attending ward meetings, conducting outpatient clinics, and writing examinations, I worked away at analysing the mountain of data I had brought back with me in large trunks from Greece. When the final tests of significance had been applied, I was surprised to discover that the statistical findings were far more persuasive than I had dared to expect, and it seemed to me that I had proof of the correctness of Bowlby's theory.

Much gratified, I turned from the analysis of nurse-infant interaction scores and began a detailed study of the typescripts of tape-recorded interviews I had personally conducted with each of the nurses to whom the children in my sample had become attached. Nothing that any of them said conflicted with the observational and statistical data. On the contrary, the data were supported and richly augmented by the nurses' responses to my questions. However, I began to feel uneasy. Although Bowlby was undoubtedly right as far as he went, it seemed to me that his theory did not pay adequate attention to certain aspects of the attachment phenomenon which increasingly I came to see as possessing great significance.

In the course of these interviews I had asked each nurse what she thought it was that had motivated her and her infant to become attached to one another. Without exception, they all replied that it was 'love'. My attempts to probe what they meant by this elusive concept suggested that they used it to describe the subjective emotion of fondness, solicitude and delight which accompanied caresses, kisses, tender words, eye-to-eye contacts, smiles, songs and tickling games. In describing what it was that caused them to love a particular child they talked freely of his personal attractiveness, popularity and charm and of his evident need, enthusiasm and jealousy for themselves. All mention of physiological functions was conspicuously absent from their replies. As far as they were concerned, attachment meant love, and love grew out of the same social, emotional and sensual experiences as those which, persisting and maturing with time, sustained the attachment once it was formed, causing it to become ever more ardent and exclusive.

Although their statements often betrayed their lack of psychological sophistication, much of what the Metera nurses said had a fresh, original quality which, naive as it sounded, possessed the virtue of being uninfluenced by psychoanalytic dogma and secondhand beliefs. Their observations provided me with a timely reminder that attachment is indeed the synonym of love. The precise definition of operational criteria, the calculation of attachment indices and separation protest scores may facilitate the study of social behaviour but cannot encompass that intangible factor which these Greek nurses called 'αγάπη, the subjective experience underlying all mother-infant interactions, prompting their origin, moulding their nature and complexity, and sustaining the bond even when no interactions occur and both partners are separated in space and time. However accurately one observes the outer manifestations of attachment or analyses verbal reports of the experiences involved, sooner or later, one is brought up short before the seemingly insurmountable difficulty of defining the mysterious experience which two lovers, whatever their age or sex, manage to communicate to each other, and of measuring the deep subjective reward which their communion seems to bring.

These thoughts compelled me to acknowledge that there are serious limitations to the application of the ethological approach to human psychology. The Metera nurses had taught me, in their innocence, that if we were not very careful, we could allow ethology to lead us into the same reductive trap as had imprisoned the behaviourists. Preoccupation with the detailed investigation of species-specific behavioural systems, fascinating though such studies can be, might well yield not a unified science of humanity so much as an arid technology which seeks to boil down the infinitely rich phenomena of life to the last innate releasing mechanism. (An inclination towards this tendency has already been demonstrated by the manner in which a growing number of biologists endorse the 'selfish gene' theory of evolution. As Richard Dawkins's book (1976) on the subject unequivocally states it: 'We are survival machines – robot vehicles blindly programmed to preserve the selfish molecules known as genes.')

Though Bowlby is the last man one could ever accuse of aridity or inhumanity, there are ethical problems involved in conceiving of a mother and her child as units in a cybernetic system – apart from the fact that it makes them sound uncomfortably like the targets of warring missiles. By concentrating on the behavioural processes through which attachments are formed, it is easy to forget that the child does not experience his mother as a mere behavioural sequence with punishing or rewarding attributes but as a person, an indispensable 'other', with recognizable features and personality characteristics which are uniquely precious to him.

Take, for example, the ethological interpretation of staring and smiling in infancy, both of which are regarded as 'sign stimuli' which release nurturant behaviour in the mother. The baby's smile has a powerful impact, which a nursing mother finds deeply gratifying – particularly when accompanied by steady visual regard – and attachment theorists conceive of this as one of nature's ways of rewarding her for the care and attention she provides. As K. S. Robson (1967) has put it: 'Nature has been wise in making both eye-to-eye contact and the social smile . . . [for they] foster positive maternal feelings and sense of payment for "services rendered". . . . Hence, though a mother's response to these achievements may be an illusion, from an evolutionary point of view it is an illusion with survival value.'

This is but one of many possible illustrations of the 'reductiveness' of a rigorously ethological approach to human psychology. For a mother, the joy she experiences when her infant stares at her, smiles and makes rapid movements with arms and legs is no illusion. Indeed, for many a woman such moments are the happiest fulfilment of her life. Who are we to tell her that her pleasure is the consequence of a confidence trick played on her by nature in order to ensure the survival of her child? A behaviouristic reluctance to attribute cognitive and affective experiences to a child smacks of academic blinkerdom and lays bare the spiritual impoverishment of a psychology based on ethology and nothing more.

However brilliant the insights obtained, the trouble with a purely ethological orientation is that it neglects the most wonderful feature of the 'primal relationship' between infant and mother – that it is ruled by Eros. It is perfused with love. The moment the mother-child dyad is formed, Eros is constellated; and it is out of love that ego-consciousness, selfhood and personal identity grow. Knowledge of the world and security in the world are based on loving relatedness, to which Bowlby's behavioural systems contribute the links. We love life inasmuch as love was present in our first great affair.

From a mother's point of view, happiness at the beginnings of personal recognition on the part of her child is entirely appropriate; from the child's, staring is not just a pourboire, an automatic technique for rewarding the care-giver for services rendered, but the means by which he begins to perceive the most important person in his universe, and his smiling and kicking are inextricably tied up with the first dimly perceived experience of delight.

The fact that staring and smiling are innate responses does not mean that they are robot mechanisms totally divorced from conscious experience: even a child of four weeks is 'conscious' when it is not asleep. The degree of consciousness may not be highly differentiated, but it is present nevertheless. Otherwise, when is the 'milestone' of consciousness achieved? Consciousness is not a commodity which up to a certain moment is absent and then suddenly makes a miraculous appearance: it is a capacity like any other which develops and differentiates with maturation. Consequently, it is detrimental to presume that a child's attachment to its mother proceeds through behaviour merely, with no concomitant affective or cognitive components.

Bowlby's use of the term 'attachment' rather than 'love' is understandable in view of his desire for precision and the need to formulate his ideas in a way that renders them amenable to verification by observation and experiment. But we as doctors, psychologists and human beings have, it seems to me, to try and comprehend *what it is like* to be a mother or a child, and how it is that the relationship between them develops the feeling and the quality that it does. We must never forget that the actual *experience* of attachment and the symbolic implications of the mother-child relationship reach far beyond mere behavioural systems and the neuro-physiological mechanisms responsible for their control.

The difference in emphasis between the Metera nurses' reports and the observational data thus presented me with a problem. How was one to bring all aspects of the attachment phenomenon within the ambit of a single theoretical formulation? What I needed was a generally comprehensive theory capable of embracing both the behavioural manifestations of attachment and the inner psychic manifestations occurring in consciousness in the form of symbols, images, intuitions, feelings, words, etc. Bowlby had made an impressive contribution by proposing a theory of human social development which satisfactorily related ontogeny (personal development) to phylogeny (the development of the species), at least as far as normal and pathological patterns of attachment behaviour are susceptible to observation. But the bias of his theory remained behaviouristic and 'outer', for all its recognition of phylogenetically determined mechanisms; and although Bowlby, as a clinician and a psychoanalyst was aware of the importance of inner affective and symbolic processes, neither he nor his followers had done much to explore the direct links between the public manifestations of attachment and their private experiential equivalents. It was evident that the procedural difficulties of achieving such a synthesis were immense. And before such work could begin, a theoretical framework was essential to guide the development of hypotheses and the design of programmes of research. The theory would have to transcend the historic split between mind and matter inaugurated by René Descartes (1596–1650) and would need to be compatible with the laws of evolution. Where was such a theory to be found?

As I thought about this, it occurred to me that the theory I was attempting to formulate had been in existence for over fifty years. I had been anticipated by Carl Gustav Jung! Jung's theory of 'archetypes' operating through a 'collective unconscious' was exactly what I was after. The only problem was that I could not be sure if I believed in it, because I had never quite grasped what he meant.

I knew enough to recognize that Jung's theory was based on an insight which came to him while he was still a colleague of Sigmund Freud's – namely, that there exist in human beings certain psychic and behavioural forms which, while achieving unique expression in each individual, are, at the same time, universally present in all members of our species. I went to the hospital library and opened Part 1 of Volume 9 of Jung's *Collected Works, Archetypes of the Collective Unconscious*. The index referred me to paragraph 3, where I read:

> I have chosen the term 'collective' because this part of the unconscious is not individual but universal; in contrast to the personal psyche, it has contents and modes of behaviour that are more or less the same everywhere and in all individuals. It is, in other words, identical in all men and thus constitutes a common psychic substrate of a suprapersonal nature which is present in every one of us.

That seemed plain enough. But as I read on, I began to suffer from the same confusion that I had experienced on other occasions when I tried to read Jung. Much of what he said was abstruse, and he had a fondness for terms like 'primordial images' which savoured of Lamarckism (i.e.

they suggested that Jung believed in the inheritance of acquired characteristics).

I browsed through all the volumes of the *Collected Works* in the library but, try as I would, I could not be clear in my mind whether Jung's ideas were compatible with a biological view of human nature. I needed authoritative advice and, fortunately, I knew exactly where I could get it. I went to see Irene Champernowne.

Irene had been my analyst for five years when I was a student. She was Jungian to the very depths of her collective unconscious, having analysed and trained with Jung, and his colleague, Toni Wolff, in Zurich during the 1930s and 1940s (when war permitted). Before training as an analyst, Irene had been a lecturer in biology at a college in London, and she still liked to keep abreast of developments in botany and zoology at the same time as running her busy analytic practice.

When my analysis ended, I had lost touch with Irene for some years; then, by chance, we met again at a conference in 1964 and rapidly became the closest of friends. She knew all about my work in Greece and so, with her Jungian and scientific background, she was an obvious person to consult with my theoretical problems.

Interestingly enough, five highly productive years of analysis had not turned me into a Jungian. In the course of our sessions together, Irene would occasionally use a concept or make an assertion whose validity I would question, but I found the whole experience of analysing with her so intensely rewarding, that I was willing to silence my intellectual qualms rather than waste time in theoretical arguments. There can be no doubt that for me Jungian analysis worked. Whether this was because of Irene's natural gifts as a therapist or because of the effectiveness of analytical psychology itself I was not sure, but that my horizons widened, that my capacity to understand myself and others grew, that my ability to share love deepened, that I felt personally enriched, was as evident to me as it was to my nearest and dearest. Indeed, the benefits of the process were so great that I was willing to 'suspend disbelief' over those aspects of Jungian theory which appeared dubious to me. The sensible thing to have done would doubtless have been to read Jung's books and papers during the course of my analysis in order to discover which of his views were acceptable to me, but there was no time to do that *and* complete university courses in academic psychology and medicine during the same period. Needless to say, no provision was made for the study of Jung either at Reading or at Oxford, where, as in most departments of psychology, he was regarded as a crank.

Before going to discuss Jung's theories with Irene, I tried to clarify in my mind what my difficulties were. I knew that Jung had coined the term *collective* unconscious in order to distinguish it from the *personal* unconscious of Freudian psychoanalysis. Whereas Freud had assumed that most of our mental equipment was acquired individually in the course of growing up, Jung asserted that all the essential psychic characteristics that distinguish us as human beings are determined by genetics and are with us from birth. These typically human attributes Jung called archetypes. He regarded archetypes as basic to all the usual phenomena of human life. While he shared Freud's view that personal experience was of critical significance for the development of each individual, he denied that this development was a process of accretion or absorption occurring in an unstructured personality. On the contrary, for Jung, the essential role of personal experience was *to develop what is already there* – to actualize the archetypal potential already present in the psychophysical organism, to activate what is latent or dormant in the very substance of the personality, to develop what is encoded in the genetic make-up of the individual, in a manner similar to that by which a photographer, through the addition of chemicals and the use of skill, brings out the image impregnated in a photographic plate.

It was this, when I looked back on it, that had given me difficulty. Bowlby, and my work at the Metera, had made me more able to appreciate the part that genetic programming could play in co-ordinating complicated sequences of *behaviour*, but what about images and ideas? How could 'primordial images', as Jung often referred to archetypes, be inscribed in the brain and later be 'developed' by experience? It was this which made one suspect that he believed that experiences acquired by one generation could be transmitted genetically to the next – the discredited view originally advanced by the French biologist, Jean-Baptiste Lamarck (1744–1829). Furthermore, the term 'collective unconscious' had always worried me, partly because of its Marxist connotations, but mostly because it seemed to have a mystical ring to it, as if Jung believed in the existence of a 'group mind'. Both these notions struck me as contrary to the accepted teachings of biology, but when I confessed as much to Irene, she made it clear that she did not share my reservations. Far from considering there to be anything 'unbiological' about Jung's theories, she made the heretical assertion that, in her view, they were a good deal more biological than Freud's. Indeed, she gave this as one of her reasons for being a Jungian. Moreover, she believed that Jung had reconciled the highest achievements of the human spirit with the base materials out of which that spirit had evolved. In other words, for her, Jung had built a bridge between Darwin and God!

More than anyone else I have known, Irene Champernowne had a reverence for life which transcended all scientific or theological preconceptions. She was too much in awe of nature to feel disturbed by the thought that human consciousness and the human personality had evolved out of 'lower' animal forms. She saw the great achievements of mankind as extensions of Darwin's evolutionary principle and in no sense as independent of it. But her essentially biological view of the emergence of our species could not diminish her religious conviction that the Almighty had a hand in it all, or that the human spirit was the medium through which creation approached Him.

She was intrigued but not surprised, therefore, by the parallels I drew between the ethological theory of mother-child attachment and Jung's. And in the course of discussing these parallels she said something which hit me with the force of a revelation. Archetypes, she declared, are *biological entities.* They are present, in related forms, throughout the animal kingdom. Like all biological entities they have a natural history: they are subject to the laws of evolution. In other words, *archetypes evolved through natural selection.*

This was a tremendous statement. And it seemed to me that in making it Irene had struck the bedrock of psychology as a biological science. Ethology teaches that each animal species is uniquely equipped with a repertoire of behaviours adapted to the environment in which it evolved. Even allowing for our greater adaptive flexibility, we are no exception. Once one conceives of archetypes as the neuropsychic centres responsible for co-ordinating the behavioural and psychic repertoires of our species in response to whatever environmental circumstances we may encounter, they become directly comparable to the 'innate releasing mechanisms' responsible for Lorenz's 'species-specific patterns of behaviour' and Bowlby's 'goal-corrected behavioural systems'.

Consider a classic ethological example. When a male stickleback encounters a female whose belly is swollen with mature eggs, he courts her by going into a smart zig-zag dance routine. The capacity to perform this famous ballet is built into the nervous system of the courting male: he does not have to attend an aquatic school of dancing to learn the necessary movements because these are already encoded in his brain. All that he needs to cue his performance is the appearance of the appropriate 'sign stimulus' – the swollen belly. No learning theorist ever taught him that 'swollen belly' means 'may I have the pleasure of this dance'. Instead, the sexual archetypal system operating in the male stickleback incorporates the precise instruction, 'Look out for fellow stickleback with swollen belly; when you see it, dance.'

It is not impossible that the maternal archetypal system is similarly programmed. A woman does not learn to love her newborn baby: within moments of delivery, she perceives its helplessness and its need for her, and is moved by irresistible feelings of love, the force of which may come as a shock to her. There is nothing Lamarckian about this. As Jung himself insisted, the term archetype

> is not meant to denote an inherited idea, but rather an inherited mode of functioning, corresponding to the inborn way in which the

> chick emerges from the egg, the bird builds its nest, a certain kind of wasp stings the motor ganglion of the caterpillar, and eels find their way to the Bermudas. In other words, it is a 'pattern of behaviour'. This aspect of the archetype, the purely biological one, is the proper concern of scientific psychology. (*CW* 18, para 1228)

Jung's most effective counter to charges of Lamarckism was the distinction which he made between what he called the *archetype-as-such* and the images, ideas, feelings and behaviours that the archetype gives rise to. The archetype-as-such is the inherent neuropsychic system – the 'innate releasing mechanism' – which is responsible for patterns of behaviour like the zig-zag dance, or patterns of experience like falling in love, when an appropriate member of the same species is encountered in the environment.

My discussion with Irene sent me back to Jung's *Collected Works* with a clearer vision, and the more I read the more convinced I became that there was indeed no incongruity between his archetypal hypothesis and the ethological approach to human psychology. Jung's assertion that the archetype does not 'denote an inherited idea, but rather an inherited mode of functioning' was biologically unimpeachable. It was no more Lamarckian than saying that the male stickleback is innately predisposed to dance when he spies a gravid female, or that a child is innately equipped to speak or to run on two legs. Naturally, the environment, and personal experience of the environment ('learning'), is no less important than the innate predisposition. But the innate predisposition must be there. Otherwise, it would be a matter of relative simplicity to persuade an elephant to dance at the sight of a pregnant stickleback, or a camel to run on two feet.

These conclusions forced me to recognize that for years I had been using two intellectual systems, which I had kept sealed off from one another, because I considered them to be logically incompatible. Thus, I had been using Jungian concepts in treating my patients and ethological concepts in conducting my research. Happily, I now realized that I was free of this dilemma: I could combine Jungian and ethological approaches to patients and research alike and achieve a deeper understanding of both. This insight is the seed out of which this book has grown.

Part I

Archetypes in theory

· 1 ·

Jung and the ethologists

With hindsight one can see that Jung suffered ostracism by the academic establishment not because he was a mystic but because his ideas ran counter to the intellectual currents of his time. The academic psychologists insisted that the behavioural repertoire of human beings was infinitely plastic, almost completely subject to the vicissitudes of the environment, and relatively uninfluenced by innate or predetermined structures, whereas Jung persisted all his life in advancing the opposite view. For Jung, a science of psychology could not be founded on the study of a seemingly infinite variety of individual differences: it was necessary, first of all, to establish the ways in which human beings are all psychologically similar. The question which seems to have been perennially at the back of his mind was, what are the *archetypal features* of human nature? What are the behavioural and psychological characteristics that are specific to us as a species? To him, there were no fundamental incompatibilities between man's spiritual attainments and his lowly biological origins, and pondering such matters induced in him no such feelings of existential nausea as seemed to afflict the academics. On the contrary, he was greatly excited by them, and the vision that these two aspects of human life – the biological and the spiritual – could be united in one scientific theory provided the impetus that drove him to become a psychiatrist in the first place.

In his autobiography, *Memories, Dreams, Reflections*, Jung describes his reaction when, as a medical student, he began reading Krafft-Ebing's *Lehrbuch der Psychiatrie*:

> My heart suddenly began to pound. I had to stand up and draw a deep breath. My excitement was intense, for it had become clear to me, in a flash of illumination, that for me the only possible goal was psychiatry. Here alone the two currents of my interest could flow together and in a united stream dig their own bed. Here was the empirical field common to biological and spiritual facts, which

> I had everywhere sought and nowhere found. Here at last was the place where the collision of nature and spirit became a reality.

With time, Jung's vision was to develop such breadth as to embrace those arch-antagonists science and religion, conceiving man's spiritual life not as a denial of his evolutionary origins but as an expression of them.

So, although ethology and analytical psychology might strike one as odd bedfellows, the incompatibility is in fact more apparent than real. Both are valid approaches to the meaning of behaviour. Where they differ, it is more a matter of observational emphasis than a fundamental contradiction, for while ethology concerns itself with behaviour which is objective, 'outer' and public, analytical psychology deals with behaviour which is subjective, 'inner' and private. The two disciplines, therefore, may be regarded as *antinomies*, in the sense that they are complementary attempts to comprehend the same universally occurring phenomena. An illustrative parallel would be provided by two teams of cartographers who set themselves to map some *terra incognita*, one team recording coastlines, estuaries, rivers, lakes and political boundaries, the other concentrating on the geological structures underlying the visible features of the landscape. The completed maps may present very different aspects to the eye of the beholder, but, in fact, both would represent equally valid interpretations of the same terrain.

The data on which Jung based his theoretical formulations came from an impressive galaxy of sources; but his main insights were derived from a heroic descent into the deeper reaches of his own personality, from a lifetime devoted to the study of mythology, comparative religion and alchemical texts, and from a careful analysis of dreams, phantasies and pictures produced by patients who came from all over the world to consult him. Much of this material has been published in the 18 volumes of Jung's *Collected Works*, and has been summarized and reinterpreted by numerous authorities other than Jung (e.g. Edinger, Henderson, Hochheimer, Jacobi, Jaffe, von Franz, Storr, and Whitmont, to name but a few). I have no wish to reduplicate this already extensive literature. The inspiration for my own approach to Jung's thought arises, as I have described, from my own research and clinical work, and from the discoveries of ethologists and sociobiologists which demonstrate impressive similarities between the behaviour apparent in animal and human societies, and between that of widely differing populations of human beings. The findings of these contemporary scientists dramatically corroborate Jung's previously despised assertion that the human psyche, like the human body, has a definable structure which shares a phylogenetic continuity with the rest of the animal kingdom.

Although it is undeniable that the cultural and environmental circumstances into which a human child is born will influence his behaviour as an adult to a greater extent than is true of members of other mammalian species, it has in the past been too easily forgotten that the forms which human cultures adopt are themselves profoundly influenced by the human genome (i.e. the characteristic genetic structure of homo sapiens). Thus, all cultures, whatever their geographical location or historical era, display a large number of social traits which are in themselves diagnostic of a specifically human culture. These have been independently catalogued by George P. Murdock (1945) and Robin Fox (1975). According to them, no human culture is known which lacked laws about the ownership, inheritance and disposal of property, procedures for settling disputes, rules governing courtship, marriage, adultery, and the adornment of women, taboos relating to food and incest, ceremonies of initiation for young men, associations of men which exclude women, gambling, athletic sports, co-operative labour, trade, the manufacture of tools and weapons, rules of etiquette prescribing forms of greeting, modes of address, use of personal names, visiting, feasting, hospitality, gift-giving, and the performance of funeral rites, status differentiation on the basis of a hierarchical social structure, superstition, belief in the supernatural, religious rituals, soul concepts, myths and legends, dancing, homicide, suicide, homosexuality, mental illness, faith healing, dream interpretation, medicine, surgery, obstetrics, and meteorology. The list could go on.

Knowledge is, after all, a matter of imposing order on chaos. Darwin's contribution is a case in point. He entered a world of infinite biological complexity, where scientists were so overwhelmed by the staggering variety of living forms that they could do little more than describe, draw, classify and annotate. (Since 1758, when formal classification was started by Carolus Linnaeus, 1707–78, almost a million different animal species have been listed.) But in his lifetime Darwin changed all that – through one tremendous insight, namely, that the guiding principle governing the structure and function of all living organisms is, quite simply, the survival of the species.

Similarly, Jung, contemplating the apparently infinite multiformity of symbolisms created by mankind, so richly complicated, so ingeniously diverse, came to realize that they were in fact variations on a number of universally recurrent themes. So, just as Darwin found homologues in anatomy, and the ethologists have demonstrated homologues in patterns of behaviour, so Jung traced homologues in symbols. It was this insight which caused him to formulate the theory of archetypes, which attributed the universal occurrence of homologous symbols and mythologems to the existence of universal structures within the human mind.

True to the same tradition, ethology has proceeded by applying the Darwinian insight to the study of behaviour, describing the behavioural characteristics which distinguish one species from another, analysing the way in which these characteristic behaviour patterns enable each species to meet the exigencies of its environment, and demonstrating the steps by which one pattern of behaviour emerged from another as species underwent genetic evolution. The dramatic achievements of this approach, which have become known to such a huge public through television documentaries and bestsellers of the Morris-Ardrey type, has at last begun to have an impact on psychology – as well as on endocrinology and neurophysiology, where it has proved helpful in studying the effects of hormones and changes in the central nervous system. Moreover, ethology has had a profound and controversial influence on sociology, with the development, in recent years, of a whole new science of *sociobiology*, which views social organization from the standpoint of genetics and ecology (the study of organisms specifically in relation to their environment), elucidating the means by which human and animal populations adapt, through genetic evolution, to the demands of their own peculiar 'ecological niche'.

Naturally, the introduction of genetics into the social sciences has met with hostility from those Romantics who still wish to believe that all human behaviour is the product of social conditioning; but, whether they like it or not, it is clear that genetics has more than its foot in the sociological door. As E. O. Wilson, the most influential of the socibiologists, has written (1978): 'The question of interest is no longer whether human social behaviour is genetically determined; it is to what extent.' Thus sociobiology is hostile to social theories, like those which have dominated university teaching until now, derived from the ideas of savants such as Jean-Jacques Rousseau, Karl Marx, or Ruth Benedict, which would have us believe that an almost infinite variety of behaviour patterns is possible for our species, depending on the social conditions which prevail at any given time or place. Ethology and sociobiology teach, on the contrary, that human behaviour is highly circumscribed by the genetic consequences of evolutionary adaptation, and that any attempt to adopt forms of social organization and ways of life other than those which are characteristic of our species must lead to personal and social disorientation, and, ultimately, to the extinction of whole populations.

Unfortunately, anthropologists have, with a few notable exceptions, proved as slow as psychologists to meet the ethological challenge. Just as in the past psychology and psychiatry sought to explain personality in terms of influences arising from the individual's personal circumstances, so anthropology increasingly occupied itself with the minutiae of how one culture differed phenomenologically from another, each being a coherent entity and a law unto itself, and how local climate, geology, child-rearing practices, and so on, combined to bring these differences about. Hardly anyone concerned himself with those things which all men and women and all cultures had in common, or asked to what extent these universal features might be susceptible to a purely biological explanation. But the ethological revolution has begun to change this, with consequences whose theoretical importance it would be hard to exaggerate: for if we can discover the archetypal structure of human nature we shall be able to define its optimum needs, and thus provide a rational basis for the practice not only of psychiatry and medicine, but of sociology and politics as well. In this momentous enterprise the comparative method will be crucial.

To take a mundane example, in the medical field epidemiological studies have established that since the human bowel evolved to process a diet rich in fibre human communities living in accordance with this 'archetypal intent' (i.e. they eat plenty of bran, fruit and vegetables) are relatively free of bowel diseases, while those communities like our own which contravene it suffer a comparatively high incidence of colonic cancer, ulcerative colitis, regional ileitis, diverticulitis, piles, and so on. Similarly, our species is not equipped to deal with a high daily intake of animal protein and fat: we evidently evolved in an environment which provided vegetables and fruit in greater abundance than animal foods. The result is that the protein-glutted northern hemisphere affords diseases of which the protein-impoverished south knows nothing. Findings such as these carry the highest significance for both therapeutic and preventive medicine.

In the same way, research into the archetypal nature of mankind must have direct impact on the theory and practice of politics. Though it has been fashionable to speak of 'political science' since early Fabian days, the term is a misnomer because hitherto no science of politics *could* exist in the absence of an epistemological foundation on which such a science might be based. It is not farfetched, however, to propose that biology and the comparative method could provide that foundation: the better we understand the essential parameters of human nature, the better we shall be able to legislate for that nature, to create societies in which human beings will feel most truly at home. Objective political science might then make us conservatives and radicals all – conservatives in the sense of wishing to preserve those political institutions which are essential, and radicals in wishing to adopt new institutions more suited to our archetypal needs than those already in existence. As it is, the political views dominating the world at the present time are based on assumptions about the fundamental nature of mankind which are hopelessly out of date.

The point is well argued by Robin Fox (1975), who is one of the few anthropologists to adopt the ethological standpoint:

> If there is no human nature, any social system is as good as any other, since there is no base line of human needs by which to judge them. If, indeed, everything is learned, then surely men can be taught to live in any kind of society. Man is at the mercy of all the tyrants – be they fascists or liberals – who think they know what is best for him. And how can he plead that they are being inhuman if he doesn't know what being human is in the first place? If, however, man can establish what the basic human satisfactions and needs are – if he knows what the human social nature is and what kinds of social systems are compatible with it – he can make a stand against the brainwashers, genetic tinkerers, totalitarians, and utopian liberals who would knock us into shape.

Jung would, I believe, have been in complete sympathy with this argument. 'All those factors,' he wrote, '. . . that were essential to our near and remote ancestors will also be essential to us, for they are embedded in the inherited organic system' (*CW* 8, para. 717).

Although Jung would have been quick to point out the 'reductionist' tendencies inherent in the ethological approach, there are many aspects of it which would have delighted him – especially the wealth of data it provides for the 'amplification' (a favourite word of Jung's) of archetypal themes. He would have found himself at home with many of the intellectual assumptions of ethology; and it is impressive to note the similarities that link Jung with the man who has done most to advance ethology to its present status, Konrad Lorenz. It is true to describe both Jung and Lorenz as 'charismatic' personalities with a zest for life, capable of inspiring intense loyalty in their adherents, both reared in the Central European mould of Germanic scholarship and holding a special respect for Kant and Goethe, both possessing an intractable penchant for swimming against the academic tides of their time in pursuit of private visions, both widely misunderstood, and both inspiring the wrath and contumely of the behaviourists. It has been persuasively suggested (Gorer, 1966) that the cultural biases which have blinded all but some (mainly European) workers to the role of innate psychic structures are due to the pre-eminence of the United States and Soviet Russia in the behavioural sciences: the egalitarian ethos prevailing in these two very different societies has resulted in a powerful commitment to the proposition that all men and women are quite literally *born* equal, and this has induced both American and Russian psychologists to devote their attention to the mechanics of learning so as to facilitate the activities of pedagogues and politicians in realizing the dream of a truly egalitarian society. Reared in a more aristocratic tradition, neither Jung nor Lorenz was constrained by any such preconceptions.

However, there exists between Lorenz and Jung a significant personal difference that needs to be emphasized, and that is the extraversion of Lorenz and the introversion of Jung: it is not surprising that their work should bear the stamp of this fundamental distinction, and the complementary nature of the two approaches makes any attempt to compare and, where possible, to synthesize them both attractive and overdue. As I hope this book will help to make clear, there is, in fact, remarkably little conflict between the Jungian and ethological positions. What is particularly striking is the way in which concepts introduced by Jung more than half a century ago anticipate with uncanny accuracy those now gaining currency in the behavioural sciences generally. Jung would have appreciated this irony, since it was the practitioners of these very sciences who, in his lifetime, persistently misunderstood his work, stigmatized him as a crank, and dismissed his concepts of the archetype and the collective unconscious with frank derision. Yet, the data which these workers are amassing are not only compatible with Jung's theories, but also serve to strengthen and amplify them to an extent that few Jungians (and certainly few behavioural scientists) appear to realize.

Nowadays, it is common to hear ethologists praised for their part in bringing psychology into the mainstream of biology; but those who deliver these accolades never give Jung his due for attempting a similar achievement, against almost universal opposition, so many years earlier. Not that he would have minded. He was too committed to the direction in which his own researches carried him ever to pay much attention to the narrow intellectual fashions that dominated academic psychology in his day. His psychological approach was, as Marie-Louise von Franz has observed, 'too fundamental, in a sense, to be modern' (1975).

Where differences do exist between Jung and the ethologists, they lie not so much in their theoretical orientation as in their primary data, the observations from which their hypotheses were derived and on the basis of which they were tested. Being a profoundly introverted and introspective man, Jung was infinitely more interested in the inner world of experience than in the outer world of observable events. What mattered to him were not 'patterns of behaviour' as much as 'patterns of awareness'. If you read his fascinating autobiography (1963) for descriptions of places he visited or people he met in the course of his long life, you will be disappointed: it is much more an account of his dreams and the development of his ideas, for dreams and ideas were the stuff of life to him.

In contrast to Jung, the ethologists are concerned with the outer manifestations of living organisms rather than with their subjective experiences. For this reason, it would be mistaken to persist in a purely ethological orientation to the study of mankind because it would effectively prevent a new scientific synthesis from occurring. There can be no unified science of humanity if it concentrates on the outer world of behaviour while ignoring the inner world of experience. For it is the inner world of experience which determines our awareness of life, and it is patently absurd that a discipline which purports to be an all-embracing science of psychology should proceed as if no such phenomenon existed.

It is precisely this absurdity that analytical psychology can rectify, for Jung still holds the bridge which spans the gulf between inner processes and outer events. The ethological revolution is fine, as far as it goes, but it fails to connect with the inside. The major contribution still to be made by Jungian psychology is, I believe, to provide the means of forging this connection through application of the archetypal hypothesis.

· 2 ·

Archetypes and meaning

No two subjects are more intrinsically fascinating than ethology and analytical psychology, yet, until now, no one has attempted to link them together in the same book. This is a strange omission, for not only do both disciplines complement one another in a number of important ways, but both command large audiences which, I suspect, overlap to a greater extent than is generally realized. Moreover, Jungians have, on the whole, tended to remain aloof from the rapid developments occurring in ethology, while ethologists have displayed grand indifference to the work of Jung. It is ironic that the lay public should perceive parallels between the two disciplines to which their practitioners remain relatively blind.

Jungians as a group have proved particularly reluctant to elucidate the biological implications of Jung's theories: so mesmerized have they been by the archetypal symbols mediating the individuation process in their patients and in themselves that they have neglected the archetype's behavioural manifestations no less than its phylogenetic roots. This, in my view, is a tragic oversight. It has ensured that their work should proceed in splendid isolation from all related disciplines and has been responsible for divorcing analytical psychology from the behavioural sciences, where its influence could be both beneficial and humanizing.

The trouble is that the triumph of scientific materialism has resulted in psychic agnosticism – a doubt that the psyche even exists. Since Jung's proofs were psychic proofs, to many of his contemporaries they were not proofs at all. But a signal advantage of stressing the biological aspect of Jung's theories, which his followers have tended to overlook, is that it makes them both credible and illuminating to the modern secular mind.

For the archetype, as Jung conceived it, is a precondition and coexistent of life itself; its manifestations not only reach upwards to the spiritual heights of religion, art and metaphysics, but also down into the dark realms of organic and inorganic matter.

However, despite the esoteric course analytical psychologists have chosen to follow, Jung continues to attract interest, and I believe that the reasons for his appeal are not unrelated to those underlying the success of books and television programmes about the findings and implications of ethology. Both Jung and ethology appear to provide some satisfaction for a fundamental human need – the need to *perceive meaning*, the need to *comprehend*.

It is a need which has been increasingly frustrated as this twentieth century, probably the most portentous in the history of mankind, has unfolded and we have witnessed the seemingly inexorable disintegration of Christendom. The loss of moral certainty accompanying the decline in Christian authority has coincided with a humiliating erosion of our sense of possessing, by Divine Right, an unassailable position at the very heart of the cosmic order, inducing in us a collective conviction of insignificance, which has made spiritual hypochondriacs of us all. So extensive is the mental turmoil characteristic of our faithless times that it is not altogether surprising that there should have been a dramatic growth in the prestige of psychiatrists, matched by a decline in the importance of priests. By the mid-1960s this trend had become apparent to everyone concerned in the 'helping professions': 'more and more patients', wrote Victor Frankl in 1965, 'are crowding our clinics and consulting rooms complaining of an inner emptiness, a sense of total and ultimate meaninglessness of their lives.' Jung had noticed the same phenomenon much earlier: 'About a third of my cases are not suffering from any clinically definable neurosis,' he wrote,' but from the senselessness and aimlessness of their lives. I should not object if this were called the general neurosis of our age' (*CW*16, para. 83).

In accounting for this cultural disaster, one cannot absolve the brilliant achievements of natural science from a large share of the blame. By sacrificing the unitary world view which dominated Christendom up to the beginning of the seventeenth century, scientists were able to free themselves from the shackles of medieval scholasticism and proceed to the development of concepts which made possible the conquest of the material world. Thus was a crucial piece of biblical rhetoric put to the test: 'What shall it profit a man, if he shall gain the whole world, and lose his own soul?' (Mark VIII: 36). The general consensus of the more articulate beneficiaries of the affluent society would seem to say 'not much'. Certainly, the price we have paid for 'gaining the whole world' has been quite literally astronomical, for not only has it meant the sacrifice of our place at the centre of the universe, and the rupture – for the first time in the history of our species – of the mythological bonds linking us to The Great Architect Of All Creation, but it has, more terrifyingly, opened the Pandora's box of technological madness, the prospect of gross overpopulation, world-wide famine, mineral exhaustion, global pollution, and nuclear catastrophe, which may well cause the demise of Christendom to coincide with the destruction of life on this planet, as the Book of Revelation so confidently predicts.

The need to escape this horrendous fate is the crucial issue of our time; but how is the escape to be accomplished? Loss of a divinely ordained purpose within the universal order denies us access to the faith of Mother Julian of Norwich that 'all manner of things shall be well'; on the contrary, we are afflicted with a sense of almost unbearable loneliness, cast adrift as we are in an infinite, totally heartless space scattered with lumps of insensate matter. We face the critical moment in the history of our species, and we face it alone.

Our wish to awake from this nightmare finds expression, even at this late date, in periodic, though ephemeral, religious revivals and the formation of esoteric cults, in the resurrection of primordial 'sciences' like astrology, and in belief in visits by UFOs, those technologically sophisticated guardian angels, emissaries of a Superior Intelligence from somewhere 'out there', keeping a friendly eye on us, ready, it is hoped, to intervene should collective insanity bring us to the brink of annihilation. There is, so it seems, a passionate, though universally frustrated, desire to replace the detached, materialistic world view imposed by modern science with a *Weltanschauung* capable of revitalizing the near-moribund notions of life's meaning and purpose, and of providing an ethical standpoint from which to face the mortal problems which confront us.

Where is such a *Weltanschauung* to be found? Few free or intelligent spirits in the Western world would subscribe any longer to the divine authenticity of scriptural texts, nor would they see much hope for humanity in the shibboleths of Karl Marx, Mao Tse Tung, or J. Maynard Keynes. Philosophy offers no comfort, since it has long abdicated all responsibility for questions of a metaphysical nature. Freudian psychoanalysis, having helped to liberate us from our sexual repressions, seems to have outlived much of its usefulness; and gurus, whether the Maharishi or Dr R. D. Laing, have their day, like daffodils, and wither all too soon. Where else is there to turn? Have the followers of Charles Darwin or Carl Jung anything more substantial to offer than the rest? Let Jung answer for himself:

> Analytical psychology is not a *Weltanschauung* but a science, and as such it provides the building-material or the implements with which a *Weltanschauung* can be built up or torn down, or else reconstructed. There are many people today who think they can smell a *Weltanschauung* in analytical psychology. I wish I were one of them, for then I should be spared the pains of investigation and doubt, and could tell you clearly and simply the way that leads to

> Paradise. Unfortunately, we are still a long way from that. (*CW* 8, para. 730)

The same can be said of Darwinian biology, or any other science: 'A science can never be a *Weltanschauung* but merely the tool with which to make one' (*CW* 8, para. 731).

But a major advantage of the Darwinian and Jungian approaches is that they essentially *are* scientific and, as a consequence, congenial to the contemporary Western temperament. Indeed, at this point in our history, no *Weltanschauung* can hope to command more than esoteric interest if it fails to take account of biology, physics, and neurophysiology. It is well that this is so. The appalling limitations of scientific materialism as a cultural dominant should not drive us to a wholesale rejection of scientific thought or deductive reasoning. Rather it should cause us to re-examine, in the modern context, the age-old metaphysical questions which are prompted by the tangible phenomena of our universe, and which concern the nature and cosmic position of our species. It is precisely because the work of biologists and analytical psychologists involves them in these matters that it brings them an increasing share of public interest, and why an attempt at a synthesis of the two approaches is timely.

The overwhelming majority of Jung's contemporaries believed, as do the majority of people today, that the essential problems facing humanity lie in the world about us. Jung, however, maintained that, on the contrary, they lie in human nature itself: 'The principal and indeed the only thing that is wrong with the world,' he wrote, 'is man' (*CW* 10, para. 441). At a time when behaviourism held undisputed sway in university departments of psychology, and effectively banished the mind from the curriculum, Jung stressed the primacy of the psyche in human affairs, affirming the truism that, as the very basis of our experience of existence, our minds are our most precious possession. And the strength of Jung's appeal lies essentially in the simple fact that alone among modern psychologists he put the human spirit first. From the time of his break with Freud, just before the First World War, his concern came to be increasingly focused on the subjective experience of the individual in his quest for meaning and value in life. As we can now see, his diagnosis of the malaise afflicting modern man went deeper than the diagnoses of those other great pioneers of analysis, Freud and Adler. To Freud, 'civilization and its discontents' was a matter of repressed sexuality and neurotic symptomatology, while Adler saw it more in terms of the industrial state's inability to satisfy the demands of man's social instincts: Jung, on the other hand, understood our cultural crisis through his research into that basic 'Self' of human nature which antedates all civilization and all technology.

Unlike Freud, Jung was not so much interested in signs and symptoms as in meanings and symbols. If man had become sick, it was because his fundamental symbolic beliefs had lost their validity, with the result that he was no longer related to the great sweeping continuum of his cultural history. Theoretically, it was true that he could be restored to health if, as the priests maintained, new life were inspired into the old symbols, but this prescription could be little more than a pious palliative in a society where collective faith in the traditional symbols was dying. In this event, Jung saw clearly that he had no other recourse than to encourage the modern individual to abandon his exclusively extraverted quest for meaning in the outer world of material objects and, instead, to attempt to put him in touch with the symbol-forming capacities latent within his own psychic nature. And that, in a nutshell, was the implicit objective of the therapy he devised, and which is still practised in his name.

In his lifetime, Jung was eclipsed by Freud, but since his death a reassessment of the two reputations has occurred, to Jung's advantage. His reasons for breaking with Freud have found much posthumous sympathy. Despite Freud's undoubted innovative genius, we can now appreciate how over-constrained was his thinking by a narrow dogmatism – Jung considered that it had a quasi-religious intensity – that the sexual libido theory must be held onto 'at all costs', imposing thereby an intellectual bondage not only on his followers and their patients, but also on those influential cultural elements so receptive to Freud's ideas. The fundamentally reductive approach which characterized the Freudian attitude to the phenomena of life – what Jung lampooned as the 'nothing but' approach, which boiled all things down to their lowest common denominator – helped to spread the disenchantment endemic in our culture. Indeed, the more perceptive of Freud's disciples recognized their complicity in this misfortune: 'we were dismayed,' wrote Erik Erikson in his book *Young Man Luther*,

> when we saw our purpose of enlightenment perverted into a widespread fatalism, according to which man is nothing but a multiplication of his parents' faults and an accumulation of his own earlier selves. We must grudgingly admit that even as we were trying to devise, with scientific determinism, a therapy for the few, we were led to promote an ethical disease among the many.

This eloquent piece of breast-beating was echoed by Karl Stern: 'Unfortunately,' he wrote, 'the reductive philosophy is the most widely acclaimed part of psycho-analytic thought. It harmonizes so excellently with a typical petit bourgeois mediocrity, which is associated with contempt for everything spiritual.'

Jung's approach to the psyche was altogether more liberal, more humanitarian, more tentative than Freud's: if psychology were to achieve scientific validity, he believed that it must eschew all Procrustean preoccupations, and attempt to encompass the whole of psychic reality. All dogmatic systems were inevitably one-sided and excluded from their matrix more than they comprised. To equate the dynamism of the human spirit with sexual libido struck him as both blasphemous and scientifically inept. Moreover, Freud's view of the unconscious as a murky pond that could be drained by analysis and redeveloped by the ego in the service of a purely rational consciousness was bitterly uncongenial to Jung: he regarded an exclusively rational view of human nature as hopelessly inadequate. The profound experiences of psychological transformation involved in the development of personality depended more on irrational than rational processes, and any psychology which failed to grant due honour to these processes would be a betrayal of mankind. Psychology was the endlessly fascinating frontier zone – the borderland where biology and spirit, knowledge and experience, body and mind, conscious and unconscious, the individual and the collective, all came crowding together. In the unconscious, Jung believed, there resided the collective wisdom of our species, the basic programme enabling us to meet all the exigent demands of life; for him, psychotherapy was a process of creative synthesis whereby the ego was informed and fructified by healing symbols arising from the unconscious; it was not a business of reductive analysis whereby the unconscious was subdued, conquered, and colonized by an imperial ego.

To Freud, analysis was essentially a medical matter: the patient came with a symptom; he was analysed, and if the symptom disappeared the analysis was concluded. Jung's view of analysis went much further than this, for he was not particularly concerned with the mere removal of symptoms. It was the duty of psychotherapy, he argued, to reach beyond the confines of medicine and psychiatry into areas which were previously the province of priests and philosophers. Many of his patients continued to analyse with him long after they had been successfully treated for their symptoms, and this enabled him to study areas of experience previously inaccessible to psychiatry; its main consequence was the discovery of what Jung believed to be the basic motive of human psychology – the quest for wholeness. It was the process of responding to this motive that he termed *individuation*.

Increasingly, Jung saw that the progressive extraversion and collectivism of modern society has proceeded to the detriment of the individual's ability to seek his own individuation. Modern man's obsession with the development and exploitation of mineral resources, labour resources, and financial resources, has been paralleled by an almost total neglect of the creative resources within his own psyche. Thus, he is trapped in the same fallacy as the alchemists, who projected their spiritual aspirations into matter, believing that in the process they were working towards the highest value. So it is that man's scientific preoccupation with physical causality and deterministic 'laws' has gone hand in glove with the impoverishment of his spiritual life and a contempt for his own priceless capacity for freedom and growth. As a result, he conceives of himself less as a spiritually sentient being and more as an economic commodity. This collectively depressing trend is exemplified by the economic slavery a man is prepared to embrace in order to compete for consumer goods, and by the money, care, and attention he is willing to invest in his car or his home rather than in his mind and his body. In a predominantly introverted society it would be otherwise.

What, then, may be in store for us now that all traditional values crumble under the weight of our materially obsessed society? A new Dark Age more terrible than anything in the past? Or a New Enlightenment in which rejuvenating symbols arise, carrying us forward into an epoque more wonderful than we can imagine? We cannot know. But Jung's is one of the few contributions that might still help to tip the balance in the direction of cultural rebirth, through the accuracy of his diagnosis of our collective ills, and the rational remedies he prescribed for them. He believed modern man to be sick because he had lost his customary access to the traditional resources of his culture: the cure, therefore, lay in enabling him to establish contact with the resources inherent in his own nature.

As Jung was the first to admit, analytical psychology could never aspire to hand us a new system of beliefs to replace the old faiths that have disintegrated: what it provides is not beliefs, but practical insights into the nature of human experience, not a philosophy, but techniques enabling individuals to achieve the perception of meaning. Jung never advocated a 'return to the Church' or a regression to the 'well-tried values of our forefathers' because he regarded such exhortations as futile attempts to reverse the tide of history. What he believed necessary was hard psychological work on the part of individuals to achieve in actuality their own potential for wholeness, thus opening the modern mind once more to an encounter with life-enhancing symbols. That such effort must result in the experience of meaning, he had no doubt, partly on the empirical grounds of his own clinical practice, and partly as a consequence of his conviction that nature is not only outside but inside; that the phylogenetic human psyche is a portion of nature itself; and that, consequently, there exists, in a very profound sense, a hidden connection between human nature and the nature of the cosmos.

The relationship between archetypes and meaning is as apparent in ethology as in analytic psychology, though for different reasons. The immense popular success of this new branch of zoology demonstrates its appeal to something deeper in us than a mere delight in animal-watching; it excites something more than a vestigial instinct left over from our early forebears with their daily imperative to eat and not be eaten. What ethology satisfies is, I believe, no less than our desire to make the mythological connection; for, latterly, people have started to turn to ethology, and to the biological sciences in general, in much the same spirit as once they turned to the Book of Genesis – from a wish to know how things began.

As long as human communities have existed they have devised mythologies, like that enshrined in Genesis, to account for the creation of the world and the origins of mankind. The mythology, once devised, was customarily handed down from one generation to the next as a corpus of factual knowledge: the myth, hallowed by the patina of lineal respect, became, in a manner of speaking, self-evidently true, a venerable account of what actually occurred. So it was with the Judeo-Christian myth of creation – until it foundered on the Galapagos Archipelago half-way through the last century. But the demand for explanations persists: like children uncertain of their parentage, we cannot rest till we know where we came from. We are more sceptical than our grandfathers, however, less willing to believe on trust precisely what we are told; we demand proof. It is a demand that Darwin was able to satisfy. By giving a coherent account of how human beings, with all their remarkable capacities, developed out of the simplest organic matter, Darwin provided us with a contemporary myth which has found wide acceptance because of its basis in scientific fact. For post-Darwinian biology, like the mythologies and religions of old, is capable of yielding a unified view of the origin and nature of existence, a view capable of encompassing and reconciling the vast diversity of living forms and their behaviour, and establishing their fundamental continuity through the living protoplasmic thread of evolution. Without being anthropomorphic or sentimental, ethology enables us to comprehend the wonderful complexity of animal life, to place ourselves in relation to it, and, in the process, to re-establish the connection between ourselves and nature, thus healing the breach which opened up, to our spiritual impoverishment, at the beginning of the scientific revolution.

No one was more aware than Jung of man's need to perceive meaning and seek explanations. Jung conceived this need as a basic characteristic of our psychic nature and saw religions, myths and sciences as direct expressions of it. Unlike the Freudians, he refused to submit to the 'typical bourgeois mediocrity' and its 'contempt for everything spiritual'. On the contrary, religious behaviour, like other forms of cultural behaviour, being an ingredient in the repertoire of our species, was something we abandoned at our peril. He had the utmost respect for myths and for man's myth-making capacity. To describe Christianity as a myth, and Christ as a mythic hero, was in no sense derogatory, for the achievement of Christ was that he became the greatest symbolical figure of all time, that he founded the guiding myth of our culture, which has shaped the lives of Europeans since the crucifixion. Jung knew that people needed myths if they were to remain vitally in touch with the archetypal core of their nature. Myths provide an entire cosmology compatible with a culture's capacity for understanding, they establish a transcendent context for our brief existence here on earth, they validate the values which rule our lives, they ensure that cohesion of cultures and the worth of individuals by releasing an archetypal response at the deepest levels of our being, and they awaken in us a sense of participation in the *mysterium tremendum et fascinans* which pervades the relationship between the cosmos and the Self.

By promoting an understanding of the significance of myths and stressing the inestimable value of man's myth-making capacities, Jungian psychology can only further the quest for a unitary world view to replace that which has been lost by Christendom. The archetypal hypothesis not only makes such a view possible but gives it depth and, rightly applied, leads directly to the experience of meaning. This is the fulfilment of Darwin's inspiration seen within the Jungian perspective: the perception of ourselves, spiritually no less than physically, as the culmination of the great, lumbering, evolutionary pageant up to this critical moment in history.

'Believing as I do,' wrote Darwin, 'that man in the distant future will be a far more perfect creature than he now is, it is an intolerable thought that he and all other sentient beings are doomed to complete annihilation after such long continued slow progress.' Is it too late to hope that we might defer that annihilation? Or are we on the threshold of the apocalypse? Is it likely that we have lived to recognize in full consciousness our place in nature only to anticipate by a fraction of biological time our self-destruction – and with it the annihilation of all creatures great and small? 'In my deepest soul,' wrote Thomas Mann, 'I hug the supposition that with God's "Let there be", which summoned the cosmos out of nothing, and with the generation of life from the inorganic, it was man who was ultimately intended, and that with him a great experiment is initiated, the failure of which because of man's guilt would be the failure of creation itself, amounting to its refutation. Whether that be so or not, it would be well for man to behave as if it were so.'

The teleological enormity of such reflections can induce panic in the most stable characters. For even though we are the first animals to begin to understand the physical processes underlying our experience of life, and though we are developing the psychological and biotechnological capacities for self-transformation, the genome still has us in its grip. We are still the animals that we were. Our ability to influence the course of history and avert the disasters just ahead is far more circumscribed than most of us care to admit. But the creation of a better, safer world will not come through political rhetoric or inhabiting a Rousseauesque cloud-cuckoo land. It can only come, if come it can, through a deep understanding of the nature of the animal we are. In his archetypal hypothesis Jung proposed a principle responsible for the articulation of all processes governing the organic and psychic processes of life; and his whole manner of approach to these phenomena demonstrated how they may be studied in such a way as not to destroy our awareness of the wonder and the mystery of living. Herein lies his abiding greatness and the justification for this book.

· 3 ·

The archetypal hypothesis

It is possible that future generations will see Jung's theory of archetypes as one of the truly seminal ideas of the twentieth century. However, like all great ideas, it was not entirely original. It has a long and respectable pedigree, which goes back at least as far as Plato.

Jung himself acknowledged his debt to Plato, describing archetypes as 'active living dispositions, *ideas in the Platonic sense*, that preform and continually influence our thoughts and feelings and actions' (*CW* 8, para. 154, italics added). For Plato, 'ideas' were mental forms which were superordinate to the objective world of phenomena. They were *collective* in the sense that they embody the *general* characteristics of groups of individuals rather than the specific peculiarities of one. Thus, a particular dog has qualities in common with all dogs (which enable us to classify him as a dog) as well as peculiarities of his own (which would enable his master to pick him out at a dog show). So it is with archetypes: they are common to all mankind, yet each person experiences them in his own particular way. But there the similarity ends, for the Jungian archetype is no mere abstract idea but a biological entity, a 'living organism, endowed with generative force' (*CW* 6, para. 6, n. 9), existing as a 'centre' in the central nervous system, acting, as we have seen, in a manner very similar to the *innate releasing mechanism* much later postulated by the ethologist, Niko Tinbergen.

Archetypes, being 'active living dispositions' or 'living organisms, endowed with generative force', have the capacity to initiate, control and mediate the common behavioural characteristics and typical experiences of our kind, even though we are, for the most part, unaware of them. As the basis of all the usual phenomena of life, the archetypes transcend culture, race and time. Thus, in Jung's view (as opposed to Plato's) the mental events experienced by every individual are determined not merely by his personal history, but by the collective history of the species as a whole (biologically encoded in the collective unconscious), reaching back into the primordial mists of evolutionary time.

The archetypal endowment with which each of us is born presupposes the natural life-cycle of our species – being mothered, exploring the environment, playing in the peer group, adolescence, being initiated, establishing a place in the social hierarchy, courting, marrying, child-rearing, hunting, gathering, fighting, participating in religious rituals, assuming the social responsibilities of advanced maturity, and preparation for death. 'Ultimately,' wrote Jung, 'every individual life is the same as the eternal life of the species' (*CW* 11, para. 146).

The human being is, therefore, a psychophysical system with a built-in 'biological clock': its structure and life-cycle is predetermined by the evolutionary history of its genes. As the biological clock ticks away and the life-cycle unfolds, so the system accepts and incorporates into itself the life-experience of the individual. But what you and I experience as the whole process is only the end result. We are aware only of the ontogenetic (personal developmental) aspects of our own maturation, being largely unconscious of the phylogenetic blueprint on whose basis it proceeds. This goes a long way to explaining our readiness to give credence to behaviourist or learning theorist accounts of human psychology, which look no further in their formulations than the conditioning to which each individual has been subjected in his lifetime.

A near-contemporary of Jung's, who must have influenced his thinking about archetypes, was Adolf Bastian (1826–1905). This German ethnologist spent many years travelling all over the world studying the myths, folklore and customs of mankind. What impressed him was the similarity which existed between many of the themes and motifs which he encountered wherever he went. He noticed, however, that these universal themes – which he called *Elementargedanken* (elementary ideas) – invariably manifested themselves in local forms, peculiar to the group of people he happened to be studying: these he called *Volksgedanken* (ethnic ideas).

Jung was encouraged towards the formulation of the archetypal hypothesis much in the same way as Bastian inferred the existence of *Elementargedanken*, though Jung did not confine himself to folklore and anthropology. It will be recalled that his decisive insights came from the study of comparative religion, mythology and alchemy on the one hand, and from the material produced by his patients and himself, on the other. Like Bastian, he was struck by the way in which analogous motifs cropped up in the most diverse cultures, as far removed from each other in geography as they were in historical time: in other words, he noted that mythological and religious themes were, as the ethologists say, 'environmentally stable'. Jung was not so naive as to deny that this universal parallelism of motifs, ideas and images could be brought about by the combined operation of tradition and migration, but he argued that some form of transmission through heredity must also occur since he was able to discover numerous instances where such motifs arose spontaneously, without any previous encounter with them on the part of the subject. Jung, therefore, concluded that they must correspond to 'typical dispositions', 'dominants' or 'nodal points' within the structure of the psyche itself.

As was often the case with Jung, confirmation of a crucial hypothesis which had been formulating in his conscious mind came to him in the form of a dream. It occurred in 1909 when, together with Freud, he was sailing across the Atlantic on his first visit to America.

> I was in a house I did not know, which had two storeys. It was 'my house'. I found myself in the upper storey, where there was a kind of salon furnished with fine old pieces in rococo style. On the walls hung a number of precious old paintings. I wondered that this should be my house, and thought, 'not bad'. But then it occurred to me that I did not know what the lower floor looked like. Descending the stairs, I reached the ground floor. There everything was much older, and I realized that this part of the house must date from about the fifteenth or sixteenth century. The furnishings were medieval; the floors were of red brick. Everywhere it was rather dark. I went from one room to another, thinking, 'Now I really must explore the whole house.' I came upon a heavy door, and opened it. Beyond it, I discovered a stone stairway that led down into the cellar. Descending again, I found myself in a beautifully vaulted room which looked exceedingly ancient. Examining the walls, I discovered layers of brick among the ordinary stone blocks, and chips of brick in the mortar. As soon as I saw this I knew that the walls dated from Roman times. My interest by now was intense. I looked more closely at the floor. It was of stone slabs, and in one of these I discovered a ring. When I pulled it, the stone slab lifted, and again I saw a stairway of narrow stone steps leading down into the depths. These, too, I descended, and entered a low cave cut into the rock. Thick dust lay on the floor, and in the dust were scattered bones and broken pottery, like remains of a primitive culture. I discovered two human skulls, obviously very old and half disintegrated. Then I awoke. *Memories, Dreams, Reflections*, 1963, p. 155)

He recounted the dream to Freud, who considered the most important symbols to be the two skulls, and he pressed Jung for his associations to them in an effort to identify an unconscious death wish against two people in Jung's life. Jung totally rejected this interpretation, but for the sake of peace kept his reservations to himself. Privately, he reflected on the dream, and its meaning became perfectly clear to him:

> It was plain to me that the house represented a kind of image of the psyche – that is to say, of my then state of consciousness, with hitherto unconscious additions. Consciousness was represented by the salon. It had an inhabited atmosphere, in spite of its antiquated style.
>
> The ground floor stood for the first level of the unconscious. The deeper I went, the more alien and the darker the scene became. In the cave, I discovered remains of a primitive culture, that is the world of the primitive man within myself – a world which can scarcely be reached or illuminated by consciousness. The primitive psyche of man borders on the life of the animal soul, just as the caves of prehistoric times were usually inhabited by animals before men laid claim to them. (1963, p. 156)

The dream of the house had a powerful effect on Jung: it revived an old interest in archaeology and heightened his passion for mythology. He spent much of 1910 engrossed in these studies, in the course of which he came across a recently edited Greek text relating to the Mithraic cult. Part of the text recorded a vision in the following words: 'And likewise the so-called tube, the origin of the ministering wind. For you will see hanging down from the disc of the sun something that looks like a tube. And towards the regions westward it is as though there were an infinite east wind. But if the other wind should prevail towards the regions of the east, you will in like manner see the vision veering in that direction.' Jung concluded that 'evidently a stream of wind is blowing through the tube out of the sun' (*CW* 8, para. 318).

This passage struck Jung as an extraordinary instance of spontaneously recurrent archetypal symbolism, for it reminded him of an incident which had occurred in the Burgholzli Psychiatric Hospital, Zurich, one day in 1906, when he came across a patient, a paranoid schizophrenic, 'blinking through the window up at the sun, and moving his head from side to side in a curious manner. He took me by the arm,' says Jung, 'and said he wanted to show me something. He said I must look at the sun with eyes half shut, and then I could see the sun's phallus. If I moved my head from side to side the sun-phallus would move too, and that was the origin of the wind.'

Commenting on the startling parallelism between these two visions, Jung admits the possibility that they could be purely fortuitous, but argues that if they were so, then

> we should expect the vision to have no connections with analogous ideas, nor any inner meaning. But this expectation is not fulfilled, for in certain medieval paintings this tube is actually depicted as a sort of hose-pipe reaching down from heaven under the robe of Mary. In it the Holy Ghost flies down in the form of a dove to

> impregnate the Virgin. As we know from the miracle of Pentecost, the Holy Ghost was originally conceived as a mighty rushing wind, the πνευμα, 'the wind that bloweth where it listeth'. In a Latin text we read: 'Animo descensus per orbem solis tribuitur' (They say that the spirit descends through the disc of the sun). This conception is common to the whole of late classical and medieval philosophy. (*CW* 8, para. 317)

And it is indeed unlikely that the patient, 'an ordinary clerk', would have been conversant with this philosophical tradition.

This finding of parallels – or 'amplification' of archetypal themes – is an example of the comparative method in action. Jung insisted that there was seldom anything fortuitous about such similarities: they represent 'the revival of possibilities of ideas that have always existed, that can be found in the most diverse minds and in all epochs, and are therefore not to be mistaken for inherited ideas' (*CW* 8, para. 320).

A position broadly similar to Jung's has subsequently been adopted, quite independently, by specialists in linguistics like Noam Chomsky and by psychologists like E. H. Lenneberg who decisively reject traditional academic assumptions concerning speech acquisition – namely, that all language develops through imitation and learning, reinforced by rewards and punishments. In Chomsky's view, every child comes into the world fully equipped with the capacity for speech: his brain contains a language acquisition device which enables him, as he grows up in the family milieu, rapidly to acquire the knack of using words and building sentences in a way that those around him will readily understand.

Many readers of this book will have had the humbling experience of spending years trying to master a foreign language only to find themselves relatively tongue-tied when they visit a city where the language is spoken as the mother tongue. Yet, the public parks are full of three-year-olds with an apparently superb command of grammar, idiom and inflection. In three brief years these tiny minds have mastered a skill which we, with our adult intelligence, cannot hope to equal for all our dedicated hours in language laboratories and classrooms. In the young child the language acquisition device is fully operational, in the adult it has largely atrophied with disuse.

Interestingly enough, one of Chomsky's most enthusiastic advocates is Konrad Lorenz, who, in his book *Behind the Mirror* (1977) quotes the case of Hellen Keller in support of Chomsky's thesis. Although blind and deaf from birth, Helen learned English in eighteen months through the simple expedient of getting her governess, Anne Sullivan, to write words in her palm with the tip of a finger.

Anne Sullivan's account of how quickly her pupil mastered the

> apparently insuperable task of learning language solely on the basis of feeling the imprint of the letters of the alphabet on her hand, and how she came to form abstract concepts of the most complex kind – all this must strike anyone biased in favour of behaviourist views on learning as utterly incredible. (p. 185)

Lorenz argues convincingly that the astonishing speed with which Helen Keller developed a facility for conceptual thought shows that it was not a question of providing something that was missing but of activating something already present. Helen's extraordinary achievement in acquiring a mastery of written and spoken language between her seventh and eighth year is, for Lorenz, 'unshakeable proof of the correctness of Chomsky's theories' (p. 189)

While it is true that specific grammars (like mythological motifs) show rich diversity throughout the world, Chomsky believes their basic forms – what he calls their *deep structures* – to be universal. Languages all perform the same essential functions in finite ways, and once their 'deep structures' have been defined, all languages should, he thinks, prove reducible to the universal (or 'archetypal') grammar on which all individual grammars are based.

In much the same way as Chomsky is seeking to define innate propensities underlying the development of articulate speech, so Lévi-Strauss and the French structuralist anthropologists are searching for innate factors which determine our perception of social relationships. What these workers have subsequently achieved for linguistics and anthropology, Jung attempted to do much earlier for psychology, through the study of mythology, comparative religion, legends and fairy tales, dreams and nightmares. He sought to define their common elements, their archetypal themes, relating these to the 'deep structures', the 'given', 'in-built' determinants of the human psyche. To the last, he remained convinced that far from being a *tabula rasa*, a blank slate passively submitting to the inscriptions of life's lessons, man was born with numerous predispositions for perceiving, feeling, behaving and conceptualizing in specific ways. He accepted, of course, that the extent to which these predispositions were developed or expressed depended largely on environmental factors and individual life-experience, but he viewed the growing child as an active, pre-programmed participant in the developmental process. For him, the slate was not blank: much was already inscribed on it before lessons began (albeit in invisible chalk); moreover, it would suffer only certain forms of information to be recorded on it; and, most of all, it was capable of doing much of the recording itself. 'There is no human experience,' he wrote,

> nor would experience be possible at all, without the intervention of a subjective aptitude. What is this subjective aptitude? Ultimately

> it consists of an innate psychic structure which allows man to have experiences of this kind. Thus the whole nature of man presupposes woman, both physically and spiritually. His system is tuned in to woman from the start, just as it is prepared for a quite definite world where there is water, light, air, salt, carbohydrates, etc. The form of the world into which he is born is already inborn in him as a virtual image. Likewise parents, wife, children, birth, and death are inborn in him as virtual images, as psychic aptitudes. These *a priori* categories have by nature a collective character; they are images of parents, wife, and children in general, and are not individual predestinations. We must therefore think of these images as lacking in solid content, hence as unconscious. They only acquire solidity, influence, and eventual consciousness in the encounter with empirical facts, which touch the unconscious aptitude and quicken it to life. They are, in a sense, the deposits of all our ancestral experiences, but they are not the experiences themselves. (*CW* 7, para. 300)

It is of considerable historical interest that the archetypal hypothesis was anticipated to some extent by the German astronomer, Johannes Kepler (1571–1630). Kepler believed that his delight in scientific discovery was due to the mental exercise of matching ideas or images already implanted in his mind by God with external events perceived through his senses. This interpretation of scientific enquiry also owed its origins to Plato but was much developed by Kepler, who spoke of his innate ideas and images as 'archetypal'. Echoes of the same notion are to be found in Kant's dictum that 'there can be no empirical knowledge that is not already caught and limited by the *a priori* structure of cognition.'

'For, to know is to compare that which is externally perceived with *inner ideas* and to judge that it agrees with them, a process which Proclus expressed very beautifully by the word "awakening", as from sleep,' wrote Kepler (1619).

> For, as the perceptible things which appear in the outside world make us remember what we knew before, so do sensory experiences, when consciously realized, call forth intellectual notions that were already present inwardly; so that which formerly was hidden in the soul, as under the *veil of potentiality*, now shines therein in actuality. How then did they (the intellectual notions) find ingress? I answer: all ideas or formal concepts of the harmonies, as I have just discussed them, lie in those beings that possess the faculty of rational cognition, and they are not all received within by discursive reasoning; rather they are *derived from a natural instinct and are inborn* in those beings as the number (an intellectual thing) of petals in a

> flower or the number of seed cells in a fruit is innate in the form of the plants. (Quoted by Pauli, 1955, italics added)

Kepler's 'inner ideas' which lie 'under the veil of potentiality' and which are 'derived from a natural instinct and are inborn' are clearly akin to Jung's 'primordial images' – the term which laid him open to accusations of Lamarckism. His later substitution of the more satisfactory term 'archetype' proved to be somewhat capricious, however, because he continued to use both terms in subsequent writings. But at least the charge of Lamarckism forced him to make the very necessary distinction between the archetype-as-such, and the archetypal images, motifs and ideas that the archetype gave rise to, thus making it clear that he did not believe archetypes to be inherited images, but purely the inherent psychic structures responsible for the production of such images. 'The archetype as such is a hypothetical and irrepresentable model,' he wrote (*CW* 8, para. 6, n. 9). 'One must constantly bear in mind that what we mean by "archetype" is in itself irrepresentable, but that it has effects which enable us to visualize it, namely, the archetypal images' (*CW* 8, para. 417). However, having made clear what he should have made clear in the first place, he was not above blaming others for the confusion he had created. 'Again and again I encounter the mistaken notion that an archetype is determined in regard to its content, in other words that it is a kind of unconscious idea (if such an expression be permissible). It is necessary to point out once more that archetypes are not determined as to their content, but only as regards their form, and then only to a very limited degree. A primordial image is determined as to its content only when it has become conscious and is therefore filled out with the material of conscious experience' (*CW* 9, pt I, para. 155).

Jung was fond of comparing the form of the archetype to the axial system of a crystal, which

> preforms the crystalline structure of the mother liquid, although it has no material existence of its own. This first appears according to the specific way in which the ions and molecules aggregate. The archetype in itself is empty and purely formal, nothing but a *facultas praeformandi*, a possibility of representation which is given *a priori*. The representations themselves are not inherited, only the forms, and in that respect they correspond in every way to the instincts, which are also determined in form only. The existence of the instincts can no more be proved than the existence of the archetypes, so long as they do not manifest themselves concretely. With regard to the definiteness of the form, our comparison with the crystal is illuminating inasmuch as the axial system determines only the stereometric structure but not the concrete form of the individual crystal. (*CW* 9, pt I, para. 155)

Jung's first use of the term 'archetype' came in 1919 (*CW* 8, para. 270). Greek in origin, it dates from classical times and means 'prime imprinter'; usually it referred to an original manuscript from which later copies were made. The etymology of the word is instructive:

> The first element 'arche' signifies 'beginning, origin, cause, primal source principle,' but it also signifies 'position of a leader, supreme rule and government' (in other words a kind of 'dominant'): the second element 'type' means 'blow and what is produced by a blow, the imprint of a coin . . . form, image, prototype, model, order, and norm', . . . in the figurative, modern sense, 'pattern underlying form, primordial form' (the form, for example, 'underlying' a number of similar human, animal or vegetable specimens). (Jacobi, 1959)

Although Jung's original insights into the existence of archetypal phenomena were personal and largely subjective, abundant corroborative evidence has come not only from mythology and psychiatry, but also, in recent times, from ethology and sociobiology. Careful examination of patterns of behaviour as they manifest themselves in diverse human societies and different species of animals leads the unbiased mind to the conclusion that Jung was right: that 'the collective unconscious contains the whole spiritual heritage of mankind's evolution, born anew in the brain structure of every individual' (*CW* 8, para. 342); that there are indeed universal forms of instinctive and social behaviour, as well as universally recurring symbols and motifs, and that these forms have been subject to the essentially biological processes of evolution no less than the anatomical and physiological structures whose homologous nature first established the truth of Darwin's theory.

· 4 ·

Archetypes and behaviour

If you hatch out a clutch of baby chicks and then pull a wooden model of a flying hawk over their heads they will crouch down against the ground and emit cries of alarm. This is an ancient defensive response, and it is innate. Moreover, one can raise generations of chicks without ever exposing them to a hawk – real or wooden – without extinguishing the response. The moment you display the hawk to members of the seventh or eighth generation, say, they cringe. An archetypal system, once it has evolved as a characteristic of a given species, breeds true as long as the species exists, and does not disappear with disuse.

A dramatic demonstration of the truth of this statement occurred in 1939, when the British ornithologist, David Lack, sent thirty caged finches, which he had trapped in the Galapagos Islands, to his colleague, Robert Orr, in California. These were descendants of the same finches which had provided Darwin with crucial evidence for the principle of natural selection, when he visited the Galapagos Archipelago in 1835 on board *HMS Beagle*. The finches had been there for hundreds of thousands of years – long enough for fourteen different species to evolve, each beautifully adapted to its own ecological niche. On the mainland, on the other hand, the original species from which the fourteen had evolved had long been extinct.

The reason why finches flourished on the remote Galapagos Islands and not on the mainland was because the Islands possessed no falcons or large birds of prey. For hundreds of thousands of years these finches had never had to cringe or demonstrate alarm as a predator flew overhead because they had not seen one. Nevertheless, when Lack's thirty specimens, drawn from four different species, arrived in California, Orr was amazed to observe that they all emitted alarm calls and cringed whenever a predatory bird, such as a raven or a red-tailed hawk, came in sight. The 'predator archetype' had lain dormant in the 'collective unconscious' of these birds for something approaching a million years. Yet, when the appropriate stimulus was encountered in the environment, the archetype was at once activated, with its related behaviour patterns and, one may infer, the experience of fear.

Few people would have difficulty in regarding behaviour of this kind as *instinctive*. But many would object violently to the suggestion that any such behaviour could occur in human beings, arguing that human behaviour, so variable from person to person and from culture to culture, cannot be described as instinctive in any respect. But this extreme position is no longer tenable. As John Bowlby, who has done so much to erode it, writes (1969):

> Man's behaviour is very variable, it is true, but not infinitely so; and, though cultural differences are great, certain commonalities can be discerned. For example, despite obvious variability, the patterns of behaviour, often very intensely motivated, that result in mating, in the care of babies and young children, and in the attachment of young to parents are found in almost all members of the human race and seem best considered as expressions of *some common plan* [italics added] and, since they are of obvious survival value, as instances of instinctive behaviour. For it must be emphasised that in all higher species, and not in man alone, instinctive behaviour is not stereotyped movement but an idiosyncratic performance by a particular individual in a particular environment – yet a performance that nonetheless follows some recognizable pattern and that in a majority of cases leads to some predictable result of benefit to individual or species.

If for 'some common plan' we substitute 'archetype' this passage is completely in accord with the Jungian position. Bowlby was the first Freudian analyst of stature to refute the notion that there can be no behaviours in man, other than sex, which are homologous with instinctive behaviours in other species – though others had questioned it, for example Hermann of the Hungarian School of psychoanalysis, Suttie, and Anna Freud of the English School. Stated quite simply, his view is that 'the basic structure of man's behavioural equipment resembles that of infra-human species but has in the course of evolution undergone special modifications that permit the same ends to be reached by a much greater diversity of means' (1969, p. 40). Human instinctive behaviours are held 'to derive from *some prototype or prototypes* [my italics] that are common to other animal species.'

As always, Bowlby is careful to define his terms. Instinctive behaviour, he maintains, is characterized by four main features:

1 it follows a recognizably similar and predictable pattern in almost all members of a species (or all members of one sex);

2 it is not a simple response to a single stimulus but a sequence of behaviour that usually runs a predictable course;

3 certain of its usual consequences are of obvious value in contributing to the preservation of an individual or the continuity of a species;
4 many examples of it develop when all the opportunities for learning it are exiguous or absent.

Bowlby believes, in my opinion quite rightly, that all arguments about whether a certain form of instinctive behaviour is 'innate' or 'acquired' are futile. 'Just as area is a product of length multiplied by width so every biological character, whether it be morphological, physiological or behavioural, is a product of genetic endowment with environment' (1969, p. 40). Indeed, the old nature versus nurture controversy represents a total misconception of the nature of behavioural processes. As has often been said, the distinction, carried to its logical conclusion, would insist that innate behaviour was that which occurred in the absence of an environment, and learning behaviour as that which required no organism. Some (e.g. Lionel Tiger, 1969, and Geoffrey Gorer, 1966), have seen the nature/nurture debate as a pseudo-scientific problem which has divided workers not so much for scientific reasons as for emotional and political prejudices, left-wingers giving total commitment to the environmentalist view, while those on the right find grist for their mill in an essentially genetic approach to racial and social differences, arguing that social inequalities are inevitable and necessary to the stability of social institutions. Konrad Lorenz, on the other hand, sees the argument as arising primarily from the human propensity for thinking in opposites – a view which Jung would have endorsed – which results in the fallacy of regarding 'nature' and 'nurture' as mutually exclusive concepts. Such polarized thinking inevitably leads to individuals adopting one-sided postures and becoming pugnacious in their defence.

To detach us from the horns of this dilemma, Professor Robert Hinde of Cambridge has made the useful suggestion that rather than wasting time arguing about which behaviours are learned and which are innate the progress of science would be better served if we conceive of a *continuum of behaviours* ranging from those which are *environmentally stable* (i.e. relatively little influenced by environmental variations) and those which are *environmentally labile.* Hinde's suggestion has been wholeheartedly adopted by Bowlby, who has never argued that human instinctive behaviour patterns are themselves innate. 'Instinctive behaviour is not inherited,' he writes: 'what is inherited is the potential to develop . . . behavioural systems, both the nature and form of which differ in some measure according to the particular environment in which development takes place' (1969, p. 45). Behaviour traditionally called instinctive belongs to the environmentally stable end of Hinde's continuum; and it remains stable as long as the environment stays within the range of that which the species normally inhabits. In such an environment the behaviour occurs in a predictable form in all members of the species and for this reason is often designated as *species-specific*.

But even at the environmentally stable end of the continuum, the stability is relative and some degree of lability exists. Of course, examples of remarkably stable instinctive behaviour abound in the ethological literature: just as baby chicks cringe when a wooden model of a hawk is pulled forwards over their heads, or male sticklebacks dance when they spy a gravid female, so mallard ducks respond amorously to the sight of a green-headed mallard drake, even when they have never seen one before. But there are also somewhat more labile instinctive behaviours which take account of environmental circumstances and are able to adapt to them: examples are the way in which the young gosling 'imprints' as 'mother' the first moving object it perceives after emerging from the egg, the manner in which furry animals grow thicker coats when the weather turns cold, or a plant, put in the shade by tall neighbours, reaches upwards so as to bathe its leaves in more sunlight. Such things occur because the genetic programme evolved by the genome – by 'trial and success', as Lorenz puts it – enables the organism to adapt appropriately to environmental variations. It is this kind of adaptive genetic programme that Ernst Mayr has called the *open programme*, and instinctive behaviours in human beings are probably all dependent upon programmes of this kind.

Courting behaviour is an example of an open programme in action in human beings, no less than in animals. In nearly all human cultures, for instance, sexual foreplay proceeds by a sequence of increasing intimacy from the moment that a couple establish eye contact, exchange words, and go on to touch and arouse one another to the point of actual copulation. The precise behavioural patterns involved are subject to some variability, but the general sequence is universally applicable. Some tribes indulge in nose-rubbing and face-pressing, others 'kiss' by slapping the lips close to the partner's face and inhaling, while others again go in for reciprocal tongue and lip-sucking. To overemphasize these minor differences is to obscure the more instructive discovery that there is marked similarity in the courting behaviour of all human beings in whatever cultural milieu they may have been reared.

The same is true of behaviours associated with kinship obligations and marriage; it also appears to be true of certain forms of political behaviour:

> the apparently endless kinds of kinship and marriage arrangements known to men are in fact variations on a few themes. The same can be said of political arrangements, which despite their cultural variety, are reducible to a few structural forms. Once one gets behind the surface manifestations, the uniformity of human behaviour and

> of human social arrangements is remarkable. (Robin Fox, 1975, p. 249)

The assumptions underlying the ethological approach to human instinctive behaviour (adopted by Bowlby, Lorenz, Fox, Eibl-Eibesfeldt, and many others) have much in common with those on which Jung based his theory of the archetype. Jung conceived of the archetypal nuclei of the phylogenetic psyche as determining and co-ordinating the basic patterns of human life in a way which was characteristic for all members of the species. Archetypes function, he maintained, at a level of cerebral activity mainly below the reach of consciousness, and, therefore, their *modus operandi* cannot be perceived. Nevertheless, their influence on our life-experience is profound, their activity achieving expression in the universal forms of behaviour, images, and ideas which characterize human communities everywhere. The primal occurrences of life – being born, forming attachments, gaining initiation into the adult state, courting, mating and rearing children, collective bonding by males for the purposes of hunting and interspecific conflict, and dying, all are subject to archetypal control and are associated with certain 'typical dispositions' both in behavioural (often ritualistic) and subjective ideational forms. Thus, throughout the whole cycle of life, the archetype stands behind the scenes, as it were, as a kind of author-director or actor-manager, producing the tangible performance that proceeds on the public (and the private) stage. The life-cycle of living organisms is the supreme example of the sophisticated and profoundly influential control which genes exert over complex biological processes. That there is a biological substratum for the most complex social and individual behaviour among all animals is now certain, and man is no exception. It is a measure of the persisting influence of theological dogma that we could imagine man to be exempt.

Consequently, there is considerable conceptual overlap between Jung's archetypes and Bowlby's species-specific behavioural systems. Indeed, it would not seem far-fetched to identify the archetypes with Ernst Mayr's 'open programmes', in that they are phylogenetically acquired, genome-bound units of information which programme the individual to behave in certain specific ways while permitting such behaviour to be adapted appropriately to environmental circumstances. As Jung himself put it:

> the instincts form very close analogues to the archetypes – so close, in fact, that there is good reason for supposing that the archetypes are the *unconscious images* [my italics] of the instincts themselves; in other words they are patterns of instinctive behaviour. The hypothesis of the collective unconscious is, therefore, no more daring than to assume that there are instincts. (*CW* 9, pt 1, para. 91)

Although the reader's initial reaction to this passage may well be one of irritation that Jung has yet again made a semantic confusion between images and archetypes, it must nevertheless be acknowledged that the notion of inherent 'images' or 'configurations' in living organisms is a recurrent one in biology. Without some such concept it is difficult to comprehend the extraordinary manner in which plants grow from seeds or how they spontaneously replace parts that have been damaged or removed. 'Somehow,' wrote the biologist Edmund Sinnott (1955), 'there must be present in the plant's living stuff, immanent in all its parts, *something that represents the natural configuration of the whole* [my italics], as a norm to which its growth conforms, a "goal" toward which development is invariably directed. This insistent fact confronts us everywhere in biology' (pp. 26–7). Or consider nest-building in birds. In human terms it is hard to assume that the bird engaged in its labour of construction has any 'idea' what it is doing, but it must have some kind of 'image' of what a completed nest should be like. The image may or may not be conscious, but clearly there is some central mechanism that 'knows' how a nest should be built and which co-ordinates the energies of the bird as it builds it.

Moreover, the concept of an 'unconscious image' in the sense of a blueprint on which behavioural systems are based is not altogether uncongenial to Bowlby, as the following passage makes clear:

> Whilst all the instinctive systems of a species are so structured that as a rule they promote the survival of the species within its own environment of adaptedness, each system differs in regard to the particular part of the environment with which it is concerned. Some behavioural systems are so structured that they bring an organism into a certain kind of habitat and retain it there; others are so structured that they lead the organism to eat particular foodstuffs; and others again that they bring the organism into special relations with other members of its own species.* On some occasions the relevant part of the environment is recognized by perception of some relatively simple character, such as a moving flash of light; far more often, however, recognition entails the perception of pattern. In all such cases, we must suppose, the individual has *a copy of that pattern in its CNS* [my italics] and is structured to react in special kinds of way when it perceives a matching pattern in the environment. (1969, pp. 47–8)

All open programmes involve cognition. Specific external stimuli may serve to 'release' the programme, but some cognitive apparatus must

* One thinks of Jung's statement that there are as many archetypes as there are common situations in life.

exist within the organism to decide which of the programme's options is to be put into effect. Lorenz believes that all adaptive modifications of instinctive behaviours occur along the same lines: 'The system always contains genetic information on all the programmes it is potentially capable of carrying out' (1977, p. 68). External events are already 'planned for' in the sense that the various possibilities are genetically built into the programme so as to permit the organism, by using its cognitive apparatus, to select that which is best suited to the environmental circumstances prevailing at any given moment.

Viewed from the strictly biological standpoint, the archetype is an ancient, genetically determined releaser or inhibiter. From the purely psychological point of view it is, of course, a good deal more than that, since the survival of the species, and the life of each member of the species, depends upon our capacity to 'know' situations, to recognize the essence of what we may find ourselves up against, and our ability to select from a vast repertoire of possible responses the behaviour and strategy most suited to the problem in hand. The relationship between the archetype and the conscious experience of individual members of the species lies at the very heart of Jungian psychology, and will be examined in the next chapter. It is now time we considered the question of archetypal influences on the psychology of perception.

Archetypes and sensory perception

Physics, at the time when psychology seized upon it as the only scientific model worthy of emulation, demanded that we believe in a material world which could be viewed with total objectivity. Biology, on the contrary, holds the view that every individual of each species inhabits an essentially subjective world – what Jacob Johann von Uexküll, the founder of ethology, called the organism's *Umwelt* – and our perception of it is dependent upon processes of which we are largely unaware. Thus biology, like Jungian psychology, asserts that we receive knowledge of the world through perceptual processes which are mostly inaccessible to consciousness and which have evolved in a manner appropriate to our *environment of evolutionary adaptedness* (i.e. the environmental circumstances in which our species originally evolved).

The term '*Umwelt*' is in many ways preferable to 'environment' because it stresses the essentially subjective quality of the world which each animal species inhabits. The *Umwelt* in which all creatures live is highly specialized, and what renders it so specialized is less the actual physical configuration of the *ecological niche* (i.e. the organism's environment of evolutionary adaptedness) than the highly selective and idiosyncratic way in which this configuration is *perceived*. We, like all other animals, perceive only what we have been equipped to perceive; and only recently have we begun to recognize that our perceptions, like many of our patterns of behaviour, have been programmed by evolutionary pressures.

The '*Umwelts*' of different species can overlap, as, for example, in the case of man and the dog, but they are usually very different. Try to imagine, for the sake of argument, what features there might be in common between the '*Umwelts*' of the elephant and the squid. And even between men and dogs there are considerable differences since man inhabits a predominantly visual *Umwelt* while the dog's world is largely dominated by smells.

The essentially subjective nature of sensory perception has by no means been the exclusive province of biologists. It is a question which has long exercised the minds of philosophers and psychologists, who have asked themselves to what extent our senses may be said to provide us with a true picture of the real world as it actually exists. One of the most notorious thinkers in this field was Bishop Berkeley (1685–1753) who went so far as to question whether in fact the real world existed at all except when someone was looking at it. Taken to the point of ultimate absurdity, Berkeley's view leads to 'solipsism' – the belief that nothing exists in the world except oneself.

A considerably more helpful contribution was made by Immanuel Kant (1724–1804) who, fortunately, had no difficulty in assuming the existence of real objects whose qualities were perceptible by our senses. What he did question, however, was whether the senses gave us a true and accurate picture of what objects were 'really' like. We cannot know, he believed, what we add to or subtract from the real world in the act of perceiving it. We experience the world as we do because our perceptions impose a certain order on it. We cannot do otherwise: we see things within the artificial categories of space and time because these *a priori* categories are like a pair of tinted spectacles which we cannot remove and they therefore colour every observation that we make. Kant's teaching on these matters deeply affected the thinking of both Lorenz and Jung, as we shall see later.

A more introverted approach, broadly in sympathy with Kant's, was adopted by Edmund Husserl (1859–1938), the phenomenologist. He considered the shapes and colours that make up our visual percepts to stand as 'symbols' of the real objects perceived. (This, too, was in line with the Platonic idealism which for centuries dominated German philosophy. One thinks of Goethe's statement: 'All transitory things are but a symbol.') Thus, for Husserl, like Kant, it is our perceptions, rather than reality, that determine what we perceive. Instead of a table imposing itself on our perceptions, we impose our perceptions on it: our unconscious perceptual mechanisms marshal the chaotic mass of information making itself available to our senses, thus rendering them comprehensible to the conscious mind.

Up to a point, Husserl's view has been confirmed by ethological research, which has demonstrated that living organisms are highly selective of those environmental stimuli to which they respond. Such selectivity is inevitable: any physical environment possesses immense perceptual complexity and it is essential that the organism should confine its attention to those aspects of the environment that are most relevant to survival. Thus, ethology teaches that all organisms are programmed to perceive the world in specific ways, to select and respond to *key stimuli* which possess special significance within the context of the organism's *Umwelt.* This highly specialized ability depends on the existence of central mechanisms for receiving and processing information so that all the stimuli bombarding the organism at any moment can be 'filtered', the significant stimuli eliciting attention while the rest are virtually ignored. In all species, stimuli capable of passing the filter possess the power to release certain specific patterns of behaviour in the organism perceiving them. It was to explain this process that Niko Tinbergen proposed his hypothesis of an *innate releasing mechanism* (IRM for short). It is through the operation of such innate mechanisms that ethologists believe many patterns of social behaviour to be activated.

For example, a male robin will recognize and attack any rival entering his territory. What perceptual qualities must the rival possess in order to elicit this hostile behaviour? The answer is quite simply a red breast. That it is specifically the red breast which releases the aggression is clear from the observation that a male robin without a red breast is not attacked while a crude bunch of red feathers (provided it is displayed within the subject's territory) is. Then again, young rhesus monkeys, reared in isolation from birth, will shrink and emit sounds of fear if a picture of a threatening adult rhesus monkey is projected onto the wall of the cage. Projections of non-threatening adults elicit no such response. Release of the fear behaviour can only be explained on the basis of an IRM because the subjects have never seen or interacted with members of their own species.

As we have already seen, a classic example is that of the courting behaviour of the male stickleback on encountering a pregnant female: it is released by two *sign* (or 'key') *stimuli* – the swollen abdomen of the female, and the special posturing movement she makes on sighting the male. For her part, the female's courting behaviour is also released by two sign stimuli – the male's red belly and his special movements, the 'zig-zag dance'.

Thus, the sign stimuli responsible for releasing their appropriate responses are both simple and immutable: they correspond to the inner readiness of the organism as precisely as the key to the lock, and for this reason IRMs have sometimes been referred to as 'key-tumbler' structures.

That IRMs are present and operative in human beings there can be no doubt. Rene Spitz's classic experiments on the staring and smiling responses in 2-month-old babies enabled him to define the sign stimuli necessary to elicit these two responses. Using dummy figures he demonstrated that the necessary configuration consists of two eyes moving up and down in the manner of a nodding head. The effect is strengthened if a hair-line is drawn on the dummy to emphasize the nodding, and if a crude mouth is added with its corners turned up to represent a smile. The human voice also helps to elicit the responses. As will be described in chapter 7, the staring and smiling responses play a crucial role in the behavioural chain which mediates development of the infant's attachment to its mother. That they are unquestionably innate can be deduced from the observation that even babies blind from birth will stare and smile in the direction of their mother when she leans over the cot and speaks.

By discerning the features out of which he will later build a concept of the mother's face, the infant reveals, in Spitz's view, 'the capacity to rediscover in reality the object which corresponds to what is present in his imagination'. Here Spitz would appear to imply that the child can recognize outer configurations which correspond to inner archetypal prefigurations – much in the same way as Kepler considered that he was able 'to compare that which is externally perceived with inner ideas and to judge that it agrees with them' (see p. 45 above).

Further examples of the influence of innate programming on perception, behaviour and experience are afforded by the study of *fear*. In both animals and man, conditions which give rise to flight, withdrawal, or other demonstrations of fear are not necessarily dangerous in themselves: on careful examination it is clear that they are, as often as not, only indirectly related to situations which are actually a hazard to life or limb. As Bowlby puts it:

> in a wide array of animal species including man, a principle condition that elicits alarm and retreat is mere strangeness. Others are noise, and objects that rapidly expand or approach; and also, for animals of some species though not for others, darkness. Yet another is isolation.
>
> Now it is obvious that none of these stimulus situations is in itself dangerous. Yet, when looked at through evolutionary spectacles, their role in promoting survival is not difficult to see. Noise, strangeness, rapid approach, isolation, and for many species darkness too – all are conditions statistically associated with an increased risk of danger. (Bowlby, 1973)

Bowlby asserts that the tendency to react with fear to such common stimulus situations is due to genetically determined biases which possess survival value in the sense that they prepare individuals to meet *real* dangers. The existence of these biases would explain how it is that in modern civilized environments fear can be aroused in a variety of situations which are not, in fact, at all dangerous. Thus, to show fear in response to the perception of height, the approach of strange people or animals, the sudden occurrence of loud noises, or the realization that one is entirely alone, may in many instances seem absurd to a rationalist, or be deemed 'neurotic' by a psychiatrist, but in fact such behaviour reflects biological wisdom. For what the individual is responding to are the *natural cues*, or 'sign stimuli', commonly associated with danger in the environment of evolutionary adaptedness. Very often these cues do not betoken any danger, but they *could* do: therefore, it is not inappropriate for the individual to respond to them with wariness or fear on the principle that it is better to be safe than sorry.

Lorenz sees the innate organizations inherent in our perceptual apparatus as 'immune to all changes' and 'the foundation of all experience' (1977, p. 26). Clearly, he considers the IRM to be as crucial to our apperception as Jung's 'subjective aptitude' ('an innate structure which allows man to have experiences of this kind' – see above, p. 45). Thus, like Jung, Lorenz believes that innate perceptual mechanisms are the necessary precondition of all cognition: 'They precede all experience, and must do so if experience is possible at all. In this respect they correspond absolutely to Kant's definition of the *a priori*' (1977, p. 26).

Throughout Jung's work there are recurring references to Kant and his *Critique of Pure Reason*, with its unequivocal statement that 'there can be no empirical knowledge that is not already caught and limited by the *a priori* structure of cognition.' Jung equated this '*a priori* structure' with the archetypal determinants of the phylogenetic psyche (what he often referred to as the *objective psyche* as well as the 'collective unconscious'): he considered that it was these archetypal structures which controlled the perceptual mechanism, determining the relative salience of differing stimuli arising from both outside and inside the individual's personal boundaries.

However, the powerful influence of Germanic idealism is seldom far from Jung's thought and at times his statements bring him dangerously close to the brink of solipsism, arguing that the only thing of which we have certain knowledge is the psychic image reflected in consciousness: 'To the extent that the world does not assume the form of a psychic image, it is virtually non-existent,' he wrote. (*CW* 11, para. 769).

By contrast, Lorenz is less a prisoner of transcendental idealism: 'I am unshakeably convinced that all the information conveyed to us by our cognitive apparatus corresponds to actual realities.' (1977, p. 7). The reason he gives as the basis for this conviction is an important one, for, if we accept it, it solves at a stroke the paradox which has haunted all philosophical discussion of sensory perception since the time of Berkeley. Lorenz's proposition is this: our cognitive apparatus is *itself* an objective reality which has acquired its present form through *evolutionary adaptation to the real world.*

> The 'spectacles' of our modes of thought and perception, such as causality, substance, quality, time and place, are functions of a neurosensory organization that has evolved in the service of survival . . . we have developed 'organs' only for those aspects of reality which, in the interests of survival, it was imperative to take account, so that selection pressure produced this particular cognitive apparatus.' (1977, p. 7)

With this insight, Lorenz, who for a period held Immanuel Kant's chair at the University of Königsberg, believes he has found the essential flaw in Kant's transcendental idealism: 'He saw clearly that the forms of apprehension available to us are determined by the pre-existing structures of the experiencing subject and not by those of the object apprehended, but he did not see that the structure of our perceiving apparatus had anything to do with reality' (1977, p. 9). Lorenz continues:

> the system of sense organs and nerves that enables living things to survive and orientate themselves in the outer world has evolved phylogenetically through confrontation with an adaptation to that form of reality which we experience as phenomenological space. The system exists *a priori* to the extent that it is present before the individual perceives anything, and, must be present if experience is to be possible.

This also applies, he believes, 'to the relationship between our innate forms of potential experience and the facts of objective reality which these forms of experience make it possible for us to experience' (1977, p. 10).

I have quoted these passages at length because I believe Lorenz's argument to be crucial and because there are many similarities between Lorenz's statements and those quoted earlier by Jung ('There is no human experience, nor would experience be possible at all, without the intervention of a subjective aptitude. . . . These *a priori* categories have a collective character'). Moreover, Jung, for all his Platonic idealism, was clearly on to a similar notion as Lorenz concerning 'the facts of objective reality' in his conception of the phylogenetic psyche as being 'objective'. What Jung failed to do, however, was to develop the necessary biological argument to substantiate his view; nor did he make the Lorenzian link between the objective psyche, the objective world, and the consequent reality of our percepts. In this respect, Lorenz's standpoint represents an advance on the Jungian position, and it is an advance that analytical psychology could heed to its advantage. In Jung's defence, it should be said that he was a doctor, a psychologist, and a philosopher, rather than a biologist, and that it was no mean feat to anticipate to such a large extent the modern ethological view. The 'transcendental reality', wrote Jung, beyond 'the world inside and outside ourselves ... is as certain as our own existence' (*CW* 14, para. 787). Yet the distinction between subjective experience and the objective reality lying beyond it remained for Jung an 'unfathomable mystery' at the epistemological foundation of his work. However, he knew that introverted reflection upon the intrapsychic phenomena of experience added to our perception a whole new dimension of meaning, and, to him, this dimension was more important than reality itself.

For his part, Lorenz is not blind to the value of the introverted as opposed to the extraverted attitude, but being an extravert himself he has little time for 'idealism', seeing his approach essentially as one of *realism*.

> The realist persists in looking outwards only, unaware that he is a mirror. The idealist persists in looking in his mirror, averting his eyes from the external world. Thus both are inhibited from seeing that there is an obverse to every mirror. But the obverse does not reflect, and to this extent the mirror is in the same category as the objects it reflects. The physiological mechanism whose function it is to understand the real world is no less real than the world itself. (1977, p. 19)

To this unexceptionable statement I think Jung might have replied: 'God preserve us from living on the obverse side of the mirror!' And that really is the salient feature of the Jungian perspective: the archetypes have indeed evolved in adaptation to outer reality, but what matters to us as sentient beings is not so much the fact of their objective nature as our *experience* of them.

It is at this point that we approach the limits of ethology's usefulness. Brilliant though ethologists have been in their analysis and elucidation of behavioural processes, they are not able to tell us much about the subjective or experiential phenomena which must accompany those processes. As Weibel has written: 'The biologist can grasp inner processes only indirectly, through their effects on surface areas of the object that are accessible to him. For this reason he must *think* these effects with the help of models and theories' (quoted in Jaffe, 1970, p. 158, n. 20).

In man, behavioural responses are associated with psychological concomitants: we know the nature and quality of our acts. Each of us is aware that he is not just a conglomerate of behavioural systems responding to a variety of environmental stimuli: we are conscious of what is happening, and we experience behaviour – both our own and other people's – as possessing certain qualities of feeling or emotion. It is quite possible that this is also true of many other animal species, but we cannot know how our experiences differ from theirs because, unfortunately, we cannot ask them.

But one distinction which it seems fair to make is that not only do we know what we are doing at the time that we are doing it, but we can, in addition, actually work out in our minds what we shall do before we do it. Monkeys can plan in this way up to a point (as Kohler's classic experiments established), but it is clear that they have never evolved the capacity to manipulate thoughts and deal with symbols to the degree that we have. This is one of the more telling reasons why they have remained monkeys while we have become men. Thinking, planning, using symbols to deputize for actions, are capacities of profound evolutionary significance, and ethology cannot, by virtue of the nature of its methodology, tell us very much about them.

Jung, on the other hand, devoted his life to the study of just these processes. While he fully accepted that archetypes had an instinctual component, what interested him much more was the archetype's psychic or 'spiritual' aspect which finds symbolic expression in consciousness. As we have seen, he defined the archetype as 'an inherited mode of functioning, corresponding to the inborn way in which the chick emerges from the egg' and equated it with 'a pattern of behaviour' (see above, pp. 17–18). In the same passage he continues:

> This aspect of the archetype is the biological one. . . . But the picture changes at once when looked at from the inside, that is, from within the realm of the subjective psyche. Here the archetype presents itself as numinous, that is, it appears as an *experience* of fundamental importance. Whenever it clothes itself in the appropriate symbols, which is not always the case, it puts the individual into a state of possessedness, the consequences of which may be incalculable. (Forward to Harding, 1948, pp. ix f)

Examples of instinctive behaviour associated with the phenomenon of archetypal possession will be presented when we come to discuss the *Shadow* concept in chapter 12 and the process of falling in love in chapter 11. At this juncture we must examine links between archetypes and conscious experience.

· 5 ·

Archetypes and experience

1 Duality and dualism

'Just as we have been compelled to postulate the concept of an instinct determining or regulating our conscious actions, so, in order to account for the uniformity and regularity of our perceptions, we must have recourse to the correlated concept of a factor determining the mode of apprehension,' wrote Jung, as if summarizing both sections of the last chapter. 'It is this factor,' he went on, 'that I call the archetype or the primordial image. The primordial image might suitably be described as *the instinct's perception of itself* [Jung's italics], or as the self-portrait of the instinct' (*CW* 8, para. 277).

Thus, the archetype possesses a fundamental duality: it is conscious and unconscious, symbolical and instinctive, psychic and non-psychic; it is the essential precondition of all psycho-physical events (for the non-psychic, material dimension Jung employed the term *psychoid archetype*, of which more later). The dual aspects of the archetype are not conceived as 'opposites' or as different modalities, but rather as self-complementary 'antinomies'. It is as a consequence of this dual nature that the archetype achieves expression – or is *actualized* as Jung would say – both on the objective level of outer behaviour and on the subjective plain of inner conscious experience. In his essay *Mind and Earth*, Jung wrote: 'the archetypes are as it were the hidden foundations of the conscious mind, or, to use another comparison, the roots which the psyche has sunk not only in the earth in the narrower sense but in the world in general. Archetypes are *systems of readiness for action*, and at the same time *images and emotions*' (my italics). In this conception of the archetype as the common origin of both behavioural and psychic events, Jung made a theoretical contribution of the highest significance, and one which deserves far wider recognition than it has hitherto received, for it permits us to escape from the pitfalls of vitalism and epiphenomenalism (see below) which have hampered the progress of all those who have attempted to unravel the mysteries of the relationship between the body and the mind.

Since the time of René Descartes (1596–1650), we have been taught to think of body and mind as if they were separate entities, either influencing one another or proceeding side by side. The various schools of thought which have evolved out of this view may be summarized under four headings:

1 *Mentalism*: this is essentially Descartes' view, namely, that body and mind are distinct entities, each of equivalent status, which are linked together in a way which it is impossible to explain. It is this position that Gilbert Ryle satirized as 'the dogma of the Ghost in the Machine'.

2 *Vitalism*: this view denies the equivalent status of body and mind. It sees mind as predominant, and capable of controlling physical processes, including those of the brain. For the vitalist, the 'Ghost' controls the 'Machine'.

3 *Epiphenomenalism*: this view is the complete antithesis of vitalism. It sees the neurophysiological processes of the brain as causal and primary: the 'Ghost' is merely the product of the 'Machine'. Mental processes have no causal agency, they are merely epiphenomena (epi=upon) accompanying the physical activities of the brain, and they make absolutely no difference to the outcome.

4 *Interactionism*: this is a compromise view which holds that body and mind can mutually influence one another.

As Bowlby has justly observed, neither Cartesianism nor any of its offshoots has done much to advance our understanding of the psyche's relationship to the soma. Mentalism has precluded the framing of testable hypotheses, whereas epiphenomenalism has usually been associated with a form of extreme behaviourism which effectively rules out investigation of 'all the more exciting reaches of human experience . . . moreover, the theoretical schema presented is found to be of little use to those, clinicians and others, who deal with ordinary people living everyday lives' (1969, p. 107). Behaviourists who are not epiphenomenalists have tended to opt out of the body-mind problem by shelving all consideration of psychic events until some imagined time in the future when it is hoped that our techniques will be sufficiently sophisticated to integrate so-called mental phenomena with the data of behavioural investigation. This is the position advocated by J. S. Haldane (in *Organism and Environment as Illustrated by the Physiology of Breathing*, 1936), and although it represents a stance of unimpeachable scientific rectitude, it is, as Bowlby points out, one which is of little assistance to the clinician whose work is largely concerned with the reports which patients make about their private experiences, only some of which can be corroborated by observation or put to an objective test. No doctor can permit himself the luxury of Haldane's elevated procrastination: every day of his working life he has to relate the objective to the subjective, the public to the private, the body to the mind. That the problem of building a bridge between these two realms is one of great methodological difficulty cannot be denied, but it should not deter us from making the attempt. Certainly, one can no longer be excused for suspending all consideration of the problem by hiving it off on to posterity. We have to go on developing psychosomatic models in the same spirit as Bowlby or Jung: they may be judged by those who come after us as absurdly crude, but then so were the early astronomers' models of the universe and the early cartographers' maps of the world. Crude models are at least a beginning. The only possible objection to devising them is that they can sometimes bewitch the inventor (and his assistants) who then identify the model with reality, believing that once and for all the riddle has been solved, that no further modification is necessary, nor should be allowed. Jung was acutely aware of this danger; one sometimes wishes that the same could be said of his disciples. ('Thank God I am Jung,' he once said, 'and not a Jungian.')

2 The Jungian model

Put in its simplest terms, Jung's psychosomatic model proposes a phylogenetic structure, the interstices of which are filled out in the course of ontogenetic development. The phylogenetic structure is made up of archetypal units which possess the dynamic property of seeking their own actualization in the behaviour and the developing personality of the individual as he lives out his life-cycle within the context of his environmental circumstances. To this overall process of archetypal actualization and personality development Jung gave the name *individuation*. 'Individuation,' he wrote, 'is an expression of that biological process – simple or complicated as the case may be – by which every living thing becomes what it was destined to become from the beginning' (*CW* 11, para. 144). And again: 'Ultimately, every individual life is at the same time the eternal life of the species' (*CW* 11, para. 146).

By way of illustration, let us take an archetype of greatest significance during the early years of life: the mother archetype. As we have already noted, Jung, unlike Freud, considered the mental equipment of the child to be highly adapted to the world into which it was born. Jung held that the neurophysiological system concerned with the perception and experience of mothering activities, as well as the behavioural repertoire necessary to relate to the figure providing them – usually the mother – gradually matured under the organizing influence of the mother archetype functioning within the child. The mother archetype is the vital nucleus of the individual's growing mother complex: originally the archetype-as-such is unconscious; then, as the child matures in close proximity to its mother, so all those behaviours, feelings, and perceptions determined by the mother archetype are 'released' or activated with the consequent development of the mother complex within the child's psyche and the associated co-ordination of the mother-infant behavioural chain in outer reality.

It is often thought – quite erroneously – that complexes are essentially pathological. In fact, complexes are as much a part of the healthy psyche as they are of the neurotic psyche. The term *complex* is one which Jung himself introduced into psychology early in his career when working on his classic word association test. By it, he inferred a collection of associated ideas and images all linked together by a common affect. Although the term has indeed acquired connotations of pathology, Jung had no such connotations in mind when he proposed it. While complexes could be pathological and contribute to neurotic suffering, Jung regarded them as normally healthy components of the psyche; complexes were, in fact, the functional units of which the ontogenetic psyche was composed. Complexes are archetypes actualized in the mind.

Jung believed that the process of archetypal actualization and complex formation occurred in accordance with the *Laws of Association* worked out by academic psychologists at the end of the last century. These take two forms: (1) the *law of similarity*, and (2) the *law of contiguity*, and normal complexes are formed when both these laws are satisfied. Thus, a normal complex develops when (1) the personal mother is 'good enough' (to use Dr D. W. Winnicott's phrase) in that her maternal qualities correspond appropriately enough to those anticipations built into the maternal archetype for her to be perceived and experienced by the child as 'mother'; and (2) when she is continuously present, or contiguous, throughout the course of childhood. On the other hand, a pathological mother complex will be formed if either of these laws is inadequately satisfied, for example, if the mother's repertoire of maternal behaviours is defective in some important way, or if there should be lengthy periods of mother-child separation.

Pathological complexes can also arise when contiguity overrides similarity in the associative process: then forms of actualization can occur which are inappropriate or antagonistic to the primary archetypal intent. Examples leap readily to mind: young goslings imprinting Lorenz or his boat rather than mother goose: Pavlov's dogs developing anorexia nervosa when given electric shocks with their dinner (the feeding behavioural system being perverted from its normal objective as a result of pathological conditioning, in which self-preservation has become associated, by contiguity, with the experience of hunger); the child who becomes attached to the rejecting and battering mother. Similarly, sexual deviations such as fetishism, sado-masochism, paedophilia, and so on, may be understood as inappropriate actualizations of archetypal determinants through contiguity with incongruous stimuli at sensitive periods of development.

Complexes are part conscious and part unconscious: they are to the personal (ontogenetic) psyche what archetypes are to the collective (phylogenetic) psyche, for they are composed of ontogenetic 'flesh' covering a phylogenetic 'skeleton'. At the core of every complex there is an archetype. From the moment of conception the possibility of individual development is inherent in the genetic structure of the new individual and, however much circumstances, both intra- and extra-uterine, may influence development, the possibilities latent in the original archetypal structure are primary *a priori* determinants of the whole life-cycle. This basic archetypal structure Jung termed *the Self*, calling it 'the archetype of archetypes', and saw it as the matrix of the individual totality, out of which the conscious individual personality emerges. It is the Self which determines the stages of ontological development, functioning as invisible guide and mentor, leading the growing child on towards consciousness, personality and effectual existence. But the archetypal purpose inherent in the Self is heavily dependent for its expression upon the presence of those figures and events normally characteristic of the human *Umwelt*, of which the presence of parents, or at least of adults *in loco parentis*, are the most crucial.

Although Jung died before much of the data on the consequences of maternal deprivation and separation became available, the often tragically sad details of these findings would not have come as a surprise to him. He was quite clear that a mother, or mother-substitute, must be present, and continuously present, if the mother archetype was to be actualized in the child. The first essential for the woman of the primal relationship was that she be *there* – to constellate in human form the 'Great Good Mother', she who nurtures, warms, grants security, and who alone makes possible the continuance of life; the unconsciously mobilized maternal behaviour of the mother then enables her to place herself in dynamic relationship with the mother archetype operating within her own psyche, no less than within her child. Jung was convinced that children actually experience their parents as personifications of the parent archetypes, thus imparting to them a magic power and significance far transcending, as often as not, their personal qualities as people. Parents are, of course, fallible creatures with their own limitations and few are sufficiently individuated to be able to actualize in their entirety all attributes of the parental archetype. But be they ever so incompetent, they will still afford the key that opens the archetypal lock, so setting in train the development of those earliest complexes which form the foundations of the personal psyche and determine the child's anticipations of his world. For parents are the 'great teachers' of mankind, the 'transmittors of culture' the living embodiments of natural existence (mother) and of order (father); and the complexes founded upon their influence play on and on throughout life like a circular tape-recording, made during crucial moments of infancy, which repeats ceaselessly till the mechanism finally runs down and stops.

Formation of the mother complex, therefore, occurs as the result of our first, most profound and, probably, most influential encounter with an archetype.

3 On encountering archetypes

Though he devoted over half a century to the study of archetypes, Jung concluded that they must defeat all attempts to grasp them academically. If you try to define the archetype objectively and fail to give its 'feeling tone' due recognition, then you 'end with nothing more than a jumble of mythological concepts, which can be strung together to show that everything means anything – or nothing at all'. (1964, p. 96). Archetypes 'gain life and meaning only when you take into account their numinosity – i.e. their relation to the living individual' (p. 98). Ultimately, you cannot define an archetype, any more than you can define meaning. You can only experience it.

Take, for example, the contra-sexual archetype. Everybody carries qualities of the opposite sex, not only in the physical sense of contra-sexual genes, hormones and anatomical vestiges, but also in the psychological realm of attitudes, feelings and ideas. As one would expect, Jung's primary interest in these contra-sexual attributes was in their psychic manifestations, which he believed to be archetypally determined. The feminine archetype in man he termed the *Anima* and the masculine archetype in woman the *Animus*, and he saw each as the means of comprehending the essential 'otherness' of the opposite sex. 'Thus the whole nature of man presupposes woman, both physically and spiritually. His system is tuned to woman from the start' (see p. 45 above). When a man experiences passionate attraction to a woman, it is because she seems to embody his Anima, and she appears to him more beautiful, more numinous than any other woman around – often to the stupefaction of his friends who completely fail to understand what he sees in her. (George Bernard Shaw once described love as 'overestimating the difference between one woman and another'!) This is the phenomenon of *archetypal projection – but only those who have had the experience of falling hopelessly in love can know* what the phenomenon is like. Enormous power seems to be possessed by the woman on to whom the archetype is projected, and the man who does the projecting is quite unable to use his critical faculties, because the archetype, once constellated, has him in its grip. Whatever conscious reasons he may advance in explanation of his choice, they are in fact secondary – rationalizations merely: the primary motivation lies in the numinous quality of the activated archetype.

It is not poetic licence that has caused artists since classical times to portray lovers as the helpless victims of Eros, that most mischievously capricious of all gods. Archetypal projection is not something one chooses to do: it happens to us, whether we like it or not. But there is evidently a natural tendency for the phenomenon to occur. Inherent in every archetype is the notion of unfulfilment: an inner awareness of need. Man needs woman, either as mother or mate, if he is to fulfil himself. The archetype ever seeks its own completion, and when activated reveals that which remains to be attained on the tortuous path forward to individuation.

The commonest guise in which the Anima is encountered is in dreams, where she frequently appears as an unknown young woman. Although she looks young, there is about her a timeless quality and often a suggestion that she has years of experience behind her. She may be connected with earth or water and is often endowed with great power. Like the mother archetype she has positive and negative aspects: on the one hand she is a loving, helpful figure, on the other a seductress or witch. Anima dreams can be extremely vivid and their numinosity may live on in the imagination long after most dreams are forgotten.

Thus, the feeling value of the archetype is every bit as important as its intellectual understanding; and feeling value is something that only an individual can experience in his private awareness. Jung saw this truth as crucial to the establishment of any humane science of psychology. 'Psychology,' he wrote, 'is the only science that has to take the factor of value (i.e. feeling) into account, because it is the link between physical events and life. Psychology is often accused of not being scientific on this account: but its critics fail to understand the scientific and practical necessity of giving due consideration to feeling' (1964, p. 99).

What did Jung mean by 'feeling'? For him, feeling was one of the four primary modes of human psychic functioning. The other three are thinking, sensation and intuition. All four are perfectly effective modes of apperception, but each individual tends to make his primary adaptations to reality through one of the four modes, that being his 'superior function'. A full description of the four functions is to be found in *Psychological Types* (*CW* 6), but a succinct summary of them is given in *Modern Man in Search of a Soul* (p. 107): 'Sensation establishes what is essentially given, thinking enables us to recognize its meaning, feeling tells us its value, and finally intuition points to the possibilities of the whence and whither that lie within the immediate facts.'

Like most of Jung's theoretical formulations, his four functional types have been widely misunderstood and attacked. While most authorities are able to accept sensation and thinking as crucial modes of apperception, many draw the line at feeling and intuition, dismissing them as embarrassing artefacts, too unsusceptible to objective verification and statistical treatment to be worthy of serious scientific investigation. Yet feeling and intuition are functions crucial to the perception of meaning; without them we are relegated to the condition of sophisticated robots.

Fortunately, not all psychologists have been disdainful of these neglected functions. Bowlby, for example, though primarily concerned with the characteristics of behavioural systems is no simple behaviourist: he acknowledges that behaviour is commonly associated with conscious awareness. Moreover, he has no doubt that awareness, acting through functions that he terms 'appraisal' and 'feeling', plays an essential role in activating, monitoring, and terminating a system's performance. For Bowlby, 'affects, feelings, and emotions are phases of an individual's *intuitive appraisals* [my italics] either of his own organismic states and urges to act or of the succession of environmental situations in which he finds himself. These appraising processes have often, but not always, the very special property of being experienced as feelings, or, to use a better terminology, as felt' (1969, p. 104). Bowlby acknowledges that his use of such terms as 'feeling' and 'intuitive appraisal' brings up questions related to the body-mind problem already touched on in the first section of this chapter. His understanding of how it is that appraising processes come to be 'felt' rests on S. Langer's philosophical approach to the problem in her book *Mind: An Essay on Human Feeling* (1967). Langer argues that 'feeling' is not a discrete entity but a process, and 'being felt is a phase of the process itself'. She uses the term 'phase' to apply to any mode in which anything may appear or disappear *without anything having been added to or subtracted from it.* As an example of what she means, Langer cites the heating and cooling of an iron: 'When iron is heated to a critical degree it becomes red; yet its redness is not a new entity' (i.e. the redness has not come from anywhere as the iron heats up, nor has it anywhere to go when the iron cools down: it is not like phlogiston!). 'It was *a phase of the iron itself* [my italics], at high temperature.' Thus, Langer concludes, 'as soon as feeling is regarded as a phase of a physiological process instead of a product of it – namely, a new entity metaphysically different from it – the paradox of the physical and the psychical disappears.'

The models of Bowlby and Jung, arrived at quite independently, accord well with Langer's proposition. Like attachment theory, archetypal theory conceives of the 'Ghost' neither as a product of the 'Machine' nor as an entity metaphysically different from the 'Machine': both objective behaviour and subjective experience are viewed, as Langer puts it, as 'phases' of the same process – the process of archetypal actualization. The living being, wrote Jung,

> appears outwardly as the material body, but inwardly as a series of images of the vital activities taking place within it. They are two sides of the same coin, and we cannot rid ourselves of the doubt that perhaps this whole separation of mind and body may finally prove to be merely a device of reason for the purpose of conscious discrimination – an intellectually necessary separation of one and the same fact into two aspects, to which we then illegitimately attribute an independent existence. (*CW* 8, para. 619)

To Jung, psyche and matter were 'two different aspects of the same thing' (*CW* 8, para. 418). This formulation is entirely compatible with Jung's whole approach to psychology which was dominated from the outset by the dual concepts of symmetry and polarity. Thus, as we have already seen, he conceived of the archetype as possessing two poles: a biological/organic pole and a psychic one. He also considered a dynamic polarity to exist within the psyche as a whole between ego-consciousness on the one hand and unconscious processes on the other, the two operating in relation to each other in the manner of a homeostatic – or self-regulating – system. Moreover, another pair of polar concepts which commended themselves to Jung were those of causality and finality, so that he understood psychic events – whether dreams, symptoms, affects, or whatever – not only in terms of their origin in childhood (as was the Freudian bias) but in terms of their goal or purpose. 'What is the dream trying to tell us?' he would ask his patients and students. 'What one-sided attitude of ego-consciousness is it seeking to redress?' Here, too, there are marked similarities with Bowlby's view that behavioural systems like those operating between a mother and her infant function cybernetically through positive and negative feedback to achieve a form of behavioural homeostasis. Of his own approach, Bowlby writes: 'By utilizing the concept of feedback, it gives as much attention to the conditions that terminate an act as to those that initiate one. . . . By being cast in terms of control theory and evolution theory, the model links psychoanalysis to the main corpus of present day biology.' In essence the same could be said of the approach of Jung, except, of course, that it was formulated much earlier and before cybernetics came of age. The fact is that Jung attributed as much significance to symbolic events as Bowlby attributes to behaviour, and he approached them in much the same spirit. Archetypes, he discovered, often achieved their most immediate, their most numinous expression in dreams; and dreaming he conceived to be *a symbolic form of goal-corrected behaviour.*

Jung made his boldest contribution to the body-mind debate when, in 1946, he extended his concept of the archetype to embrace its 'psychoid' nature. Until then, he had regarded the two poles – or 'antinomies' – of the archetype to be 'instinct' and 'spirit'. Now, with this new development, he added an extraordinary dimension to the whole hypothesis: for, in fact, what he now proposed was that archetypal structures were fundamental to the existence of all living organisms, and that they were continuous with structures controlling the behaviour of inorganic matter. The archetype had become for him 'the bridge to matter in general' (*CW* 8, para. 420). The psychoid archetype was thus the essential organic nucleus.

> The deeper 'layers' of the psyche lose their individual uniqueness as they retreat farther and farther into the darkness. 'Lower down', that is to say as they approach the autonomous functional systems, they become increasingly collective until they are universalized and extinguished in the body's materiality, i.e. in chemical substances. The body's carbon is simply carbon. Hence, 'at bottom' the psyche is simply 'world'. (*CW* 9, pt 1, para. 291)

Ultimately, the distinction between organic and inorganic matter is artificial, like the distinction between mind and body, a hypothetical construct developed to assist our comprehension of reality. Thus, the theory of evolution will not have been properly worked out until it has been carried back beyond the emergence of the simplest living organisms to encompass the changes occurring in the inorganic substances from which these organisms arose.

This work is already well advanced. Of the 92 naturally occurring elements, the curiously 'Jungian' number of four are basic to the structure of all living organisms: hydrogen, oxygen, nitrogen, and carbon. At the time when life on this planet began the prevalent raw materials on the earth's surface were again four in number: water, carbon dioxide, methane, and ammonia. As long ago as 1922, the Russian scientist Oparin suggested that these simple inorganic substances were the precursors of the more complex organic molecules of sugars, fats and proteins, out of which living organisms evolved. Like Oparin, the British biologist J. B. S. Haldane believed that vast numbers of organic structures could have been naturally synthesized from the earth's primeval atmosphere when its elements were exposed to the rays of the sun and the great flashes of lightning which characterized the climatic conditions of primordial times. These organic compounds, he believed, would have accumulated 'till the primitive oceans reached the consistency of hot dilute soup'.

This hypothesis was not tested experimentally until 1953, when Professor Urey, in America, subjected a mixture of methane, ammonia, hydrogen, and water vapour to a series of electrical discharges over the course of a week. When he analysed the resulting mixture, Urey found an astounding variety of organic substances, including amino-acids, which are the 'building blocks' of living cells. Similar laboratory experiments have subsequently demonstrated that all the organic substances necessary for the creation of life – proteins, the energy-liberating ATP, and the vital nucleic acids (the purines and pyrimidines) out of which the genetic molecule DNA is made – all can be produced out of simple inorganic gases without the intervention of human, or divine, ingenuity.

A crucial step in the evolutionary process occurred when organic molecules thus formed acquired the capacity *to replicate themselves*. This need only have happened in the case of one such molecule by the sort of stupendous fluke that is only conceivable in the seeming eternity of evolutionary time. But once formed, this original replicator would have functioned as a mould or template from which other molecules in the 'hot dilute soup' were made as identical or reciprocal copies. Whether the original replicator operated on a positive-to-positive basis, or whether, like its modern equivalent – the DNA molecule – it used positive-to-negative replication, its advent brought an entirely new order of stability into the world. Until then there would have existed an infinite variety of organic forms, but once the replicator emerged it would have changed all that by spreading its copies rapidly throughout the seas. Thus the replicator was the original biological archetype – the first structure from which copies could be made; and we see in the replicator and its copies the primordial archetypal quality, namely, that of stability and invariance.

That the million or so different species at present inhabiting our planet reproduce themselves so faithfully still depends on this simple archetypal device. In every cell of every living organism there exists a highly specific blueprint drawn up by a further quaternity of substances – the nucleotides adenine, thymine, cytosine and guanine – which together make the genes. Combined in assorted pairs, these remarkable compounds compose the language through which matter communicates with matter in a perpetual renewal of the miracle we call life. Like the steps of a spiral staircase, the nucleotide pairs, linked by two spiralling sugar-phosphate supports, form the 'double helix' of each molecule of DNA, their sequential order conveying the code which determines how every cell in an organism, be it gorilla, cabbage, or paramecium, must develop. The unique property of these molecules is replication. The staircase splits down the middle, using itself as a template for the creation of a new molecule, the sequential order of the nucleotide pairs being reduplicated each time the cell divides.

The archetypal significance of this extraordinary propensity was not lost on Francis Crick who, together with James Watson, obtained a Nobel Prize for discovering the structure of DNA. In his book, *The*

Double Helix (1968, p. 102), Watson describes a pub conversation in which Crick fell to discussing the existence of a 'perfect biological principle': suddenly, he 'popped out with the idea that the perfect biological principle was the self-replication of the gene – that is, the ability of the gene to be exactly copied when the chromosome number doubles during cell division'. The operation of this 'perfect biological principle' assures the perpetuation of each species, whose characteristics are encoded in the genotype. Perpetuation of the genotype depends upon perpetuation of matter, but with one important proviso – that what is passed from generation to generation is a structure, a *characteristic patterning* of matter: it is this pattern which forms the *replicable archetype* of the species.

Unicellular organisms reproduce themselves by dividing into two new individuals, the chromosomes simply splitting in half. Most higher forms of plant and animal life, however, have differentiated into males and females and use sexual reproduction, with the result that the DNA carried by progeny is derived half from the father and half from the mother, thus achieving a new genetic synthesis with each generation. Once fertilized, the ovum begins to divide, the one cell becoming two, two becoming four, and so on, until the new organism is completed in every detail in strict accordance with the dictates of the genotype. How this miraculous transformation comes about molecular biologists are beginning to discover. It seems that the DNA molecule is a minute control system co-ordinating the activities of enzymes and other biochemical agents through the use of positive and negative feedback in accordance with the developmental programme laid down in the nucleotide sequence. The genotype functions as an 'open programme': for example, the ectoderm cells of an embryo can develop into skin, the parts of an eye, brain cells, or the spinal cord. What decides which of these tissues a particular ectodermal cell will become? The decision seems to reside with the cytoplasmic substances which are produced in the neighbourhood of the cell concerned. If you take a piece of ectoderm from a part normally destined to become skin and place it in the region of the developing eye, it will lose its epidermal propensities and become an eye cell. It appears that every ectoderm cell possesses the information required to form all ectodermal tissues (as Spemann, the great embryologist, would have phrased it, its 'prospective potency' is greater than its 'prospective significance'): which of the potential programmes is actually put into effect depends entirely on the environmental influences to which the cell is subjected. All adaptive processes, whether behavioural or embryonic, probably function along the same lines. The system incorporates genetic instructions for all the programmes it is potentially capable of executing: the exigencies of life are already 'planned for', the apparent goal being *the wholeness of the individual organism.*

Followed to its logical conclusion, Jung's seminal concept takes us beyond the confines of biology: his view of the archetype's 'psychoid' aspect has been taken up by the physicist, Wolfgang Pauli, who saw it as a major contribution to our understanding of the 'laws' of nature. For Pauli, the psychoid archetype represented a sort of 'missing link' between the world which is the legitimate study of science, and the mind of the scientist who studies it. Jung's postulate was not just 'the bridge to matter in general' but to 'a cosmic order independent of our choice and distinct from the world of phenomena' (1955, p. 152). The relationship between the physical reality we perceive and our cognitive formulations concerning that reality is 'predicated upon the fact that the soul of the perceiver and that which is recognized by perception are subject to an order thought to be objective' (p. 152). The archetypes which order our perceptions and ideas are themselves the product of an objective order which transcends the human mind and the external world. Thus, Pauli reaffirms Kepler's original insight that scientific discovery proceeds on the basis of 'matching' observations of external phenomena with forms pre-existent in the human psyche. A position which, as we have seen, has been further developed by Lorenz in his proposal that 'our cognitive apparatus corresponds to actual realities' because it bears the stamp or imprint ('archetype') of the outer world to which, in the course of evolution, it has become intimately and specifically adapted.

Essentially, Pauli believed that the psychologist and the physicist were engaged on a complementary quest, advocating that

> the investigation of scientific knowledge directed outwards should be supplemented by an investigation of this knowledge directed inwards. The former process is directed to adjusting our knowledge to external objects; the latter should bring to light the archetypal images used in the creation of our scientific theories. Only by combining both these directions of research may complete understanding be obtained. (p. 208)

Thus, Pauli argued that psychoid archetypes function 'as the sought-for bridge between sense perceptions and ideas and are, accordingly, a necessary presupposition even for evolving a scientific theory of nature' (p. 153). Seen in this light, therefore, Jung's archetypal model offers a potential basis not only for the unification of the biological sciences but of science as a whole.

This innovative extension of the archetypal hypothesis represents a significant step forward in the direction of establishing the epistemological roots of Jung's individuation principle: that it is not merely a process confined to patients undergoing analysis, but an evolutionary principle universally present throughout nature; a dynamic potentiality active within the cells of every organism working towards the goal of self-completion. The clearly discernible life-cycles of all living systems demonstrate the existence of a self-regulating propensity moving ever forwards on a predetermined course which ensures that the growth and activity of the organism will occur in accordance with the archetypal intentions encoded in the genes. This process of individuation, 'by which every living thing becomes what it was destined to become from the beginning', enshrined for Jung the fundamental meaning of life. The ultimate goal of the process, both for the evolution of the species as a whole and for the development of the individual personality, Jung saw, quite simply, as 'consciousness'.

Just as he assumed archetypal structures to be operative in animals as well as humans,* thus possessing an evolutionary history, so Jung declined to attribute to human beings a monopoly on consciousness. He rejected the ruthlessly anthropocentric prejudice which maintains that the only mental phenomena are human and that, therefore, such phenomena, by definition, cannot be experienced by animals. This Humpty-Dumpty logic has blinded us to the obvious truth that animal consciousness and human consciousness are evolutionary extensions of the same thing. Edmund Sinnott has breached this monstrous anthropocentric bastion by a daring redefinition of mind, not in terms of human awareness, but as 'whatever directs the development and activity of an organism towards goals set up within its living stuff' (1957, p. 85). Sinnott considered protoplasm, 'the basic stuff of life', to be a system orientated towards specific goals which were precisely defined by the genome. The course of evolution has been marked by a movement forwards on the part of protoplasmic systems to develop cognitive or 'mental' functions as an increasingly efficient means of regulating appropriate, adaptive behaviour. In other words, Sinnott conceives of mind as an executive organ which has evolved to co-ordinate the activities of protoplasmic systems in the service of survival thus permitting the more certain achievement of their inherent goals. Mind and body have their source together in the basic protoplasmic system. Both, in Sinnott's view, are 'coextensive with life itself'; or, as Langer might say, both are 'phases' of the same process.

For Sinnott, such 'instinctive' behaviour as that demonstrated by a humming bird building its nest represents 'the dim beginnings of mind'. These tiny birds are never taught the rudiments of nest-building, yet they set about the immensely complicated task of constructing their first home like 'a human craftsman, sizing up a particular problem, trying this means and that, and finally reaching a satisfactory solution' (1957,

* Archetypes are 'inherited, instinctive impulses and forms that can be observed in all living creatures' (CW 3, para. 565).

p. 44). Nest-building is a form of goal-corrected behaviour implicit in the structure of the organism, yet, as they work, birds function *as though* they were conscious of what they are doing. This, Sinnott regards as a psychic process in simple form, and cites it as an example of primitive psychic activity clearly associated with the functioning of organic structures – 'the dim beginnings of mind'. Man's mental experience, in essence and origin, he sees as an evolutionary extension of such activities. 'In behaviour protoplasmic purpose grows to instinct, and with dawning consciousness this leads to thought and the higher elements of mind' (1957, pp. 43–4).

In man, as a result of evolution, the 'basic protoplasmic process working towards goals' has developed the potential for wide consciousness of its own activity, and it was this capacity which so deeply excited Jung. And it is to Jung that we owe the extraordinary insight that *we can ourselves perceive our own phylogeny as a personal revelation*: that we can extend consciousness so as to intervene creatively at the juncture where phylogeny becomes ontogeny. Biology, archeology and anthropology offer objective, scientific descriptions of the evolutionary process: but in our personal ontological development we can, each and every one of us, catch glimpses of this process as a subjective psychic experience. As the archetypal sequences (the basic 'protoplasmic pattern') unfolds in the life-cycle of the individual, it is at the same time represented in consciousness as archetypal images and ideas: the symbolisms thus brought into being are not mere luxuries to be shared in an analytic hour, but an integral expression of the 'basic protoplasmic purpose' in man. The total archetypal system – what Jung termed 'the Self' – has programmed within it the complete scenario for individual life. As the story unfolds, new archetypal motifs emerge, expressing the point which the action has reached. Much of the time we pay little attention to this inner theatre, which will never close till the very end of the last act, but occasionally – more often if in analysis – one finds oneself suddenly on stage, committed to a part of the performance. At such moments an archetype has taken hold and one is transfigured by its numinous intensity.

Part II

Archetypes in practice

· 6 ·

The family

Once upon a time, and not so long ago, the family was regarded as a sacred institution. Marriage sealed a life-long bond between a man and a woman, the purpose of which was the procreation and rearing of their children. In recent decades, however, the family has taken a severe battering: rapid social and economic changes attendant upon the industrial revolution have resulted in a disintegration of the traditional 'extended' family with its built-in emotional and social support systems, while architectural fads and the phantasies of post-war town planners have turned our inner cities into psychiatric disaster areas by shattering the kinship networks that formerly held people together within distinctive territorial bounds. All this has coincided with widespread dissemination of the narcissistic belief that every individual has a right to personal fulfilment which transcends the vows of marriage and which justifies the termination of marriages in which such fulfilment can no longer be adequately found. As if this were not enough, the family has also come under ideological attack, being held responsible for the systematic exploitation of women and children and stigmatized as the cause of practically all the psychiatric ills that man is heir to. (Those interested in such polemics will find plenty of ammunition in the writings of Germaine Greer, David Cooper, Ronald Laing, etc. While gratefully acknowledging the validity of many of their insights, I stop short of any radical rejection of the family as an institution. To argue that families should be done away with because they cause neurosis seems to me about as logical as advocating the abolition of houses because people die in them, or the prohibition of breasts because women get cancer there. True, growing up in a particular family may make you neurotic, but the probability of being neurotic is far greater if you grow up with no family at all.)

However, despite this inimical barrage the family is still with us, albeit in its truncated 'nuclear' form of parents and dependent children. Indeed it shows remarkable resilience. It has even survived systematic attempts to dismantle it. In Soviet Russia, for example, soon after the 1917 Revolution, it was decided to free the family of all legal constraints: registration of marriages was no longer obligatory, birth control was advocated and legal abortion made freely available on demand. Divorce was easy, free love accepted, and no rules or regulations were tolerated concerning how couples should behave to one another or to their children. And yet, as Maurice Hindus records in his book *Mother Russia* (1943), the family remained. Its roots were never shaken and were never in danger of being torn out. Despite easy divorce, the right to free and frequent abortions, the overwhelming mass of Russian humanity, in the village almost all of them, fell in love, married, and even when they did not record the union in the registration office, they stayed married. They raised children. They built a home in the best way they could. Stripped of the family compulsions that their grandfathers had known, they chose of their own accord to continue the ancestral habit and tradition of family life.

A more concerted effort to restructure the family was undertaken in the kibbutzim of Israel. Here the intention was to end the division of labour along gender lines, to establish complete equality between the sexes, to overthrow the authority traditionally vested in the father, and to emancipate the woman from her responsibilities as housewife and mother by entrusting the community with the duties of cleaning, cooking and rearing the children. For the first few years things seemed to work much as the founders intended: women drove tractors and serviced them while men who so wished cooked and did the laundry. It was apparent that a majority of the women were less efficient at arduous tasks than most men (e.g. harvesting and driving heavy machinery) but outdoor jobs could usually be found for them – at least until they became pregnant. Then the ideologically imposed structure began to break down. Pregnant women, it was found, could not work for long, even in the kitchen garden. Moreover, once the baby was born, mothers usually wanted to breastfeed and consequently had to remain within earshot of the crèche. Thus, motherhood resulted in a steady shift of women from the productive branches of the economy to the service branches, their original jobs being taken over by men, and within a generation the traditional division of labour had all but reasserted itself. Although mothers continued to share their responsibilities for child-rearing with the kibbutz nurses, there was seldom any doubt about the intensity of their parental feelings or about the children's primary attachment to their mothers. For men and women the hours at the end of the working day became family hours, time to be spent in their own accommodation, at home with the children. Gradually, and quite spontaneously, the customary family structure was restored.

That the family should prove to be so tough a survivor is not perhaps surprising when one considers that it has probably existed since our species began. Anthropology demonstrates that family formation is a universal characteristic of mankind. Different cultures favour different kinds of family, it is true, but all societies support family ties of one sort or another, where at least one man and at least one woman care for children – whether they be their own or not. It seems, therefore, that the family is an expression of archetypal functioning; its very universality and persistence indicates that the family is biologically established as a species-specific characteristic and that it is only secondarily modified by cultural or ecological factors as to the indigenous form that it takes.

If we look at cultures other than our own, we find that monogamy is 'officially' more common than polygamy (many wives), while polyandry (many husbands) is extremely rare. In the majority of monogamous societies, however, men take secondary, unofficial spouses whereas women generally do not. A wide survey of non-industrial cultures undertaken by Murdock and White (1969) revealed that 68 per cent of them practised monogamy, 31 per cent polygamy, and only 1 per cent polyandry. However, of the monogamous cultures no less than 51 per cent were found to practise occasional polygyny. This raises the question of whether, as the old adage has it, woman is monogamous by nature while man is polygynous – a touchy issue to which we will return in a later chapter.

How did families evolve and why is it that they are such a striking feature of human ethology? As we shall see, family-like groupings exist in other primates, but in no other animal is family life so highly structured and 'institutionalized' as in man.

Our sub-human ancestors are thought to have been predators who developed the knack of running about upright on two feet and using their hands (freed from the chores of locomotion) to fling projectiles at their prey. Tool- and weapon-making, collaborative hunting and the use of speech gradually evolved in the struggle for existence together with the greatly enlarged brain which made such things possible. In evolutionary terms, the emergence of the early hominids represented a huge leap forward, but it presented nature with mechanical and social problems which had to be solved if this bright, predatory biped was to survive and continue on his progress towards full humanity: swift motion in the upright posture required the development of a strong, narrow pelvis, while greatly increased brain size demanded a much bigger skull – an easy enough transformation for natural selection to arrange, but it meant that childbirth became hazardous for both mother and child, especially when the mother had a more than usually narrow pelvis or the baby an exceptionally large head. If the course of human obstetric history was not to become a bloody battle between irresistible forces and totally immovable objects some sort of compromise had to be reached.

The compromise selected by nature was elegantly simple: pregnant women were caused to go into labour after a gestation period of only nine months when the baby's head was still sufficiently immature to pass through the pelvic opening. This sensible solution gave rise to logistical difficulties, however, for it meant that, in comparison with the offspring of other mammals, human babies were born in a state of considerable prematurity. Who was to feed and care for this helpless but promising creature?

The answer was, of course, the mother – as it always had been throughout the mammalian kingdom. But the excessive prematurity of the human infant, the long years of succour and nurturance needed to bring it to adulthood, placed a far greater burden on the human mother than that endured by any of her mammalian sisters. To bear it alone and without support would, in the environment of evolutionary adaptedness, have been fatal, especially for a woman who, in the absence of contraception, gave birth to a new child every two or three years. The well-being of her young and the survival of the species demanded she be provided with a protector and helpmate. Seen in this light, the family seems the obvious solution.

Clearly, some form of protective alliance is necessary for the care of offspring in animals like man, monkeys and the apes where growth and development of the young proceeds at a slow pace and adult skills must to a greater or less degree be learned. It is probably for this reason that the formation of enduring heterosexual bonds is common in primates but relatively rare in mammals as a whole, where the young are born reasonably mature and grow to independence comparatively quickly (though even here, some kind of family structure may be apparent as among wolves, foxes, and wild dogs).

Among primates, sexual bonds vary from the strict monogamy of some species of New World monkey (the titi monkey is a very model of marital fidelity and parental responsibility), through the polygyny of Hamadryas baboons, where one male jealously guards a harem of up to nine females and their young, to the relative promiscuity of chimpanzees (where, nevertheless, kinship ties are strong: for example, Jane Goodall has described the case of a two-year-old male chimpanzee who, when his mother died, was promptly adopted by his sister and thereafter protected by his brother).

However, despite this extensive variation, all primate populations have one feature in common: invariably a strong bond is formed between a mother and her child; what varies is the degree to which the male involves himself in this relationship. But that he does involve himself with females in forming relatively permanent associations for the care and protection of infants is not open to question, and it is a characteristic more commonly found in primates than in any other order of mammal.

Thus it would seem that the imperative to form families is rooted in our primate nature. That our notions concerning kith and kin are more sophisticated than those of other apes is due in part to our superior cerebral functioning and partly to the fact that populations which have assumed ordered patterns of family life have possessed a selective advantage over those which have not. They tended to survive while the others went to the wall.

No less important for survival and no less an extension of our primate nature is the differentiation of function which has always existed in our species between the male and female partners in the familial bond. This 'division of labour' freed women to devote their energies to the indispensable business of bearing and rearing children, while their menfolk played politics, waged war, hunted game and brought home the protein, so as to feed and protect the mothers and children for whom they accepted responsibility.

Since family ties are so clearly a matter of life and death for all human societies, it is hardly surprising that several factors have evolved in the course of human development whose function is to sustain mature heterosexual partnerships once they have been formed. These are partly biological and partly 'cultural':

1 The genetic acquisition of a tendency to form lasting heterosexual bonds – whether monogamous, polygamous or polyandrous – can be understood in terms of Jung's Anima and Animus archetypes: males and females are born with an innate anticipation of each others' nature, with an *a priori* capacity for mutual understanding and relatedness – for 'symbiosis'.

2 The 'hypersexuality' of human beings – the ready potency of males and the year-round receptivity of females which is independent of oestrus – makes it possible for husbands and wives perpetually to gratify one another.

3 The development of marriage laws which served (a) to hold partners together despite the frictions and misunderstandings of everyday life, and (b) to reduce sexual jealousy and competition between males, thus enabling them to go about their essentially *collaborative* business of hunting, protection and warfare without having to waste too much time keeping an eye on their women. Marriage promotes the cohesiveness of a society and its competitive efficiency, and it is not hard to see why such an invaluable institution should have evolved.

It is highly probable, therefore, that for as long as our species has existed and wherever on this planet human populations have taken up their abode children have been reared in families. And if, as Jung believed, the human infant is born with a psyche already structured and programmed to meet the typical circumstances of its *Umwelt*, then it is reasonable to assume that this innate structure will anticipate in some measure the presence and the behaviour of parents.

There is a huge and growing volume of evidence that this is indeed the case, some of which we shall now examine.

· 7 ·

The mother

Just as the seedling, newly ejected from its pod, enters the world in the assurance that it will contain soil, so the infant, expelled from the womb, approaches life on the assumption that it will provide a mother; for the mother is to the child what 'mother earth' is to the seed: without her it would perish. As we have seen, the human infant at birth is one of the most helpless of creatures, as though 'from his mother's womb untimely ripp'd' a good nine months too soon. Much of the first year of human life may, therefore, be regarded as a 'post-uterine embryonic phase'. Such a degree of helplessness renders the mother absolutely indispensable: she is the baby's 'life-support system' in a dangerous, inhospitable world. As Erich Neumann has put it: 'the mother's existence is the absolute life-giving and life-regulating precondition of infant existence, which alone makes its development possible' (1973, p. 17). At first the infant takes this ministering angel entirely for granted; it is only towards the end of the 'post-uterine embryonic phase' that he begins to perceive her as a person in her own right and a genuine relationship between them becomes possible. Nevertheless, even before a specific attachment bond can be said to have formed, a great deal of social interaction goes on during which the child develops the repertory of behaviours which he will later use to express the love and need he has for the person he recognizes as his mother.

If one were to attempt to write out in words the archetypal programme for the first two years of life, it would go something like this:

1 First distinguish your mother from yourself and from everybody else at the same time as forming a secure bond with her; then form bonds with the other people around you who will subsequently reveal themselves to you as father, uncle, aunt, brother, sister, grandmother, etc.

2 Having formed a bond with your mother and having started to take your place in the family, begin as a matter of urgency to distinguish people and objects that are familiar to you from those which are strange; then approach and socialize with the familiar and withdraw and escape

from those which are strange – they could harm you, attack you, or eat you alive.

3 Having registered and acted on these instructions, proceed to explore and familiarize yourself with your immediate environment and, when possible, play with your peers, never straying very far from mother, frequently checking that she is near, and returning to her directly you encounter anything frightening or strange.

These three sets of instructions predominate during the first years of life, when bond formation, stranger avoidance and exploratory activities are the most apparent features of every child's developing behavioural repertoire. In this, children are no different from any other mammal (except in the relative slowness with which the programme proceeds): it is the archetypal programme with which all young mammals are born.

In the normal course of events, a mother is well prepared to become attached to her baby by the months of waiting for its arrival. Her libidinal investment is apparent from the moment of birth. In all species of mammal the mother rapidly learns to recognize her own baby and develops a tenacious proprietorial right to it. If any attempt is made to take the infant away she will display violent hostility. Equally, if she is presented with an infant belonging to another female she will decisively reject it.

As soon as the infant is born, the mother sniffs and nuzzles it, licks the membranes free, and gives it her undivided attention. If she is not permitted to go through this ritual, the baby being removed from her at birth, then there is a real danger that when it is later presented to her she will not recognize it as her own and will refuse to care for it. This has been experimentally established in ewes and sea-lions, and it has also been demonstrated that the period immediately following birth is a sensitive one for the successful formation of the mother-infant bond in humans (Klaus *et al.*, 1972).

Thus, the frequently expressed anxiety of mothers in maternity wards that their child might get swapped for somebody else's is no neurotic foible: it is probably genetically based. It is an expression of the fundamentally biological nature of the individualized bond. A mother can feed and care for only a finite number of young. If she adopted babies indiscriminately, or attempted to kidnap those belonging to other females, the chances are that her own might die of neglect and the social order be fatally disrupted by a never-ending series of feminine squabbles, baby-snatchings and general mayhem. Moreover, such a chronic state of affairs could only hinder the development of trust and security in the offspring. Clearly, the personal mother-child bond has great advantages both for the individuals intimately concerned and for the population at large.

As time goes on, the mother's attachment to her child is confirmed and strengthened in response to the numerous signals which he emits (because he is programmed to do so) which release in her feelings of love and tenderness as well as the appropriate 'maternal' behaviour that her role demands. From the very beginning, the infant is powerfully motivated to seek physical contact with the mother and not to relinquish contact once it has been obtained. In the 'environment of evolutionary adaptedness' human mothers and infants spend as much time in close physical contact as do gorillas and chimpanzees. This has been observed in hunter-gatherer societies which have survived into the present century: babies are not kept in a cradle or a pram as with us but, as with monkeys and apes, are carried about piggie-back fashion. Although human infants are less able to hang on to their mothers than infant primates – they are not so strong and their mothers lack a natural easy-grip fur coat – nevertheless all human babies have vestigial grasp reflexes strong enough to support their own weight. This primary need to be cuddled, when fully satisfied, forms the foundation of the child's developing 'basic trust', and it is a need which persists into adulthood. When held, one experiences security, protection and comfort; holding is a gesture which has great therapeutic potency in the treatment of pain or despair. Perhaps the most destructive aspect of loneliness is that one lacks access to such effective balm. As Professor George Brown and his colleagues have shown from studies based on their Social Research Unit in London, individuals who can depend upon the physical and verbal expression of attachment from an intimate enjoy a vital social asset protecting them from depression and neurotic distress.

The need for physical contact is, therefore, something which goes beyond mere sexuality. There is in all mammals – especially in mammalian infants – an *appetitive* need for the establishment of contact, for the maintenance of contact, and for the restoration of contact once it is lost. This is the very essence of the attachment bond; and the purpose of this fundamental behavioural system is clear: *survival.*

The child's physical orientation to its mother is soon augmented by the establishment of visual and auditory links. Within but a few hours of birth, babies begin to single out the human voice – particularly the higher pitched human voice – from other sounds in the environment. Thus, they will quieten and reduce spontaneous movements more reliably in response to the sound of female speech than to other auditory stimuli of like intensity. Similarly, the visual apparatus appears to be programmed to respond to the 'faceness' of stimuli, so that some crude representation of two eyes, a nose and a mouth will be attended to more readily than visual stimuli organized in other configurations. Most effective of all in quietening a newborn infant are the combined stimuli of human face, human voice, and the tactile and proprioceptive stimuli of being held. These observations all support the Jungian contention that the child is prepared by its genetic endownment to interact appropriately with the world, and that its early existence is dominated by the controlling influence of the mother archetype.

Without doubt, the most potent social assets with which the human infant is endowed are its innate ability to cry and to smile. The baby's cry is analogous to the 'lost call' of young mammals and ground nesting birds which has the effect of releasing retrieval behaviour in the parents. It is no accident that few sounds are more disturbing to a human being than the sound of a baby crying. Some inner imperative tells one that it must not be allowed to continue: something must be done to stop it. (The normal maternal response of gathering up the protesting infant into her arms while speaking to it soothingly usually does the trick.)

Smiling has a no less powerful effect on maternal responsiveness. At first, smiling is apparently indiscriminate – little more than a reflex which can be elicited by rocking or feeding or the sound of a gentle female voice. Indeed, in the earliest months of life the infant does not seem to mind who looks after him as long as he is fed, kept warm and dry, and cuddled. As we have already noted, it is only very slowly that he manages to form a percept of his personal mother and show the beginnings of a personalized bond with the 'mother-out-there'. The earliest sign that this is starting to happen occurs at about the fourth week when he is prone to spend time staring up at his mother's face; and this can have a profound emotional impact on her if he happens to smile at the same time.

I have already given my reasons for my reluctance to adopt a purely ethological view of staring and smiling as being 'sign stimuli' which trigger the innate mechanism responsible for releasing nurturant behaviour in the mother (see pp. 12–13). Instead, I prefer the Jungian view that the evolving repertoire of behaviours apparent in both mother and child represent stages in the progressive actualization of the mother-child archetypal system, and that these stages are associated with subjective experiences in both participants, conscious and differentiated in the mother, much less so in the child. What each experiences at any moment in the maturation of the primal relationship is in no sense illusory or automatic, but a necessary expression of the *a priori* nature of the archetype.

There is, I believe, no fundamental incompatibility between Jung's maternal archetype and Bowlby's 'goal-corrected behavioural system', but I consider that the theory of archetypes can augment what Bowlby has achieved with his attachment theory. In the first place, it can correct the behavioural bias of the ethological approach by promoting a shift in the direction of an equal concern with both behaviour *and* experience. The passage in which Jung relates archetypes to patterns of behaviour has already been quoted (p. 18). In the same passage, he continues: 'This aspect of the archetype is the biological one. . . . But the picture changes at once when looked at from the inside, that is, from within the realm of the subjective psyche. Here the archetype presents itself as numinous, that is, it appears as an *experience* of fundamental importance.'

Secondly, by emphasizing the fact that both psychic events and behavioural events possess a common phylogenetic origin, archetypal theory places the whole of human psychology within the evolutionary scheme of biological reality and, at the same time, transcends the pitfalls of epiphenomenalism and Cartesian dualism.

Thirdly, by accepting, but not overemphasizing, the operational criteria of attachment and the behavioural systems mediating the bond, archetypal theory permits us to give due weight to the essentially loving and intuitive nature of the primal relationship, without impairing scientific objectivity or undermining procedural precision in research or clinical practice. For, to leave out the love, the mutual fascination, the intuitive rapport, and the poetry, is to leave out the crucial thing – the actual consequences for *experience* of mothering and being mothered. It is just not good enough to argue that these matters have little to do with science, because they are the very essence of human psychology; and if psychology claims to be a science, it *has* to take them into account.

The mother archetype

It is necessary to repeat that when Jungians speak of a mother archetype, they are not referring to an innate image but to an inner dynamic at work in the phylogenetic psyche. The 'artefacts' of this dynamic – its symbolic residues – are to be found in the myths and artistic creations of mankind. The 'symbolic canon' of the mother archetype is very extensive and those wishing to approach it are referred to Erich Neumann's book on the subject (*The Great Mother: An Analysis of the Archetype*, 1955). However, some expressions are so universally encountered that they can be mentioned here: as Mother Nature and Earth Mother she is goddess of fertility and dispenser of nourishment; as water or sea she represents the origins of all life as well as a symbol of the unconscious, the fount of all psychic creativity; as Moon Goddess she exemplifies the essential periodicity of womanhood. She also takes the form of divine animals: the bear (jealous guardian of her children), the celestial cow, who nourishes the earth with milky rain.

The Great Mother is thus an aspect – the central aspect – of the Archetypal Feminine. 'Great' expresses her timelessness and her numinous superiority over everything mundane and merely human. Like all archetypes, the Great Mother possesses both positive and negative attributes, and this 'union of opposites' within the same archetype is characteristic of all preconscious components which the ego has not yet divided into its antitheses. Neumann has argued that for scores of millennia early man experienced this paradoxical duality within the godhead, and that it was only with cultural sophistication that a distinction was made between good goddesses and bad. The same was probably true of God the Father until Judeo-Christianity split Him into all-good Almighty God and all-evil Satan.

While, on the one hand, the Great Mother is creative and loving, on the other, she is destructive and hateful. This paradox on the mythological plane corresponds to the observation shared by all schools of analysis that children are deeply ambivalent in their feelings and behaviour towards their mothers. Where the schools differ is in their explanations of how the 'good' and 'bad' images of the mother are formed. The 'object-relations' school, for example, sees them as 'introjected' images of the mother in contrary moods (i.e. both are 'internal objects' based on the child's actual experiences of the personal mother). Jungians, however, see them as symbolic actualizations of the Good Great Mother and Terrible Mother archetypes respectively (i.e. the child is phylogenetically forewarned of the mother's inevitably dual nature – that she who caresses also slaps; she who gives also witholds; she who grants life may also take it away). Thus, where the Good Mother's symbols are the flowing breast, the abundant cornucopia, the fruitful womb, the Terrible Mother is the bloodstained goddess of death and destruction; she is Kali dancing on the hapless form of Shiva (Neumann, plate 65), she is 'dark, all-devouring time, the bone-wreathed lady of the place of skulls', the Mayan goddess Ixchel, with deadly snake on head, animal claws, and crossed bones on her mantle – the emblem of death (Neumann, p. 189, fig. 45). She is Rangda who steals children (Neumann, plate 71) and the Gorgon with writhing snakes round her head (at whom men have merely to glance to be instantly turned to stone). The animal forms which she most characteristically adopts are the dragon and the devouring sea serpent, with whom the heroes of countless mythologies have grappled down the eons of man-made time. Universally, the negative aspect of the mother has been personified in monsters, gorgons, witches, ghouls, who have murdered the sleep of children (and adults) since the dawning of mankind.

Both 'Good' and 'Terrible' aspects of the mother archetype condition the behaviour of mother and child at a predominantly unconscious level of psychic activity. Constellation of either aspect results in what Neumann calls 'a state of biopsychical seizure', a compelling state of possession which drives the behaviour and experience of the subject and is associated with powerful emotional accompaniments. When the Good Mother rules all is peace and contentment; but should the Terrible Mother be activated pandemonium is the result – inconsolable screaming in the child (often rationalized as 'teething' or 'wind'), fury, even battering, in the mother (who, in retrospect, may find her own behaviour incredible and deeply shaming when the 'biopsychic seizure' has passed). Clearly, it is important for the stability of the attachment bond and the health of the child that the mother should succeed overall in constellating the Good rather than the Terrible Mother. When one appreciates the symbolic power of the archetypes involved, the truth of this statement is apparent. Yet, in his neglect of the archetypal psychic background to the attachment bond, Bowlby excludes a dimension of enormous prognostic significance. While it is undeniable that he has made a highly impressive contribution to psychopathology by explaining neurosis and personality disturbances as a consequence of prolonged separations, loss and threatened loss of primary attachment figures, he is to be criticized for his failure to attribute significance to the symbolical or feeling quality of the attachment formed. For him, the crucial variables are the availability or unavailability of the mother figure; and where mother figures are available he tends in his theoretical formulations to assume that they are 'good enough'. This is a serious limitation. Fortunately for humanity, most mothers are 'good enough'. But some mothers are 'too good', not in the sense that they bind their child to them through a neurotic fear of losing him, but because their maternal bounty is so profligate as to retard his growing independence and ability to cope with the world; while others are bad, even 'terrible', because their resentment and hostility deny the child satisfaction of his legitimate needs. Moreover, a 'good' personal mother can be experienced as 'terrible' through no fault of her own but through the misfortune of accident or illness which may render her maternally incompetent. What matters from the point of view of healthy psychic development is not so much the actual behaviour and personality of the mother, as Bowlby supposes, as *the archetypal experiences actualized by her* in the child.

The critical factor for psychopathology is not the actual mother but the mother complex which is formed within the individual's psyche, and this complex – the queen of all complexes – is no inner reproduction or 'video-recording' of the personal mother-out-there, but a product of her interaction with specific phylogenetic components in the child's maturing psyche. This fact, with all its implications, has to be grasped if success is to be achieved in the psychotherapy of individuals with dysfunctional parental complexes. We shall return to these matters in chapter 9.

The mother, ego-consciousness and the Self

Inasmuch as the mother-child bond is forged through a mutual archetypal constellation, much of it proceeds at an unconscious level: each participant constitutes the perceptual field responsible for evoking the archetype in the other. Initially, there is a full *participation mystique* between the child and its mother out of which the child's ego and differentiated consciousness gradually emerge. In the beginning is the Self. And the Self bears within it the seeds of the total personality – a fact which finds symbolic expression in the astrological notion that the probabilities of a person's life experience are ordained at the moment of his birth.

All those attributes which will later make up the psychology of a unique individual are thus prefigured in the Self, and the ego (the necessary precondition of the perception of one's own personal identity) is no exception. 'The ego,' wrote Jung, 'stands to the Self as the moved to the mover. . . . The Self . . . is an *a priori* existent out of which the ego evolves. It is, so to speak, an unconscious prefiguration of the ego' (CW 11, para. 391). With maturation, the ego develops a subjectively experienced independence from the Self, but in reality it remains intimately related to it: this relationship Neumann has called the *ego-Self axis*. In a sense, the Self is to the ego what the parent is to the child; it also resembles the relationship envisaged by the great world religions as existing between God and man, for the ego is, in a manner of speaking, the Self's representative 'on earth' (i.e. in outer reality). Thus, to start with, the Self and the parental archetypes are so closely interrelated as to be one. Only gradually, as the child's ego-consciousness grows and he begins to recognize his parents as persons in their own right distinct from himself, do the parental archetypes – Mother (in both her Good and Terrible aspects) and Father – differentiate out of the archetypal totality which is the Self.

Mythologically, this dawning of consciousness, with its associated capacity for differentiation, is symbolized as the *Separation of the World Parents* (Father Heaven from Mother Earth) and the creation of light out of darkness. To quote Frazer:

> It is a common belief of primitive peoples that sky and earth were originally joined together, the sky either lying flat on the earth or being raised so little above it that there was not room between them for people to walk upright. Where such beliefs prevail, the present elevation of the sky above the earth is often ascribed to the might of some god or hero, who gave the firmament such a shove that it shot up and has remained up above ever since. (1924–5, p. 26)

An indispensable feature of such creation myths is the coming of light – the quintessential symbol of consciousness and 'illumination' – which follows separation of the archetypal Parents. Light is represented as an attribute of masculine Heaven, while darkness persists in the fastness of feminine Earth. Thus, the archetypal matrix of ego-consciousness is essentially masculine (as is the ego's activity in willing, asserting, deciding and discriminating), while the archetypal ground of the unconscious is essentially feminine. This is true for both sexes: 'The correlation "consciousness-light-day" and "unconsciousness-darkness-night" holds true regardless of sex. . . . Consciousness, as such, is masculine even in women, just as the unconscious is feminine in men' (Neumann, 1954, p. 42).

The individual development of ego-consciousness and the growth of the ego-Self axis is represented diagrammatically in Figure 7.1. At birth, Self is all. As yet, ego-consciousness exists only *in potentia*. Neumann's extensive mythological and ethnographic researches led him to the conclusion that the archetypal image most evocative of the pre-ego stage of infancy is the *uroborus* – the circular snake biting its tail. Jung, who was hardly less concerned with the forms in which human beings gave tangible expression to the Self archetype, found that, in the second half of life, the most typical mode of Self-objectification was the *mandala*. Mandalas are to be seen all over the world and from most known periods of history. Like the uroborus they are basically circular in form, though the centre is emphasized and, in addition, they normally incorporate some symbolic representation of the quaternity (e.g. a cross or a square). They are age-old symbols of 'wholeness', 'totality' and 'deity'. Moreover, it is particularly interesting to note in this context that Rhoda Kellog's studies of the spontaneous drawings of pre-school children have demonstrated that the basic forms produced are mandala-like, especially when the young artists attempt to draw themselves or their parents.

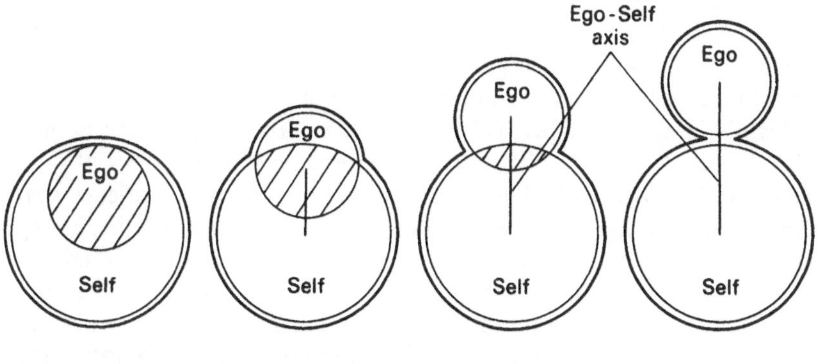

FIGURE 7.1 Diagrammatic representation of the development of the ego-Self axis. At first the ego exists only *in potentia* as a component of the Self. Then, as ontological development proceeds, the ego gradually differentiates itself out from the Self. The perpendicular line connecting them represents the ego-Self axis, the vital link which sustains the integrity of the personality. The shaded areas of the ego represent the relative degree of ego-Self identity persisting at stages in the developmental process (adapted from Edinger, 1972)

Growth of the ego-Self axis begins in the first month of post-uterine life. For most of the time, the infant slumbers in the coils of the uroborus – 'the Great Round, in whose womb centre the ego-germ lies sheltered' (Neumann, 1973, p. 10). Periodically, he surfaces and establishes, however momentarily, islands of consciousness. When the mother is 'good enough', early infancy is only marginally less secure and tension-free than the intra-uterine phase of life. Should tension arise in the form of hunger, cold, wetness, or the need for physical contact, the child has but to signal the event by crying. Normally, the mother then responds appropriately through her intuitive understanding of his need; satisfied, he sinks back into slumber.

In all probability, the child, as yet, makes no distinction between 'inside' and 'outside', between his mother and himself. And because this earliest phase of extra-uterine life is predominantly a period of well-being and security, it is commonly symbolized as 'paradise'. The story of Adam and Eve and their expulsion from the Garden of Eden can be understood as a parable of the emergence of ego-consciousness, and the replacement of harmonious unity with the conflicts born of awareness of opposing categories of experience (e.g. good and evil, love and hate, pleasure and pain). The Garden of Eden is, of course, a mandala, with its four rivers and Tree of Life at the centre.

Many other myths portray the original state of man as one of roundness, wholeness and paradise. In the *Symposium* Plato tells us: 'The primeval man was round, his back and sides forming a circle.' But this Self-sufficient creature got above himself – he displayed that kind of psychic 'inflation' or hypomania which regularly occurs when the ego is identified with the Self – and the gods punished him by dividing him into male and female portions, thus condemning him to an eternal quest for his 'other half'. Similarly, in the Greek myth describing the Four Ages of Man, the first, original age is depicted as the Golden Age, a paradise, in which man lived in blissful union with the gods.

Plato's image of the original 'round' man corresponds to the hermaphroditism of the Self, within which the psychic characteristics of both sexes are 'planned for' (though, as we shall see, there is evidence that gender and sex are genetically linked so that from the very beginning masculine characteristics dominate in males and feminine characteristics in females. These fundamental differences are highlighted by cultural influences in the child's upbringing thus affirming the ego's identification with the monosexual propensities of the personality and promoting the suppression of the contrasexual characteristics, which become incorporated in the Anima/Animus). The hermaphroditic unity of the Self, from which the male-female duality later emerges is also exemplified by the account in *Genesis* of how the Lord created Eve out of Adam's rib. The Platonic notion is also echoed in the Upanishads:

> In the beginning this world was Soul [Atman] alone in the form of a person. Looking around, he saw nothing else than himself. He said first: 'I am'.... He was, indeed, as large as a woman and a man closely embraced. He caused that self to fall [pat] into two pieces. Therefrom arose a husband [pati] and a wife [patni]. (*Brihadaranyaka Upanishad* 1. 4. 1–3)

The ego's initial oneness with the Self is thus conceived mythologically as a historically tangible beginning when the human soul lived at one with nature and the deity. This state is paradisical because full consciousness has not yet appeared to disrupt bliss with conflict. As growth of the ego-Self axis proceeds, however, the original undifferentiated unity is left behind 'in paradise' and the world is encountered increasingly as a realm of tensions. Distressing though this may be, steady development of the ego-Self axis is a matter of great consequence for the mental health of the growing individual. The Self, as central co-ordinating nucleus of the total psyche, instigates and homeostatically controls the emergence of the maturing ego, and on this process the whole future integrity of the personality stands or falls. If it goes wrong, the consequences can prove catastrophic; that it should not go wrong largely depends on the presence and appropriate responsiveness of the mother, for the normal development of the ego-Self axis occurs only where there is normal development of the mother-child bond.

As Bowlby stresses, the first and most essential requirement of the mother figure is that she be there – and lastingly there. But, as Neumann says: 'it is not the personal individual, but the generically maternal that is the indispensable foundation of the child's life.... In this sense she is anonymous and transpersonal, in other words archetypal' (1973, p. 21). As far as the young infant is concerned, the mother is not an individual human being with an identity of her own: she is the living embodiment of the Great Mother archetype. For this reason early development proceeds independently of the mother's personal characteristics provided that she lives with her child 'in accordance with her archetypal role' (p. 24). It is on the basis of this mutual *participation* that all mothers and children work out their own particular variations on the archetypally composed theme. Gradually, with the emergence of the child's ego-consciousness, the mother's functions of cherishing, nourishing and protecting lose their anonymous features and 'personate' as the attributes of 'Mum'.

Consistent and appropriate mothering confers upon the child the priceless experience of living in a predictably reliable world, and it is this experience which is the essence of Erikson's 'basic trust' – the feeling that life, people and society can be relied upon; that they are worthy of trust and positive collaboration. In fulfilling this function, the mother-child bond has deep social and political implications: 'confidence in the mother is identical with confidence in the society she represents' (p. 40). Attachment to her is 'the foundation of every feeling of being at home in the social group' (p. 41). It is the nucleus round which all human (and primate) communities have formed. It is indeed the *primal relationship*.

The growth of love

As I have argued, the most wonderful feature of the primal relationship, which Jungians accentuate and behaviourists tend to ignore, is that it is ruled by Eros: it is perfused with love. The moment the mother-child dyad is formed, Eros is constellated. And it is out of what Jungians call the 'Eros of relationship' that ego-consciousness grows. Knowledge of the world and security in the world are thus based on loving relatedness. We love life inasmuch as love was present in this first great affair of our lives.

To the formation of the mother-child bond, Eros provides the indispensable catalyst. 'It is as if,' wrote Bowlby, 'maternal care were as necessary for the proper development of personality as Vitamin D for the development of bones' (1951). Just as children suffering from vitamin D deficiency grow up with bowed and distorted limbs, so children deprived of a mother's love develop rickets of the soul. As Bowlby's monograph made abundantly clear, children reared in institutions without love are retarded in their physical, intellectual and social development when compared with children reared in normal families, and are more susceptible to physical and mental disease. Signs of retardation begin to manifest themselves early and the damage, once done, is probably irreversible. Many workers have pointed to an association between institutional care, maternal deprivation, and the later development of an 'affectionless character' with its feeble superego and disagreeable penchant for impulsive antisocial behaviour. Such characters, once formed, are often beyond redemption since their inability to make human relationships deprives the therapist of his most important instrument. Thus, you can provide an orphaned child with 'mothering' by paying caretakers to feed him and keep him clean and warm; but should you fail to provide him also with the Eros-experience of a lasting relationship with one loved mother figure you risk exposing him, at best, to a future rich in psychopathology and, at worst, death.

Similarly, numerous experimental studies of a variety of social mammals have demonstrated that failure or impairment of the bond to mother results in predictable abnormalities in the offspring. For example, as the Harlows have shown, rhesus infants, deprived of their mothers but provided with mechanical substitutes, may survive into adult life but their social and sexual capacities are permanently damaged: both males and females are sexually incompetent and make hopeless parents, treating their young with the same concern as inanimate objects. The British paediatrician Sir James Spence once observed that one of the principle purposes of the family was the preservation of the art of parenthood. This dictum would seem to be as true of monkeys as it is of man. The Harlows have provided many dramatic instances of the pathology which can result when environmental distortions hamper the progression of the archetypal programme for ontogenesis.

Loss or absence of mother, therefore, means more to the stricken infant than loss of someone to care for his bodily needs. To be sure, the necessary ingredient of love does not have to be provided by the biological mother; any woman will do provided her feeling is sufficiently touched by the child to allow herself to be drawn into the mother-child archetypal field (which has often been compared to a magnetic field) and provided she is willing to stay there long enough to see the child through to maturity. But any woman so tempted should be warned: it is not a role to be undertaken lightly. Should she be prepared only to *play* at mothering, or should she after a while tire of the role and decide to hand the child on to someone else, then her action will be experienced by him as the ultimate betrayal and his ability to trust life and human society may be permanently impaired. An intelligent young man in his late twenties was once referred to me for treatment of agoraphobia and a severe obsessional neurosis. Analysis revealed that his symptoms dated from when he was eight years old. At that time his mother had left home to live with another man. The boy, who preferred his mother to his father, followed her and begged to be taken into her new ménage. Her man refused to consider it, and weakly she sent the lad home to his father. His suffering was terrible; and, although angry with his mother, he became convinced that the fault lay primarily within himself – that there must be something essentially unacceptable about him if his beloved mother could reject him so totally. This conviction blighted the next twenty years of his life.

Premature rupture of the mother-child bond is something to be avoided.

Separation

The power of the maternal archetype's impetus to full actualization is never more apparent than when a young animal or child is separated involuntarily from its mother. As Bowlby has amply demonstrated, the loud protest and dreadful despair which such forced separations induce are *primary responses* not reducible to other causes: they are due directly to the *a priori* nature of the attachment bond. The extent of the infant's suffering and of the damage caused is broadly related to the duration of the separation: brief separations are bad enough; long ones can be quite devastating. The archetypal longing of mothers and children for the proximity of each other is apparent in all mammals and is pathetically exemplified on those occasions when behavioural scientists try to prize them apart. Because they cling so tightly to one another they cannot be separated except by deception or the use of brutal force. The following account of such atrocities is given by Jensen and Tolman (1962) and quoted by Bowlby (1973, p. 85):

> Separation of mother and infant monkeys is an extremely stressful event for both mother and infant as well as for the attendants and for all other monkeys within sight or earshot of the experience. The mother becomes ferocious towards attendants and extremely protective of her infant. The infant's screams can be heard over almost the entire building. The mother struggles and attacks the separators. The baby clings tightly to the mother and to any object which it can grasp to avoid being held or removed by the attendant. With the baby gone, the mother paces the cage almost constantly, charges the cage occasionally, bites at it, and makes continual attempts to escape. She also lets out occasional mooing-like sounds. The infant emits high pitched shrill screams intermittently and almost continuously for the period of separation.

Since the above passage was published many of these horrible experiments have been performed, the victims being subjected to separations lasting from minutes to months, and their sufferings meticulously recorded. For example, in 1967 Kaufman and Rosenblum reported the results of separation studies on bonnet and pigtail infants whose mothers were removed for four weeks.

> The *initial* reaction in all was one of extreme *agitation* with screaming, distress calls, pacing, searching head movements, frequent trips to the door and window, and movements towards other group members. In most pigtails studied this reaction persisted for about a day, during which time the infant neither ate nor slept; but the next day the infant showed a *severe depression*, sitting hunched over, almost rolled into a ball with the head often between the knees. When the face could be seen it had the appearance of dejection and sadness Darwin described and believed 'to be universally and instantly recognized as that of grief'. The infant became very inactive, did not play, and seemed disengaged from this environment. After five to six days of persistent depression the reaction began to lift with gradual re-engagement of, first, the inanimate

environment, and then, of peers. By the end of the four weeks of separation the infant appeared fairly normal in his behaviour. In these pigtails, then, during the mother's absence, there were three successive stages – agitation, depression, and finally recovery.

Protracted separations between mother and child are rightly regarded as 'unethical' by behavioural scientists in the case of humans but not apparently in the case of non-human primates, though when one reads of the anguish that such experiments cause one feels justified in asking why. It is, presumably, a further example of the anthropocentric fallacy, lingering on as a hangover of medieval theology, which assumes that because, unlike monkeys, we have 'immortal souls' our sufferings matter while theirs do not.

Evidence concerning the responses of young humans on separation from their mothers comes mostly from observations of children in hospitals and nurseries. These findings are eloquently summarized by Bowlby in his book *Attachment* (1969). The children studied (mostly by James Robertson) were between 15 and 30 months of age. They had been removed from their mothers and their familiar environment and placed for a limited period in a residential nursery or hospital ward, where they were cared for by a succession of unfamiliar people. All the children had previously formed secure attachments to their mothers and had never before been separated from them. From the moment separation began a predictable sequence of behaviour was observed; it corresponds closely to that noted by Kaufman in pigtail monkeys and reported above. Bowlby summarizes the stages of the sequence as follows:

> The initial phase, that of protest, may begin immediately or may be delayed; it lasts from a few hours to a week or more. During it the young child appears acutely distressed at having lost his mother and seeks to recapture her by the full exercise of his limited resources. He will often cry loudly, shake his cot, throw himself about, and look eagerly towards any sight or sound which might prove to be his missing mother. All his behaviour suggests strong expectation that she will return. Meantime he is apt to reject all alternative figures who offer to do things for him, though some children will cling desperately to a nurse.
>
> During the phase of despair, which succeeds protest, the child's preoccupation with his missing mother is still evident, though his behaviour suggests increasing hopelessness. The active physical movements diminish or come to an end, and he may cry monotonously or intermittently. He is withdrawn and inactive, makes no demands on people in the environment, and appears to be in a state of deep mourning. This is a quiet stage, and sometimes, clearly erroneously, is presumed to indicate a diminution of distress.

> Because the child shows more interest in his surroundings, the phase of detachment which sooner or later succeeds protest and despair is often welcomed as a sign of recovery. The child no longer rejects the nurses; he accepts their care and the food and toys they bring, and may even smile and be sociable. To some this change seems satisfactory. When his mother visits, however, it can be seen that all is not well, for there is a striking absence of the behaviour characteristic of the strong attachment normal at this age. So far from greeting his mother he may remain remote and apathetic; instead of tears there is a listless turning away. He seems to have lost all interest in her.
>
> Should his stay in hospital or residential nursery be prolonged and should he, as is usual, have the experience of becoming transiently attached to a series of nurses each of whom leaves and so repeats for him the experience of the original loss of his mother, he will in time act as if neither mothering nor contact with humans has much significance for him. After a series of upsets at losing several mother-figures to whom in turn he has given some trust and affection, he will gradually commit himself less and less to succeeding figures and in time will stop altogether attaching himself to anyone. He will become increasingly self-centred and, instead of directing his desires and feelings towards people, will become preoccupied with material things such as sweets, toys, and food. A child living in an institution or hospital who has reached this stage will no longer be upset when nurses change or leave. He will cease to show feelings when his parents come and go on visiting day; and it may cause them pain when they realize that, although he has an avid interest in the presents they bring, he has little interest in them as special people. He will appear cheerful and adapted to his unusual situation and apparently easy and unafraid of anyone. But this sociability is superficial: he appears no longer to care for anyone. (1973, pp. 27–8)

As Bowlby has subsequently pointed out, each of these three phases of response to separation is related to a central issue of psychoanalytic theory: *protest* raises the problems of separation anxiety; *despair* that of grief or mourning; *detachment* that of defence. He then proceeds to suggest that attachment theory is able to give a more coherent account of these phenomena than conventional psychoanalysis. Personally, I find this suggestion most persuasive. But I would go further and argue that all these crucial areas of psychopathology can be better understood as *natural consequences of thwarting archetypal intent.* I shall develop this argument in subsequent chapters because I believe it to provide a sound theoretical orientation from which a truly biological psychiatry might most profitably proceed.

Exploration: distinguishing the familiar from the strange

Uninterrupted, loving proximity is, then, the essence of the healthy mother-child bond: through it the child learns to trust in the continuity of existence – that whatever happens, short of total disaster, life will go on. Provided his mother succeeds in constellating the Good Mother, rather than her Terrible alternative, the child will be able to cope with even distressing and frightening experiences through repeated maternal assistance in dealing with them. For, as the child experiences the mother so, by analogy and extension, he experiences life and the world. Not that the child 'identifies' mother with world: for him she *is* the world. Only later, with the use of his progressively differentiating consciousness, does he begin to make the distinction between the two. 'This connection between mother and world explains why in mythology the archetype of the Great Mother takes the form of the spinner who makes the web (that is, the varied structure of the world and of life), and guards over it' (Neumann, 1973, p. 52). That this connection is made *through love* has profound consequences for the child's future happiness: it is the basis of his capacity to love life; to extend his investment of libido in the mother to an investment in the world, and in a positive image of himself-in-the-world. It means that the child's first perceptions of reality are verified through feeling, relatedness, and nearness (in contrast to the later paternal influence which will encourage concept formation, objectivity, and abstraction). Love of mother, love of world, and love of self are necessary conditions for the stable development of the ego-Self axis – the spinal column of future individuality and autonomy. The tentative emergence of this positive self-concept then facilitates the dissolution of the child's original identity with mother and enables him to begin his first hesitant explorations of the numinous, enticing world beyond the mother's body. In this manner, the mother becomes a 'secure base' to and from which the infant crawls in the course of his explorations, reassuring himself, as it were, of her continued existence. At times of real or imagined danger he scuttles rapidly back to her as to a bolt hole. Such behaviour is to be observed in all young mammals. 'Probably for all,' wrote Bowlby, 'the haven of safety which terminates escape responses and brings a sense of security is the proximity of mother.'

In a sense, attachment behaviour and exploratory behaviour are antithetical to each other. The intense curiosity which motivates all young creatures to explore may be understood as a primary expression of the individuation principle, a basic drive of the Self to seek encounter with the environment and achieve actualization, through such encounter, of the Self's archetypal endowment. Before going off on any exploratory foray, however, the infant will invariably first satisfy himself that his mother is present, settled, and not likely for the time being to move away. Only then will he cease to display attachment behaviour and begin to investigate his surroundings, familiarizing himself with the local topography, and building up in the process a coherent picture (or inner 'model') of the environment which may subsequently prove essential for survival.

No less important for survival is an ability to perceive objects and situations in the environment which are threatening or potentially dangerous. As has already been noted in chapter 4, young mammals display fear and avoidance behaviour in response to a number of natural cues, any of which could be associated with danger. In human infants, a striking example of this innate warning system is the marked uneasiness they show from six or seven months onwards in the presence of persons unfamiliar to them. By the end of the first year, this initial wariness has developed into full-blooded fear. If a stranger approaches and makes social overtures, the child will avert his head and try to escape. Should his flight be impeded, he will show considerable distress, crying and screaming, however much proud parents seek to reassure him that there is little to fear and that the nice lady or gentleman has nothing but kind intentions. There can no longer be any doubt that the behaviour system mediating withdrawal from strangers is innately determined in the same way as that promoting attachment to familiars, and some have argued convincingly that stranger-phobia in human infants is an evolutionary vestige of the flight response in lower mammals. That such social responses as crying, smiling, laughing, babbling, social withdrawal, and facial expressions denoting anger, fear and sadness are innately determined has been demonstrated by studies of children blind and deaf from birth, all of whom display these behaviours at the appropriate phase of ontogenesis. Professor Irenaus Eibl-Eibesfeldt of Germany, who has done much of this work, has film of a little blind and deaf girl who distinguished strangers from familiars by sniffing their hands. She shows obvious signs of stranger-phobia despite the fact that visitors were invariably kind and gentle to her out of pity for her condition. Further evidence has been obtained from normal, sighted children who display fear responses (turning away, crying, and screaming) at about fourteen months of age when presented with masks displaying vertical 'threat wrinkles' on the forehead. The innate responses of young rhesus monkeys to threat images have already been mentioned.

Early establishment of the familiar-unfamiliar dichotomy has evident survival value for all mammals: it results in behaviour which maintains proximity to conspecifics who are friendly and places which are safe, and withdrawal from subjects which are potentially hostile and situations which could be dangerous. This innate propensity for classifying all creatures in one of two categories according to whether they be perceived as friend or foe is the phylogenetic basis for all later xenophilia and xenophobia, all in-group/out-group dichotomizing, all social conflicts and wars. These apocalyptic matters will be returned to in chapter 12.

The first year of life is, therefore, a busy time. Far from being a *tabula rasa*, the newborn infant enters the world equipped to encounter what it can expect to encounter in 'the environment of evolutionary adaptedness'. The great achievement of this period is the formation of attachments with consciously perceived figures, and in this rich social experience the child is himself a highly active participant, demonstrating by his whole attitude and behaviour the presence of a strong inner imperative prompting him ceaselessly to seek dialogue with his mother and the world. It is on the outcome of this dialogue that his future health and happiness depend.

· 8 ·

The father

While a vast literature has grown up in recent decades on the significance of the mother-child bond, fathers have been relatively neglected. This is, perhaps, only to be expected as our culture continues to recoil from the 'patrism' of nineteenth-century life towards the 'matrism' of the present time. However, it is surely going too far to assert, as some social scientists and women's liberationists have done, that fathers are largely irrelevant to the well-being of their progeny, that their sex is immaterial, and their sole useful contribution to child-rearing is to function from time to time as breastless mother-substitutes. Such a degree of contempt for the paternal virtues would contrast sharply with the clinical experience of psychiatrists and the personal experience of most of us that fathers do indeed have great influence on the lives of their sons and daughters. Fortunately, this dissonance between theory and fact has led to some interesting research in recent years, the implications of which we shall be examining in this chapter. Broadly speaking, the findings are in keeping with Jung's (1909) belief that the father plays a crucial psychological role in 'the destiny of the individual'.

The father archetype

It was in his 1909 paper that Jung first stated his opinion that the seemingly 'magical' hold and influence that parents have over their children was not merely a function of their individual personalities, or of the child's relative helplessness, but was primarily due to the numinosity of the parental archetypes activated by them in the child's psyche. 'The personal father inevitably embodies the archetype, which is what endows this figure with its fascinating power. The archetype acts as an amplifier, enhancing beyond measure the effects that proceed from the father, so far as these conform to the inherited pattern' (*CW* 4, para. 744).

In myth, legend and dreams, the father archetype personifies as the Elder, the King, the Father in Heaven. As Lawgiver he speaks with the voice of collective authority and is the living embodiment of the *Logos* principle: his word is law. As Defender of the Faith and of the Realm he is the guardian of the *status quo* and bastion against all enemies. His attributes are activity and penetration, differentiation and judgment, fecundity and destruction. His symbols are heaven and the sun, lightening and wind, the phallus and the weapon. Heaven symbolizes the spiritual aspirations of the masculine principle, of which the Father is the primal carrier, but in nearly all religions and mythologies heaven is by no means the realm of universal Good: it is also the origin of natural disasters and human catastrophes, the seat from which the godhead passes judgment and from which he punishes with thunderbolts and rewards with boons; it is the throne room of the primordial patriarch, where he freely exercises his powers of life and death over his wives and children. For like the Mother, the Father has a Terrible side: he possesses the dual aspect of Jehovah and of the fecundating and destructive Hindu god, Shiva. He is Kronos who prevents his sons from replacing him by eating them alive.

As far as the growing child is concerned, Jungians all agree that the father archetype is activated later in the ontological sequence than the mother archetype, though rather vague opinions are expressed about when this may be said to occur. Jung was of the opinion that the father archetype showed little sign of activity until about the fifth year, but thereafter it assumed greater influence over the developing personality than the mother archetype and that this influence persisted well into puberty. As we shall see, however, there is good reason for supposing that the father becomes of considerable importance much earlier than Jung believed.

Clearly, the first archetypal constellation through which the Self gropes its way out of the uroborus into conscious reality is the Mother, but it seems probable that the post-uroboric 'Mother' is, in fact, still at the stage of the (undifferentiated) 'Parent': only later, with the emergence of ego-consciousness and the formation of attachment bonds with both parents, is it likely that 'Separation of the Parents' occurs, the parental archetype becoming differentiated into its maternal and paternal poles.

That this process of parental distinction is already started by the second year, and is well advanced by the fourth, is indicated by a number of studies. For example, Biller (1974) has consistently found that paternal deprivation beginning before the age of four has a more disruptive effect on a child's development than father absence commencing at a later date. In a study by Leichty (1960) college men whose fathers were at home during their childhood were compared with a group whose fathers were away in the Army when they were between three and five years old. These 'paternally deprived' men had considerable difficulty in adjusting to the return of their fathers, some finding it impossible to identify with them or to accept them as a masculine ideal. Burton (1972) studied the effects of father absence on the development of gender identity in children in Barbados and found that the presence of the father during the first two years of childhood was critical if the development of a feminine orientation in boys was to be avoided. Moreover, Money and Erhardt (1972) and others have assembled evidence which strongly suggests that gender identity has usually been accomplished by *eighteen months*. Attempts to correct a wrong gender attribution after this age gave rise to impressive difficulties. It is clear, therefore, that the father is much more to the child than an occasional mother-substitute and that the father archetype becomes both differentiated and active at an earlier stage than Jung supposed.

But where Jung was not mistaken was in his view of the contribution which the father makes to psychogenesis: it is through the father-child relationship that gender-consciousness emerges. Slowly the boy comes to recognize that his bond to father is based on *identity* ('I and the father are one'), while the girl comes to appreciate that it is based on *difference* (i.e. the father constitutes, both spiritually and sexually, her first profound experience of the essential 'otherness' of the male). Jung believed that the father's presence was crucial if the boy was to actualize in consciousness and in behaviour his own masculine potential. Since formation of the mother bond predates the onset of gender consciousness, it is based on mother-identity for the boy no less than for the girl. The girl, therefore, has to make no readjustment to her original sense of identity with mother, while the boy has to undergo the revolutionary transformation from mother-identity to identification-with-father. Lack of a father makes this transition hard, and sometimes impossible, to achieve. Many studies confirm the high incidence of sex-role confusion in boys who grow up without fathers, and the relative absence of such confusion in fatherless girls.

However, there is little doubt that fathers do influence in significant degree the manner in which their daughters *experience* their femininity *vis-à-vis* the man. His loving affirmation can greatly assist her to happy acceptance of her female role, while his rejection or mockery can cause deep injury which may never heal. Girls who grow to maturity without fathers may have few doubts that they are women, but when it comes to living with a man as his partner they can feel hopelessly lost and unprepared.

The father's influence over the development of his children extends far beyond the question of sexual identity and relationships, however. In the great majority of patrilineal societies, he acts as the bridge between family life and the life of society at large. This is what Talcott Parsons

(1955) calls the father's *instrumental* role, which he distinguishes from the mother's *expressive* role. Almost universally, the father possesses a centrifugal orientation (i.e. towards society and the outside world) in contrast to the mother's centripetal concern (i.e. with home and family), and our culture is no exception, despite attempts in some quarters to change it. By representing society to the family and his family to society, the father facilitates the transition of the child from home to the world at large. He encourages the development of skills necessary for successful adult adaptation, while at the same time communicating to the child the values and mores prevailing in the social system. That he performs this function is no mere accident of culture: it rests on an archetypal foundation. 'Whereas mother in her eternal aspect represents the earth that does not change, the transpersonal [i.e. archetypal] father represents consciousness as it moves and changes. In this sense father is subject to time, subject to ageing and death; his image changes with the culture he represents' (Von der Heydt, 1973). The Mother is outside time and dominates the realm of feelings, instincts and the unconscious; the Father is concerned with events occurring in the tangible world in the context of space and time – events which are approached, controlled and modified through consciousness and the use of will. It is not just that a father's attitudes to work, social achievement, politics and the law condition the developing attitudes of his children, but that he constellates for them the whole extraverted potential of the world as place-to-be-known-and-lived-in. Inasmuch as he succeeds in this role, he sets them free from their involvement with mother and fosters the necessary autonomy (ego-Self axis) for effective living. For her part, the mother's *expressive* function continues to provide the emotional support and security enabling them to go out and meet the world's challenges.

That fathers and mothers are constitutionally geared to their respective social and personal roles does not, of course, deny the existence of 'instrumental' capacities in the mother or of 'expressive' ones in the father. What we are discussing are those typical dispositions and modes of functioning which are the hallmarks of archetypal expression. Certainly, men can function in the same roles as women, and vice versa, but that is not what they are best equipped for. When it comes to the expression of Eros, for example, the archetype is characteristically actualized differently by men and women in relation to their children. It is as if, as Wolfgang Lederer (1964) says, fathers and mothers stand for two different modes of loving: for the mother it is usually sufficient that her child *exists* – her love is absolute and largely unconditional; a father's love, however, is more demanding – it is *contingent* love, love which is conditional upon performance in the world. Thus, Eros is actualized by the mother directly through her expressive role; while in the father it is inextricably linked to his instrumental function. Mother-love is an *a priori* precondition of the bond to her child; father-love is something that has to be won through achievement. And since the father's love has to be earned, it is an incentive to the development of autonomy, and an affirmation of that autonomy once it is attained. Growth of the ego-Self axis, therefore, which begins through the relationship to mother is consolidated and confirmed through the bond to father.

Paternal behaviour in animals

From the standpoint of biology, fathers are clearly of less importance than mothers once fertilization has taken place. However, it would be surprising if the paternal role, so important in our own species, were not evident in other mammals as well. Allowing for the fact that conjugal relationships in most mammalian species tend to be nothing if not promiscuous and that it is consequently often impossible to decide which male has sired which infant, it is nevertheless true that mature males in many species show a degree of interest and personal involvement in the lives of mothers and babies to warrant application of the term *paternal*, even if the behaviour concerned is somewhat less discriminating in its expression than that which characterizes the human father.

In most primate species, for example, adult males associate freely with the young, showing their personal concern by such behaviour as grooming, playful wrestling and biting, retrieving, providing food, protecting from attack, and so on. Some species are more paternalistic than others. The New World titi monkey, for instance, which lives in monogamous union with its mate, spends most of his time carrying or cuddling his infant, only handing over to the mother when it needs to be fed. The gibbon, a small Asian ape which is also 'monogamous', has a less exclusive relationship with its progeny but is none the less intimately involved in their care up to about eighteen months of age, when his paternal interest wanes. Male hamadryas baboons, normally tough and assertive in their relations with each other, often display behaviour which seems almost maternal in dealing with their young, carrying and cuddling them with obvious signs of interest and affection. In this species, infants unfortunate enough to lose their mothers, are invariably adopted by young adult males. Moreover, in all baboon populations a transfer of attachment from mother to adult male appears to occur in the second year, at the time when the mother commonly gives birth to another infant and loses interest in the one she has been nursing. This paternal solicitude persists until about thirty months when the juvenile begins to seek his position in the dominance hierarchy of the troop. A similar form of male adoption occurs when a younger sibling is born among Japanese macaques, the 'adopting father' tending to be an animal of high rank in the dominance hierarchy. Except for his inability to suckle the infant, his behaviour for some months closely resembles that of the mother. In most species of primate, males act as a source of refuge for young when they are frightened, and will intervene when squabbles break out between them. Less directly, male adults also contribute to the welfare of the young by defending the troop and its territory from conspecifics and predators.

As in human cultures, therefore, there is considerable variation in the form that paternal behaviour may take in primate species, but it seems that the potential for such behaviour is present in most of them. Even among those species where males are normally indifferent or hostile to the young, there is evidence that, under certain conditions, they will form close attachments with infants. It is thus reasonable to conclude that paternal behaviour is 'planned for' in the genome of all primate males: it depends on the exigencies of the environment whether or not it is activated and expressed. When it *is* activated, the father archetype appears to have many features in common in both animals and men.

· 9 ·

On the frustration of archetypal intent

Although fears are commonly expressed for the health of Western society, it is still fortunately true to say that the majority of our children grow up in reasonably stable families where they receive care which is 'good enough' from both parents. Developmental psychology is sufficiently advanced for us to know that such children are likely to enjoy mental health in that they are free of incapacitating neurotic symptoms, and that they tend to become secure, self-reliant adults who display social maturity through their ability to be helpful and co-operative with others. It is these characters that psychiatry and the various schools of analysis regard as 'normal': psychoanalysts speak of them as possessing a 'strong ego'; Kleinians consider them to have 'introjected a good object'; in Erikson's terms, they have established 'basic trust'; Fairbairn would have described them as displaying 'mature dependence' (i.e. we all need people we know we can 'depend on', but without being anxious or compulsive about it, without 'clinging on' to them); for Bowlby and the attachment theorists, they have succeeded in constructing a representative model of themselves as being able to provide self-help and as being worthy of receiving help from others should the need arise. In Jungian terms, they are well started on the path to individuation.

However a large section of the population is less fortunate. Neurotic illness, which disturbs the emotional and mental well-being of people without depriving them of their reason, is without doubt one of the greatest scourges of contemporary man. Just how common it is cannot be accurately determined; those statistics which do exist are almost certainly underestimates since they are derived from the minority of sufferers who present themselves for treatment. Even so, on the most conservative estimates, neurotics account for at least one third of all patients consulting family doctors and are responsible in Great Britain alone for the loss of about 17 million working days each year. In the majority of such people who are actually seen by psychiatrists, a history is elicited of deficient parental care – deficient in the sense that the quality of the care provided was such as to frustrate those archetypal imperatives, inherent within the biogrammar of the maturing Self, which are concerned with the formation of attachment bonds, the establishment of basic trust, and the development of a secure ego conceiving of itself as being both acceptable to others and capable of coping with the eventualities of life. The characteristic patterns of deficient parenting which neurotic subjects commonly reveal in their histories may be summarized as follows:

1 parental absence or separation from the child: one or both parents may go away and leave the child, or put him in hospital or an institution; the earlier the loss and the longer or more frequent the separations, the more serious are the consequences for the mental health of the child and future adult;

2 parental unresponsiveness to the child's attachment needs: one or both parents are persistently unresponsive to the child's care-eliciting behaviour, and they may, indeed, actively disparage or reject him;

3 parental threats of abandonment used as sanctions to coerce or discipline the child: one or other parent makes a practice of threatening to withdraw love, to abandon the family, to commit suicide, or even to kill the spouse or child;

4 parental induction of guilt in the child: assertions are made that the child's behaviour is or will be responsible for the illness or death of one or other parent;

5 parental 'clinging' on to the child: the parent (usually the mother) displays 'anxious attachment' to the child, exerting pressure on him to be the primary care-giver in their relationship, thus inverting the normal pattern, and forcing the child to be responsible and grown up beyond his years.

Any one of these forms of parental distortion of archetypal intent can result in anxious, insecure individuals who report themselves to be 'lacking in confidence', 'shy', 'inadequate' and 'unable to cope'. They often have difficulty in forming and maintaining lasting relationships, and are characteristically described by psychiatrists and social workers as 'over-dependent' or 'immature'. Under stress they are prone to 'break down' and develop neurotic symptoms, such as persistent anxiety, depression, obsessive-compulsive phenomena and phobias.

The actual kind of distortion to which an individual patient may have been subjected in childhood can sometimes be deduced from the manner in which he relates to emotionally significant persons in his environment – including the psychiatrist. The commonest manifestation of pathogenic parenting is what Bowlby describes as *anxious attachment* – a nagging anxiety that one's attachment figures might be lost; this coincides with a low threshold for the release of care-eliciting behaviour. Typically, such patients become extremely anxious when their psychiatrist goes away on holiday, or if they fear they may have displeased or annoyed him in some way. Moreover, all five variants of pathogenic parental behaviour listed above are prone to *release anger* in the archetypally frustrated child. Since the parents are infinitely more powerful than the child, however, and since the care and protection they provide is essential to his survival, he usually feels obliged to control his anger and inhibit its expression. The (largely unconscious) resentment which this induces tends to persist into adult life as a 'chip on the shoulder': the hostility which could not be directed against the parents is displaced on to some other group (e.g. the bosses, the unions, the blacks, etc.) or on to someone perceived as weaker (e.g. the spouse, child, or employee). Such people also commonly have strong unconscious *yearnings for love* which may reveal themselves in some aberrant form of care-eliciting behaviour which, as often as not, is modelled on the aberrant form of care-giving behaviour displayed by the parents (e.g. half-hearted suicide attempts, threats to leave, malingering, hypochondria, guilt-induction, and so on).

A brief case history will serve to illustrate these points. Tancred, described by his family doctor as 'a very immature chap in his late twenties', was referred with attacks of acute anxiety, acute depression, and recurrent attempts at suicide. His mother was an alcoholic socialite who put parties before maternity, with the result that all her children grew up to be neurotic and unstable. Her attitude to Tancred had been deeply ambivalent from the start: sometimes she treated him like a pet, but generally was content to leave him in the care of a string of indifferent nannies. When Tancred responded to this treatment with behaviour disturbances, such as bed-wetting, head-banging, food-refusal, nightmares, and so on, his mother became incensed, subjecting him to ridicule and frank rejection: 'I wish you'd never been born,' she would scream.

Tancred's father, a high-ranking naval officer, was a kind but retiring man, who tended to avoid family scenes by immersing himself in his work. Although Tancred loved him, he did little to ease his mounting insecurity: he was essentially a 'fair-weather father' who never seemed to be available when he was desperately needed.

As his therapist, it was difficult to make any contact with him initially, but slowly a relationship formed between us which, on his side, bore all the signs of anxious attachment. The trouble was that he could never bring himself to believe that I would tolerate him as a patient. He had recurrent nightmares in which I said how much I loathed him and that I intended to put him to death. During consultations he would misconstrue harmless remarks as mockery and rejection. At times he found the relationship too much of a responsibility and would behave badly in a way clearly designed to provoke me into terminating his treatment.

Analysis revealed that this pattern was repeated with all emotionally significant figures in his life. Invariably, he alternated between demonstrations of love and appreciation (gifts, letters, cards, etc.), demands for care and protection (telephone calls for help, suicide attempts, the manufacture of dramatic incidents, etc.), resentful hostility ('You can fuck off; I never want to see you again'), which would be followed by panic lest he had totally alienated one, and episodes of deep dejection when he felt worthless and essentially unlovable.

Yet, underlying this profoundly disturbed behaviour there was an apparent longing for a relationship with a strong, dependable figure who could be relied on to be kind, reassuring, attentive and permanently available. In other words, he was embarked on a forlorn quest for someone to make accessible to him all those parental qualities which his father, and above all his mother, had conspicuously failed to provide. That he despaired of ever attaining his goal was entirely attributable to his personal history which had conditioned him to believe that people could never be trusted to be loving and available when you needed them.

As this sad story makes clear, those archetypal components which our personal parents succeed in actualizing for us may not be as crucial for our individual destiny as those archetypal components which they *fail* to actualize. As children, we all begin by experiencing our parents as infallible, vividly numinous embodiments of the Mother and Father archetypes; only later, as we attain years of discretion, do we recognize them as fallible human beings with their own personal limitations, which we, in our youthful arrogance, believe we can transcend. It was this eternal truth that Oscar Wilde saw when he said: 'Children begin by loving their parents; as they grow older they judge them; sometimes they forgive them.'

In theory, at any rate, every archetype possesses a totality; individual parents, however, being human and not gods, are by their very nature imperfect and incomplete: consequently, they can never hope to embody in their own lives all the attributes of a parental archetype. All that any parent can ever realistically aim to be is 'good enough' to provide the key that opens the archetypal lock and, in doing so, realize that the parental archetype so released will profoundly influence the child's expectations. As we ourselves discover when we grow up, children always expect more of us than we have to give them, and when we disappoint them, they go off to seek what they want elsewhere. It would be cruel and ungrateful were it not that each generation repays what it owes to the last by giving to the next.

Whatever archetypal potential we as parents fail to activate in our child still persists there *as potential* and, by definition, must continue to seek actualization in reality. The extent of this unactualized potential is inversely proportional to our effectiveness as parents, the more incompetent we are, the greater the archetypal energy seeking to be discharged, and the greater the 'parental hunger' manifested by the child (hence, for example, the 'clinging' children one encounters in institutions).

Jung's insights as to how this process occurs arose from his early researches on the word association test. He came to the conclusion that elements capable of constellating an archetype activated not just the corresponding portions of the archetype but the total archetypal system. The system, once activated, then seeks encounter with associated elements *other* than those which brought about the original activation. This hypothesis is entirely in line with Jung's overall concept of a Self which seeks its own completion in the individuation process. In clinical practice one comes across many instances which are compatible with it.

Take, for example, the case cited by Dr Edward Whitmont (1969) of the male patient whose father was a dictatorial despot and who, in the course of growing up, developed a pathological father-complex which expressed itself in fear and resentment of authority figures, especially those possessing characteristics reminiscent of the father. Such cases are encountered almost daily by practising psychotherapists. But they are crucial to our argument because of an interesting detail which they all seem to share. As Whitmont noted, deeper probing of the parental complex reveals the patient's essential ambivalence about the hated authority figures: instead of avoiding them like the plague, he seems positively to be drawn to them, repeatedly getting himself trapped in their clutches. It is a pattern which he is apparently powerless to change, like a moth battering itself again and again against a lamp. Whitmont reflects:

> This means that our contact with the actualized aspect of the archetype in any form associated with the real father tends to trigger not only the response of its corresponding, actualized complex but also the total archetype; the parts which have *not* been actualized but which strive for actualization are touched through the channels which are already available, although they are insufficient and inadequate for appropriate expression. There is a sort of vacuum effect, with a compensatory suction toward the unexperienced portion, the 'search for the external object never seen before'. Then we are drawn by a longing for the 'ideal' father, mother, lover, etc., which is the more unattainable or unrealistic as the discrepancy increases between the actual experience or lack of it and the unrealized elements. (1969, p. 122)

The phrase 'search for the object never seen before', Whitmont borrows from Adolf Portmann, who first used it to describe the behaviour of the young cuckoo which, although reared by foster-parents of a different species, nevertheless seeks out and mates with one of its own kind, which it has never before encountered. Evidently, argues Portmann, within the central nervous system of the cuckoo there are structures 'waiting to be activated' which subserve 'preformed patterns of behaviour' which make possible the recognition and acquisition of a mate 'never seen before'. So it is with the archetypes of the human phylogenetic psyche. When actualization has been deficient, an individual finds himself, despite his conscious will in the matter, 'sucked into' personal involvements and situations which promise to possess characteristics adequate to constellate, or bring to birth, the unlived archetypal elements. The resultant clinical picture is so common as to warrant a name: the term *Flying Dutchman Syndrome* would seem appropriate. For those thus afflicted roam endlessly about the world searching for the 'ideal' figure who will grant them what they crave – the warm, devoted mother, the effectively masculine father – whom they never knew as children.

Thus the man with the despotic father was drawn repeatedly to tyrants because of his need to find something more in them. What attracted him was the masculine unknown, a yearning for 'the never seen before', those unactualized parts of the father archetype concerned with loving guidance and support in the outer world.

Let me illustrate this theme with a further, highly instructive case. When he came to see me first, Colin was thirty-four, an intelligent, articulate, well-educated man, a university lecturer in German. He was not depressed or anxious; indeed, he struck me as rather content with his lot: he had many interests, numerous friends, and spent most of the university vacations in Germany, where his boyfriend, an NCO serving with NATO Forces, was stationed.

The reason why he consulted me was essentially curiosity about his own sexual make-up. In addition to being homosexual, he was a uniform and boot fetishist and a masochist. The sort of men who attracted him were toughly masculine and unequivocally working class; soldiers were his special penchant. The affair with Peter, his army sergeant, had been going on for two years. It was, he said, the happiest of his life and he wanted to do nothing to spoil it. Essentially, theirs was a 'master-slave' relationship, though evident affection existed between them. For the duration of each vacation, Colin rented accommodation near Peter's camp. During the daytime, while Peter was on duty, Colin did the housework and shopping, and subsidized his income by giving private English and German lessons. In the late afternoon, Peter would come home in uniform and conduct a thorough military-type inspection of their quarters. If he found anything dirty or out of place, he would give Colin a sound dressing down, and order him to lower his trousers and bend over the back of a chair. He would then beat him on the naked buttocks with a long, flexible cane kept specially for the purpose. All this Colin found deeply satisfying. He had no wish to give it up, but he wondered why.

The clinically significant features of the family history were as follows: he was by far the youngest of three gifted children, a welcome afterthought, as it turned out. His mother, who described his arrival as 'my loveliest surprise', was a warm-hearted, loving woman who had always adored Colin and he her. The security of their relationship was never in doubt, and there were no separations until he went away to the university at the age of eighteen. The father was a mild, gentle, retiring, rather obsessional man of impeccable middle-class outlook, whose business took him repeatedly away from home during Colin's childhood. From things that his mother said, Colin gathered that his father's potency had always been uncertain and that any display of erotic affection acutely embarrassed him. He was prone to fuss about trivia and, although a kindly and entirely reliable breadwinner, he sounds to have been something of an old woman: his fussiness was a standing joke between Colin and his mother.

As far as discipline in the home was concerned, there seems to have been little or none. Despite the father's fussiness there were few rules and regulations, and Colin was encouraged to indulge his artistic and intellectual gifts to his heart's content, provided he did not make too much noise or mess when his father was at home. The only matters that he could recall his father being firm about were that he should not consort with the rough working-class boys who sometimes penetrated their residential suburb from a nearby council housing estate, and that he was never allowed to wear boots, shoes being regarded as the only appropriate wear for a nicely brought up young boy. Corporal punishment was out of the question and, indeed, the whole subject was strictly taboo, since the mother felt the practice to be barbaric and talk about it deeply upset her. When I asked if his father had ever spanked him, Colin laughed, saying that the idea was comic since the poor man couldn't hurt a fly. A few days later, however, he recalled that his father had on one occasion given him a hard slap on the bare bottom when he had refused to get out of his mother's bed!

What discipline there was in the home was maintained by the mother – in the most gentle and loving way. If ever Colin did anything disreputable or aggressive, she would respond by becoming hurt and upset. This had the effect of making Colin feel extremely guilty, and he would do all that lay in his power to mollify her and atone for his churlishness.

His erotic phantasies began early. He recalled that from about five years onwards he had phantasies of big, tough labourers in hobnailed boots rubbing against his naked body with their coarse overalls and beating him with sticks. These phantasies persisted largely unchanged until he was ten or eleven, when an interesting event occurred. Colin did or said something – what exactly he could not remember – that must have shocked his father's sense of proper masculine decorum, for it resulted in him reproving Colin for 'behaving like a sissy'; and he added, with uncharacteristic severity, 'You wait till you are called up, my boy. The army will make a man of you!' Following this incident, the erotic phantasies changed and, instead of being man-handled by labourers, he was inspected and hounded about parade grounds by drill sergeants, who swore at him and belaboured him with their pace-sticks. These new military phantasies coincided with the onset of puberty and Colin's first conscious experience of orgasm.

How then may we formulate this case in terms of archetypal theory? As has already been indicated (p. 106 above), for a boy to become possessed of his own masculinity, he requires a lasting, intimate relationship with an effectively masculine father-figure. It follows that absence or masculine deficiency on the part of the father will fail to activate the Father archetype within the boy's psyche, with the result that the masculine principle, an archetype sequentially linked to the Father archetype, also remains unactivated, and the boy is left *uninitiated* into the masculine world, doomed irredeemably to languish under the dominance of his mother complex. This, I believe, is precisely what happened to Colin.

The clue to his erotic phantasies lies in the unactivated portions of the Father archetype. The lack of masculine toughness, aggression and authority in the father, combined with his frequent absences from home, turned Colin into a homosexual Flying Dutchman, forever questing after the man (whom he eventually found for a while in Peter) to actualize for him what his father could not. What attracted him were men who caricatured those masculine qualities that his father, in his bourgeois effeteness, looked down on and condemned – tough, working-class men, who wore coarse overalls, rough uniforms and boots.

His masochism arose from two sources: his desire for an authority who could maintain order in an explicitly masculine way (in contrast to the old-maidish fussiness of his father), and out of a desire for punishment (which he never received from either of his gentle, loving parents) to absolve the extreme guilt he felt whenever his spontaneous (masculine) aggression upset his mother. The fact that the masculine quest became eroticized meant that he sought punishment in a form regarded in the family as taboo, namely, caning. Moreover, the cane also had obvious phallic significance – the weapon that the personal father could not bring himself to use and which, as a consequence, the unactualized father *would*. Furthermore, the choice of the army as the setting in which his phantasies proceeded, symbolically represented Colin's need to be initiated into the adult male world, the parade ground providing the *temenos* on which the drill sergeant would 'make a man of him'.

One important consequence of inadequate parenting, therefore, is failure to develop. There is not only a critical period during which parents must be available, but a critical degree to which the parental archetypes must be actualized if the child is to move on to maturity. Failure to receive adequate parenting at the correct time results in 'parent hunger' and embarcation on a Flying Dutchman quest which may never attain its goal. Bowlby has performed an inestimable service in demonstrating that healthy development depends on the presence of parents who are not only available but who also refrain from threatening to make themselves unavailable as a means of coercion. What is just as important, however, is the *quality* of the parents who are available, that is to say, the extent to which they have individuated as men and women by the time they come to raise a family.

Individuation and the relative salience of parents

The impact of parental personality on the development of the child is a subject requiring much research and many volumes to describe. It is certainly far too enormous to be touched on here, except in the broad sense of how *adequate* a father or mother a man or woman may be by virtue of their personal qualities. While it is fortunately true that the majority of parents are apparently 'good enough', it is equally true that a substantial minority are not. As we have seen in the case of Colin's father, one way in which it is possible to be deficient as a parent is to *lack salience*, that is, to be insufficiently *there* either physically (through absence) or symbolically (through lack of personal effectiveness). However, it is also possible for a parent to err in the opposite direction and be *too salient*, that is, too assertive and powerful and unwilling to grant the child sufficient space in which to develop his autonomy. Such parents tend to interfere unnecessarily in their children's lives, seeking to control and regulate their behaviour, or to overprotect them from real or imagined dangers, when it would be better to let them find their own feet and test out their own abilities in the face of life's ordinary challenges. In the Jungian literature, these parents are described as 'devouring'.

Parents who lack salience

The most obvious way in which a parent can lack salience is through failure to be physically present. The potentially disastrous consequences of lacking a mother have already been mentioned in chapter 7. Contrary to the assertions of some feminists, we now know, in addition, that the consequences of growing up without a father can be almost as catastrophic for the child's chances of achieving a happy and fulfilled adult life. 'Behavioural systems,' writes Bowlby, 'develop within an individual through the interaction during ontogeny of genetically determined biases and the environment in which the individual is reared; the further the *rearing environment* departs from that of evolutionary adaptedness the more likely are that individual's behavioural systems to develop atypically' (1973, p. 106). As has been suggested in chapter 6, the 'rearing environment' to which human infants are evolutionarily adapted is characterized by the presence of at least one female and at least one male living in some form of familial association whose function is to protect and care for children. If Bowlby's proposal, quoted above, is correct, then it follows that the more the social environment deviates from the family model the more probability there is that the child will develop atypically. On the basis of this assumption, one would predict that children who grow up without families (e.g. in orphanages and other institutions) would tend to show marked developmental disturbances, those growing up in single-parent families would tend to be better off but atypical maturation in some areas would occur, while children reaching maturity in a stable family environment would tend to show healthy development provided both parents possessed sufficient personal salience to activate crucial archetypal potential in the child's psyche.

A great number of research findings are in line with these predictions. For example, in recent years it has been established that children reared without fathers are likely to show deficits not only in their sexual and social development, but in their moral and cognitive development as well. This is particularly true when the father's absence is due to separation, desertion or divorce. This is a vast and growing problem. In the United States more than 10 per cent of all children (a total population in excess of 8 million) live in fatherless families (Herzog and Sudia, 1970). In some ghettoes the figure is as high as 50 per cent (Moynihan, 1965). More and more marriages are being terminated by divorce, and increasingly large numbers of children are growing up in single-parent families, many of them being brought up by substitute caretakers rather than their own parents (Bronfenbrenner, 1975). Moreover, even those children who are fortunate enough to have parents who stay together often tend in our society to have fathers who are *relatively* absent: a growing number of fathers work at places a long way from home and have very little time to be with their children – a mode of life which contrasts starkly with that prevailing in the 'environment of evolutionary adaptedness', where children had ready access to their fathers and a wealth of opportunity to observe them in the practice of those social and physical skills characteristic of adult males in their community (e.g. the conditions which prevail among the !Kung Bushmen of Botswana). The consequence for modern children is that they have little practical experience of what it is to live and function as a man, and boys are seldom in a position to actualize their masculine potential by the simple expedient of living out their ontogeny in their father's presence. Moreover, both boys and girls are customarily in the presence of their mother as she carries out her female role: this makes it easy for the girl to acquire an adult feminine identity, but further complicates the masculine problem for the boy.

I am, of course, aware that not everyone will regard these facts with dismay. After all, we live at a time when it has become increasingly fashionable to regard gender-consciousness and sex-linked patterns of behaviour as crippling stereotypes whose disintegration is to be encouraged in the interests of individual liberty. Few, I imagine, would wish any longer to see women as subservient chattels, to be used and exploited by their menfolk, nor would they seek to deny that men and women should be treated equally in society and before the law. However it has to be said that feminine militants do themselves and humanity a disservice when they try to minimize basic differences between the sexes; for this results paradoxically in denigration of the archetypal feminine and over-valuation of the masculine: it leads directly to a perverse cultural climate in which women feel guilty and humiliated rather than gratified and fulfilled by the role of wife or mother, and in which they unconsciously saddle themselves with a stereotype of womanhood which is in fact more restrictive than that prescribed by tradition – a stereotype that Tiger and Fox have wickedly lampooned as the belief that women are really men who periodically take time off from work to have babies.

In chapter 11 I shall develop the argument that certain differences between the sexes are fundamental in the sense that they are biologically grounded. In a manner of speaking, men and women are different animals: they have evolved in special ways which enable each to make their peculiarly male and peculiarly female contribution to the propagation and welfare of the species; these differences are psychic and social no less than somatic and reproductive. To attempt to abolish them on ideological grounds is not just plain silly, it is impossible: it represents a preposterous violation of archetypal intent. One might revel in the comic absurdity of the exercise were it not for the fear that it will create more confusion and unhappiness than already exists in the discordant world of contemporary marital relations.

Not that one is in a position any longer to incite women, even if they wished it, to a life of unbridled maternity. The population explosion demands reproductive restraint. In any case, medical progress has decreed that motherhood need absorb less of a woman's life-span than hitherto: the dramatic decline in infant mortality means that she can ensure survival of her clan by having fewer children, while extension of the average life-expectancy from around 40 to 70 means that she can look forward to many vigorous years after she has reared her children.

Times are changing for our species and we must keep abreast of them or perish. Women are being freed to make increasingly significant contributions to our society and to discover new possibilities within themselves which reach far beyond their reproductive function. But it is imperative that this new female expansiveness should take due cognizance of what is *archetypally feminine* and not seek to achieve fulfiment by mimicking the male. The woman who negates or overrides her feminine nature in order to become a pseudo-male sustains critical injury to the ego-Self axis, a self-inflicted wound which causes sterility on the psychic no less than on the physical plane; she risks becoming alienated from her own inherent resources and from the meaning of her life. Archetypes are the decrees of nature; we flout them at our peril.

The contemporary decline in the position of the father has coincided with a most interesting cultural development: the emergence of an anti-authoritarian *Zeitgeist*, especially amongst the young, which manifests itself in a blanket hostility towards the traditional patriarchal values enshrined in Judeo-Christian civilization for millennia. This phenomenon must engage our attention here because it affords an example of what may happen when a society of individuals collectively shares in the rejection or repression of integral components of an archetype. What have been rejected in this instance are those aspects of the Father and the archetypal Masculine which relate to the maintenance of law and order, discipline and self-control, morality and responsibility, courage and patriotism, loyalty and obligation, the exercise of authority and command, all of which have been under attack throughout the last two decades as being inimical to individual freedom and creativity.

Yet an archetype cannot be hacked off from the Self and disposed of like an amputated limb. If it is rejected by a negative conscious attitude it returns to the unconscious only to re-emerge in some other form. The fact is that, whether we like it or not, authority, order, discipline and responsibility are intrinsic components of the paternal archetypal nucleus. They are there because natural selection has put them there; because without them no population could hope to survive. If our civilization declines to encourage their actualization, or even more if it actively represses them, they will not go away: they will persist as unconscious archetypal potential which will continue to seek actualization in other subversive or antisocial forms.

Revolutionary movements in liberal democracies exemplify this process. First they caricature the liberal establishment as a group of 'fascist oppressors' which they declare they have a 'moral duty' to attack. Then, 'in the name of humanity' they proceed to organize themselves with ruthless efficiency to destroy, mutilate and terrorize in an effort to overthrow the hated social order, actualizing in the life of their own organisation the very 'Father' qualities of power, force, order, discipline and 'loyalty to the group' that they affect to despise in their 'oppressors'. One hesitates to imagine what kind of a regime the IRA, the Baader-Meinhof gang or the Red Brigade would establish if they ever succeeded in achieving their objectives. 'In the name of the people' they would doubtless round up all 'enemies of society' and treat them with the same consideration as did Hitler, Stalin or Pol Pot. Repressed archetypal components tend to erupt in primitive, destructive ways, primarily because they emerge in undifferentiated form from the unconscious; it can take decades or centuries for consciousness to perceive their essential characteristics and bring about some new integration of their power. The rise and fall of Nazi Germany with the subsequent establishment of the Federal Republic may be interpreted as an example of this process operating on a national scale.

Until the *Ragnorok* which brought the Third Reich to its cataclysmic end, Germany had been a rigidly patriarchal society in which fathers demanded *Ehrfurcht* (lit. 'honour-fear') from their children and induced in them the type of compulsive, 'authoritarian' personality which is described later in this chapter. Jung believed that the Father archetype in the German collective unconscious was powerfully contaminated by the Teutonic myth of Wotan, the Lord of Hosts, but that vitally dynamic aspects of the Wotan figure had been repressed under the unyielding hierarchical structure of the '*Ehrfurcht*' society. Order, discipline and a slavish respect for masculine authority were clearly in evidence at all levels of society; what was repressed was the passionate, irrational god of storm and frenzy, the god of war whose violent spirit takes possession of the hearts of men and drives them berserk with the lust for blood and destruction. Jung held that these terrible archetypal vestiges had lain dormant for centuries, repressed in the name of Christendom (which regarded Wotan, like Pan and Dionysos, as Satanic) and sterilized by the bright rationalism of the Enlightenment.

With uncanny prescience, Jung made his diagnosis of the condition and prognosis for its outcome in a paper written fourteen years before Hitler came to power:

> Christianity split the Germanic barbarian into an upper and a lower half, and enabled him, by repressing the dark side, to domesticate the brighter half and fit it for civilization. But the lower, darker half still awaits redemption and a second spell of domestication. Until then, it will remain associated with the vestiges of the prehistoric age, with the collective unconscious, which is subject to a peculiar and ever-increasing activation. As the Christian view of the world loses its authority, the more menacingly will the 'blond beast' be heard prowling about in its underground prison, ready at any mo-

> ment to burst out with devastating consequences. (*CW* 10, para. 17)

When, in the mid-1930s, the world stood mesmerized by Hitler's political success, Jung had no doubts as to its real nature and origins.

> We are always convinced that the modern world is a reasonable world, basing our opinion on economic, political and psychological factors. But if we may forget for a moment that we are living in the Year of Our Lord 1936 . . . we would find Wotan quite suitable as a causal hypothesis. In fact I venture the heretical suggestion that the unfathomable depths of Wotan's character explain more of National Socialism than all three reasonable factors put together. (*CW* 10, para. 385)

Hitler, Jung believed, was himself in the grip of the repressed Wotanic elements: 'The impressive thing about the German phenomenon is that one man, who is obviously "possessed", has infected a whole nation to such an extent that everything is set in motion and has started rolling on its course towards perdition' (*CW* 10, para. 388).

In a passage from the same (1936) paper, Jung expresses in metaphors his understanding of how it is that archetypal components never disintegrate but lie dormant in the unconscious, waiting to be re-activated:

> It was not in Wotan's nature to linger on and show signs of old age. He simply disappeared when the times turned against him, and remained invisible for more than a thousand years, working anonymously and indirectly. Archetypes are like river beds which dry up when the water deserts them, but which it can find again at any time. An archetype is like an old water-course along which the water of life has flowed for centuries digging a deep channel for itself. The longer it has flowed in this channel the more likely it is that sooner or later the water will return to its old bed. The life of the individual as a member of society and particularly as part of the State may be regulated like a canal, but the life of nations is a great rushing river which is utterly beyond human control. . . . Thus the life of nations rolls on unchecked, without guidance, unconscious of where it is going, like a rock crashing down the side of a hill, until it is stopped by an obstacle stronger than itself. Political events move from one impasse to the next, like a torrent caught in gullies, creeks, and marshes. All human control comes to an end when the individual is caught in a mass movement. Then the archetypes begin to function, as happens also in the lives of individuals when they are confronted with situations that cannot be dealt with in any of the familiar ways. (*CW* 10, para. 395)

The moment when the 'blond beast' burst out of its 'underground prison' came when the German people were subjected to intolerable stresses – the defeat of 1918, the post-war revolution, the Versailles Treaty with its punitive obligation to pay crippling reparations, galloping inflation followed by the Depression – which could no longer 'be dealt with in any of the familiar ways'. '*Deutschland erwache!*' the Nazis cried, and the call brought forth Wotan from his slumber.

The true awakening came, however, with the savage trauma of the Nuremburg trials which brought to the Germans their first awareness of what had possessed them, and to their great credit they were able to use the insight to create out of the rubble of Valhalla a humane and vigorous democracy. But, at the same time, a dramatic change was inaugurated in the mode of actualization of the Father archetype: there was an almost total abandonment of the '*Ehrfurcht*' concept and a virtual collapse in the authority of the personal father. The German psychoanalyst, Alexander Mitscherlich, sees this as a disaster, and he is possibly right in that such sudden and radical abandonment of a whole mode of archetypal functioning can only store up trouble for future generations. Moreover, one should never forget that it is 'not in Wotan's nature to linger on and show signs of old age' and that once more, after his 'second spell of domestication', he is slumbering in the Kyffhäuser mountain waiting for the ravens to call him and announce the breaking of a new day. 'He is a fundamental attribute of the German psyche, an irrational psychic factor which acts on the high pressure of civilization like a cyclone and blows it away' (*CW* 10, para. 389).

Though a Freudian, Mitscherlich views the post-Nazi decline of the patriarch in an almost Jungian perspective: he sees the image of the Father as embedded in the very roots of Western civilization, and believes that its disappearance exposes us collectively to the ills of alienation, social and personal irresponsibility, neurotic anxiety and uncontrolled aggression. In the absence of direct paternal instruction in practical life and the loss of a dependable paternalistic tradition, individuals orientate themselves by reference to each other, thus giving the peer group its contemporary significance, with its concomitant infantilisms of envy, rivalry, and trendy 'other-directedness'. Increasingly, the state takes over the paternal roles of protector and provider without encouraging the development of individual autonomy and self-sufficiency, and without teaching the economic fact that all things, whether luxuries or necessities, have to be earned. This causes a form of fixated and collective adolescence.

Certainly, clinical impression would confirm that various forms of arrested development at the adolescent stage of the life-cycle are extremely common in our society and apparently on the increase. In Jungian circles it has become customary in recent years to group these adolescent difficulties together and to refer to them as 'the problem of the *puer aeternus*', after a seminal work with this title by Dr Marie-Louise von Franz (1970).

In her book, von Franz describes the puer aeternus syndrome as one occurring in individuals who, whatever their chronological age, have remained adolescent in the sense that they display characteristics which are normal in a youth of seventeen or eighteen. The condition is almost invariably associated with a bond to mother which persists with pre-pubertal intensity. A high proportion of such people tend to have been only children or the youngest son, and their mothers tend to have been single or divorced, or else married to men who were unloving, unfaithful, or impotent.

The main features of the syndrome are to be noted in the sexual sphere and in the lifestyle that the individual tends to adopt. Typically, two forms of sexual disturbance are found in the male puer: homosexuality and Don Juanism. 'In the case of the former,' says von Franz, 'the heterosexual libido is still tied up with the mother, who is really the only beloved object, with the result that sex cannot be experienced with another woman.' Usually such men lack masculinity and seek it symbolically in their male partners. In the case of Don Juanism, the image of the mother – the perfect woman who will give her all to a man – is sought in every woman. 'He is looking for a mother goddess, so that each time he is fascinated by a woman he has later to discover that she is an ordinary human being. Having lived with her sexually the whole fascination vanishes and he turns away disappointed, only to project the image anew on to one woman after another.'

Puer Aeternus was an archaic god. His name is taken from Ovid's *Metamorphoses*, book IV, where he is apostrophized thus: 'For thine is unending youth, eternal boyhood: thou art the most lovely in the lofty sky; thy face is virgin-seeming, if without horns thou stand before us.' This gives poetic expression to the narcissism of the puer and his reluctance to grow up. It goes with failure to achieve a mature social adaptation together with a compensatory arrogance and false individualism which would have us believe that there is no need for 'hidden genius' to adapt to mundane realities.

> Such people usually have great difficulty in finding the right kind of job, for whatever they find is never quite right or quite what they wanted. There is always 'a hair in the soup'. The woman is never quite the right woman; she is nice as a girl friend, but –. There is always a 'but' which prevents marriage or any kind of definite commitment.

The puer's sense that he is 'not yet in real life', that he cannot yet be expected to establish himself in the world, is usually associated with the phantasy that one day he will 'make it', become famous and show people what he is really made of. But, in the meantime, his fear of commitment, his inability to assume adult responsibilities, forces him to live what Baynes (1949) called 'the provisional life' – at some time in the future he will enter life, become the person he is, but 'not yet'. The frustration of living the provisional life often finds relief in a delight in dangerous sports – especially flying and mountaineering, 'so as to get as high as possible, the symbolism being to get away from reality, from the earth, from ordinary life'. One could find similarities in those who are not averse to getting high on drugs.

In some ways the puer aeternus resembles the trickster figure common to many tribal mythologies. In the Winnebago hero myths, for example, the trickster appears as an impulsive, self-centred character, who is controlled and dominated by his appetites and makes absolutely no contribution to the common good. However, there the comparison ends; for as the story unfolds and the trickster passes from one exploit to another he becomes less capricious and irresponsible, is less prone to turn himself into animal forms, and begins to assume the behaviour and more regular characteristics of a man. In the Jungian view, mythical hero cycles reflect on the transpersonal plane the normal development of ego-consciousness from infancy to manhood; it is not until adolescence that transition from trickster to hero may occur. It was in order to promote this transition at the personal level that primitive man developed rites of initiation.

For many young people, the way of the trickster exercises a powerful attraction and it provides the strongest resistance to initiation into the responsibilities of adult life, especially when indulged by a weak father or over-solicitous mother. Henderson (1967) sees this as one of the hardest problems that education has to solve, since the trickster principle offers 'a kind of divinely sanctioned lawlessness that promises to become heroic'. It is tempting to link this view with the contemporary phenomena of vandalism, football hooliganism, punk rock, indiscipline in schools, inner-city rioting, and so on. But that would be an oversimplification. As Erik Erikson suggests (1959), the modern adolescent who struggles to free himself from mother and family is in danger of falling victim to what he terms 'identity diffusion', at a time when biological and social pressures are on him to commit himself to a partner and an occupation, to compete energetically for both these resources with his peers, and to accomplish a socially acceptable definition of himself as an individual. Little wonder that for many regression seems the better part of valour.

It is precisely at this stage that a strong, competent and loving father can perform his 'instrumental' function to greatest effect. By his example he can encourage his son and daughter to sacrifice the trickster puer/

puella position and enable them to become *initiated* into the adult world. He can also render them invaluable assistance to escape from the power of a possessive mother should she wish to resist their growth into maturity. The question of initiation will be examined in the next chapter. It is time that we turned now from the problems of weak parents to consider those of mothers and fathers who are so committed to the parental role as to be in danger of emulating Kronos and devouring their children alive.

The devouring parent

Parents who 'devour' their children do so with the best intentions: fathers do it in the name of justice, mothers in the name of love. Of course, no one would argue that love and justice are in themselves bad things – each of them is obviously a very good thing; but one can have too much of a good thing.

Take love, for example. Is it possible for a mother to love her child too much? Freud certainly thought so: 'an excess of parental affection does harm by causing precocious sexual maturity and also because, by spoiling the child, it makes him incapable in later life of temporarily doing without love or of being content with a smaller amount of it' (*SE* 7, p. 223). So did Neumann: 'The effects of too much or too little attention to the child are equally negative' (1973, p. 21). Though later in the same book he backtracks somewhat: 'Actually, too much love on the mother's part is by no means as dangerous or as harmful as a negative mother-child relationship and too little love' (p. 62). Spoiling, he says, 'does not produce serious disorders until it becomes necessary for the child to relax its ties with its mother and this process is impeded or prevented by the fact that the mother has spoiled her child' (p. 62).

Bowlby, on the other hand, rejects the notion of spoiling altogether. He does not believe that overdependency (which he prefers to call 'anxious attachment') is caused by loving children too well: on the contrary, he thinks the reverse is the case. However, Bowlby does not examine the hypothesis proposed by Neumann (and many others) that too much love may make it hard for the child to free itself sufficiently from the tie to mother to be able to leave the family nest and find a spouse. This is an odd oversight in one who began life as a Freudian, because it is an issue which relates directly to the Oedipal problem – the central myth of psychoanalysis.

Freud was himself in no doubt that future marital happiness depends on the formation of a secure, loving bond to mother in infancy. He regarded the mother-child relationship as 'unique, without parallel . . . the prototype of all other love relationships – for both sexes'. Jungians agree: 'A child's later personal relationship to its mother, as the basis for every subsequent love relationship and indeed of every human relationship, stands or falls with the primal relationship' (Neumann, 1973, p. 41). Bowlby, like Harlow, endorses these views: the formation of an infant-mother bond is an essential prerequisite to formation of a successful mating bond.

However, *attenuation* or loosening of the mother bond is necessary before mating can occur. From the ethological standpoint it seems probable that the instructions inherent in the archetypal biogrammar are no less precise on the need to reduce the intensity of the bond to mother than they are on the need to form it in the first place. If the mother, because she is lonely or has a sexually disinterested or deviant husband, chooses to override the instruction to attenuate the bond, or if the child through 'anxious attachment' cannot bring itself to break away, then the adolescent's ability to relate to his peers (especially to those of the opposite sex) is impaired. Whether 'spoiling' arises from anxious attachment of the mother to the child, or whether it is the expression of fiercely possessive maternal love, the result for the child is the same: an archetypal relationship appropriate to childhood is pathologically perpetuated into maturity thus inhibiting further emotional and social development by obstructing the activation of bonding programmes appropriate to later stages in the ontological sequence. This problem – an increasingly prevalent one in our society – is considered in greater detail in the next chapter.

Jung regarded undue perpetuation or intensity of the mother-son bond as a 'secret conspiracy' between both partners through which 'each helps the other to betray life' (*CW* 9, pt 2, para. 21). To break free would make demands on the boy which he is unable to meet, especially in the absence of a salient father. To leave her,

> he would need a faithless Eros, one capable of forgetting his mother and undergoing the pain of relinquishing the first love of his life. The mother, foreseeing this danger, has carefully inculcated into him the virtues of faithfulness, devotion, loyalty, so as to protect him from the moral disruption which is the risk of every life adventure. He has learnt these lessons only too well, and remains true to his mother. This naturally causes her the deepest anxiety (when, to her greater glory, he turns out to be a homosexual, for example) and at the same time affords her an unconscious satisfaction that is positively mythological. . . . At this level the mother is both old and young, Demeter and Persephone, and the son is spouse and sleeping suckling rolled into one. (*CW* 9, pt 2, paras 22–3)

A son trapped in this position cannot break free. Psychologically speaking, he is locked in the mother, devoured by his mother complex. The universality of this danger for the young male may be deduced from the ubiquitous mythological motif of the devouring monster that has to be slain if the hero is to win the 'damsel in distress'. The monster may be a dragon which lives in a cave or a monster of the deep. Sometimes the hero slays the monster after a long struggle; sometimes he is devoured by a huge sea-serpent and after a period in the monster's belly succeeds in cutting his way out in a sort of auto-Caesarian section, or causes the monster to vomit him up in a regurgitation 'rebirth'.

Hero myths all have a great deal in common (Campbell, 1949). The hero sets out from his commonplace home and receives the call to adventure. He usually crosses some kind of threshold and is then subjected to a series of tests and ordeals. Eventually, he undergoes the 'supreme ordeal' – the fight with the dragon or encounter with the sea monster is a common example – and his triumph is rewarded with 'the treasure hard to obtain', e.g. the throne of a kingdom and a beautiful princess for his bride. Such myths express in symbolic form the experience of Everyman: to embark on the adventure of life he has to free himself from his parents' tutelage and win a place for himself in the world (the kingdom); if he is to win a mate (the princess) he must undergo a second birth from his mother, a final breaking of the psychic umbilical cord (victory over the dragon-mother often involves entry into her to permit a symbolical transformation in the hero through which he 'dies' as his mother's son and is 'reborn' as a man worthy of the princess and the kingdom). Failure to overcome the monster signifies failure to get free of the mother: the hero languishes in her belly forever, ingested, engulfed, 'absorbed', and the damsel (the Anima) is never liberated from the monster's clutches (jailed by the mother complex, she is trapped *in perpetuity* in the unconscious).

The hero asserts his masculinity through his combativeness, his readiness to overcome the fearful obstacle which the dragon symbolizes, and he demonstrates his courage by his willingness to conquer the unknown abyss, the terrifying *otherness* of the female, to penetrate her, to 'know' her. Jungians regard the young male's fear of the female in her sexual aspect as primordial in nature and not primarily due to the Freudian 'castration complex'. Freud believed that boys feared loss of the penis as a punishment for sexual activities of which their fathers disapproved; he argued that this fear was accentuated by the discovery that female genitalia are 'different', since the difference is rationalized by the assumption that girls once had penises which were subsequently removed in retribution for erotic delinquencies. This piece of Freudian mythology came to assume as important a place in psychoanalytic dogma as the Oedipus complex, but there can be little doubt that the aetiological significance of both complexes has been exaggerated and their implications for human psychology wildly overgeneralized.

For the boy, the *sexual* female is the unknown 'other', the 'never seen before' which has to be encountered at puberty. The mother is, of course, the most familiar figure in the world and through her the maternal aspects of the archetypal feminine are intimately familiar – what is strange and unknown is her sexuality. Thus, puberty is a critical threshold. The sharp increase in male hormone heralds a passionate interest in female sexuality which is experienced initially in relation to the most loved female, the mother. But the incest taboo, which is itself biological and primordial, makes her, though loved, a forbidden object. The boy's emergent masculinity renders it imperative, therefore, that he conquer his fear, turn from the mother, and seek the feminine sexuality which he now craves in the receptive female not yet encountered in the outer world.

Just as his whole nature had been prepared for the formation of his bond to mother, so also is he psychically prepared for the encounter with his mate. As the mother archetype wanes so the Anima, a sequentially linked nucleus of the archetypal feminine, waxes. Once the youth is free of the mother, his dragon-fight won, the Anima comes into the psychic ascendant, and under this powerfully numinous archetypal influence the quest for the soul-mate begins.

The powerful, domineering mother can wreck the hero's precarious progress just as surely as the possessive, 'spoiling' mother. Such women tend to be Animus-ridden (they live and function much more than most women through the masculine elements in their personality) and are consequently prone to activate in their sons the destructive masculine attributes inherent in the Terrible Mother archetype. These male characteristics are apparent in the dragon/sea-monster and are plainly evident in the more human representations of the archetype.

The Animus-dominated mother thus enhances the male's primordial fear of woman, and she can so sap his masculine confidence as to make it impossible for him even to attempt the dragon-fight. To survive, he may adopt a posture of meek submissiveness to veil his smouldering resentment, his beleaguered sexuality achieving some relief in a masochistic and onanistic glorification of his servitude, as the phallic attributes of the Terrible Mother become eroticized *faute de mieux*.

A man once consulted me with potency problems. His mother was a domineering puritan who had habitually professed disgust at all manifestations of sexuality, thus inducing profound guilt about sex in her son. He was heterosexually orientated, but could only be aroused if his partner, whom he preferred to be older than himself, castigated him when he undressed for being 'a nasty, dirty boy' and threatened to spank him soundly if he dared to get an erection. This usually did the trick, and provided she continued to reprove him and occasionally slapped him during intercourse he was able to sustain an erection to the point of orgasm. By this subterfuge he managed to bypass his guilt. He turned the tyrannical female authority into a sexual object who, by promising him punishment for being 'dirty' implicitly allowed him to have sex.

Domineering mothers are particularly effective at promoting sexual deviations in their sons through their exemplification of womanhood as something too dangerous to be approached with any degree of trust or desire for intimacy. Deprived of its normal goal, the boy's sexuality is forced to seek other modes of expression, such as exhibitionism, transvestism, fetishism, sado-masochism, or homosexuality.

Whereas spoiling mothers tend to devour their sons whole, domineering mothers are more selectively voracious: they go for the will and the genitals; they are 'castrating' mothers *par excellence*. On the whole their daughters are somewhat less damaged than their sons, for sexual deviation is primarily a masculine prerogative, but they do not escape unscathed. Like their brothers they tend to have problems in forming satisfactory heterosexual attachments. In particular, they are prone to develop a pattern of behaviour apparently the opposite of anxious attachment, namely, what Dr Colin Murray Parkes (1973) calls *compulsive self-reliance*. A woman living in accordance with this pattern eschews the whole minefield of affectional relationships, maintaining a detached, prickly independence, denying all need for love and support, and rigidly insisting on doing everything for herself, whatever the odds.

A closely related form of behaviour, which does at least allow some form of attachment to occur, is *compulsive care-giving*. Here the individual may actually enter into a close relationship, but always in the role of the care-giver, never that of one receiving care. While it is true that people showing either of these 'compulsive' attitudes to attachment have often had mothers of a domineering kind, both forms of behaviour can also be found in individuals whose mothers gave them inadequate love and attention, irrespective of whether or not they were 'Animus-dominated'. Such mothers may have been chronic depressives, for example, or may themselves have been the victims of maternal deprivation. Instead of caring adequately for their children and fulfilling their archetypally determined attachment needs, these mothers are likely to have demanded support for themselves and assistance in caring for other members of the family. Not uncommonly, children reared in institutions show similar 'compulsive' patterns in their social behaviour. From early childhood they are conditioned to believe that the only relationships possible for them are ones in which they remain fiercely independent or in which they provide all the care and repress their longings to receive care in return. While compulsive self-reliance is found in men as well as women, clinical impression would suggest that women are more prone than men to be compulsive care-givers. In both sexes, however, these forms of compulsiveness are usually the result of pathogenic mothering.

On the whole it is true to say that parents who devour their children are, whatever they may say to the contrary, motivated more by power than by love. They are possessed by the need to dominate, to control, to assert their authority. As we have just seen, this pattern can certainly occur in mothers who are Animus-dominated, but it is a pattern much more frequently encountered in fathers. The reason for this is partly cultural, in that patriarchal societies encourage fathers to behave in this way, and partly archetypal, in that men are naturally more assertive and competitive than women. The dominance-submission archetype is evidently a crucial determinant of masculine behaviour in all social mammals, not only in the way in which males seek to dominate each other, but also in the manner that males dominate their mates and their offspring.

Thus, domineering parents are people who are more in the grip of the dominance archetype than they are in the grip of Eros. As a result, their family life is more a matter of power struggles than of mutual love and support. Inevitably, such families tend to actualize in their progeny the one archetype at the expense of the other, and domineering parents are likely to produce children who, when they grow up to be parents (always assuming, of course, that they are not too sexually perverse or compulsively self-reliant to mate), are themselves domineering. As Bowlby says: 'each of us is apt to do unto others as we *have been* done by. The bullying adult is the bullied child grown bigger' (1979, p. 141). In the psychoanalytic literature such individuals are described as possessing an *authoritarian character*. The authoritarian character is essentially sado-masochistic: 'He admires authority and tends to submit to it, but at the same time he wants to be an authority himself and have others submit to him' (Erich Fromm, 1942, p. 141). Basically, he distinguishes two kinds of people: the strong and the weak. He worships the former; for the latter he has nothing but contempt. Power fascinates him with all the numinosity of a naked archetype – not because of any principle for which it may stand, but simply because it is powerful. Just as a predatory animal will pounce at the precise moment when its prey turns and flees, so an authoritarian character becomes predatory at the first sign of weakness. 'The very sight of a powerless person makes him want to attack, dominate and humiliate him' (p. 145). Whereas a loved child is appalled by the notion of attacking someone who is helpless, the dominated child's aggression is aroused the more helpless he perceives his victim to be.

In the same way as all sadists have a masochistic side, so the authoritarian has a need to respect an authority greater than himself. He not only likes to constrain the freedom of those whom he controls but also enjoys the sense of submitting himself to a leader, God or Fate. As a soldier this kind of man is a martinet to his subordinates but, at the same time, finds deep satisfaction in submitting himself with unquestioning obedience to his superiors. As a monk he will be dictatorial with the lay bretheren but totally submissive to the Abbot and the Rule of the Order. The authoritarian character is thus the individual basis of a collective fascism, where the social and political structure is dominated by an order imposed by a single masculine authority. Fascism is the ultimate expression of father-dominance; the ultimate expression of mother-dominance is communism: it is perhaps not without significance that Nazism took root in the German 'Fatherland' while communism found its home in 'Mother' Russia.

In so far as authoritarian characters make pathogenic parents, it is not just by providing too much coercion and not enough love, but also through their customary hostility to two fundamental attributes of the maturing Self, namely, sexuality and aggression. This hostility has the unfortunate effect of interrupting vital lines of communication between the ego and the Self, and, in turn, sabotages the efforts of key areas of the Self to seek actualization in reality. As a consequence, the coerced individual is blocked in the realization of much of his emotional, sexual and cognitive potential. What is more, in the interests of a quiet life, he develops a false persona – one which is modelled on the demands of the parents and not on the needs of the Self.

Good parents facilitate their child's attempts to explore, for the drive to explore the environment and the drive to actualize the Self are two aspects of the same thing, and both require aggression. Undevoured children are naturally assertive: they play freely and their games and phantasies are about being grown up, strong and effective. Inasmuch as they have established confidence in a secure base, they can normally sustain an easy balance between their wish to be free (exploration) and their wish to be loved (attachment). Thus they are both attached *and* aggressive. Inevitably, these two propensities come into conflict, for even the most permissive parents periodically frustrate their children and become the objects of their hostility. How the parents deal with anger when it arises can have profound consequences for the personality development of the child. Provided they can tolerate the expression of appropriate aggression it tends to become integrated as an acceptable part of the child's conscious personality and his security in relation to his attachment figures remains unthreatened. On the other hand, should they find all forms of assertiveness intolerable, the child's security will be seriously at risk, and he will be constrained to inhibit all expression of the forbidden behaviour whenever possible. However, this is not always easy to achieve, particularly when a child's attachment needs and his aggression are aroused at the same time and in relation to the same parental figure. Were this to recur often the cumulative anxiety in the child would prove unendurable. How is such a conflict to be resolved? Clearly, if the child is not to alienate the parent he must dispose of his unacceptable aggression. Where is it to go? There are several possibilities:

1 *It can be turned inwards as Self-loathing*: this strategy, by no means uncommon, has a profoundly disruptive influence on development of the ego-Self axis and can result in protracted neurotic suffering in the form of guilty rumination, obsessive, gloomy thoughts, compulsive acts, and chronic depression.

2 *It can be displaced on to a scapegoat*: usually the choice falls on someone weaker or on a group perceived as 'inferior' – racial minorities, for example, homosexuals, etc. Not infrequently the target group is selected by the dominant parent: prejudiced fathers tend to have similarly prejudiced sons.

3 *It can be transformed into worship of the oppressor*: there may be a family conspiracy that the tyrannical parent is 'wonderful' and above all criticism. 'The Fuhrer is always right,' cried Dr Goebbels. The hero of *1984* ends up declaring his love for Orwell's hateful 'Big Brother'.

4 *It can be eroticized*: the two forbidden impulses, sex and aggression, achieve a shared discharge in sado-masochistic phantasies and practices. The sexualized aggression is then linked either with strategy 2 or with strategies 1 and 3: eroticized aggression directed against weaker individuals is the essence of *sadism*, while that directed against the Self in deference to the worshipped tyrant is the essence of *masochism*. The sadist is one who has incorporated the coercive parent; the masochist one whom the parent has devoured. Sadism seeks unrestricted power through Self-identification with authority; masochism seeks to be absorbed by authority so as passively to participate in its power and its glory and atone for sin.

Bondage symbolism, which often accompanies sado-masochistic practices, is an extension of the same principle: the sadist who trusses up his sexual partner is *parodying the behaviour of his parents* who habitually restricted his desire to be free and to explore; the masochist who has himself tied up is *parodying his own acquiescence* to the same parental restrictions. Sado-masochism is a ritual, a game for the discharge of impulses prohibited from achieving their normal goals. As such, it affords a dramatic and instructive illustration of the possible consequences of thwarting archetypal intent.

That parents are often not in fact as good or as bad, as powerful or as weak, as their children *experience* them is yet further evidence of the power and psychic significance of the archetypes. All psychotherapists know what a shock it can be to meet a couple of parents after working with their son or daughter for some time: not infrequently these ordinary, decent people bear little resemblance to the ogres (or saints) whose images the patient has presented during the months of treatment. Psychologically speaking, what matters is not how the parents actually behave, but how the child experiences their behaviour; what possesses lasting psychodynamic power in the life of the individual is not the parents' actual personalities in the outer world but the parental complexes built up within the child's psyche from a unique combination of cues derived from the personal parents and the archetypal elements which these cues evoke.

Mothers and fathers

Although the parental complexes possess greater significance for psychic development than the parents themselves, no one – not even the most archetypally committed Jungian – would wish to argue that the character of the personal parents has no importance at all. On the contrary, the psychic climate which they create in the home profoundly conditions the archetypal processes constellated and the complexes formed, and what is just as important as the parents' individual relationships with their child is the quality of the relationship that they establish with each other. So it is that one's success or failure in relating to members of the opposite sex is largely determined by extensive experience gathered in childhood of repeated interactions between one's father and mother. All schools of analysis agree that there is no finer start in life than to have been born to parents who loved, trusted and respected one another, who were open and honest in their personal dealings, and consistent in their attitudes to each other and to their children.

On the other hand, chronic marital conflict can greatly distort a child's view of normal heterosexual relationships and can engender a deep sense of personal insecurity which may manifest itself in crippling neurotic problems in later life. Thus, as we have already noted, Dr Bowlby has called attention to the frequency of parental conflict and threats to abandon the home in the history of patients suffering from phobias and depression, most of whom display the unmistakable signs of anxious attachment to all important figures in their lives.

What is particularly significant for the child's sexual development is the personal value attributed by each parent to the other. The authoritarian father who patronizes his wife and denigrates her position will have a damaging effect on his daughters' self-concept and will encourage equally 'chauvinistic' attitudes in his sons. The weak father, on the other hand, who adopts a submissive or ineffectual role in relation to his wife invariably forfeits her respect and undermines his position with his children who are archetypally conditioned to expect him to be strong and who consequently, aided by the conscious or unconscious influence of their mother, come to despise him. In this situation the mother is forced on to her 'instrumental' side with the result that the children increasingly depend on her Animus and on each other for the authoritative guidance normally (and archetypally) provided by the father. In our society this latter constellation is becoming more and more evident with the decreased salience and availability of the modern father, and accounts in some measure for the contemporary emphasis on female rights and on peer relationships.

Thus, while the archetypal potential for heterosexual and parental behaviour and experience is part of the constitutional endowment of us all, the degree to which we succeed in realizing that potential is largely determined by the personalities of our parents, and is every bit as dependent on how they treated each other as on how they treated us. Inasmuch as one's parents loved one another, so can one love one's spouse; inasmuch as our parents loved us for ourselves so can we love our children.

Patrism and matrism

The study of comparative religion reveals that it is characteristic of some cultures to believe in father gods who live in heaven, while others have mother goddesses who inhabit the earth. The Judeo-Christian-Muslim religions are all examples of a father-based theology. The Mediterranean world, on the other hand, provided many examples of mother-based theologies – those centred on Ceres, Astarte, Cybele, Demeter, the Magna Mater, and so on. Some of these cultures – the Greeks, for example – had father gods as well as mother goddesses, the rains from heaven being necessary to fructify the earth.

Now the interesting thing is that cultures with a father-orientated religion are also found on examination to have a father-dominated social structure, in which patterns of behaviour and systems of values reflect the characteristics of the father archetype. Similarly, mother-based theologies go with a mother-orientated social structure, which reflects the characteristics of the mother archetype. The features of these contrasting forms of society have been graphically summarized by Gordon Rattray Taylor (1972) who designates them 'patrist' and 'matrist' societies respectively.

Where members of a society believe primarily in a sky god, their culture tends to be puritanical in sexual matters, to assign a low status to women and to exhibit an authoritarian political structure. Where an earth mother is worshipped, on the other hand, the culture tends to be permissive in sexual matters, grants women high status, and its politics are broadly egalitarian.

> Patrism combines two ideas: hierarchy and discipline. The individual fits into an organizational structure, in which orders come from above, and rules exist to cover almost every kind of situation. The Army is the classic example of the patrist structure; the Roman Catholic Church is another. Each is organized in ranks, or layers, individuals at one level being in charge of those immediately below, and responsible to someone immediately above. In contrast, matrism sees the individual as free from all external compulsions and hence obviously equal to all other individuals, in the sense of having no authority over them, nor recognizing any. The contrast is between Discipline and Spontaneity. (pp. 49–50)

This is perhaps a stark and oversimplified differentiation but broadly speaking it holds true over a large number of the societies known to anthropology. Taylor's description echoes, in many ways, that of Bachofen in his book, *Mother Right*, though he is careful to drop Bachofen's 'patriarchal/matriarchal' terminology, for we now know that a truly matriarchal society has in all probability never existed. But it would be unwarranted to suppose that societies get stuck forever in their matrist or patrist orientation. Many change in the course of history, while others manage to maintain both orientations at the same time. Western culture, for example, was unequivocally patrist in the late nineteenth century (though it was modified to some extent in England through the influential presence of Queen Victoria), whereas since the First World War it has become increasingly matrist. It can be convincingly argued that the most inventive and creative cultures are those like Ancient Greece in which a balance between matrism and patrism is achieved. Thus, the most productive periods in English history have been times when a firm belief in God coincided with the reign of a powerful Queen. It is unlikely that the resurgence of energy which characterized Britons in Elizabethan and Victorian times was due to pure historical accident. Nor does it seem far-fetched to speculate that Britain's disappointing performance since the accession of Queen Elizabeth II in 1952 could be linked with an excess of matrism consequent upon a loss of faith in God the Father. No Jungian would be shocked by the suggestion that the history of the British nation may have been different if King George VI had been succeeded by a son. The socio-political significance of a monarch lies in the archetypal elements which this salient figure activates in the unconscious of his or her subjects. The truth of this statement can be verified when patients in analysis dream – as British patients invariably do from time to time – of encounters with the Royal Family. Not infrequently, these dreams are associated with the activation of archetypal components of clear relevance to the individuals' living circumstances.

As Taylor rightly argues, the evidence for the swing to matrism in modern times is overwhelming – the increase in sexual permissiveness, the tolerance of homosexuality, the progressive improvement in the status of women, the prevalence of egalitarian attitudes, the rejection of class distinctions in dress, speech and behaviour, the political impetus to dismantle hierarchically organized institutions, the contempt for patriotism and the military 'virtues', the orgiastic desire for euphoria through rock music and drugs, the provision of 'nurturant' welfare services to ensure that everyone is nourished, clothed and given medical care, and the advance of the notion that everyone has a 'right' to these things whether they work for them or not, the emphasis on consultation between government and governed, employers and employed, teachers and pupils, the importance of 'fairness' and 'sharing', the belief that crime is as much the fault of society as it is of the criminal and the progressive abandonment of punishment as an appropriate means of dealing with him, the emergence of spontaneous 'formless' art, the contempt for history, tradition and the past, and so on. The list could be greatly extended.

Where one must take issue with Taylor, however, is over his explanation of how the matrist or patrist tendency comes into being, for he understands it merely in terms of the psychological mechanism of 'introjection'. Taylor argues that since the modern father lacks salience (for reasons we have already examined) children cannot easily model themselves on his behaviour or introject his values and attitudes:

> even the boy who introjects his father today is likely to introject a weak or indulgent father, deprived of the authoritarian and conservative attributes we associate with our fathers in principle. This therefore contributes to the matrist trend, for it weakens the father-figure at a time when the mother-figure is being strengthened. (1972, p. 67)

This is true as far as it goes, but in leaving out the archetypal dimension Taylor puts the cart before the horse. All cultures are potentially both patrist *and* matrist. What determines whether one constellation predominates over the other does indeed depend on the relative salience of mothers and fathers in that culture at any given time in its history; but it is not so much a matter of 'introjection' as of archetypal actualization. When they grow up, father-absent children modify society in the direction of matrism because the patristic attributes of the father archetype remain unactivated in their psyches.

The unbiased reader is to be forgiven if he inquires whether this distinction matters. Is it not after all a matter of theory, how one looks at these things? It is indeed. But the function of theories is to explain facts. Any given set of facts may be susceptible to any number of theoretical explanations; who is to say that any one theory is any better than the rest? The answer is that some theoretical explanations are good and some are bad. The best theory is the one that most satisfactorily explains all the facts. So which facts does the archetypal theory explain which 'introjection' cannot?

The answer is the *enantiodromia*, and the longing for enantiodromia, that a one-sided matrism or patrism creates. In our matrist society too many masculine archetypal imperatives are unfulfilled for matrism to prevail indefinitely. Indeed, as this book goes to press one can already discern signs of an impending swing of the pendulum back in the patrist direction – the demand for law and order, financial realism, greater socio-economic efficiency, calls for the reintroduction of conscription and the build up of military strength. If this is so, then it can only be unwelcome to those who have fallen into the error of conceiving matrism as an ideal to be aimed at. In fact, matrism seems to be the chief component of most Utopian ideals, based as they are on the phantasy of recreating in adult life the blissful security of a Golden Age (the primal relationship). Take Zeno's Utopia, for example – a 'world state' where there would be no conflicts and all the citizens would be generous and wise. All trappings of rank would be abolished, all prestigious buildings pulled down, armies demobilized, and all causes for inter-state rivalry removed. There would be no competition for wealth because there would be no money. No distinctions would be permitted between men and women, even in dress, and sexual promiscuity encouraged. The predominant ethic would demand the expression and the exchange of love. Eros would rule over all.

Zeno's is just one of many visions of a matrist paradise which have beguiled men's minds, but which, alas, have never been realized on earth. That they have not, and never can be, has little to do with introjection and everything to do with archetypes. Matrist Utopias cannot exist because the father archetype prevents them. They may come within a hair's breadth of realization – as in some hippie communes in the 1960s – but the father archetype inevitably takes his revenge on them, and they perish. A matrist society is fine for the women (as long as there is enough protein and shelter, and no war to be fought); but it is emasculating for the men, and the father archetype just will not stand for it, and that is that.

· 10 ·

Personal identity and the stages of life

The crucial fact on which the whole experience of life rests is a sense of continuing personal identity: 'I am me; I have been me since the moment I was born and I shall go on being me till the day I die.' This central conviction of 'ego' as a unique continuum through mortal existence is the indispensable condition of human awareness, and it is also a miracle – especially when you consider that many body cells are periodically renewed in the course of the life-cycle, so that whole chunks of you as you sit reading this book were not in existence ten years ago. Moreover, you will have lived a number of different 'lives' before you reached the present stage on your life's journey – infant, school child, soul-mate, parent, 'professional', etc. Yet through all the years of physical, psychic and social transformation the golden thread of personal identity persists.

Of course, your uniqueness as an individual is older than your awareness of being the person that you are: the die was cast at the moment of your conception. Your Self was, therefore, in existence for some considerable time before your ego developed sufficient maturity to grant recognition to the fact. Like many people, I cherish a memory of when this awareness came most vividly to me. I must have been four or five years old. I had been put to bed, kissed and tucked in; the light was out, but I was not yet asleep. As I lay quietly in the darkness an extraordinary thing happened: I was transfixed by the knowledge, the absolute certainty of my own existence. For the first time ever, apparently, I realized that I belonged body and soul to myself. When the shock of recognition passed, I seemed to wander about in my body, into my hands, up into my head, and down to the tips of my toes. I was intoxicated with pride, like a man strolling through some great estate which he had just inherited. 'This is me,' I thought, 'all me; and it's been here all the time.'

Thus does the Self accord itself recognition through that organ of consciousness – the ego – which it has given rise to. In one place Jung defines the ego as 'a relatively constant personification of the unconscious itself, or as the Schopenhauerian mirror in which the unconscious becomes aware of its own face' (*CW* 14, para. 129). The ego, having established a sense of unity of body and mind, and a sense of continuity in time, is then cast in the role of executant of the archetypal blue print for the whole life-cycle which is systematically encoded within the Self. This function the ego proceeds to perform in the illusion that it is a free agent, the master of its fate, the captain of its soul. In fact, it is only a 'deintegrate' as Dr Michael Fordham (1964) has called it, the aspect of the Self which is manifest in space and time. Jung saw this 'self-realization of the unconscious' as the primary purpose of psychic evolution. 'Everything in the unconscious seeks outward manifestation, and the personality too desires to evolve out of its unconscious conditions to experience itself as a whole' (1963, p. 3). 'The Self, like the unconscious is an *a priori* existent out of which the ego evolves. It is . . . an unconscious prefiguration of the ego. It is not I who create myself, rather I happen to myself' (*CW* 11, para. 391).

This view dramatically contrasts with all other approaches in psychology, all of which assume the ego to be the central nucleus of the human personality. What Jung proposed was nothing short of psychology's Copernican revolution: instead of personality centred on the ego, he maintained that the ego is a satellite of the Self. 'The ego stands to the Self as the moved to the mover, or as object to subject, because the determining factors which radiate out from the Self surround the ego on all sides and are therefore supraordinate to it' (*CW* 11, para. 391).

However, in the course of being actualized the Self is inevitably constrained by the living circumstances of the growing individual, especially by the personality and culture of his parents and the nature of his relationship to them. Just as no parent can ever hope to actualize the totality of the parental archetype, so no ego can ever incorporate the wholeness of the Self. Incarnation entails sacrifice: it means fragmentation ('deintegration') and distortion of the original undifferentiated archetypal state: many aspects of the Self will prove unacceptable to the family milieu and consequently are relegated to the Shadow (Freud's personal unconscious), while others will remain unactualized and will persist as unconscious and latent archetypal potential, which may or may not be activated at a later date. Thus, in every individual life-span some distortion of primary archetypal intent is unavoidable: we are all of us, to a greater or lesser degree, only a 'good enough' version of the Self. This fact is of the utmost psychiatric significance, because the extent of the distortion is the factor that makes all the difference between neurosis and mental health. Moreover, the life-long struggle of each individual to achieve some resolution of the dissonance between the needs of the conscious personality and the dictates of the Self is at the very heart of the individuation process.

Here lies the essence of the critical distinction which must be made between *individuation* and the biological unfolding of the *life-cycle*. The two processes are, of course, interdependent in the sense that one cannot possibly occur without the other, yet they are fundamentally different. The life-cycle is the indispensable *condition* of individuation; but individuation is not blindly living out the life-cycle: it is living it consciously and responsibly, and is ultimately a matter of ethics. Individuation is a conscious attempt to bring the universal programme of human existence to its fullest possible expression in the life of the individual.

What we *seem* to be – to ourselves and to others – is only a fraction of what there is in us to be. And as a result the Self is never satisfied: it *knows* that the ego could do better if it tried. For this reason it never stops prompting and advising; it is forever tugging in new directions, always seeking to expand and readapt the habits and clichés of consciousness, sending us bad dreams and disturbing thoughts, making us question the value of things we hold dear, mocking our complacent pretensions to have 'arrived'. This is the secret of man's 'Divine discontent'. For all of us, so much more is 'planned for' than we can ever hope to realize in conscious actuality: our lives are crowded with lost opportunities. Yet, for those who have ears to hear, the call to individuate ('the voice of God within') is constantly transmitted to the ego by the Self. Unfortunately, reception is often jammed by interference from the parental complexes; and such is our extraverted concern with the material world that few of us heed these inner incitements to greater Self-fulfilment.

But Jung's major contribution to psychology has been his elucidation of the principle of Self-actualization, and one cannot but admire the boldness and imaginative profundity of his conception. Before the days of computers and before any detailed studies had been made of the mechanisms underlying innate rituals in lower animals it was extremely difficult to comprehend how complex sequences of behaviour and ideation could possibly be genetically programmed into an organism in such a way as to be 'released' by 'planned for' events occurring at critical periods in the life-cycle. Yet that is precisely what Jung proposed, and it is only now, decades later, that people begin to appreciate what he meant and understand how it could possibly be so. In this, as in other areas, Jung was an outstanding pioneer. Whereas many of the original concepts of Freud have been superseded, those of Jung are just beginning to receive the attention they deserve: in many respects it is true to say that it has taken science until now to catch up with him.

Bowlby's view of ontogenesis

Without knowing it, Bowlby has probably done most to change the climate of psychology in such a way as to make Jung's Self concept and the principle of individuation acceptable. Like Jung, but quite independently, Bowlby conceives of the human organism as a system constructed in such a way as always to be ready, at successive stages of the life-cycle, to process certain kinds of data, to experience certain psychophysical states, and produce certain kinds of behaviour. Maturation dictates that, like any good modern computer, the organism be capable of storing the data once it has been processed and, having stored it, of progressing to the next stage to deal with the next set of circumstances that might arise. In this manner, development proceeds by way of a largely predetermined series of sequences, each of which is linked to a stage in the natural life-cycle of the species, and each manifested in species-specific patterns of behaviour, such as maternal bonding, speech acquisition, peer play, puberty initiation ceremonies, hunting and warfare, sex bonding, and so on. 'The result is that in any given population of *homo sapiens* at any specific moment there are individuals who have reached different stages in the developmental sequence, each will possess a certain "store" of data and will consequently emit behaviours which will stimulate others who have reached a stage appropriate to respond to them' (Henry and Stephens, 1977). The product of interaction between such individuals will be certain typical – or as Jung would have put it, archetypal – relationships or attachments. Thus, as Bowlby points out,

> behaviour patterns mediating attachment of young to adults are complementary to those mediating care of the young by adults; in the same way, systems mediating adult masculine behaviour in one individual are complementary to those mediating adult feminine behaviour in another. This emphasizes afresh that instinctive behaviour is never intelligible in terms of a single individual but in terms of a population of individuals collaborating together. (1969, p. 179)

Once again we are led into a concern with intraspecific behaviour patterns and away from the subjective experience of people, an orientation which Jung would find uncongenial, but Bowlby is nevertheless putting into contemporary terms the basic principles on which Jung believed that the Self organized what he called 'the stages of life'. The fact is that Jung's concept of personality development largely anticipated Waddington's *theory of epigenesis*, now widely adopted by developmental biologists, and on which Bowlby bases his view of human ontogeny. As we have noted, Jung spoke of the archetypes as determining pathways of development or as river beds along which environmental circumstances might induce libido to flow. These pathways or riverbeds are the 'time extended properties', to use Waddington's phrase, of the Self. Thus the Self 'proposes' pathways of which the environment 'disposes' in the course of development. The archetypes of the phylogenetic psyche are actualized in the complexes (pathological or normal as the environment disposes) of the ontogenetic psyche, and tend to maintain the individual on whatever developmental pathway he is already on. In this way, the complexes come to possess the enduring self-regulatory property which Waddington termed *homeorhesis*.

Bowlby's own understanding of these processes owes as much to animal studies as it does to cybernetics and computer technology. For example, in considering the stages through which the social adaptation of the individual proceeds, Bowlby quotes with approval the Harlows' (1965) contention that five distinct affectional systems are called into function in the course of ontogeny. Though these postulates are based on experiments with rhesus monkeys, Bowlby considers that broadly similar ontological steps occur in the social maturation of human beings. They are as follows:

1 *The maternal system*: this ensures survival by providing nurturance and protection, encourages security through body contact, and promotes social development as a consequence of infant-mother interaction.

2 *The infant-mother system*: this integrates the pre-programmed behaviours of the infant, prompting him to seek the mother's proximity and to maintain it through activation of the maternal system in her.

3 *The peer system*: this plays a crucial role in promoting exploration of the environment and in developing social and motor skills. Moreover, it is indispensable to the emergence of appropriate sexual responsiveness, for in all primates sexual promiscuity between peers, both homosexual and heterosexual, seems to be a necessary preliminary to the development of mating bonds.

4 *The heterosexual system*: this operates intermittently in some species and more durably in others. Thus, while many birds mate for life, most mammals are promiscuous. The heterosexual affectional system also varies between species with regard to its activation and its reliance on previous learning. For example, in birds and rodents mating is primarily determined by hormonal rhythms, whereas in primates the formation of heterosexual bonds is influenced by the success or failure of bonds previously formed with mother or peers. As the Harlows put it: 'Primates which have never loved early, never love late.'

5 *The paternal system*: this is more important and widespread in mammals and primates than was formerly understood. It has the function of providing protection against predators, of preventing infants from falling victim to aggression within the group, and of assuring the privileged position of mothers and infants and controlling their behaviour within

certain limits. It manifests itself in a paternal interest in infants and in a willingness to play with them.

As will be readily appreciated, these five affectional systems accord well with the facts presented in the previous four chapters of this book. It seems probable, however, in the light of Lionel Tiger's (1969) work on bonding in male groups that, at least in the case of males, the peer affectional system continues to remain active for much longer than Bowlby or the Harlows imagined. For bonds between males not only persist in many primate and human societies long after the heterosexual affectional system has been activated but, in Tiger's (1969) view, form the 'spinal column' of the group's political and social anatomy.

Each of these systems is probably separate and distinct in its mode of operation, in that each 'develops through its own maturational stages and differs in the underlying variables which produce and control its particular response patterns' (Harlow and Harlow, 1965). But, as Bowlby points out, the systems are apt to influence the development of each other, particularly in the case of human beings.

> For example, it is not uncommon for one individual to treat a sexual partner as though the partner were a parent, and the partner may reciprocate by adopting a parental attitude in return. A possible, indeed probable, explanation of the behaviour of the partner who takes the juvenile role is that, in that partner, not only has attachment behaviour [i.e. attachment behaviour as directed to parental figures] persisted into adult life, which is usual, but it has, for some reason, continued to be almost as readily elicited as it is in a young child, which is not usual. (1969, p. 285)

This raises two important questions, one for psychology and one for psychiatry. The question which psychology has to answer is how the usual sequences of ontological development come about; while the question for psychiatry is how it is in certain individual cases that these sequences fail to proceed normally. In considering these crucial issues, Bowlby asks himself how we are to understand, for example, the absence of courting behaviour in infancy. He suggests three theoretical possibilities:

1 The neural substrate for courting behaviour may not yet have developed, so that the behavioural system cannot, in any circumstances, be activated.

2 The neural substrate could, on the other hand, be fully developed but the behavioural system lies dormant because some of the causal factors necessary to activate it are not present.

3 The neural substrate responsible for the behaviour might be only partially developed (or causal factors for only some of the component

systems may be present) so that, although bits of the behaviour are seen, the full functional pattern is still absent.

Of the three possibilities, the last would seem to accord most closely with the observed facts. It could explain, for example, how it is that certain component patterns of adult sexual behaviour (e.g. clasping and pelvic thrust) are to be noted at a surprisingly early age, in line with Freud's concept of the *component instincts* which make up 'infantile sexuality'. Fragments of sexual behaviour of a non-functional kind occur in many, perhaps all, primate species. Indeed, it seems probable that throughout the mammalian kingdom, infantile sexuality is the rule.

In addition to developments proceeding within the neural substrate, there can be little doubt that many changes in behaviour that are seen in the course of the life-cycle are due to shifts in the relative levels of hormones circulating in the bloodstream. Bowlby, like Jung, starts from the theoretical standpoint that the behavioural systems responsible for both masculine and feminine behaviour are present in *all* members of the species long before puberty. A critical factor determining which of these two behavioural systems will predominate at any particular stage in the life-cycle is the relative level of male and female hormones. Numerous experiments justify this assumption: castrate a male rat at birth and inject him with oestrogens (female hormones) and he will display a full range of feminine behaviour patterns as he grows to maturity; treat a female monkey with testosterone (male hormone) shortly before birth and her behaviour will remain typically masculine throughout her life. In clinical practice, a marked tendency to tomboyishness has been noted in girls whose mothers had high levels of circulating testosterone during pregnancy.

It is not surprising, therefore, that changes in the behavioural repertoire, associated with a sharp emphasis on sex-role orientation, occurs at puberty, when there is a sudden dramatic increase in the quantities of testosterone liberated into the bloodstream. Young men, for example, secrete as much as thirty times more testosterone than they did as boys.

But there is clearly much more to the whole process than just that. If maturation were purely a question of neural growth and hormone manufacture, then the overwhelming majority of our fellow men and women would make a series of easy, regular and predictable transitions from one phase of the life-cycle to the next, and psychiatrists would be put out of business. The facts, as we know, are very different. Clinically, one encounters a large and, I believe, growing population of individuals whose development into maturity is neither easy, regular, nor predictable; and in the majority of cases one is led, on investigation, to the same conclusion: that there is unfinished business with the parents.

Not that the problem is confined to having been loved too little or too well by one's mother, or to growing up with too weak or too domineering a father: everyone is at risk. Dim memories of the uroborus fill us all with paradise longings, and no one is entirely free from anxiety about what may lie ahead. All change carries with it a measure of dread: 'better the devil you know than the devil you don't know.' The parental complexes, established in our most impressionable years, at the critical period of learning basic trust, form a bedrock of certainty which cannot be relinquished without panic. It is not surprising that many people cling on to the comforting assurances of childhood, hoping thereby to halt the inexorable forward motion of the Self, and escape the ordeals of adult life. Such craven attempts to stop the clock, 'drop out', and play hookey from the cycle of life, is no individual aberration in our culture but is in danger of becoming an epidemic: no one any longer wishes to grow old; everybody wants to stay young. The collective trend is not to grow away from the all-containing mother, but to cling on to her.

Whitmont's law of psychic inertia and the need for initiation rites

In order to account for this collective juvenility, Whitmont (1969) proposes a psychic law corresponding to Newton's law of inertia. Newton's law, it will be recalled, relates to a fundamental rule of bodies, namely, that every body perseveres in its state of rest or motion unless compelled to change that state by external forces impinging on it. Whitmont argues that this law applies not only to physical bodies but to any entity existing in space and time including the psyche. 'In the psyche', he writes, 'inertia is seen as a tendency towards habit formation and ritualization.' He believes it to be 'characteristic of all complexes' and argues that it is 'essential for the sense of stability and permanence which is the basis of consciousness' (1969, p. 123). Psychic inertia manifests itself as *resistance to change*, however desirable such change may be. 'Every pattern of adaptation, outer and inner, is maintained in essentially the same unaltered form and anxiously defended against change until an equally strong or stronger impulse is able to displace it.' An impulse of this kind may arise from the Self or the environment, but 'every such displacement or alteration is reacted to as a death-like threat to the ego' (p. 246).

Whitmont's law of psychic inertia would certainly account for the need which almost everywhere seems to have impelled mankind to invent initiation ceremonies to mark the passage of individuals from one stage of the life-cycle to the next. Such rites would help to overcome psychic inertia by providing the symbols and the group impetus needed to carry the libido forward and loosen the ties holding it back. And it may well be that the widespread forms of puerility apparent in our own society are associated with the decline among us of these invaluable aids to maturity.

Moreover, as we have seen in chapter 4, an essential part of our genetic endowment is designed to promote the experience of fear when confronted by the strange or unknown and is linked to a behavioural system whose goal is the avoidance of potentially dangerous situations. Such fear and avoidance behaviour would clearly tend to operate in the same direction as Whitmont's inertia principle to discourage abandonment of the home in order to risk the inescapable dangers of adult life. Yet, if the population is to survive, these regressive tendencies must be mastered, and the next generation of father-warriors made ready to meet their biological destiny in procreation and defence. This, it seems, is what initiation is designed to do. Initiation, like military training (which is in some ways its modern equivalent) is hard, dangerous and frightening: by surviving it a boy proves his manliness to the collective; by bearing it he masters his fear and earns his own masculine confidence; by submitting to it he relinquishes the way of the Trickster and demonstrates his willingness to accept the mores imposed on him by his elders in the name of the gods. In this manner a divinely sanctioned morality is perpetuated, with profound biological consequences for the cohesion, stability and fecundity of the group.

Historically, Jung was the first to correct the retrospective biases of psychopathology, which sought to explain all psychic disturbances in terms of childhood traumata and phantasies. Abandoning Freud's rigidly determinist model of the psyche, Jung maintained that development could be arrested and distorted not only by events in the history of the maturing individual, but also by his fear of taking the next step along the path of individuation. Should that fear attain high intensity, then the psychic reaction is one of recoil to an earlier stage of development at which the individual may remain fixated and, without some form of social or psychotherapeutic intervention, be incapable of further maturation.

With the evolution of culture, initiation rituals apparently became necessary because individual willingness to submit to the demands and disciplines of outer reality is not something which occurs automatically with the normal processes of growth. It has to be imposed with sufficient determination to overcome what Baynes called 'the renegade tendency', that combination of inertia, fear, and resistance to change which characterizes the Trickster, who clings to the *status quo* and 'knows no difference between right and wrong and accepts no discipline other than his own experimental attitude to life' (Henderson, 1967, p. 36).

For the sake of the collective, adolescence *has* to be a time of declining parental archetypal activity, when the child begins to withdraw his *projections* of the parental archetypes from his personal parents and begins to come to terms with them as real people, accepting their deficiencies as well as their strengths. If the outcome is to be happy, and activation of archetypes later in the ontogenetic sequence is to occur (the Hero, the Anima, the dominance and proprietorial archetypes in the boy, the Haitera and Animus archetypes in the girl), then the parents must also give up their *identification* with the parental archetypes and withdraw *their* projection of the Child archetype from the adolescent. At this crucial point in the life-cycle, therefore, four different outcomes are theoretically possible: (1) the child withdraws his projection, but the parents do not; (2) the parents withdraw their projections, but the child does not; (3) both sides withdraw their projections synchronously; and (4) both sides persist in their projections and decline to withdraw them. Clearly, the third possibility is the most devoutly to be wished. It is also the most unlikely, since it is highly improbable that such powerful archetypal constellations could undergo a sudden change at precisely the same moment – unless some dramatic event should occur which affected them all equally. This, of course, is the event which intiation provided.

In our own society, which has virtually allowed the institution of initiation to disappear, possibilities (1) and (2) are more prone to characterize the loosening of parental bonds in adolescence. In possibility (1), where the child withdraws his projection but the parents do not, the adolescent is left with no alternative than to rebel against the parents and fight for his freedom; in possibility (2), where the parents withdraw their projections but not the child, the result is anxious attachment on the part of the adolescent, who then embarks on a 'Flying Dutchman' quest for parental substitutes, and remains fixated at the Trickster stage or the 'puer aeternus'. From the point of view of the group, the most disastrous possibility of all is the fourth, where neither child nor parents withdraw their projections, the child remaining forever fixated at the pre-pubertal stage.

Initiation, therefore, rendered superfluous the adolescent rebelliousness so characteristic of our time, and largely circumvented the production of pueri aeterni which has become endemic in Western culture. Thus, it is hard to escape the conclusion that initiation rituals possess biological, as well as psycho-social, significance in that their practice would evidently promote the survival of those populations in which they occurred.

Initiation: threshold between the sacred and the profane

It was van Gennep (1960), in his classic work on the subject, who first argued that rites of passage had evolved in human societies to mark the individual's 'life crises' as he moved from one stage of the life-cycle to the next. From his extensive analysis of such ceremonies, he concluded that they all proceed through three stages: separation, transition, and incorporation. Certain kinds of ceremony emphasize one of these three stages more than the others: e.g. funerals are predominantly rites of separation, while marriages are basically rites of incorporation, and initiation rites are rites of transition. But all of them nevertheless exemplify the three stages. Baptismal initiation, for example, proceeds through the stages of baptism, chrism, and communion; and these correspond to the three degrees of the mystic life: purification, illumination, and union. 'The three stages of initiation in the pagan mystery-cults,' wrote Godwin Baynes (1949), 'were sometimes symbolized by three concentric rings. The outer ring represented the rite of purification or lustration; the middle ring, the ordeals and the sacrifice; and the inner ring, the identification with god. The same symbol could express the three stages of realization – experience, reflection, and understanding' (p. 749).

The whole of life may, of course, be viewed as one long process of transition; but it is never a steady progression, and the way is strewn with markers, like milestones which have been eccentrically placed, some fairly close together, others widely apart, and the journey between them is often tedious and uneventful. People all over the world have apparently always regarded attainment of a milestone as a cause for celebration, for a rite of passage designed to bring home to the traveller that one part of the journey has been completed, and to prepare him for the next stage which is about to begin. Van Gennep considered rites of passage to be an example of what he believed to be a fundamental law of life, the *law of regeneration*: the energy present in any system displays a tendency to discharge itself and, as a consequence, must recharge itself at intervals. Thus, the living energy of the individual is recharged as he is initiated into each new phase of his life, and the process is symbolized by the rites of death and rebirth, through which the individual 'dies' to his previous circumstances (separation) and is 'born into' the new (incorporation). In some tribes the novice is considered dead, and he remains 'dead' for the duration of his noviciate. Later, he is 'resurrected' and taught how to live, no longer as a child, but as a man. He is instructed in tribal law, totem ceremonies, tribal myths, and so on, and the final act of the initiation process is a religious ceremony during which the novice is ritually mutilated so as to make him forever identical with the adult representatives of his own sex.

Inherent in van Gennep's concept is the dichotomy of the sacred and the profane – the sacred being a temporary or transitional state through which the individual passes at special moments in his life. For as long as he is in this special state, he is 'sacred' to those of his fellows who remain in the usual mundane state, and are therefore 'profane'. Once he has passed through the transitional state, he then has to be *incorporated* into his new status and returned to the profane realities of life. Rites of passage enable both the individual and society to cope with this transition without undue disturbance, and they afford public recognition and confirmation of the fact that the transition has occurred. At the psychic level, the realm of the sacred corresponds, of course, to the activity of the phylogenetic psyche and the profane to that of the ontogenetic psyche: the symbolic and ritual elements of the rites possess intense ('sacred') numinosity for the candidate because of the archetypes that they constellate; return to the profane world, and acceptance of the new status, indicates that the ego, having been exposed to impact of hitherto unencountered archetypal processes has begun to integrate them within the personal psyche in the form of complexes which have been transmuted by the intensity of the ritual experience.

Traditionally, boys were prepared for the initiatory ordeal by frequent recitals of tribal myths and legends which recounted the deeds of heroes of the past. These stories had the teleological function of establishing a gradient along which the masculine libido might flow towards the goal of mature and responsible manhood. The hero's entry into the supernatural (archetypal) world and his return was the prefiguration of the boy's 'death' and 'rebirth' in the initiation ritual: 'The maternal universe was that of the profane world,' wrote Eliade (1958). 'The universe the novices now enter is that of the sacred world. Between the two there is a break, a rupture of continuity.' Thus, initiation did not just separate the boy from his mother and turn him into a hunter/warrior: it also attributed a divinely sanctioned meaning to his life by relating him personally to the myths, totems and spirits of his tribe.

As van Gennep put it:

> to the semicivilized mind no act is entirely free of the sacred. . . . Transitions from group to group and from one social situation to the next are looked on as implicit in the very fact of existence, so that a man's life comes to be made up of a succession of stages with similar ends and beginnings: birth, social puberty, marriage, fatherhood, advancement to a higher class, occupational specialization, and death. For every one of these events there are ceremonies whose essential purpose is to enable the person to pass from one defined position to another which is equally well defined. (1960, p. 3)

The virtual disappearance of rites of passage from our own culture has been accompanied by a decline in the importance accorded to sacred ceremonial. Until comparatively recent times, however, rites of passage were customarily linked with supernatural sanctions which greatly enhanced their 'sacred' potency. From the ethological standpoint they can be seen as promoting effects which clearly possessed survival value for the population in that they contributed powerfully to social cohesiveness. Rites linked the individual to the group and the group to the individual; they ensured group recognition of, and group participation in, the great events of the individual's life; they heightened his consciousness of the transformation he was undergoing; and they made the transformation more inevitable, more likely to be accomplished, by giving the individual the courage to move on to the next stage ordained for him, and to overcome the 'regressive' tendencies which might otherwise turn him back towards immature patterns and dependencies instead of progressing towards greater maturity. Thus, rites ensured the psychiatric health of the individual as well as the community.

Modern psychology and psychiatry have been no less negligent than sociology in appreciating the significance of rites of passage for normal development and group survival. The 'medical model' which has dominated psychiatry up to the present time has caused us to view deviations from 'normal' behaviour as 'neurotic', 'psychotic' or 'psychopathic'. Once they have examined a patient and attached one of these labels to him, there is a tendency amongst psychiatrists to feel that they have done something scientifically respectable, that they have diagnosed a pathological entity which, like diabetes mellitus or tubercular meningitis, possesses a known origin, a definable course, and an established cure. In fact, psychiatric diagnoses lack the precision and the validity of medical diagnoses (except in those conditions such as Alzheimer's disease or general paresis of the insane where a pathological cause is clearly demonstrable) and they are too often applied with a professional dogmatism which betrays the nosological uncertainties on which they are based. The trouble is that the 'medical model' – the idea that it is the doctor's function to examine, to diagnose, and to treat – is too rigidly deterministic, too 'outer' and 'objective' to be therapeutically helpful in the treatment of psychiatric patients because it usually fails to take into account the *meaning* of their symptoms in terms of the archetypal needs appropriate to the stage they have reached in the life-cycle. A whole new psychiatric approach opens up, however, possessing great aetiological and therapeutic potential, if one but adopts van Gennep's view of the mode of progression which characterizes the human life-cycle. Then, emotional disturbance and social maladjustment may be seen as arising directly from individual failure to meet one's archetypal destiny, to link the sacred with the profane, and pass from one phase of the life-cycle to the next – in other words, from a failure of initiation.

Inasmuch as psychoanalysis has considered the significance of rites of passage, it has focused attention on puberty initiation ceremonies to the exclusion of all other rites, seeing them purely as a reinforcement of the incest taboo: the elders inflict painful mutilation on the genitals of the young initiates so as to heighten their 'castration anxiety' and so make them leave their mothers alone (i.e. to their fathers). Bruno Bettelheim (1955), on the other hand, sees puberty initiation rites as a means of reducing castration anxiety and of minimizing envy of the attributes of the opposite sex. But such formulations miss the main point of initiation rites – that of bringing to an end one phase of the life-cycle and initiating the next phase of the archetypal sequence. The function of initiation ceremonies is to initiate.

Psychoanalysis was right to consider the older generation of males to be threatened by the rising generation of young adults, but wrong to attribute it entirely to sexual rivalry. The sudden dramatic increase in the quantities of male hormone circulating in the blood of young braves greatly heightens their aggressiveness as well as their sexual appetites. They are not, therefore, a threat just to the sexual prerogatives of the elders but to their proprietorial claims and their position in the social dominance hierarchy as well. More important still, they constitute a major threat to the stability and viability of the group, which cannot hope to compete in the struggle for existence if torn with internecine strife between the generations. All successful societies in the history of our species, therefore, have had to develop means of disciplining the young men and coercing their energies into the service of the social system. From the viewpoint of the theory of archetypes, it is striking that the forms of discipline and education which have evolved should have so many features in common. Theoretically, there are any number of ways in which constraints might be applied, but in fact the variety used is small. The archetypal structure inherent in human nature imposes upon us a relatively simple social vocabulary. Thus, although the initiation procedures used in different cultures vary, there are a number of standard elements:

1 initiation is primarily an all-male concern;
2 the young initiates are removed from all contact with females;
3 they are subjected to ordeals and trials of endurance by the older males, they are hazed and humiliated, sometimes beaten and homosexually assaulted, and physically mutilated, usually in the genital region (e.g. circumcision or subincision) but sometimes by tattooing or by knocking out teeth;
4 they are instructed in tribal lore, myths and traditions;
5 they are ritually slain and brought back to life;
6 everything is done in the name of tradition, hallowed by the tribal gods.

Initiates usually know what is to happen to them, but are brought up in the knowledge that it is 'ordained' and therefore inescapable.

> The elders could no longer rely on their physical weight to keep the young men in check, but they could rely on the weight of tradition.

> Without a knowledge of the traditions of the group, a man was as helpless as a lower animal that by some genetic quirk had failed to acquire its proper instincts. Without a knowledge of male secrets and male rituals and taboos, a boy could not be a man. This was the trick. One could not simply *become* a man, one had to *know how* to become a man. The first schools, in the technical sense, were initiation schools. Their overt function was to pass on knowledge and to 'make men'; their covert function was to preserve the ascendancy of the elders. (Tiger and Fox, 1972, p. 191)

In primates, learning performs many of the functions of instinct in lower mammals, albeit with far greater flexibility. Development of the cerebral cortex, particularly in the region of the forebrain, has made possible both extensive learning and the modification of genetically programmed drives. Initiation is, therefore, in many respects an educational procedure, as Tiger and Fox suggest, which evolved through the biological necessity of replacing rigidly organized instinctive behaviour with more adaptive habits of co-operation between members of the group. In primates, education and learning have become indispensable to survival, for through their agency the individual must acquire patterns of response which possess, in their biological consequences, the appropriateness and the power of instincts. For this reason they have to be so deeply ingrained as to *seem* 'instinctive' (i.e. automatic, invariable, and common to all members of the group). In no sphere of primate life is this more true than in the organization of dominance patterns among males for the purposes of mating, hunting, and defence.

Female initiation, on the other hand, is a far from usual occurrence and where it is found, it is usually a less serious and protracted business, consisting more of a recognition that menstruation has begun and that the young woman has now entered the reproductive phase of her life. (The appalling practice of female circumcision is fortunately a relatively rare cultural aberration.) There are probably two main reasons for this difference. In the first place, girls do not have to achieve a transformation of sex-role identification from mother to father, as is the case with boys; and in the second place, females do not constitute a threat to the masculine hierarchy. For the girl to achieve the status of an adult woman, it is sufficient for her to achieve sexual maturity, to mate and bear a child. Whereas nature turns girls into women, society has to make boys into men.

> There is, however, one common element: it is always a profound religious experience that is the basis of all these rites and mysteries. It is the *access to the sacred*, as it reveals itself upon assuming the condition of woman, that constitutes the aim and object, both of

> the initiatory rites of puberty and of . . . feminine secret societies. (Eliade, 1960, p. 213)

Not infrequently, female initiation occurs in stages:

> For example, among the Yao, initiation begins with the first menstruation, is renewed and deepened during the first pregnancy, and completed after the birth of the first child. The mystery of giving birth – that is, the woman's discovery that *she is creative upon the plane of life* – amounts to a religious experience untranslatable in terms of masculine experience. One can understand, then, why childbirth has given rise to secret feminine rituals, sometimes developed into veritable mysteries. (p. 216)

The initiatory experience for the male is altogether more extraverted, more public in its forms. For the female it is an introverted dawning of awareness of herself as woman. In many cultures this new feminine consciousness is marked by no rites at all, for it is the initiated male who brings it about by his recognition and pursuit of her womanhood; it is the man who puts the child to rest and awakens the woman. This explains the ubiquitous existence, in myth, legend, and fairy tale, of the heroine who lies sleeping until her prince comes to waken her. She is the Sleeping Beauty, the lady of Tubber Tintye, and Brynhild, who slumbers for years within a circle of fire, placed round her by Wotan, till Siegfried comes to her. She is the goal of the Hero's quest; and, in the male psyche, she is the Anima who waits patiently in the unconscious for the son to win his liberation from the mother.

Male initiation at puberty is the call to be a hero: it begins with *separation* from the old, familiar world of mother, women and children, and, as Howitt says of the Kurnai Tribe of South East Australia,

> The intention of all that is done at this ceremony is to make a momentous change in the boy's life; the past is to be cut off from him by a gulf which he can never repass. His connection with his mother as her child is broken off, and he becomes henceforth attached to the men. All the sports and games of his boyhood are to be abandoned with the severance of the old domestic ties to his mother and sisters. He is now to be a man, instructed in and sensible of his duties which devolve upon him as a member of the Murring community. (quoted by van Gennep, 1960, p. 75)

In terms of attachment theory, therefore, initiation can be seen as a means of facilitating the *transfer of attachment* from mother and family to the male group and the tribal gods. And in place of the conventional psychoanalytic explanation of the function of these rites, it would seem reasonable to propose the hypothesis that male initiation is an institution 'ordained by God' (or, if you prefer, by evolution) for the attenuation of the maternal bond when it has outlived its usefulness for survival. For the boy, however, this is no passive or empty ritual. The ordeals to which he must subject himself are harsh and designed specifically to test his metal. Neumann believed that boys, unlike girls, have to fight their way out of the original ego-Self identity, that masculine consciousness develops by *opposing* mother and Self and ultimately overcoming them by force (symbolized mythologically as the dragon fight). The young woman, on the other hand, finds herself through re-affirmation of her original mother/Self identity. Accordingly, she remains closer to her instincts and the unconscious than her brothers. As Henderson puts it:

> the woman, purely as mother, cannot see the reason for the masculine initiation, which touches on things outside her immediate experience of the feminine world with its emphasis on relatedness. For this reason the masculine *Logos*, as discriminatory function, tends to be antithetical to the feminine *Eros*, as the function of relatedness. (1967, p. 124)

Primate 'adolescence'

Parallel differences between males and females are to be found in the social development of primates growing up in their natural habitat. In most primate societies, males take nearly twice as long as females to assume full adult status. The reasons for this are partly physical and partly 'educational'. Adult males are usually much bigger than females and consequently need more time to grow up; furthermore, male skills necessary for hunting, fighting and defence take much longer to acquire than the skills of mothercraft. Female savannah baboons, for example, have usually had their first infant by the time they are four years old; young males of this age, on the other hand, are still unruly adolescents squabbling and playing rough games on the periphery of the group. In a sense, this is their period of initiation, for the elders drive them out to the edge of the troop away from their own enclave at the centre, where the dominant males keep their mates and young offspring. At the periphery, the young males do their 'national service', fighting off predators and learning how to establish a position for themselves in the dominance hierarchy. Usually it is several years before they are permitted to return to the centre, and only then if they make themselves acceptable to the older dominant males. Having established a worthy position in the hierarchy and/or acquired territory, they are then ready to mate.

This 'initiatory' period is every bit as challenging to the masculine spirit as any human initiation rites, and is certainly far more dangerous.

Mortality rates in primate groups are much higher among males than among females: in some baboon troops, for example, as many as 80 per cent of the males are killed before they reach maturity. Biologically speaking, this appalling carnage is of little consequence because the individual male is less important than the individual female: only a relatively small number of males is necessary to fertilize the females and defend the troop. The adolescent years thus constitute a period of ruthless selection which only the toughest survive to become members of the ruling party. Although this is undoubtedly extremely hard on the weaker juveniles, it has the important biological result that only the males with the 'fittest' genes sire the next generation.

For the females, growing up is altogether safer and easier. Unlike the males, they are not banished from the central area, where they continue to mix freely with their mothers and the dominant male elite, learning how to relate to males and care for infants by first-hand experience.

There are, therefore, striking similarities in sex-role development between human and primate societies. True, no 'religious' tradition is apparent among primates to provide divine authenticity for the way things are done, though one may, perhaps, detect the beginnings of religious dogma in the corpus of species-specific rituals (including self-sacrifice in the interests of the group) which are learned and handed on by 'cultural' transmission, as opposed to those 'unreligious' rituals which are genetically determined and organized without the necessity for learning or cultural tradition; e.g. dominance behaviour in a cockerel is of a much more primitive and 'untutored' order than that of a hamadryas baboon or 'divinely anointed' king. Religion, too, must have an evolutionary history.

The problem of the uninitiated

When it comes to growing up in a primate group, males have a much harder time of it. Nature, as well as 'society', it seems, is putting them to the test, and weeding out of the gene pool those that are found wanting. For not only among savannah baboons are 'failed initiates' barred from breeding: human societies can be just as ruthless in denying the right to mate to those who fail to make the grade. In some cultures, for example, failed initiates become 'berdaches' – shamans who must dress as females and if they are permitted to mate the union has to be a homosexual one. In our own society, the vast and, I believe, growing population of homosexual males may be seen as the result of failed initiation – not through any innate deficiencies of masculinity, but because, it seems, the masculine principle *requires* culturally sanctioned trials and ordeals if it is to be actualized in maturity. It is as if initiation were 'planned for' in the genome: the Self actually anticipates that some form of initiation procedure will be vested in the culture. If this is so, then it is reasonable to assume that societies which provide no puberty rites will produce a large population of males in whom the masculine principle is only partially actualized. Certainly, this would seem to be the case in contemporary Western Society.

How has this come about? Tiger and Fox (1972) believe it is because our educational practices and modes of apprenticeship no longer accord with the initiatory requirements encoded in the biogrammar. Schools and universities, they argue, are sophisticated temeni of initiation: they evolved as exclusively masculine establishments for the making of men. When they were tough, few in number and of great reputation, they succeeded in their function and produced a ruling elite of dominant males. (The British Empire, like the Battle of Waterloo, was won on the playing fields of Eton.) Modern academic institutions, on the other hand, are too mundane to challenge the spirit of aggressive young males, who see no glory in the acquisition of a school leaving certificate; they prefer to drop out and, *faute de mieux*, seek initiation into a peer group (commune, delinquent gang, mods, punk rockers, etc.), not subject to the control of elders and therefore discontinuous with the ordered fabric of society. Tiger and Fox (1972) believe that this breakdown in the initiatory process is bound to have social repercussions far more extensive than those implied by the rising statistics of juvenile crime, arguing that it will disrupt even further the already shaky family matrix in which the coming generation is reared. Education they see as only partially an intellectual matter: in its initiatory function it is also a political procedure designed to bring turbulent youngsters within the balanced hierarchical structure of the group. They quote with approval Patricia Sexton's argument that the increasing employment of female teachers to instruct and discipline boys results in the production of 'feminized males': when the educational system is dominated by women, the male initiation archetype is broken and 'feminine' rather than 'masculine' characteristics are rewarded in pupils of whichever sex. Thus, the male characteristics of greater aggression, wider-ranging physical activity and environmental exploration are thwarted by the schoolmarm's insistence on sitting still, walking sedately, keeping quiet, being courteous and listening carefully to what teacher says. Not surprisingly, this causes rebelliousness amongst the boys, and their aggression, instead of being channelled in directions useful to the community, is displaced into socially disruptive behaviour. The outcome is that contemporary educational trends foster contemporary social ills: instead of producing mature males inspired with the common ideals of the community, our educational system is loosing upon the world whole generations of morally and sexually ambivalent 'Tricksters'.

This, I think, is a little hard on the teaching profession. It is not so much academia as society at large that has abdicated responsibility for initiating the young. Traditional initiatory procedures have been allowed to atrophy with disuse because our 'elders' have lost confidence in the values of which they are the custodians and no longer possess any certain knowledge as to what it may be that they are initiating young people for. Ultimately, it is the fault of neither teacher nor pupil, elder nor novice, but the consequence of a collective crisis of confidence in our culture. The loss of respect for traditional values, the progressive relativization of all canons and ethics, results in a conceptual miasma in which one television interviewee's opinion is as good as another. So far, all attempts to replace traditional procedures with pragmatic ones has met with little success, largely, I believe, because they are based on a shallow, one-sided and biologically ignorant view of human nature. Liberal, egalitarian values are the major contribution of our civilization to the ethical progress of mankind, but they cannot in themselves ensure individual happiness or communal harmony if they fail to take into account those fundamental archetypal determinants which demand that religious forms of experience, family integrity, stability and continuity in relationships between the generations, hierarchical social structures, gender differences, initiatory procedures, and so on, be respected and allowed expression. This is not to argue that we should abandon Western civilization and revert to the life of the hunter-gatherer, but simply that our social and political policies, as well as our psychiatric interventions, should take due note of the intentions of the Self. The truth of this statement might seem glaringly obvious were we not so mesmerized by our own cultural illusions. In some ways it is as if Voltaire and the Enlightenment had never happened; for ours is an age when religious dogma has been replaced by political dogma. Everywhere political theories are embraced with little consideration for their epistemological foundation and then applied indiscriminately to ancient institutions, economic practices and traditional relationships, often with the most humane motives and in a spirit of high idealism. But this Procrustean imposition of political belief can do violence to human nature. Contemporary fashions in education are merely a case in point. They are, for example, self-righteously anti-sexist, anti-elitist, and anti-authoritarian. Although the intentions behind these attitudes are indisputably humane and therefore unexceptionable, they have unfortunately been elevated to the status of sacred lore: thus to question the wisdom of educational policies based on them is to invite persecution as a heretic and to risk banishment from university campuses all over the world. Even to consider the argument that there might be something to be said for educating boys and girls separately, teaching them different curricula and preparing them for different roles in life, or that the intellectually bright might be given different kinds of instruction from the less able, is to reveal oneself as a self-convicted reactionary who deserves to be ostracized by all right-thinking people. Yet it was not always so. What has changed?

A key to this puzzle was provided by David Riesman in his justly influential book, *The Lonely Crowd* (1952). Riesman distinguished between three different cultural types, which he characterized as 'tradition-directed', 'other-directed', and 'inner-directed'. Since our earliest cultural beginnings, the great majority of our kind have lived in tradition-directed cultures, where values, attitudes and beliefs were passed on unquestioningly from generation to generation. Any evolution that occurred in the canons of such cultures proceeded very gradually and a profound sense of historical continuity permeated the lives of all its members.

In modern times, practically all tradition-directed cultures, including our own, have been overwhelmed and transformed by 'other-directed' values, which reject the traditions of the past as suffocating and oppressive and seek new meanings in modern ideas and movements. In these cultures, the centre of gravity shifts backwards along the life-cycle of its members from old age to youth, from senex to puer. The emphasis is on rebellion against the tradition of the fathers and on solidarity with the peer group. Instead of respect for the old institutions hallowed by the gods, a restless passion arises for 'revolutionary' notions which change with each new generation, basing their currency not on what has 'always been' but on what 'everybody thinks'. Hence the rapid spread of 'popular' mass movements like the Campaign For Nuclear Disarmament in the 1950s, the revolutionary student movements in the 1960s, and the Women's Liberation Movement of the 1970s, the successive generations of 'Teds', 'Mods', 'Rockers', 'Hippies', 'Punks', and so on, and the popularity of subversive drug cultures, Maoists, Trotskyists, etc. The speed with which contemporary fads and fashions catch on is, of course, a function of the omnipotent media, with their power to influence new trends, define what 'everybody thinks' and ensure, whatever the 'in-thing' may be, that 'everybody's doing it'. Unfortunately, a life of undiluted 'other-directedness' is deeply unsatisfactory, since the emphasis on ephemera promotes alienation of the ego from the Self; it encourages the adoption of a pseudo-identity, distracting the 'with-it' adolescent from the development of a mature character securely rooted in the reality of his own nature. The intensity of the desire to heal this alienation can be judged from the huge nostalgia industry that has grown up in the 1960s and 1970s, the immensely popular books, television serials and films which hark back to the 'tradition-directedness' of the past.

To the humanist, a more satisfactory alternative to tradition-directedness and other-directedness is Riesman's third orientation, which he terms 'inner-directedness'. The inner-directed person does not derive his sense of value or identity from tradition or from conformity to peer group fashions, but from the resources of his own nature. His 'centre of gravity' is not in society but in the Self. This third orientation is the most difficult to attain because it requires courage and determination and can only be achieved by each individual in the course of developing his own character. The most original, creative, and outstanding men and women are invariably of this type, and yet it is no 'elitist' condition, for it represents a mode of adjustment which is available to every human being. It is the way of life that takes individuation as its goal.

Tradition-directed cultures are, of course, 'patrist' in character while other-directed cultures conform to the 'matrist' pattern discussed in chapter 9. Inner-directedness, on the other hand, affords a means of transcending both these cultural forms through awareness and respect for the fundamental characteristics of the creature that we are, the essence of which is crystallized in the Self. Jung believed that our species had reached a critical point in its history when acceptance of traditional values alone could no longer guarantee survival. For mass movements and 'collectivist' solutions he had deep suspicion, mixed with a fair measure of contempt. Only through inner-directed research, Self-knowledge and a sensitive approach to the assets inherent in man's archetypal constitution might a new consciousness arise capable of solving the horrendous problems which the greed and ingenuity of our species have created.

Of the three types described by Riesman, inner-directedness has more in common with the traditional than with the other-directed form. The reason for this is not hard to divine. Traditional cultures evolve slowly and achieve a homeostatic balance with the archetypal imperatives of the Self so as to achieve 'goodness of fit'. Feedback between an other-directed culture and the individual Self of each member is intermittent and sporadic, however, since values change from generation to generation, and there is no time for the relative 'goodness of fit' of one set of values to be tested before fashion rushes on to embrace the next. Clearly, at a time of triumphant other-directedness like the present, there is an urgent need to give priority to demands arising from the Self. Only then can traditional canons which are of eternal value be reaffirmed and the hectic vagaries of the other-directed orientation be corrected and brought back into a cultural synthesis appropriate both to human nature and to the terrible implications of our time.

On giving priority to the Self

The primary demand of the Self is for incarnation, to be made manifest in consciousness, in personality, and in action ('behaviour'). It is a demand which is constantly repeated throughout the whole life-cycle and is not silenced until the very last breath (many would maintain that it continues beyond it). For most people, distracted by 'other-directed' preoccupations, the imperatives of the Self are obeyed blindly, largely unheeded by consciousness. They are, however, readily accessible to consciousness: one has but to choose the 'inner-directed' path, to pay attention to one's dreams and spontaneous phantasies, to become acutely aware of the incessant stream of images emanating from the Self.

The first encounter with the Self which I can recall in a dream came at about the same time as my first awareness of my own existence, which I described on page 140. I dreamed that I opened a cupboard in the room in which I was sleeping. Instead of finding clothes there as I expected, I was amazed to see a stone staircase spiralling down into a deep, dark basement. The shock of this discovery filled me with awe and a certain uncanny fear. Then I looked up and saw that the staircase continued upwards and upwards, spiralling round a central axis, reaching, it seemed, almost to infinity. At the very highest point I could dimly make out a far distant light. In some manner, without clearly formulating it in words, I knew that this staircase represented my life.

Years later the memory of this experience was vividly revived for me when I read Jung's account of the first dream he could remember from his childhood, when he was about three or four years old. He dreamed that he was in a meadow near his home at Laufen. 'Suddenly I discovered a dark, rectangular, stone-lined hole in the ground. I had never seen it before. I ran forward curiously and peered down into it. Then I saw a stone stairway leading down' (1963, p. 26).

Much later still I came across the following passage from Romain Rolland quoted by Henderson (1967): 'I have just recovered the key of the lost staircase. . . . The staircase in the wall, spiral like the coils of a serpent, winds from the subterranean depths of the Ego to the high terraces crowned by the stars. But nothing that I saw there was unknown country. I had seen it all before and I knew it well' (p. 175). This, notes Henderson, is typical of archetypal imagery: something eternal and numinous, yet familiar.

The symbolism of descent and ascent via staircase, ladder, pole or tree, of going down into the maternal underworld and up into the paternal heavens, is probably as old as our species. It has always found particular association with rites of initiation, whose function it is to synthesize biological imperatives with social necessity and personal aspiration. Thus, the initiation both of warriors and of shamans commonly involves descent into caves or deep ravines and the ritual climbing of ladders, trees or poles.

The Australian rites of the Man's House, for example, assimilate

> the novice to the sky-god Daramulun by means of the symbol of a pole or tree which he is supposed to mount in order to reach the ancestors of the Alcheringa Time, whereas the Pueblo Indians descend to an underground chamber (*kiva*) in order to communicate through an opening in the ground (*sipapu*) with the spirits of the ancestors living below. An intermediate symbol is the totem pole of the Indians of the Pacific Northwest, which seems to join Earth and Heaven in an ancestral symbol of totemic nature. (1967, p. 103)

Here the symbolism is also clearly phallic, uniting Father (Heaven) with Mother (Earth), but to stress this fecundating element of the ritual would be to detract from its crucial *religious* implications. In Asia the ascent to Heaven via the Cosmic Tree, the *axis mundi*, 'represents one of the oldest religious means of . . . participating in the sacred order to transcend the human condition.' The candidate for initiation makes his symbolic ascent in order to 'transmute his ontological status, and to make himself like the archetype of *homo religiosus*, the shaman' (Eliade, 1958, pp. 77–8). As Eliade has demonstrated, the archetypal pattern of shamanic initiation invariably combines descent to the underworld with ascent to Heaven, and the accomplishment of this dual feat both in ritual and in dreams is the necessary condition of shamanism: 'he who has undergone them has transcended the secular condition of humanity'; that is, he has become holy, sacred, numinous through his encounter with the archetype in himself and his consequent ability to constellate it for others.

Consistently, the archetypal symbols of descent and ascent recur as often in the pages of history as in the records of anthropologists and archeologists. The Kwakiutl youth climbing and descending the 'copper pillar' projecting high above the ceremonial house of his initiation inevitably conjures up the image in English minds of boys being initiated as sailors by the 'elders', the officers and petty officers of *HMS Ganges*, who imposed on them the ordeal and trial of strength of climbing a 100 foot high mast. Ritual climbing of a ladder probably formed part of Orphic initiation ceremonies, and the mystical ladder occurs in the Mithraic mysteries and in the monotheistic religions (e.g. Jacob's dream of a ladder reaching up to heaven, and Mohammed's vision of a ladder rising upwards from the temple in Jerusalem). This monotheistic aspiration for ascent, symbolized no less in temples, cathedrals and tall spires, was anticipated by the pyramids and ziggurats (steps again), built to simulate mountains reaching up and away from Mother Earth towards the realm of the Father in Heaven.

Henderson believes that the structure of the initiation archetype itself inheres the notion of steps or stages: in ancient mystical traditions these stages were represented as being seven in number and they appear on the walls of ancient Egyptian and Mesopotamian tombs as the ladder of seven rungs. This symbolism recurs in the seven steps of the alchemical process leading up to the water bath in which the King and the Queen perform their *coniunctio* – the creative union of the masculine and feminine archetypal principles. Belief in reincarnation is also an expression of the initiation archetype – the notion that through a series of deaths and rebirths the soul transcends its baser condition as lived in previous incarnations and aspires to ever higher degrees of spiritual perfection.

The archetype of initiation is re-evoked every time that one passes from one stage of the life-cycle to the next. The symbols linked with each stage are constellated by the rituals culturally ordained as appropriate to that stage, and through the medium of a rite of passage provide a safe and reliable means for further development. For this reason the unfolding life-cycle is well conceived of as a spiral staircase, each stage of the cycle being a landing or 'secure base' which, once reached, provides a temporary resting place before yet another rite of passage moves one onwards and upwards to the next. Initiation rituals are cultural techniques for overcoming psychic inertia. As Henderson says:

> We do not find normal children developing in a measured, progressive forward direction; they show equally a chaotic, retrogressive need to recapitulate old patterns. Presumably they would progress and regress equally and interminably if the influence of some educational agency from without or some strong motivation of the archetype from within did not instigate a new cycle. (1967, pp. 188–9)

Although our culture has allowed initiation rituals to atrophy with disuse, there persists in all of us an *archetypal need to be initiated.* This need is very evident in patients undergoing analysis; archetypal symbols of initiation arise spontaneously in dreams at critical periods in the life-cycle – at puberty, betrothal, marriage, childbirth, at divorce, separation, or death of a spouse, at the betrothal and marriage of one's children, at the approach of old age and death. Campbell (1949) and Henderson (1967) give many striking instances of this, all of them examples of that mysterious and fascinating process which Neumann calls 'the personal evocation of the archetype'. It seems that the attainment of a new stage of life demands that the initiation symbols appropriate to that stage must be experienced. If culture fails to provide these symbols in institutional form then the Self is forced to provide them *faute de mieux*. Let me give some examples from my own practice.

Cliff, an 'eternal student' in his thirties, consulted me because he was depressed and frustrated by his inability to get on with his doctorate thesis. I was much intrigued to learn that the subject he had chosen for his thesis was the development of student brotherhoods since the middle ages. He had long since run out of grant money for the project and was supported by his mother who went out to work specifically to earn enough to keep him in the indolence to which he was accustomed. His father was a recessive figure who had never taken much interest in Cliff's development or given him any advice or encouragement concerning his choice of career. Analysis soon revealed that behind his academic inertia there lay fears that he would never be able to meet the challenge of the adult male world when the time came for him to relinquish his protected status of 'post-graduate student'. Sexually he was interested in women but never allowed himself to become involved in a lasting attachment: the moment a girlfriend began to demand some statement of his intentions he dropped her and found someone else. He was, in other words, a classic puer aeternus, and his problem was essentially one of failed (or unattempted) initiation.

Shortly before Cliff first came to see me had had the following dream:

> I am standing with three or four friends in the early evening dusk round a hole in the ground. It is rather like a manhole covered with a circular disc. When this is lifted back a dim light radiates from the shaft below. I step into the opening and begin to descend by means of a steel ladder, still aware of the glow coming from below me.
>
> When I reach the bottom of the ladder I turn towards the left from which the light is coming and I become aware of a female presence just behind my left shoulder. She is a young woman dressed in medieval costume. I stand there dressed in a cloak, with an oval shield on my left arm, and with flowing blond locks of hair. It occurs to me that I am like Siegfried.
>
> Straight ahead of me there extends a tunnel from the end of which light continues to glow. I seem to be in a kind of anteroom, and between me and the entrance to the tunnel there is some kind of threshold. Somewhere in the centre of the glowing light I discern a frightening head: I think it is female and like the Medusa.
>
> In my hand there appears a glowing green sword. Grasping it, I spring past the threshold into the tunnel. But I am immediately confounded. I am paralysed. I cannot move forward, nor do I know where or how to strike with my sword if I should ever get within range of the Medusa.

At first sight, this is an extraordinary dream for a modern student to have, so redolent is it of heroic themes from a bygone age. Yet such dreams are far from uncommon. This one expresses Cliff's plight in archetypal terms, relating his personal predicament to the collective experience of mankind on the 'threshold of initiation'. While the Princess (the Anima) waits patiently on his left (the unconscious side) he must commit himself to the ordeal of the dragon-fight. If he is to win his manhood and release the Anima from her confinement in the unconscious, he must cross the threshold and slay the Medusa. But he cannot. He has a sword but does not know how to use it, and the fear is too great. As in life, he is paralysed, and his manliness remains both untested and uninitiated.

Another example of a (failed) initiation dream was provided by Hamish, a professional man of forty, who was suffering from a mid-life crisis: he had lost interest in his professional life and his marriage was in ruins. In the past year he had fallen in love with two different women and the experience had wakened in him a passion for life which made his previous existence seem desiccated and barren. He now wanted to leave his wife in order to live with one of the other women, but he could not bring himself to face the upheaval and the renewed commitment that this dramatic change in his circumstances would involve.

In his dream he witnessed a strange ceremony: people were circling round a heap of evergreen branches and coal which they themselves were building higher and higher. He realized that there was some secret significance in what they were doing and tried to find out what it was.

> Eventually, I and some other young men (I seem to be younger than my real age) are told that the secret will be revealed to us if we accompany some people on a journey downwards through a tunnel whose mouth is near the coal heap.
>
> We start downwards, but there is something sinister about our guides, one of whom has a long iron spoon. I am afraid we shall not be allowed to return – and in fact, when we have got really deep, we are indeed told that we cannot return. But I refuse to accept this, and I lead my companions back towards the surface. No one tries to hinder us; those above part to let us through, while those below pursue us in a rather ineffectual way, rising up as if through water but then slipping back and becoming more and more shadowy.
>
> When we reach the surface I see some of our erstwhile guides. One is a young boy who is weeping, because unlike us he did not decide to return and now he has been captured and turned into some kind of zombie. The coal heap is still there, and I feel that I have not fully understood its significance.

The sacred aspect of initiation is stressed in this dream through the symbolism of death and rebirth – the ceremony of interspersing layers of coal (death, but in a form filled with potential energy) with branches of evergreen (life and eternal renewal) in order to build a kind of altar. Although Hamish was trapped in a crisis of middle life, he nevertheless finds himself in his dream involved in a rite more appropriate to puberty. This was psychologically correct because important aspects of his masculinity remained uninitiated ('I seem to be younger than my real age') and this accounted for the failure of his marital and professional life and for his inability to make any firm decision about what action he should take.

Faced with this outer situation, the Self recognizes the need for further initiation and, in the absence of cultural assistance (Hamish having lost his religious faith) the necessary symbols and rituals are provided by the phylogenetic psyche in the dream. Hamish finds himself embarking on the archetypally familiar journey down into the underworld in the company of his fellow initiates. (Although Cliff apparently made his descent alone, it will be remembered that he too started off in the company of 'three or four friends'.) The idea of death as a necessary preliminary to rebirth is further accentuated by the *rite de sortie* of leaving the 'surface' world and descending into the underworld, where the guides (the 'elders' or witch doctors who are the masters of initiation) are associated with devils with whom it is advisable to sup with a long spoon. The numbers of mythologies in which the 'underworld' is the repository of the dead points to the potency and durability of this archetypal notion. We have already noted the descent made by Pueblo initiates into *kiva* (the underground chamber) to communicate with ancestral spirits through *sipapu* (the opening in the ground). The Christian equation of the underworld with Hell is but one of many examples of how the symbols of earlier religions are associated with evil when taken over by a later faith: thus, Hades becomes Hell, and the good god Pan, with cloven hoof, tail, horns and goatee beard, is transformed into the devil. But the archetypes are no respecters of fashion, religious or otherwise, for they express the collective experience of mankind since our time began. And in terms of archetypal reality, the underworld is neither 'Hades' nor 'Hell' but the great womb of the earth whither souls descend in order to be reborn. Hamish's strict Catholic upbringing had, however, affected him deeply enough for him to associate the guides to the underworld with the servants of Satan, which can only have heightened his fear of what might befall him if he went on.

His fear, combined with his lack of understanding of the nature or necessity of the ritual he has embarked upon, causes Hamish to 'chicken out' and return to the surface. He thus loses a chance to become initiated. His failure highlights the drawback of growing up in a culture which has few publicly acknowledged means of initiation. It is as a consequence of this absence of traditional procedures that the mantle of 'elder', or initiatory grand master, often falls on the shoulders of the analyst, who must point out to the dreamer the archetypal significance of the symbols he is experiencing, and strengthen his resolve to press on when fear would dispose him to turn back. For this there is ample precedent: even cultures possessing an elaborate repertoire of *rites de passage* attribute great importance to the dreams of the initiate. In shamanic initiations, for example, the postulate's dreams constitute an integral part of the ritual, while in many societies a candidate's readiness to undergo any form of initiation is judged from the content of his dreams. Thus, the first occurrence of ascent/descent symbolism, or a dream involving arrows or canoes, will be taken as a sign that a youth is ready to be initiated as a shaman, a hunter, or a warrior. (Teit, 1900).

In Hamish's dream, the boy who is capable of going through with the initiation is found weeping, and Hamish fears that he has been 'turned into some kind of zombie'. Weeping is common in initiates and is presumably expressive of fear, and sorrow at the loss of mother and of childhood. The fear that initiation into manhood will turn one into a zombie is the classic complaint of the puer aeternus and the commonest justification he gives for 'dropping out of the rat race' and declining to be 'incorporated' into the social structure. The puer fears giving up the security of being his mother's child, the egalitarian comradeship of his peers, and his dreams and phantasies of greatness which are never put to the test, precisely because of an intuition that this would mean 'death'. The absence of ritual, and the preparation for ritual, denies him the knowledge that 'death' is followed by 'rebirth', and that to be initiated represents renewal of life rather than decay into a zombie-like state.

The natural fear and reluctance of the initiate is commonly personified in myths and fairy tales by a weak or dubious character who goes off with the hero on his adventures. An amusing example of this figure occurs in Mozart's opera of initiation, *The Magic Flute*, in which the hero, Tamino, is accompanied by the cowardly, indolent, pleasure-loving Papageno, who shamelessly attempts to flee from the initiatory ordeals imposed by the father-priest, Sarastro, in order to return to his cosy billet with the Queen of the Night (a devouring mother, if ever there was one). 'Papageno' invariably crops up in analysis in the form of the patient's doubts about his capacity to go on, to pass the 'trial of strength' and achieve maturity.

To submit oneself to the ritual, however, requires the sacrificial dedication which comes of adequate preparation. Hence the importance of fairy tales and hero myths, whose frequent recital forewarns children of the trials and ordeals to come and provides numinous examples of how steadfastness, loyalty and courage result in triumph. In our own time, television and cinema heroes can perform similar functions, though not always with felicitous consequences – not least because the sacral, sacrificial element is missing. There is no cultural follow-through, no sacral confirmation of the initiatory ordeal, no exposition of the necessity or the meaning of the sacrifice required. Perception of the meaning and necessity of the ritual is indispensable if the fear of the novice is to be overcome.

The individual who persists in clinging unconsciously to the mother and refuses to sacrifice the comforts of boyhood will usually compensate for his failure to achieve a genuine position among his peers by falling prey to phantasies of heroic deeds, the attainment of high status, and the conquest of fair maidens. What has in fact been achieved is no more than an inflated identification with the hero archetype. Should this eventually lead to action it is action linked with a heroic, and often solitary, obsession with trials of strength like that of a young man described by Marie-Louise von Franz who lived on mountainsides with no more covering than a nylon sheet because he could not bear the burden of belongings and the responsibilities of 'dull reality', or like the solitary flights of such pueri aeterni as Lindbergh, Saint-Exupéry and Mollison. Such heroic ascents are not purely compensatory, however, nor do they merely represent a desire to escape mundane reality; they are, like climbing the sacred pole or *axis mundi*, an expression of the imperative arising from the Self to prove one's worth and 'get initiated'.

Those relics of initiatory ritual that remain with us – the 'hazing', the tests of endurance, the trivial humiliations of student fraternities and of recruits in *corps d'élites* – are strictly secular; they are conducted by youths little older than the neophytes, and all participants know that life is seldom, if ever, really in danger. In tribal initiations, however, the neophytes are left in little doubt that they will actually be killed, and by resigning themselves to this terrifying ordeal they convincingly demonstrate their willingness and their capacity to brave death. The physical mutilations to which they are customarily subjected are not just a test of courage: they symbolize total dismemberment. Thus, Daramulun, the Supreme Being of the Yuin tribe of Australia, is believed to cut the young initiates up into pieces, burn them, and then to restore them to life as men, but each with a tooth missing (which a medicine man knocks out with a chisel in the course of the ritual). Essentially, the physical ordeal is a means of heightening the psychic ordeal, so as to accentuate the meaning of the whole initiatory process and ensure its efficiency as a technique of transformation. The significance of ritual is that it constellates a profound *experience*: it provides a traditionally sanctioned opportunity to accomplish a *transformation of the ego's experience of the Self* – an inner mutation of awareness with collective consequences. The collective *knows* what the subject is experiencing, and then renders due recognition that he has experienced it and that he is thereby transformed. Undoubtedly, initiation has immense sociobiological importance, but the essential features of the phenomenon are experiential: 'Now I am a boy belonging to my mother – Now I am a boy leaving my mother and submitting myself to the ritual that the gods have decreed – Now I die as a boy and am ritually dismembered – Now I am born as a man among men.'

In the modern world, one of the few socially sanctioned 'rituals' capable of providing a 'temenos' for such transformations to occur, when they fail to occur spontaneously, is analysis. Indeed, the success of analysis not infrequently depends on the capacity of the analyst to constellate the priestly master of initiation in his own person. Then, when the Self, responding to outer demands for change, produces the archetypal symbols of initiation, it is up to the analyst to make their meaning clear, to strengthen the novice's determination to 'put away childish things' and get on with the next stage of the phylogenetic sequence we call life.

When it comes to systematic, institutionalized initiation, however, the only form to have survived relatively intact into modern times is that of the warrior. Military recruit training still embodies the archetypal stages of *separation* from family, *transition* through a period of testing, indoctrinating and inculcating skills, followed by a ceremony of *incorporation* (the passing-out parade) into the corps or regiment of trained (i.e. 'initiated') fighting men. In all services the emphasis on tradition is strong, as is the sense of allegiance to a suprapersonal ideal (i.e. king/queen or president and country). The 'elders' (the officers and NCOs) are firmly in charge: they know the rules and see that they are obeyed.

The new recruit joining his unit for basic training ('boot camp') is subjected to a full-scale *rite d'entrée.* He sacrifices his civilian persona as his mother's son, is assigned a military identity and number, made to don the uniform of the initiate ('rookie', 'sprog' or 'ant') and treated to the notorious military haircut (a symbolic – or perhaps not so symbolic – mutilation). Then the transition begins. He is put through a series of ordeals, humiliations, and trials of strength – inspections, the parade ground, assault course, battle PT, unarmed combat, tactical exercises with long periods without food or sleep (the 'watch and wake' of knightly initiation), forced route marches in full battle order, etc., constantly hounded and harassed, criticized and assessed by the elders who, through the rigidly hierarchical military social structure, impose discipline from above and demand ritual expressions of deference and submission (e.g. saluting, standing to attention, using respectful forms of address, and so on). Only when the recruit has satisfied these impressive masculine authorities that he is indeed worthy of 'incorporation' is he permitted to 'pass out'. In the training ritual of a British Royal Marine there is even a terrifying tunnel (filled with water) through which the recruit must pass as an inescapable ordeal before he is awarded his badge of initiation into superior manhood, the prized green beret.

Despite their persisting patriarchal rigour, however, military institutions have not entirely escaped the 'matrist' influences at work in our society. One must treat with caution what the 'elders' themselves tell us about these matters since it was ever the cry of old soldiers that the younger generation is 'soft' and that 'things are made too easy for 'em nowadays', but it is hard to deny that the introduction of female non-combatant personnel and the encroachment of sophisticated technology into military affairs has made a soldier's life 'gentler', more academic, and less 'initiatory' than hitherto. Hair has got longer, discipline milder, regulations about dress and 'correct' behaviour more relaxed, social integration with the civilian population easier, and so on. Yet the traditional initiatory form remains, and its survival provides living witness to the strength of its archetypal hold on the masculine imagination: the production of warriors, it seems is inconceivable unless some such process is gone through.

However willing public opinion may be to acknowledge the necessity for initiatory procedures in the armed forces, it is nowadays much less inclined to take a tolerant view of their application in a civilian context. To matrist eyes, initiation is an essentially 'fascist' practice – a cruel method of indoctrination, a brutal imposition on helpless boys of a traditional ideology by sadistic lackeys of the establishment. Yet the truth is that initiation, as it has been customarily employed is as much a support for the adolescent seeking to define his identity as it is a means of promoting traditional forms of hierarchical cohesiveness and order. In this sense, initiation rituals function as public health measures in those societies where they are practised, thus largely obviating the need for the psychiatric services increasingly demanded for our own adolescent populations. The sudden increase in testosterone, that rising of the sap which is the spring of puberty, heralds the most dramatic phase of the life-cycle. Until then the child has confined his explorations of the world to the immediate vicinity of home, within the ambit of parental watchfulness. Now, on the crest of the hormonal wave, he is carried out of his depth; it is a thrilling and frightening adventure, and it is usually a struggle to find less turbulent waters where he can swim at ease or see the ground beneath him and stand on his own feet – a goal which it is the function of initiation to help him to achieve.

Little wonder that in the absence of traditional rituals, modern adolescents manifest what one might term 'initiation hunger'. Henderson quotes the following passage from Erikson:

> Young persons often indicate in rather pathetic ways a feeling that only a merging with a 'leader' can save them – an adult who is able and willing to offer himself as a safe object for experimental surrender and as a guide in the relearning of the very first steps toward an intimate mutuality. . . . To such a person the late adolescent wants to be an apprentice or a disciple. . . . Where this fails, as it

> often must from its very intensity and absoluteness, the young individual recoils to a position of strenuous introspection and self-testing which . . . can lead him into a paralyzing borderline state . . . a painfully heightened sense of isolation . . . a basic mistrust, which leaves it to the world, to society, and indeed to psychiatry to prove that the patient does exist in a psychosocial sense, i.e. can count on an invitation to become himself. (E. H. Erikson, 1959, pp. 125–6)

Initiation hunger is also shown by members of gangs like the 'Hell's Angels' with their daring bravado, their distinctive tattoos and dress. The piercing and automutilations practised by punk rockers also reveals obvious initiatory symbolism. Among the huge population of male homosexuals, the 1970s saw a great increase in the number of 'leather bars' frequented by men 'into S/M' (sado-masochism), dressed in the required 'uniform' of heavy boots, black leather jackets decorated with chains, and denim or black leather trousers, the sadistically inclined wearing keys clipped to their studded belts on the left side, the masochists wearing their keys on the right. In these bars assignations are made, often with the aim, seldom achieved, of establishing lasting 'master-slave' relationships.

As we saw in the case of Colin (pp. 115–17) homosexual sado-masochism can be best understood as an eroticization of the initiation archetype. Again and again the masochist puts himself through the 'ordeal' and 'trial of strength' of punishment, torture and abuse, sacrificing and submitting himself to the dominant 'master'. The ritual is repeated *ad infinitum* because of the essentially repetitious nature of all sexual acts. It is precisely because the initiation archetype has been contaminated by sexuality that the individual is caught in the ritual and cannot move on.

The same is true for the homosexual sadist, who identifies his ego with the 'master of initiation' while projecting his own uninitiated masculine potential which is latent in the Self on to the person of the masochist. By subjecting this partner to painful and humiliating rituals, he is in effect *symbolically initiating himself*. The fact that he derives sexual pleasure from this is an incidental bonus. Understandably, homosexual sadists are attracted to professions with surviving initiatory functions, such as the army, schoolteaching, the training of competitive sportsmen, etc. We shall return to this subject in chapter 11.

Phenomena such as these all accord well with the observations of analysts such as Edinger, Henderson and Neumann that the maturing psyche is itself motivated in late adolescence to put an end to childish identification with the lone trickster/hero figure and gain entry to the adult masculine group. What I have termed 'initiation hunger' is but an expression of this motivation towards maturity and is compatible with Neumann's 'personal evocation of the [initiation] archetype'. The importance of *rites de passage* is that they satisfy initiation hunger in socially productive ways:

> they strive, within an atmosphere of mythical timelessness, to combine some form of sacrifice or submission with an energetic guidance toward sanctioned and circumscribed ways of action – a combination which assures the development in the novice of an optimum of compliance with a maximum sense of fellowship and free choice. (Erikson, 1959, p. 144).

The purpose of initiation is, like that of myth, to achieve what Campbell terms 'the reconciliation of individual consciousness with the universal will'. It is a reconciliation which has to be made at each of the stages of life. For both at the personal and the collective level there is a continuing and inexorable cycle of death and rebirth: stasis is unthinkable because it is unbiological and therefore contrary to the archetypal nature of things. He who is uninitiated is lost.

· 11 ·

The archetypal masculine and feminine

In recent years many billions of words have been uttered on the fashionable topic of sexual equality and, in common with the 'culturalist' views which have dominated discussion of other psychological issues, differences between the roles and status of men and women have been squarely attributed to environmental and social influences. The traditional belief that women naturally differ from men has met with widespread rejection, it being argued that the relative scarcity of leading women politicians, composers, painters and generals is due to masculine repression and lack of feminine opportunity rather than innate feminine characteristics. As a consequence, it has become customary to exaggerate the similarities between men and women while blaming those disparities which persist between them on to the evils of social conditioning. This trend has brought Jung's generalizations concerning the fundamental differences between masculine and feminine psychology into disrepute and has led in some quarters to wholesale rejection of his Anima and Animus postulates. It affords yet another example of disharmony between Jungian theory and the popular notions of our time.

However, a careful sifting of the available evidence makes it clear that sexual differentiation is not nearly as malleable or culturally relative as contemporary prejudices would have us believe. Indeed, both the ethological and the anthropological data tend to vindicate the Jungian position: it seems probable that significant differences between the political, social and economic roles of men and women are determined by genetics. Contemporary confusions over gender roles, and the sexual aberration and social insecurity to which these confusions give rise, provide a vivid illustration of the misery that can be caused when biological reality is perverted in the cause of political dogma. That women should be forced by delusory theories to compete with men, on masculine terms and on masculine territory, is a madness generated by a culture whose members have become alienated from their archetypal roots.

As far as personal identity is concerned, nothing is of greater importance than gender: the Self does not actualize merely as a human being but as a *male* or *female* human being. As soon as the ego is old enough to give itself a name ('I', 'me') it conceives itself quite distinctly as either 'little boy' or 'little girl'. This fundamental distinction then colours one's whole psychosexual development and understanding of the meaning of one's role in life. While Jung was in no doubt that many of the psychic differences traditionally understood to exist between men and women had as much reality as their physical differences, he did not for one moment deny that male and female personality characteristics and behaviour patterns were subject to cultural influences. But he stoutly maintained that there were limits to the modifications that these influences could achieve and that underlying these modifications were certain universal features of behaviour and experience which distinguished men from women whatever culture they had grown up in and whichever historical epoch they happened to live in. The masculine and feminine principles are fundamental archetypes which have dominated the life of our species since its emergence, as indeed they had dominated the lives of our forebears long before our species evolved. To deny their profound significance is about as sensible as denying the existence of the penis or the womb.

Jung was no male Chauvinist, however. Not only did he hold both masculine and feminine principles in equal respect (there is no question of one being 'superior' to the other; both are mutually complementary, homeostatically balanced and mutually interdependent), but he argued that *both* were at work in every human individual, regardless of his or her biologically assigned sexual identity. In this latter respect he was close to Sigmund Freud who wrote: 'All human beings, because of their bisexual constitution and crossed inheritance, unite male and female characteristics.' It is a view which is justified by recent experiments which prove that both male and female behaviour patterns are 'planned for' in individual members of a number of species and that either pattern of behaviour may be elicited by manipulating male and female hormone concentrations at critical periods of development. It also coincides with the ancient Chinese Taoist concepts of Yin and Yang, those fundamental feminine and masculine principles which are held to permeate all reality and to be present and active in both men and women.

Yang and Yin

The basic principle of Taoism is uncongenial to the modern temperament, for although it shares with the contemporary spirit a concern with transition and change, its fundamental teaching centres on the immutable, eternal law underlying all states of becoming, 'the principle of the one in the many' as Wilhelm (1951) put it (*Introduction to the I Ching or Book of Changes*, p. xxxv). 'Everything flows on and on like this river,' said Confucius, 'without pause, day and night.' But the flux, like the river, has a source: the 'great primal beginning', *t'ai chi*, had a still earlier beginning, *wu chi*. *Wu chi* was traditionally represented by a circle; *t'ai chi* by a circle divided into interlocking elements of light and dark, yang and yin whose distinctive characteristics persist as omnipresent polarities underlying all changes and all transitions. The yang principle is characterized as energetic, dynamic and assertive; its attributes are heat and light (symbolized by the sun and its rays); its realms are heaven and the spirit; in its phallic, penetrating aspect it arouses, fructifies and creates; in its aggressive form it combats and destroys; its orientation is essentially centrifugal, out-going, extraverted; it is positive and impulsive, but also disciplined and ascetic.

FIGURE 11.1

Whereas yang is assertive and initiating, the yin principle is passive and containing (symbolized by the moon and the cave); its realms are earth, nature and the womb, for it is essentially concerned with gestation, giving form to the energy of yang and bringing life out of darkness; its movement is centripetal, in-turning and introverted.

It is not our culture alone that has traditionally regarded assertiveness, creativity, physical aggression and destructiveness as male attributes, and gestation, nurturance and life-enhancement as female. Neither is the yang/yin dichotomy peculiar to ancient China. These are universally apparent distinctions, and their very universality betrays their archetypal origins. This is not to say that men cannot be passive or yielding or women dynamic and assertive, for yin and yang propensities are in us all; but the universal experience of mankind is that yang is more highly developed (more conscious) in men and yin more highly developed in women. The complementary principle is nevertheless still present and functional in both sexes, and it was to these contrasexual propensities that Jung gave the names Animus (the yang in women) and Anima (the yin in men), knowing them to be vitally important factors in the psychic economy of us all.

The contemporary wish to develop the yin principle in man and the yang in woman is praiseworthy inasmuch as it promotes individuation towards psychic wholeness. However, it can all too easily result in stagnation and neurosis when males and females seek to develop the contrasexual principle before they have adequately brought to birth in living reality the principle appropriate to their sex. Hence the growing populations of dreamy, ineffectual men, and bossy, unloving women that characterize many sections of modern society. Traditionally, one of the prime functions of male initiation rites was to heighten the initiate's identification with the yang principle and to reduce or eliminate his mother-induced identification with the yin. As we saw in the last chapter, failure to achieve this crucial stage of development results in 'the problem of the puer aeternus'. The man who has insufficiently actualized the masculine principle is in danger of becoming too closely identified with the Anima, and then he lives and behaves like a second-rate woman; *mutatis mutandis*, the complementary fate awaits the woman who has not adequately lived out her feminity – she becomes 'Animus-dominated'. Success in the first half of life demands actualization of the potential appropriate to one's sex; integration of the contrasexual elements is better left to the second half.

Both yin and yang principles can be differentiated into two poles: dynamic at one pole and static at the other. The psychological implications of this distinction are well developed by Whitmont (1969). The four aspects of the masculine/feminine continuum thus derived may be summarized as follows:

1 *Dynamic yang*: aggressive, combative, phallic, striving for dominance and self-assertion. This pole Whitmont labels the *Martian pole* after Mars, god of war.

2 *Static yang*: reason, reflection, discernment, respect for order, justice and discipline, abstraction and objectivity. This pole corresponds to what Jung called the *Logos principle*, which he saw as the primary characteristic of masculine psychology (a biased supposition which owed its origins to his own personality type – an introverted thinking type – and his education).

3 *Dynamic yin*: expresses itself in the need to become involved with individuals rather than things or abstract ideas; it is intensely subjective and personal, and it corresponds to Jung's *Eros principle*, which he believed (again somewhat narrowly) to be the primary characteristic of feminine psychology. Aphrodite stands as an exemplar of this archetypal aspect.

4 *Static yin*: this is the gestating, womb-like aspect of yin: it is unconscious and instinctive as in Nature (*physis*) where it finds expression in the unending cycle of life and death in all living things. 'It is impersonal, nonindividual and collective; it is also averse to consciousness and to discipline'. Whitmont calls it the 'gestative motherly pole of yin' and sees its chief representative in the Great Mother.

These four elemental poles can be represented schematically as in Figure 11.2.

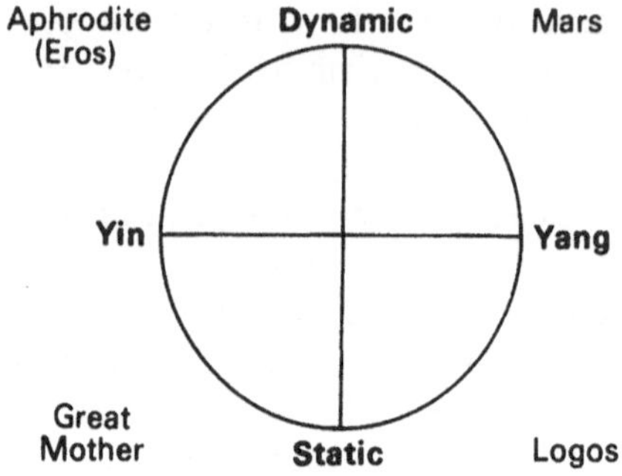

FIGURE 11.2

With their delight in teasing out the polarities in things, Jungians have attempted to formulate further theoretical differentiations of these archetypal elements. Taking the archetypal Feminine as the starting point, Toni Wolff (1956) agreed that one set of polarities existed between the Great Mother and Love Goddess figures, but believed these to be transected by another set of polarities which she termed Amazon and Medium. Once again, therefore, we derive four basic types:

1 *The Mother*: this aspect tends to be impersonal or collective in its functioning in the sense of being instinctive and conventional in its concern with gestation, nurturance, child-rearing and home-making. The pole is represented by the Great Mother, Natura, Demeter, etc.

2 *The Hetaira or 'Love Goddess'*: this aspect, exemplified by Aphrodite stands at the opposite pole to the Mother. She is concerned with getting her man and relating to him at the intensely personal level rather than taking on the social role and responsibilities implicit in becoming a wife and a mother. A woman who remains too closely identified with this pole remains the eternal daughter or sister, the puella aeterna, she eschews commitment and lives the provisional life.

3 *The Amazon*: this type tends to be independent and self-sufficient; in modern life she is the career woman. She functions as comrade or competitor rather than wife or mother. The orientation is not towards individuals but rather tends to be impersonal and objective. It is hard to distinguish this aspect of the archetypal feminine from the Animus, since it clearly has masculine overtones. When integrated with the conscious personality it can enable a woman to achieve her goals in life and further her own individuation; however, should she become unconsciously identified with it, or 'possessed' by it, the result can be a demonic 'organization' lady, who tyrannizes and manipulates her underlings so as to implement her will.

4 *The Medium*: this type lives in close relationship with the collective

unconscious: she is immersed in her subjective experience and speaks with the conviction of an oracle. There is something essentially uncanny about her, as if she had access to knowledge denied to most of us. Such women may turn their gifts to professional use as clairvoyants or psychotherapists, but many more of them live less self-conscious lives, occasionally startling their friends and relations by the power and unusual nature of their insights.

These four aspects of the archetypal Feminine can also be schematically represented as in Figure 11.3.

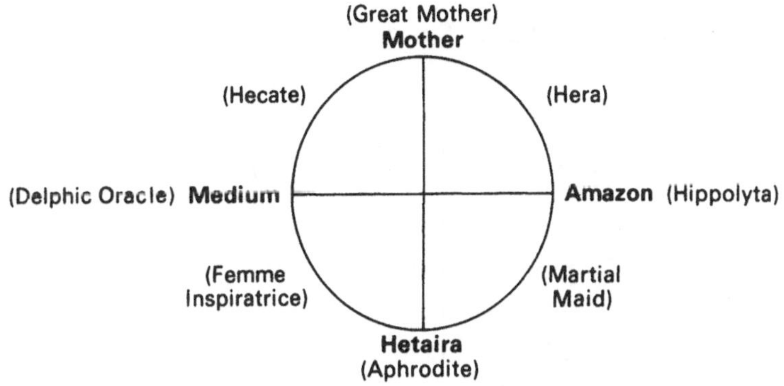

FIGURE 11.3

Examples of 'pure' types are put in brackets at the end of each coordinate and examples of intermediate types are placed between them.

A similar job has been done on the yang principle by Whitmont (1969) who believes that there are predominant traits in masculine psychology which correspond to those designated by Wolff in the feminine: these he calls the Father, Son, Hero and Wise Man.

1 *The Father*: 'This is the archetypal leader, the voice of collective authority, the Lord, King or Tyrant, but also Protector, the figure concerned with hierarchical social order, whose word is law. He directs and protects, but knows only children or subjects, not individuals' (1969, pp. 181–2). He seeks to sustain the *status quo* and stands at the static or 'Logos' pole of the yang principle – that concerned with law and order.

2 *The Son*: this is the puer aeternus. Like the Hetaira type of female he is preoccupied with his personal concerns and cares little for social responsibilities: he is thus obviously at loggerheads with the opposite pole, the Father. 'The son goes his own way, seeks individual relationships and his own individuality, his own inner treasure, in ever new settings, and he does not concern himself very much with authority or permanence' (p. 182).

3 *The Hero*: this figure stands at the dynamic, out-going pole of the

yang principle. Like the Father, he too is orientated to collective values. As soldier, ambitious professional or thrusting businessman he strives for prestige within a social context. Inasmuch as he attains his goals it is through courage, determination, aggression and the assertion of will. He is not so much concerned with maintaining the *status quo* as making use of it, or if necessary overthrowing it, in order to achieve his own ambitions.

4 *The Wise Man*: this type is concerned with meanings and ideas rather than the actions and personalities of people. He is scholar, teacher, sage and philosopher.

These can be schematized as in Figure 11.4

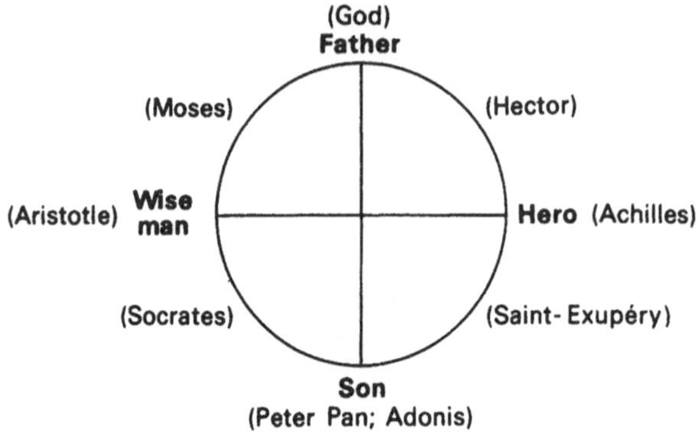

FIGURE 11.4

Like all schemata and typologies, the above are not advanced as finite descriptions of actual people, but merely as a guide or 'compass' with which one may achieve an orientation to the rich complexities of masculine and feminine psychology. To what extent may the accuracy of the compass be assumed? It is time we examined the evidence.

Evidence for the biological basis of sex differences

Hitherto, Jungians have based their generalizations relating to the archetypal nature of psychosexual differences on little more than clinical intuition. It is not surprising, therefore, that these formulations have been neglected on the grounds that they possess little scientific validity. However, there now exists a wealth of objective evidence which goes a long way to confirming the essential accuracy of Jung's assertions; yet one searches the Jungian literature in vain to find this material reviewed or discussed in the light of Jung's theories. It is high time that this were attempted.

In the brief resumé of the evidence which follows, I am heavily indebted to the invaluable work of Corinne Hutt (1972), whose interest in sex differences was aroused, she tells us, 'by some quite unexpected findings obtained in studies of the exploratory behaviour of pre-school children'. She was, of course, aware that in the majority of mammalian species males are the most dedicated and intrepid explorers, but she certainly did not expect to find that, 'even by three or four years of age, many boys and girls engage in characteristically different patterns of exploration'. When she presented her subjects with a new toy, she noted that the interest of both boys and girls was equally excited by it, but that the boys tended to be more original and inventive in the uses that they put it to. Moreover, when she obtained independent assessments of these children from their teachers, she was clearly fascinated to discover that it was the more inventive of the boys who were most frequently reported by the teachers to be 'disruptive influences in the classroom'. Follow up studies established that scores on tests of creative abilities remained consistently high for these boys while the girls' scores were lower and more variable. Hutt concluded that creativity, assertiveness and divergent thinking are linked masculine characteristics, and that outstanding abilities in these areas are likely to be manifested early in life. 'Attempts to understand these results and to interpret them plausibly', she says, 'inevitably led to a consideration of the genetics and neuroendocrinology of sexual differentiation'.

Genetics and neuroendocrinology are indeed the nub of the matter. Physical differences between men and women in height, weight, fat and hair distribution, body contour, bone structure and muscular development are so obvious that not even the most fanatical behaviourist would attempt to argue that they are other than genetically determined. Moreover, the growth and development of boys and girls are clearly programmed differently from the moment of conception, for the physical superiority of the male begins to manifest itself even in the womb: male foetuses grow faster than females and at birth male infants are both heavier and longer. Thenceforth, from infancy to old age, males have larger and more powerful muscles, their hearts are bigger and stronger, their lungs have greater vital capacity and their basal metabolic rate is higher. They make better athletes, their pectoral girdle renders overarm throwing stronger and more accurate, and their hand grip is, on average, twice as strong as in women.

Although the resting heart rate of males is lower than in females, their systolic blood pressure is higher, which means that the cardiovascular system of men is better able to adapt to stress and physical exertion. Moreover, one of the many crucial effects of the male hormone, testosterone, is to promote the formation of red blood cells, with the result that, after puberty, male blood has more haemoglobin than female blood and can, as a consequence, carry more oxygen. Males are also more efficient at eliminating metabolites like lactic acid, which are the by-products of muscular activity.

These facts lead the unbiased inquirer to the inescapable conclusion that, in the course of evolution, men have adapted to a more physically demanding mode of existence. This is evidently the biological basis of the division of labour and *has nothing to do with 'stereotyping' or cultural influences.*

Yang and yin principles are evidently at work in the very act of conception. It is the male who penetrates and the female who receives: in virtually all species which procreate by copulation, sperms are introduced into the female and not ova into the male. The 'yin' nature of the ovum is to be passive and to wait; the 'yang' nature of the sperms is to be active and to seek. Feminine nurturance is provided from the very beginning, for in nearly all species it is the ovum and not the sperm which stores the nutrients necessary for the growth and development of the embryo. For this reason, the ovum is much bigger (an astonishing 85 thousand times bigger, in fact) and more precious: a woman produces only about 400 ova in her lifetime, whereas a man produces about 100 million sperms every time he ejaculates. Thus, a single male is capable of fertilizing the ova of many females, while the most compulsively maternal female is unlikely to produce more than twenty children before the end of her reproductive life. Moreover, there is gross inequality between men and women in the demands which child-rearing makes on their personal resources: the cost to a mother of bringing a child to term, and nurturing it afterwards, is vastly greater than the cost to the father in terms of time, libido, pain, calories, etc., yet his genes benefit equally with hers. If men were not constrained by custom and by law it would be possible for the more dominant among them to fertilize literally thousands of women in their lifetime. Taken together, these facts give the biological explanation for the anthropological finding that male polygamy is very common, female polygamy (polyandry) extremely rare, and male monogamy more honoured in the breach than the observance.

When conception has occurred, and cell division begins, an immensely complicated architectural development scheme is commissioned which follows a distinctively male or female ground plan. The architects of this extraordinary project are the genes, contained in the nucleus of every cell, and arranged sequentially along pairs of chromosomes, one member of each pair being derived from the mother and one from the father. Altogether, there are in every cell nucleus 46 chromosomes (23 from the mother and 23 from the father); 22 of these pairs of chromosomes are called *autosomes* and are concerned with general structural development; the twenty-third pair are the *sex chromosomes*. Female chromosomes are designated *X-chromosomes* and male chromosomes are called

Y-chromosomes. X-chromosomes are bigger than Y-chromosomes, probably because they carry more genes. Women have two X-chromosomes whereas men have one X and one Y.

A most critical stage in the development of the embryo, determined by the presence or absence of the Y-chromosome, occurs with the formation of the gonads (the ovaries in the female and the testes in the male), because from then onwards the foetus *begins to manufacture its own sex hormones.* These have a radical effect on all later development because the gonads are formed (and become productive) before the external genital organs and the brain. At the Oregon Primate Centre it has been established that this early critical period for gonad formation causes infant monkeys to be *already psychosexually differentiated at birth.* Thus, the masculine behaviour of genetically normal (XY) males is little affected if they are castrated at birth; whereas the administration of male hormones to genetically female (XX) foetuses early in pregnancy has a decisive influence on the development of the external genitalia and the central nervous sytem which results in genetic females looking and behaving like genetic males. The human clinical finding of masculinization in girls who have been exposed to abnormally high concentrations of male hormone *in utero* has already been mentioned.

It seems that the crucial factor in the organization of structures in the central nervous system responsible for the co-ordination of male and female behaviour patterns is the male hormone, testosterone. If the embryo develops functioning testes, or if it is subjected to high concentrations of testosterone in the maternal blood stream, the result is masculine appearance and behaviour; if, on the other hand, functioning ovaries develop and there is an absence of testosterone, feminine appearance and behaviour are the result. As Hutt says: 'It seems that nature has provided that when the equipment necessary for masculine differentiation is lacking, development shall proceed according to the feminine pattern' (1972, p. 23). This is also true in genetic anomalies where individuals are born with abnormal numbers of X or Y-chromosomes: the critical factor is the presence or absence of the Y-chromosome, however many X-chromosomes there may be. If the Y-chromosome is present, masculine development will occur; if it is absent, feminine development is the inevitable result. 'In other words,' concludes Hutt, 'masculine differentiation is an active process, female differentiation is a passive one' (p. 62). Which brings us back to yang and yin again. It is the same old archetypal story: man does, woman is: men have to be *made.*

Sensorimotor differences between male and female infants are apparent long before they could possibly be induced by 'social conditioning.' Girls are clearly programmed to approach the world through a primary reliance upon different senses from boys: from the moment of birth females are more sensitive to touch, pain and sound, and throughout life they remain better able to localize sounds and differentiate between their intensity. Males, on the other hand, possess superior visuo-spatial abilities. At a few weeks of age, boys will attend more readily to visual patterns, girls to tonal sequences. The sound of other babies crying is always liable to trigger off crying in others, but female infants are more susceptible to this contagion than males.

It is true that from the very beginning mothers behave differently towards their male and female children: they are more prone to look at their sons and physically stimulate or pacify them while they spend more time talking to their daughters and, later on, indulging in verbal exchanges ('babbling dialogues') with them. Feminists would argue that mothers look at their sons more than their daughters because our culture is biased in favour of boys and places a higher value on them; but if this were the only reason then mothers would also devote more time to babbling and talking to their boys, which they do not. Thus, it seems that *some degree of sexual differentiation is actually built into the mother-child archetypal system.*

Other innate behavioural differences become evident in the first few days of life: the bodily movements of boys are more vigorous, gross and 'global' than those of girls, which tend to be finer and confined to small muscle groups (i.e. lip-twitching, smiling, sucking or raising the brows). On the whole, girls are quieter and more placid, while boys are more fretful and irritable.

So, although the extent to which basic sex differences are archetypally determined is still open to debate, that archetypal systems are involved can no longer be doubted. As with humans, infant rhesus monkeys display a number of gender-related characteristics: from an early age males are more prone to indulge in threat behaviour and 'rough-and-tumble' play, whereas females are more inclined to pass the time sitting about quietly and doing a bit of grooming. That these sex-linked behaviours tell us something of the archetypal programme encoded within the rhesus brain has, as we have noted, been demonstrated by the Harlows (1965). Deprived of all opportunity to acquire such behaviour patterns through learning or imitation, infants reared in isolation will nevertheless manifest the behaviours typical of their sex when given the chance to do so. 'It is extremely difficult for us to believe,' wrote Harlow, 'that these differences are cultural, for we cannot imagine how our inanimate surrogate mothers [made of wire and terry-cloth] could transmit culture to their infants.'

While unquestionably belonging to the same species, males and females are nevertheless 'different animals' in the sense that they have evolved different anatomical, physiological and psychic features in order to perform their biologically appropriate functions. This sexual dimorphism has resulted in females being responsible for bearing and succouring embryos, brooding eggs, and nurturing the young, and in males being responsible for driving off intruders, maintaining the food supply and dispersing populations over the available terrain. Moreover, males display two distinct patterns of sex-related behaviours, one which is orientated to other males and is concerned with masculine rivalry and co-operation, territory and position in the dominance hierarchy (*epidietic displays*), and another which is orientated to females and is concerned with courtship and mating (*epigamic displays*). Because of these added responsibilities, the males of most species have evolved accessory structures (combs, plumage, antlers, etc) and related patterns of behaviour which result in them being more striking in appearance and varied in conduct than the females. However, lest one be accused of carrying these distinctions too far, a word of caution is timely. While it is undoubtedly true that some morphological characteristics and behaviour patterns are peculiar to one sex, it cannot be denied that many are common to both (though in differing degrees). Sexual dimorphism is not about absolute sexual distinctions but about *relative* distinctions. Certain structures and functions are more *typical* of one sex than the other. Thus, the penis is an exclusively masculine feature, while mounting and pelvic thrust are not, since both behaviours can be observed in females on heat; but in general both mounting and pelvic thrust are more typical of male sexual behaviour than of female.

A good example of this sex-typical difference of emphasis is to be found in the area of mechanical and visuo-spatial skills. Although some women make good mechanics, archers and navigators, on the whole men are more proficient at these things. Men are not only better at maintaining machinery but they are also more readily able to comprehend mechanical relationships – as is demonstrated by their vastly superior scores on the Mechanical Comprehension Test. Men are also better at mathematics, have a better sense of direction, are more successful at aiming at targets and can arrange objects with greater certainty in pre-determined patterns. This visuo-spatial superiority is by no means confined to human males: it has been demonstrated in species as diverse as rats and chimpanzees. It is a special ability that seems to develop quite independently of cultural influences, since it has been found to exist in males from many different societies. In particular, male visual perceptual abilities are less 'field dependent' than female – men are less distracted by camouflage and misleading cues than women; they succeed better in ignoring irrelevant environmental characteristics and maintaining their orientation despite them. Arguments about whether these differences are entirely attributable to cultural conditioning seem irrelevant when they are placed in a biological perspective: such special abilities are patently of selective advantage in male members of a species which depends on hunting for survival. It is far more likely that they are genetically determined than socially induced, though social pressures can of course influence the extent to which males will be encouraged to develop their superior potential for the performance of these skills.

The biologically determined special aptitudes which distinguish males from females are further reflected in intelligence test scores. While males on average score higher, as one would expect, on arithmetical, design, and visuo-spatial tests, females tend to obtain higher scores on tests demanding verbal facility, a good short-term memory, and speed and deftness with the fingers. These higher female scores correlate well with the observation that schoolgirls are invariably ahead of boys in verbal fluency, are better at learning things 'by heart' and, when they grow up, are much more proficient at delicate tasks such as assembling electronic components, doing fine needlework or typing accurately and fast. No distinction is found, however, in overall intelligence scores, which average out to be about the same for both sexes. So, in no way can one sex be said to be more intelligent than the other; there are just some important differences in the forms that it takes.

But by far the most interesting distinction between males and females in connection with intelligence tests concerns the actual *distribution* of scores in the population at large. A glance at the normal distribution curves in Figure 11.5 makes this distinction clear: female intelligence is more 'average', more confined to the middle score range; male intelli-

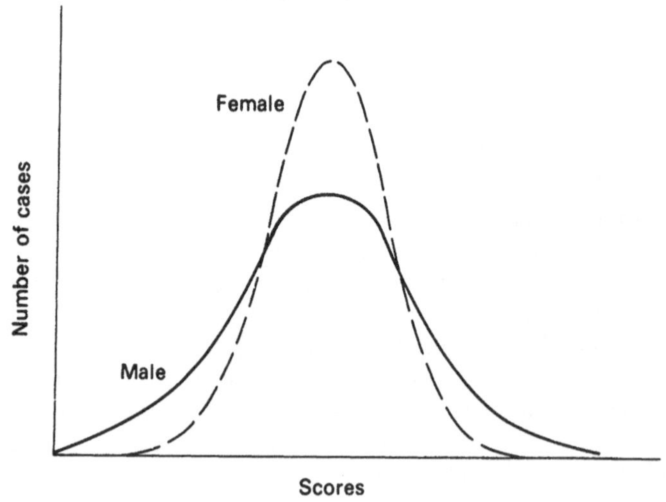

FIGURE 11.5 Normal distribution curves of male and female intelligence scores (from Tyler, 1965)

gence is more 'spread out' across a wider range, reaching from very stupid to extremely bright or 'genius'.

This greater masculine range is by no means confined to intelligence; it is true of all biological characteristics which can be measured (e.g. height, weight, muscular development, strength, etc.), and amounts to a law – the *law of greater masculine variability*. In academic examinations, for example, women students tend to obtain more second class degrees, while men get proportionately more firsts and thirds. In personality, no less than in height and intelligence, males are more variable than females and more apt to run to extremes: just as there are more male geniuses and mental defectives so there are more male criminals, sex deviants, drug addicts, murderers and suicides. Men provide the vast majority of terrorists, urban guerillas, revolutionaries and social reformers; they are also found in all known cultures to predominate in 'the establishment' as the patriarchal protectors of the *status quo*.

The human male's political proclivities are not merely an expression of greater variability, however; they are a direct expression of his biological nature. As he evolved as a hunter, man developed a sophisticated social propensity for close association in masculine groups. Attention has already been drawn to Lionel Tiger's fascinating study of bonding in males, and his view that bonds between men form 'the spinal column of a community'. His review of the cross-cultural evidence led him to argue that 'from a hierarchical linkage of significant males, communities derive their intra-dependence, their structure, their social coherence, and in good part their continuity through the past to the future'. The universal anthropological finding is that politics, like warfare, is an essentially masculine concern, and the business of politics is everywhere the same: the occupation of territory, establishment of the power structure, and the maintenance of the law (the law being a cumulative tradition laid down by generations of dominant males).

By contrast, women display a marked lack of enthusiasm for public affairs: for many years now it has been possible for them to enter politics as well as professional and business organizations, but seldom do they reach the pinnacles of power. In his classic UNESCO publication, *The Political Role of Women*, Maurice Duverger (1955) wrote:

> The progressive decline in women's influence as the higher levels of leadership are reached is not only noticeable in the structure of the state and political organs but also to be found in the government service, the political parties, the trade unions, private business, etc. Nor are there any perceptible signs of improvement in this respect. . . . The percentage of women members of parliament, for instance, is hardly increasing. On the contrary, it tends to fall after

the first elections in which women have the suffrage, and to become stabilized at a very low level.

The interesting fact is that on those rare occasions when a woman does achieve supreme power it is usually as a consequence of being the wife, widow or daughter of a politically eminent man: examples are Mrs Bandaranaike of Ceylon, Mrs Ghandi (Nehru's daughter), Eleanor Roosevelt, and the two Mrs Perons. This corresponds to the ethological finding that in many vertebrate societies, and particularly primate societies, females assume the status of their mates. Tiger believes that women are capable of releasing 'follower' behaviour in members of the community only if they have shared the 'charisma of dominance' of a closely related male. 'Otherwise they neither inspire the confidence nor channel the energies of potential supporters.' In other words, without the masculine connection, they fail to constellate the authority aspect of the father archetype. This is not only true for males, but also for females: women not only tend to vote for the same political party as their husbands, but they vote for male candidates in preference to female candidates. According to the psephologists, this pattern is consistently found in all democratic countries.

In his book, *The Inevitability of Patriarchy* (1973), Dr Steven Goldberg marshals much persuasive evidence to support his thesis that male dominance is a manifestation of 'the psychophysiological reality' of our species. In addition to advancing the genetic and neurophysiological evidence relating to the biology of sexual differentiation already summarized above, he observes that 'authority and leadership are, and always have been, associated with the male in every society, and I refer to this when I say that patriarchy is universal and that there has never been a matriarchy.' Patriarchy, it seems, is the natural condition of mankind. 'There is not, nor has there ever been, any society that even remotely failed to associate authority and leadership in suprafamilial areas with the male. (*Ibid*, pp. 28–9).

Apart from daughters, wives and widows, the only modern exceptions to the rule of universal masculine pre-eminence in political life are Golda Meir (whom one of her colleagues once unchivalrously described as the best man in the Israeli cabinet) and Margaret Thatcher. The selection of Mrs Thatcher as leader of the British Conservatives was an interesting fluke of history: it represented a gamble on the part of a defeated party, disillusioned with its male leader (a bachelor, unfairly accused of misogyny) and with no obvious male heir to the leadership. Humiliated by the powerful national trade union movement, the Conservatives, for the first time in their long history, lost confidence in themselves as the 'natural Party of Government'. If they were ever to rule again, it was essential to do something imaginative to prove to a sceptical electorate that, whatever their failings, they were at least thoroughly up to date. One of the ablest people in their ranks was a woman and, very astutely as it turned out, they judged the moment right to choose her. It was the novelty of her position as much as her handling of the political circumstances that brought Margaret Thatcher in triumph to 10 Downing Street in 1979. However, within a year of becoming Prime Minister, much of the novelty had worn off, and increasingly she became the object of much hostile (and predominantly masculine) criticism, not a little of it from her own supporters, who applied to her such unkind sobriquets as 'Attila the Hen'. Her political opponents went much further, calling her 'Boadicea' and 'The Iron Lady', thus caricaturing the almost 'masculine' determination with which she pursued her policies. Indeed, like Golda Meir, Mrs Thatcher appears to be made of tougher stuff than the men in her cabinet (or in the shadow cabinet, for that matter); she is certainly the most resolute Prime Minister Britain has had since Winston Churchill, and no one can be in any doubt as to the power of her Animus or the sharpness of her mind. It will be an interesting reflection on Tiger's theories to observe how long she can continue to carry her followers with her.

Male dominance is by no means confined to politics. In all cultures, the creative artists, composers, scientists and philosophers are predominantly men, and overwhelmingly so. It is only in literature – presumably because of their superior verbal skills – and in the performing arts that women have made a significant contribution, though, here again, men are overwhelmingly in the ascendant. The women's movement would seek to explain this as the result of masculine 'privilege' and the constraints imposed on women by male chauvinism. But this facile argument does not bear scrutiny. Even in those occupations which are traditionally the métier of women – hairdressing, cookery, dress-making, and so on – it is men who are the innovators and chief exponents. In the arts, moreover, women have been encouraged to paint pictures and make music by their menfolk since the time of the Renaissance, yet, to date, there has been no woman Beethoven or Stravinsky, Picasso or Leonardo da Vinci.

Though it is indisputable that women have, until recently, endured low status in our society and have been subject to masculine exploitation, it is hard to avoid the conclusion that men are better equipped by nature to excel in a vast range of political, cultural and physical activities. There are and always have been women of outstanding ability, but even the brightest of them seem to lack those para-intellectual qualities which determine success in creative work, namely, perseverance, aggression and ambition – all of which are known to be enhanced by the presence of testosterone in the bloodstream and are probably due to differences in cerebral development as well. Both Hutt and Goldberg argue that men also have a greater capacity for abstract and innovative thinking as well as being more powerfully motivated to bring their ideas to fruition.

So much for the areas in which men have natural advantages over women. Are there no areas in which women have the edge on men? The answer to this question is so obviously in the affirmative that it is indicative of the power of feminist prejudice that one should even have to ask it. As Goldberg (1973) puts it:

> The central role will forever belong to women: they set the rhythm of things. . . one of the most stunning regularities one notices when studying cross-cultural data closely is the extent to which women in all societies view male preoccupation with dominance and supra-familial pursuits in the same way as the wife in Western society views her husband's obsession with professional football – with a loving condescension and an understanding that men embrace the surrogate and forget the source. Nature has bestowed on women the biological abilities and psychophysiological propensities that enable the species to sustain itself. Men must forever stand at the periphery, questing after the surrogate powers, creativity and meaning, that nature has not seen fit to make innate functions in *their* physiology. Each man knows that he can never again be the most important person in another's life for long, and that he must reassert superiority in enough areas often enough to justify nature's allowing him to stay. There is no alternative; this is simply the way it is. At the bottom of it all, man's job it to protect woman, and woman's is to protect her infant; in nature all else is luxury. p. 218)

Woman creates and nurtures life; man can never parallel her triumphant achievement except in the use of ideas and technology. Alchemy, that esoteric discipline out of which all science grew, represented a systematic masculine attempt to emulate the great feminine mystery: to introduce 'base' materials into a womb-like retort and, after a period of gestation, to bring them forth as gold.

In line with their amazing and miraculous ability to create living individuals, females of all mammalian species are by nature more protective and nurturing than males: they are also more generous, more considerate, more altruistic and more devoted to personal intimacies. Throughout childhood, girls are more *affiliative* than boys in that they are much more prone to seek the proximity of others and to display pleasure in doing so. Boys, on the other hand, are less concerned with social interaction and spend most of their time in some form of physical activity such as running, chasing, woodwork, playing with large movable toys, and so on (Hutt, 1972).

These differences are relatively independent of the type of society in which individuals are reared. Whiting (1963) studied the behaviour of boys and girls in six cultures, as varied as India, Okinawa, the Philippines, Mexico, Kenya and New England and found essentially similar patterns of male and female behaviour in all of them. A factorial analysis of data obtained from observing girls revealed three predominant characteristics in their conduct: dominance, nurturance and the assumption of personal responsibility; he explained this cluster of traits as being indispensable to the development of skills appropriate to motherhood. If she is to be a satisfactory mother, a woman must be dominant and responsible in relation to her brood and capable of giving succour and care.

> We find that girls show these types of behaviour in each of the six cultures which are located in six parts of the world entirely unrelated to one another. . . . Conversely, in each of these six cultures, boys are characterized by more physical attack, more physical aggression than are girls. This seems to me to indicate an underlying difference in the physiological wiring of the two sexes. (Quoted by Hutt, 1972, p. 131)

Personally, I find this testimony convincing. But I am aware that studies revealing differences in behaviour between girls and boys, however scrupulously conducted, will carry little weight with committed feminists who argue that children are 'brainwashed' by their parents from a very early age to adopt the masculine and feminine 'stereotypes' prevailing in their culture. However, they never seem to ask themselves why these stereotypes should have arisen in the first place, or why it is that different cultures in different parts of the world should 'choose' to adopt essentially the same stereotypes. As Corinne Hutt asks, why should parents universally encourage aggressiveness in their sons and nurturance in their daughters? How can these universal 'stereotypes' come into being if they do not reflect some deeper biological origin? Unfortunately, it is anathema to the feminist creed to ask whether it is possible that 'stereotype' reflects archetype, that socialization works in the direction of bringing out sexual differences which are naturally present. Indeed, nothing is more likely to induce apoplexy in a feminist than the suggestion that society could conceivably encourage or condone aggression in boys and reward nurturance in girls because boys *really are* more aggressive and girls more nurturant, and that nature (rather than society) might have made them so for good reason.

Instead of addressing their attention to these possibilities, feminists invariably counter them by advancing the one possible exception to the rule of universal, species-characteristic sexual dimorphism – the *Tchambuli*, a people described by Margaret Mead (1935) whose women tend to be more assertive and men more passive or 'effeminate' than in other cultures. But the Tchambuli are a unique exception. No one wishes to assert that masculine and feminine characteristics are discontinuous with one another; on the contrary, they are clearly continua, at one end of which males tend to cluster and, at the other, females. Naturally, there is a great deal of overlap in the middle of each continuum, and it is always easy to find some men who are more nurturant than some women, and individual women who are more aggressive than individual men. It would be surprising if the same were not true of individual cultures which in theory can also be ranged on the same continua. But what must concern us as scientists are the *typical* characteristics of males and females: when these have been clearly defined, we shall be in a better position to understand individual differences and to explain how unusual cultures like the Tchambuli could have arisen. However, it is mischievous to use the aberrant Tchambuli as a mine to explode any theory that would seek to establish a biological basis for masculine and feminine psychology. It is a piece of polemical chicanery for which Dr Mead herself has little patience. In her review of Goldberg's book she declared that 'all the claims so glibly made about societies ruled by women are nonsense. We have no reason to believe that they ever existed . . . men everywhere have been in charge of running the show . . . men have been the leaders in public affairs and the final authorities at home' (quoted by Goldberg, 1973, p. 49). Elsewhere she writes: 'Nowhere do I suggest that I have found any material which disproves the existence of sex differences' (p. 49). Clearly, the ethnographer who made the Tchambuli known did not consider them to disprove the rule of universal sexual dimorphism. On the contrary, like Jung, Talcott Parsons, and many others, she has made fundamental generalizations about sex-typical functions which she has no hesitation in attributing to biology. The female's activities, she believes, are characteristically centred in her own person and her immediate environment – she is concerned with making clothes and utensils, with preparing and dispensing food; the man, on the other hand, uses his superior strength, aggression and visuo-spatial abilities to co-operate and compete with other men and animals and to manipulate materials, such as stone, wood and metal, to further his fascination with the external environment and his desire to exploit it. It is hard to fault these assumptions. In the evolutionary history of our species, man has depended for his security and sustenance on the environment; woman for hers on man. This crucial differentiation of function has engraved itself on culture no less than on our genes. That parents have a profound influence in shaping the attitudes and values of the young cannot be doubted, but the child is as far from being a simple product of these influences as his body a simple product of the food he eats, for they impinge on an already sexually differentiated organism with definite sex-linked archetypal potential. Society, through its representatives the parents, may modify, repress or exaggerate patterns of sexual behaviour and consciousness, but what these influences modify, repress or exaggerate are gender predispositions which are already *there.*

Animus and anima: the contrasexual complex

Enough evidence has been presented in the last section to indicate that Jung's generalizations about the differences between the masculine Logos and feminine Eros have a solid foundation in biological fact. But what about the contrasexual archetype and the complex in the personal unconscious to which, in the course of development, it gives rise? The evidence for this, it must be frankly admitted, is less objectively persuasive, more inferential in substance, derived, as it is, from a comparative study of the dreams reported by men and women, from the phenomenology of heterosexual relationships and from characterological observations of Anima-dominated men and Animus-dominated women.

However, if one is willing to entertain Jung's assertion that the individual is constitutionally equipped with an inborn set of psychophysical systems which enable him to meet and deal effectively with the typical events of human life, then it is but a small step to an acceptance of Jung's hypothesis that one of the most crucial of these archetypal systems is that concerned with relating to the opposite sex. Jung's researches left him in no doubt on this matter. Examination of thousands of dreams revealed the presence of figures carrying the archetypal features of the opposite sex to the dreamer, and these figures functioned as part personalities with all the power and influence of autonomous complexes, often being experienced by the individual as mysterious, numinous, and essentially 'other'.

> Every man carries within him the eternal image of the woman, not the image of this or that woman, but a definite feminine image. This image is fundamentally unconscious, an hereditary factor of primordial origin engraved in the living organic system of the man, an imprint or archetype of all the ancestral experiences of the female, a deposit, as it were, of all the impressions ever made by woman. . . . Since this image is unconscious, it is always unconsciously projected upon the person of the beloved, and is one of the chief reasons for passionate attraction or aversion. (CW 17, para. 338)

As a phylogenetically structured system responsible for the instigation, consummation and maintenance of the heterosexual bond, the contrasexual archetype clearly possesses profound implications for the survival of the species as a whole as well as conditioning the most crucial life-experiences of every member of it. At its most basic, the archetype represents the psychic equivalent of the physical contrasexual features present in all men and women (oestrogens and breasts in men, for example, and androgens and the clitoris in women); but it is no inert vestige: it is a dynamic system which plays an indispensable social role in mediating life between the sexes and an equally vital symbolic role in the psychic life of the individual.

Like all archetypes, the contrasexual archetype is actualized through personal experience – in this instance, experience of the significant males and females in one's life. Thus, the Animus is actualized in the first instance through the girl's living experience of her father, and the Anima through the boy's experience of his mother; these first activators of the contrasexual archetype have a profound influence on the phenomenological characteristics it acquires in the personal unconscious of the child, and it persists throughout life. At birth, as we have seen, the Self is largely undifferentiated and 'hermaphroditic', though, even so, a number of sexually related features are apparent. During childhood these features are increasingly accentuated, while those of the opposite sex remain relatively undeveloped:

> in the development of masculine consciousness the feminine side is left behind and so remains in a 'natural state'. The same thing happens in the differentiation of the psychological functions; the so-called inferior function remains behind and, as a result is undifferentiated and unconscious. Therefore, in the man it is usually connected with the likewise unconscious anima. Redemption is achieved by recognizing and integrating these unknown elements of the soul. (Emma Jung, 1957, pp. 57–8)

I would ask the reader to notice this use of the word 'redemption' for we shall return to it later.

Although it is seldom stressed in the Jungian literature, observation would strongly indicate that two of the four Jungian psychic functions

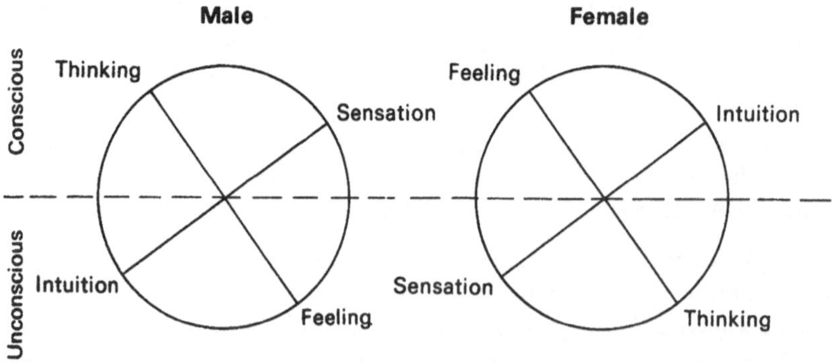

FIGURE 11.6

are characteristic of masculine psychology and two of feminine psychology: thus men are predominantly thinking or sensation types while women tend to be feeling or intuitive types, the opposite characteristics (which are latent in everybody) being associated with the contrasexual complex.

In describing the Animus concept, Jung wrote: 'Woman is compensated by a masculine element and therefore her unconscious has, so to speak, a masculine imprint. . . . The animus corresponds to the paternal Logos, just as the anima corresponds to the maternal Eros.' Not wishing to be too dogmatic about this distinction, he says:

> I use Eros and Logos merely as conceptual aids to describe the fact that woman's consciousness is characterized more by the connective quality of Eros than by the discrimination and cognition associated with Logos. In men, Eros, the function of relationship, is usually less developed than Logos. In women, on the other hand, Eros is an expression of their true nature. (CW 9, pt ii, para. 29)

Jung maintained that whereas the Anima was singular, the Animus was represented by a plurality of figures:

> With regard to the plurality of the animus as distinguished from what we call the 'uni-personality' of the anima, this remarkable fact seems to me to be a correlate of the conscious attitude. The conscious attitude of woman is in general far more exclusively personal than that of man. Her world is made up of fathers and mothers, brothers and sisters, husbands and children. The rest of the world consists likewise of families, who nod to each other but are, in the main, interested essentially in themselves. The man's world is the nation, the state, business concerns, etc. His family is simply a means to an end, one of the foundations of the state, and his wife is not necessarily *the* woman for him (at any rate not as the woman means it when she says 'my man'). The general means more to him than the personal; his world consists of a multitude of co-ordinated factors, whereas her world, outside her husband, terminates in a sort of cosmic mist. A passionate exclusiveness therefore attaches to the man's anima, and an indefinite variety to the woman's animus. Whereas the man has, floating before him, in clear outlines, the significant form of a Circe or a Calypso, the animus is better expressed as a bevy of Flying Dutchmen or unknown wanderers from over the sea, never quite clearly grasped, protean, given to persistent and violent motion. These expressions appear especially in dreams, though in concrete reality they can be famous tenors, boxing champions, or great men in far-away, unknown cities. (CW 7, para. 338)

For what it is worth, my own clinical experience does not accord with Jung's in this particular: the contrasexual image can occur as a plurality in men as well as women. Moreover, women are unquestionably more prone to centre their emotions and phantasies on a single male figure than are men to focus their attentions on a solitary female. The male sexual response is altogether more labile and capricious than the female: women are more faithful *by nature*. That this is biologically determined may be deduced from two pieces of evidence: (1) the great majority of primate societies, human and non-human, show a tendency to promiscuous relationships, but more on the part of males than females; and this would explain the predominance of male polygamy as a practice. The biological explanation of this in terms of nature's profligacy with male semen and her extreme miserliness with female ova has already been examined; and (2) there is an overwhelming tendency to promiscuity among male homosexuals, which contrasts dramatically with the jealous, possessive fidelity demonstrated by lesbians. Inasmuch as the monogamous bond holds firm, it is the female partner who provides most of the cement. The critical factor in lasting heterosexual relationships would seem to be less related to the plurality or singularity of the contrasexual image than to the monotropic insistence of Eros.

Behind the Animus and Anima there lies an archetype of even greater importance – the archetype of sex. Sexuality is better conceived as an archetypal system than as mere 'drive' or 'instinct' in view of its complexity, its universality, its numinosity and its power. The significance of sexuality in personal life extends far beyond the process of reproduction: it begins in infancy and continues to the grave; it is not confined to the sexual act but is manifested in all forms of sexual excitement, whether as heterosexual or homosexual foreplay, masturbation, erotic phantasy, voyeurism, exhibitionism, fetishism, sado-masochism or interest in any kind of pornography. Indeed, reproduction is, in terms of individual gratification, little more than an artefact of sexuality, since people seldom, if ever, mix sexual enjoyment with the conscious intent to produce offspring. Sexuality is every bit as much concerned with pleasure and with bonding as it is with procreation.

That so much of our time is spent in erotic dreams and phantasies attests to the symbolic power of the sexual archetype. So possessed was he by its *numinosum*, that Freud over-generalized the importance of sex, seeing it as the foundation of the human psyche instead of just one important archetype among many. Jungians have eschewed this fallacy, without relegating sex to the status of mere biological necessity. For one Jungian authority, it is a 'symbol for something that relates us to the meaning of our lives, to our striving and longing for the divine', and, as such, is crucial to the individuation process:

> The individuational aspect of sexuality reveals itself most compellingly in the loving, intense encounter between man and woman, in the momentary, ecstatic fusing together in the love act. This most deeply moving of human experiences cannot be grasped as merely biological copulation. This powerful event in which man and woman become one, physically or psychologically, is to be understood as a living symbol of the *mysterium coniunctionis*, the goal of the way of individuation. The sexual union of the King and Queen was considered by the alchemists to be the crowning of their work. Sexual fusion expresses the bridging in us of all the prevailing oppositions and incompatibilities. (Adolf Guggenbuhl-Craig, 1977 p. 91)

Marriage, as a sacred institution 'till death do us part', is to be understood as

> a special path for discovering the soul, as a special form of individuation. One of the essential features of this soteriological pathway is the absence of avenues for escape. Just as the saintly hermits cannot evade themselves, so the married persons cannot avoid their partners. In this partially uplifting, partially tormenting evasionlessness lies the specific character of this path. (p. 41)

But marriage is not the only path to salvation. Acceptance of the biological orientation to human life must not allow the customary course of the life-cycle to become an orthodox tyranny. The human frontal cortex, together with the differentiated ego-consciousness which it permits, renders the human being more free of the archetypal programme than any other animal. We can be much more flexible about which aspects of the programme we live out in reality. Archetypal imperatives are not absolute: experience transforms them into modes compatible with the living circumstances of the individual. Thus, the unmarried man or childless woman is not doomed to a life of emotional sterility or frustration: other archetypal possibilities are always available if they but put themselves in the way of experiencing them. Moreover, the breakdown of sexual taboos makes it increasingly possible for men and women to enjoy attachments and erotic pleasures outside the conventional model of 'married life'. The crucial thing is that they consciously embrace the realities of their situation and actively make use of whatever archetypal opportunities there are. This includes embracing modes of life previously regarded as perverse.

As young children we are all 'polymorphous perverse' in that all forms of sexual experience are 'planned for' and appear as 'partial instincts' in the course of ontogeny. 'Perverse' sexuality is therefore *normal* in the sense that all sexuality exists as potential within the Self. What Judeo-

Christianity taught us to regard with abhorrence as 'perversions' are, in fact, alternative actualizations of the sexual archetype. In the course of 'normal' maturation, potentially 'perverse' partial instincts are repressed or left unactivated on account of the cultural attitudes which prevail at critical periods of the child's development. In view of the variety of 'perverse' elements of which human sexuality is composed, the attainment of 'normality' (Freud's 'genital primacy') must be regarded as a triumph of ontogeny over phylogenetic complexity. Little wonder that many people never make it. Homosexuals are a case in point.

In the past it has been customary to view homosexuality as a form of arrested development, a failure of ontogeny, detrimental to the welfare of the species. Nowadays, this argument is less often encountered, partly because many articulate homosexuals object to it, and partly because it appears increasingly irrelevant in a grossly overpopulated world in which our species is proliferating like an incurable cancer, systematically destroying the natural ecology of the globe. If a nuclear catastrophe should occur, it seems highly probable that it will be the direct result of overpopulation, and the bitter competition for vital resources that overpopulation inevitably brings. In these circumstances, it can be persuasively argued that the more men and women who adopt a homosexual adjustment the better, for a decisive tip of the hetero-homosexual balance in the homosexual direction, far from being detrimental to our species, could help to save it, and all other terrestrial species, from extinction.

From the purely psychological standpoint, the homosexual relationship, like its heterosexual counterpart, is a perfectly valid way of working out the individuation process. At the risk of shocking some readers, I would propose that the same may be said of the sado-masochistic, 'master-slave' relationship. In all such intensely experienced relationships, a person projects on to the partner, and actively *seeks* in him or her, the unactualized or inadequately incarnated archetypal potential (masculine/feminine or dominance/submission components) of the Self. The rich phantasies which are interwoven with the relationship further the symbolic exchanges through which projections are made and withdrawn and, in so doing, promote the individuation process. For both sexes, and especially in adolescence (the period of the 'crush'), a beloved person of the same sex is experienced as a living embodiment of the Self, in much the same way as a beloved person of the opposite sex is experienced as an embodiment of the Animus/Anima. In homosexual love, the partner, as carrier of the Self, is not only perceived as having actualized important Self-potential inaccessible to his lover, but, through the highly charged medium of the relationship, unconsciously assists his lover to bring similar potential to birth in himself. This is the very essence of the 'individuation relationship'. For individuation to occur, marriage and reproduction are not essential, but relationship (attachment) and sexuality are.

However, people, unlike other animals, have a choice between 'inner' and 'outer' individuation. The reason why psychology must not confine itself to the behaviour patterns which characterize certain phases of the life-cycle is that in human beings psychic functions are *more important*. The Self expresses itself in behaviour *and* symbols; it can also express itself in behaviour *or* symbols. What it seeks is expression; what individuation demands is that such expression be achieved in full consciousness. Ultimately, it matters little whether such conscious expression is also acted out in 'behaviour'. Consciousness is the key. Frequently, behaviour and psyche proceed coincidentally and in harmony, but they do not have to; and, what is more, one mode can dominate or even replace the other. Such 'one-sidedness' may result in neurosis or arrested development, but not necessarily so: it can also result in greater personality integration and 'wholeness'. Thus, the majority of men and women feel called upon to marry and have children, but many do not. Are we to regard all unmarried or childless people as sick, as stunted individuates? Some may be, but many are not. The heterosexual bond is not *de rigueur*. There is not only one road to Rome.

Whether or not they end in marriage, all heterosexual relationships are initiated through the influence of the Animus/Anima. The projection can be instantaneous (as in 'love at first sight') or can be more gradually established over weeks or months. A true and lasting bond, however, requires more than sexual interest and mutual unconscious projections: it demands a growing recognition by each partner of the other as a real personality possessing qualities and expectations over and beyond those projected. Most couples experience difficulties in this area; but the strength and viability of their union depends on the extent to which each can forgive the other for those respects in which they *do not* embody the Animus/Anima and on the extent to which each is capable of learning to love and accept the other for being the person they happen to be.

The primacy of the contrasexual complex in mediating sexual relationships explains how it is that the 'reasons' given, for example, by a young woman for falling in love with her history tutor, are, in fact, rationalizations, which her friends, however understanding, may have difficulty in taking at their face value ('What on earth can she see in him?'). The mere use of the idiom 'to *fall* in love' expresses the notion of lost balance and impaired autonomy; it equates the strength of the experience of being attracted to someone with the force of gravity. This sense of being 'taken over' by an irresistible force is typically encountered when the ego comes under the influence of an archetypally based complex.

The autonomous power of the archetype is also vividly apparent in the quarrels which arise between couples. This is particularly true when the complex centred on the archetype is relatively undifferentiated and unconscious. Writing from the man's standpoint, Jung says of the Animus:

> It gives rise to misunderstandings and annoying interpretations in the family circle and among friends. This is because it consists of *opinions* instead of reflections, and by opinions I mean *a priori* assumptions that lay claim to absolute truth. Such assumptions, as every one knows, can be extremely irritating. . . . The 'Father' (i.e., the sum of conventional opinions) always plays a great role in female argumentation. No matter how friendly and obliging a woman's Eros may be, no logic on earth can shake her if she is ridden by the animus. Often the man has the feeling – and he is not altogether wrong – that only seduction or a beating or rape would have the necessary power of persuasion . . . because no man can converse with an animus for five minutes without becoming the victim of his own anima. Anyone who still had enough sense of humour to listen objectively to the ensuing dialogue would be staggered by the vast number of commonplaces, misapplied truisms, clichés from newspapers and novels, shop-soiled platitudes of every description interspersed with vulgar abuse and brain-splitting lack of logic. It is a dialogue which, irrespective of its participants, is repeated millions and millions of times in all the languages of the world and always remains essentially the same. (*CW* 9, pt ii, para. 29)

The problem is one of defective consciousness. Why should it recur so predictably? Why is it that in the great majority of men and women vital psychic components (such as the Animus/Anima, inferior function, and the Shadow) remain predominantly unconscious, with the result that few move along the path of individuation as far as they might? Whitmont's psychic inertia principle provides a partial answer, as does the homeorhetic propensity (Waddington) of the parental complexes. But a more compelling factor is to be found in the Freudian *superego*, the importance of which most Jungians seem to ignore: this inner parental figure and moral judge perpetually strives to censor and 'jail' any aspects of the Self which it has learned through experience may prove unacceptable to significant others and result in the subject being rejected and thrust beyond the pale (the ultimate terror of all social animals). The result is that the contrasexual complex and Shadow components are repressed whenever the superego receives intimations of their presence, and they go on being repressed again and again unless one can have the moral courage to 'have them out' and, eventually, befriend them.

Cultural influences are paramount in superego formation – the parents being in this respect little more than the stooges of society – and patrist societies tend to be particularly tough on the contrasexual complex. Patrism, as has already been noted, goes along with devaluation of the feminine and the exaggeration of such masculine qualities as authority, order and discipline. Patrism dictates that men be men and women be women, that the latter know their place and never try to ape their betters. In these societies, pejorative terms such as 'sissy' and 'tomboy' have a sharp cutting edge, capable of severing all psychic links between the ego and the contrasexual aspect of the Self. Although recent moves in the matrist direction have corrected this repressive tendency to a large extent, it is, nevertheless, an interesting paradox that the women's movement is unwittingly compounding the patrist felony by extolling the virtues of work and ambition while disparaging those of love, caregiving and motherhood: in other words, they are worshipping masculine attributes and condemning feminine ones. Clearly, there are drawbacks in societies which are coercive in their insistence on 'masculine' and 'feminine' ideals, because it leads to 'splitting' and to repression of large and deeply important portions of the Self. Nevertheless, it is crucial that boys become men and girls become women and are clear about their roles and identity. A mature culture would ensure this, while at the same time permitting members of both sexes to acknowledge and integrate the contrasexual aspects of their Selves.

The unfortunate Jungian tendency to overlook the significance of the superego is compounded by a greater perversity in attributing many of its functions to the Animus – e.g. the manner in which the Animus is described as giving rise to dogmatic moral assertions, and as having a penchant for such words as 'must', 'ought', and 'should'. That this confusion has occurred is understandable in that the father, in patrist cultures, is the parent who represents moral authority, and, as a consequence, that it is he who has the pre-eminent influence over the form and character of his daughter's superego as well as her Animus. But this begs the question of the extent to which the father-son relationship affects the development of masculine moral notions and the masculine use of such injunctions as 'ought'. The superego is, as Freud demonstrated, an institution common to the psychic make-up of *both* sexes (though he did regard it as less differentiated and potent in the female), and it can, therefore, be an effective repressor of the Animus no less than the Anima, and act as a serious obstacle to the attainment of psycho-sexual maturity. In fact, it can make heterosexual relationships virtually impossible.

When heterosexual bonds cannot be formed, or fail to last, it is usually due to pathological development of the contrasexual complex. Such pathology is generally the result of unfortunate childhood experiences in relation to the parent of the opposite sex, and it can manifest itself in any of the following ways:

1 An insufficient or one-sided activation of the Animus or Anima results in a quest for the ideal partner 'never seen before.'

2 The Animus or Anima fails to become detached from the parental complex at puberty, with the result that the heterosexual libido remains tied to the parent of the opposite sex.

3 Through an intense identification with the parent of the opposite sex, the ego becomes inflated with the contrasexual archetype and there is a failure to actualize the sexual principle corresponding to the individual's biological gender. The result is either a 'butch', Animus-dominated woman or a weak, Anima-dominated man.

4 Repression of the Animus or Anima under the prohibitive influence of the superego can result in 'flight' from all members and attributes of the opposite sex and a compulsive identification with the members and attributes of one's own. 'Confirmed' bachelors and spinsters are often of this type.

The first manifestation of pathology listed above has already been touched on in earlier chapters, where it was noted that parental deprivation can result in a later inability to form lasting relationships. The psychodynamic explanation of this incapacity lies in the failure of the contrasexual complex to achieve adequate differentiation: maternally deprived boys and paternally deprived girls suffer from atrophy of the Anima and Animus respectively, and consequently lack the psychic organs of heterosexual love.

An agreeable man in his late forties once consulted me complaining of a sense of emotional isolation and a complete inability to form lasting relationships with women, despite a strong heterosexual orientation. In the past he had been through no less than five lengthy analyses with representatives of different analytic schools, but apparently with little benefit. Coming to see me was a last desperate throw.

Unfortunately, I was unable to help him: the history was too disastrous. His mother had died at the moment of his birth, and his childhood was spent in the care of a succession of nannies, hired and fired by his capricious though well-meaning father. As soon as the boy began to form an attachment to a caretaker, she was either dismissed or departed of her own accord. The result was that, out of sheer self-defence, the child became chronically detached and so his Anima never achieved sufficient actualization for him to be able to relate properly to women. Since years of analysis with a very maternal, warm-hearted analyst had not succeeded in awaking his Anima, I saw no reason to believe that I could succeed in this case. That he had persevered with so many therapists for so long was less a function of his confidence in analytic treatment than the expression of a need for a relationship which, unlike those with his childhood caretakers, would last. The only way in which he could escape from his fear of desertion or rejection was by entering into a formal relationship for which he paid regular fees.

In marked contrast to this case, however, too close and enduring an involvement with the parent of the opposite sex can lead to hypertrophic development of the contrasexual complex and a degree of ego-identification with it, especially if the parent of the same sex has been absent during critical periods of childhood, or if the relationship with that parent has been distant or strained. Males of this type tend to be moody, unpredictable, soft and unassertive, while Animus-dominated women are characteristically aggressive, dogmatic, stubborn, moralistic and self-righteous. In its more extreme forms, contrasexual identification can result in transexualism – the compelling desire to renounce all the attributes of one's own sex and adopt those of the other.

Healthy psycho-sexual development, therefore, is primarily a matter of balance between Yin and Yang. With adequate parenting, the Animus or Anima is activated to form a well differentiated complex which, provided it escapes cultural distortion or superego repression, takes its place in the ontogenetic psyche, its influence being benevolent and constructive both in the personality and the sex life of the individual. Inasmuch as a woman is active, energetic and brave, it is evidence of a well-developed Animus, and is no bad thing as long as it does not displace her conscious feminine orientation or sustain itself at the expense of her normal instinctive life. The crucial factor, in Jung's view, was that the Animus should be harmoniously integrated with the rest of the personality and should not become so powerful as to shake the woman's affirmation of her biological identity. It is when the Animus overshadows the conscious personality that we have Hippolyta or Xantippe – the battleaxe who is not only energetic, but ruthless and brutal as well. But in health, both Animus and Anima are dynamic systems which perform a vital homeostatic function in maintaining psychic equilibrium. Each behaves in a manner which is compensatory to the conscious personality, in some measure making good its deficiencies, and seeking to balance any one-sided hypertrophies or exaggerations which may develop.

Creativity and the contrasexual dimension

In no realm of human endeavour is the contrasexual complex more crucial than that of creativity. The achievements of men as prophets, seers, artists and creative thinkers is not entirely attributable to the law of greater variability of masculine talents or to greater masculine powers of perseverance; it is also dependent upon the successful adoption of a receptive attitude to ideas and symbols emerging from normally unconscious regions of the personality. Hence the emphasis on 'gestation' and 'incubation' made by innovative men when they describe their methods of work and the manner by which their major insights came to birth.

> Because the Anima, as the feminine aspect of man, possesses this receptivity and absence of prejudice toward the irrational, she is designated the mediator between conscious and the unconscious. In the creative man, especially, this feminine attitude plays an important role; it is not without cause that we speak of the conception of a work . . . delivering oneself of it, or brooding over it. (Emma Jung, 1957, p. 56)

As we have noted, much Alchemical practice and symbolism is in accord with this insight: the *prima materia* (spermatazoon and ovum) combine in the sealed retort (womb) and by their mutual influence (chromosomal division, cell differentiation, and so on) are transformed into the treasure hard to attain (the miracle of the living child).

As the bridge between the conscious and unconscious personality, the contrasexual complex mediates the relationship between the ego and the Self. For this reason, the development of a conscious relationship with the Animus or Anima is an essential part of any Jungian analysis; and it can have profound and often radical consequences for the analysand. This procedure is not as difficult or mysterious as it may sound, for most men and women are familiar with certain aspects of their contrasexual complex long before they come into analysis: this is because from puberty onwards the majority of people, especially men, enjoy erotic phantasies. Examination of these phantasies reveals that the partners created in imagination have certain well-defined characteristics which recur again and again. It is these characteristics which typify the contrasexual complex of the phantasist.

Jungians encourage their patients to indulge these phantasies, not as an exercise in erotic manipulation, but as a technique for making the contrasexual complex accessible to consciousness. A man will be advised to imagine his erotic partner, but to stop short of subjecting her to his sexual will. Instead, he is invited to grant her freedom to act and speak as she wishes, and to observe and record what happens. As often as not, extremely revealing exchanges ensue between the ego and the Anima, and Jung conceived these dialogues as an indispensable means of furthering the process of Self-actualization. Individuation is advanced by making the Anima conscious because this enables the potential inherent in the archetypal substrate of the complex to be activated, experienced and integrated within the personality as a whole. This can be a long and demanding business. But the rewards are great; and if it is shirked, there is a danger for many patients that the Anima or Animus will remain primitive and predominantly unconscious, a sort of crude alien spirit capable of seizing consciousness from time to time and forcing its victim into modes of behaviour reminiscent of an immature or incompetent member of the opposite sex.

For this technique to succeed, it is essential that the ego exercise humility and restraint. The Anima cannot be bullied into revealing her secrets, for she is autonomous, a 'personality' in her own right, and she demands that we treat her as such – otherwise, as harassed women will, she clams up and refuses to co-operate. This is a hard lesson to learn, and to begin with one makes tactless mistakes. To acknowledge the autonomy of a woman within oneself does not come easily to a man. It contradicts all the assumptions with which one has grown up, namely, that one is an entirely conscious entity with a unitary identity, possessing free will and an absolute right to self-determination. The discovery that there are in fact parts of oneself that function independently of ego-consciousness can come as a nasty shock; and it is not surprising that many people stop short of this realization or, having made it, choose to forget about it for fear of going mad. It requires courage to press on in the teeth of this fear, as Jung himself was to find when he embarked on his own inner quest after his break with Sigmund Freud: 'the insinuations of the anima, the mouthpiece of the unconscious, can utterly destroy a man.' He realized that by taking his phantasies seriously and granting them free rein he was running

> into the same psychic material which is the stuff of psychosis and is found in the insane. This is the fund of unconscious images which fatally confuse the mental patient. But it is also the matrix of a mythopoeitic imagination which has vanished from our rational age. Though such imagination is present everywhere, it is both tabooed and dreaded, so that it even appears to be a risky experiment or a questionable adventure to entrust oneself to the uncertain path that leads into the depths of the unconscious. It is considered the path of error, of equivocation and misunderstanding. I am reminded of Goethe's words: 'Now let me dare to open wide the gate Past which men's steps have never flinching trod.'

At times he feared he was losing his sanity and had to make a conscious effort to reassert his existence in the real world. He would remind himself that he had a wife and children and repeat to himself: 'I have a medical diploma from a Swiss university, I must help my patients, I have a wife and five children, I live at 228 Seestrasse in Kusnacht.' In this manner, he survived: 'In the final analysis the decisive factor is always consciousness, which can understand the manifestations of the unconscious and take up a position towards them' (1963, pp. 212–14).

The effort was unquestionably worth it:

> For decades I always turned to the anima when I felt that my emotional behaviour was disturbed, and that something had been constellated in the unconscious. I would then ask the anima: 'Now what are you up to? What do you see? I should like to know.' After some resistance she regularly produced an image. As soon as the image was there, the unrest or the sense of oppression vanished. The whole energy of these emotions was transformed into interest in and curiosity about the image. I would speak with the anima about the images she communicated to me, for I had to try to understand them as best I could, just like a dream.

'Today,' he wrote towards the end of his life,

> I no longer need these conversations with the anima, for I no longer have such emotions. But if I did have them, I would deal with them in the same way. Today I am directly conscious of the anima's ideas because I have learned to accept the contents of the unconscious and to understand them. I know how I must behave towards the inner images. I can read their meaning directly from my dreams, and therefore no longer need a mediator to communicate them. (1963, p. 212)

Acceptance of the Anima or Animus as an independent reality, and development of the commitment to respect that reality, transforms the figure from a dangerous threat into a familiar ally. The contrasexual attributes then begin to become available to the conscious personality and a significant step has been taken on the way of individuation. A man on good terms with his Anima has Logos complemented by a refined capacity for intimate relationship; a woman in touch with her Animus has Eros nicely tempered with rational purposiveness and intellectual understanding. As Jung's wife wrote of her own experience of this process:

> above all it makes possible the development of a spiritual attitude which sets us free from the limitation and imprisonment of a narrowly personal standpoint . . . to raise ourselves out of our personal troubles to suprapersonal thoughts and feelings, which, by comparison, make our misfortunes seem trivial and unimportant. (1957, p. 40)

It is this integration of 'unknown elements of the soul' that Emma Jung refers to in the passage quoted on page 194 above as 'redemption', and it is undeniably true that men and women who have achieved it in some measure, either in analysis or through the circumstances of their lives, do seem to possess qualities of personal warmth and psychological insight that distinguish them from the ordinary run of people. Jung himself was just such a figure and a good advertisement for the value of his own techniques.

Men who are in close conscious relationship to a well-differentiated Anima tend to be highly creative individuals; very often they have in childhood been deeply loved by a powerfully maternal mother and this has resulted in a sense of being 'special' as well as in the development of a strongly positive mother complex and a state of relative Anima 'inflation'. Men of this type are blessed with much energy and strike their contemporaries as both charismatic and overwhelmingly gifted. Two obvious examples from the theatre are Noel Coward and Ivor Novello; it is possible that William Shakespeare was another. Goethe was certainly like this, and it seems very likely that Jesus Christ was too.

In her book, Emma Jung describes the case of an English author, William Sharp, who wrote under the name of Fiona Macleod. When asked why he wrote under a woman's name, Sharp once replied:

> I can write out of my heart in a way I could not do as William Sharp. . . . This rapt sense of oneness with nature, this cosmic ecstacy and elation, this wayfaring along the extreme verges of the common world, all this is so wrought up with the romance of life that I could not bring myself to expression by my outer self.

To his wife, Sharp wrote: 'More and more absolutely, in one sense, are W.S. and F.M. becoming two persons – often married in mind and one in nature, but often absolutely distinct.' On his birthday each year he would exchange letters with Fiona: he would express the extent of his gratitude to her and she would reply with helpful advice. When writing his books, it was as if Fiona 'took over' and wrote them for him. Sharp affords an interesting example of a man who, quite spontaneously, developed a 'Jungian' attitude to his Anima – though had he been a patient, Jung may have shown some concern as to the degree to which Sharp was at times both inflated by and identified with his Anima, for such individuals can come dangerously near the brink of psychosis, as Jung did himself.

That Jesus of Nazareth was a man much under the influence of a highly differentiated Anima there can be little doubt; his life and teaching were uniquely concerned with the 'Eros' of love and relationship: 'Where two or three are gathered together in my name, there am I in the midst of them.' Though he respected the patriarchal order in society and wished to do nothing to change it ('Render unto Caesar the things which are Caesar's, and unto God the things that are God's'), maintaining, like Jung, that the essential changes were those occurring in men's hearts, he was opposed, nevertheless, to the masculine struggle for dominance and 'status' – something that his disciples did not quite understand:

> He asked them, What was it that ye disputed among yourselves by the way? But they held their peace: for by the way they had disputed among themselves, who should be the greatest. And he sat down, and called the twelve, and saith unto them, If any man desire to be first, the same shall be last, and servant of all. And he took a child, and set him in the midst of them: and when he had taken him in his arms, he said unto them, Whosoever shall receive one of such children in my name, receiveth me: and whosoever shall receive me, receiveth me not, but him that sent me.

These are the words of a man whose Logos and Eros are in splendid harmony. He understood that a man's life, unredeemed by the power of *agape* was a souless charade – in St Paul's phrase, a 'sounding brass or tinkling cymbal'.

Again like Jung, Jesus was deeply committed to the individuation quest, which he conceived as the coming of the Kingdom of God:

> When he was demanded of the Pharisees, when the Kingdom of God should come, he answered them and said, The Kingdom of God cometh not with observation: neither shall they say, Lo here! or, Lo there!, for, behold, the Kingdom of God is within you.

The goal is the Self, individuation is the way, and redemption by the 'spirit' (Anima/Animus) is the means. 'Verily, verily, I say unto thee, Except a man be born of water and the Spirit, he cannot enter into the Kingdom of God.' But being autonomous, as Jung discovered, it cannot be bidden: we cannot bend the spirit to our will, it is as free as air: 'The wind bloweth where it listeth, and men heareth the sound thereof, but cannot tell whence it cometh, or whither it goeth: so is everyone that is born of the spirit.'

One cannot command the Anima, or conjure her, therefore, only approach her respectfully and ask for help. If one attends her in the right manner, she will respond abundantly: 'Ask, and it shall be given you; seek and ye shall find; knock and it shall be opened unto you: for everyone that asketh receiveth; and he that seeketh findeth; and to him that knocketh it shall be opened.' The whole of the Sermon on the Mount is a testament to the power of psychic homeostasis and enantiodromia: 'Blessed are the poor in spirit: for theirs is the Kingdom of Heaven.' Perception of the need is the clue to its fulfilment.

However, the journey is not to be undertaken lightly, for it entails sacrificing the old ego position; one must 'die' to one's identity with the masculine side of the Self and be 'born again' through the redeeming power of the Anima: 'Whosoever will save his life shall lose it: but whosoever will lose his life for my sake, the same shall save it. For what is a man advantaged, if he gain the whole world and lose himself, or be cast away.'

But once in, the commitment must be total; there can be no going back: 'No man, having put his hand to the plough, and looking back, is fit for the Kingdom of God.' Ultimately, nothing else matters – career, status, success, the bubble reputation – 'Lay not up for yourselves treasures upon earth'. Only 'treasures in heaven' (the Self) and realization of the Kingdom of God (individuation) are worth the labour. It is not what we achieve in the world, but what we actualize in ourselves that is the true test of whether or not we may truly be said to have *lived.*

· 12 ·

Shadow: the archetypal enemy

The impact of Christ's Anima on the Western world was so impressive that to this day, nearly two thousand years after his death, not one of us is untouched by it. The great gift that it brought to our civilization was a living witness to the power of love. But, based as it was on an Old Testament morality, the Christian injunction to 'love one another' in the spirit (Anima) of Christ came to be linked with an imperative to repress those propensities in our nature which were thought inimical to spiritual love, namely, *sex* and *aggression*. Moreover, the division of the Godhead into two morally opposed principles – the divine and the satanic – was a direct incitement to all Christians to extol the one and eschew the other, so that, with time, the divided Godhead became incarnated in the divided Self. This historic split between Good and Evil still profoundly conditions our lives, despite the contemporary decline in Christian conviction, for it represents a cultural actualization of the archetypal need to dichotomize.

Man has always distinguished 'bad' from 'good' – as he has distinguished enemy from friend and strange from familiar – because as a social mammal he is programmed to do so. What Judeo-Christianity has done is to provide him with the moral data for the programme to work on. We enter life equipped with the neurological substrate for superego formation (Dr David Galin's views on the possible neurophysiological mechanism involved will be discussed in the next chapter); our parents activate this system and shape the ethical complex which results in the light of their own upbringing, religious beliefs, moral standards, and so on.

It seems increasingly probable, in view of Bowlby's work, that the impetus to effective superego development is not, as Freud believed, fear of being castrated by father as a reprisal for entertaining incestuous desires, but fear of being *abandoned* by mother for being unacceptable. The horrendous prospect of being totally rejected because of some partial revelation of the Self is at the bottom of all feelings of guilt, all desire for punishment, and all longings for atonement and reconciliation.

As a defence against the catastrophe of abandonment, the superego is established as an inner watchdog whose function is to monitor our behaviour so as to ensure relative conformity to the values of the culture into which we happen to have been born. If this were not so, anarchy would be the inevitable result; individually we should all be aggressive psychopaths, incapable of co-operation and mutual trust, and the species would probably never have come into existence in the first place. The superego is, therefore, the bedrock of character and culture; it is the psychic organ that makes society possible.

The personal price we pay for acquiring a superego is a serious loss of freedom for the Self; for this inner policeman bugs the lines of communication along the ego-Self axis, and, when he hears anything he deems disreputable, dangerous or subversive, he intervenes to make us feel guilty and, not infrequently, he cuts the wires. Thus, the very milieu that makes actualization of the Self possible also demands that certain components of the Self remain unactualized in the unconscious or be actively repressed there. In our own culture these 'unacceptable' elements have been traditionally stigmatized as man's 'animal nature' or 'the beast within'; Jung called them, collectively the *Shadow*.

To equate the Shadow with the animal in us is justified inasmuch as it relates to neuropsychic functions of considerable phylogenetic antiquity; but inasmuch as the term 'animal' carries a pejorative meaning it is a gross slander on the beasts of creation. For the truth is, when we face up to it, that we are far more 'beastly' than they. As Anthony Storr says in the introduction to his book on *Human Aggression* (1968):

> The sombre fact is that we are the cruellest and most ruthless species that has ever walked the earth; and that, although we may recoil in horror when we read in newspaper or history book of the atrocities committed by man upon man, we know in our hearts that each one of us harbours within himself those same savage impulses which lead to murder, to torture and to war. (p. 9)

In the course of discussing these issues in her admirable *Beast and Man* (1979), the philosopher Mary Midgley draws attention to the fiendish medieval practice of flaying alive captured wolves as punishment for their 'wickedness'; yet, careful ethological studies have established that wolves are

> by human standards, paragons of steadiness and good conduct. They pair for life, they are faithful and affectionate spouses and parents, they show great loyalty to their pack and great courage and persistence in the face of difficulties, they carefully respect one

> another's territories, keep their dens clean, and extremely seldom kill anything that they do not need for dinner. If they fight with another wolf, the encounter normally ends with submission. They have an inhibition about killing the suppliant and about attacking females and cubs. They have also, like all social animals, a fairly elaborate etiquette, including subtly varied ceremonies of greeting and reassurance, by which friendship is strengthened, cooperation achieved, and the wheels of social life generally oiled. (p. 26)

Certainly, it would never occur to a wolf, if he cornered a human being, to incite the pack to skin him alive with all manner of hideous refinements in retaliation for all the wolves men kill. Nor would it occur to him to blind 15,000 Bulgarian captives as did Basil II in 1014; boil Turkish children alive, as did the twelfth century Greeks of Adramyttium; strap mutineers across the mouths of cannon, as did the British in India; or send six million Jews to the gas chambers.

That we, as human beings, are capable of perpetuating such horrendous acts cannot be blamed on our 'animal nature' because animals never do such things. On the contrary, the cause clearly resides in our own 'human' nature and the greatly increased capacity for ingenious evil possessed by our enlarged and much vaunted brains. The propensity for cruel, obscene and brutal acts is in all of us; that it is usually not much in evidence in 'polite society' is due to the supervision of the superego, which insists that it be kept hidden and under control, locked away in the Shadow. But if we are honest with ourselves, we know that it is there. And the fear that it might somehow 'get out' is one of the oldest fears to haunt mankind.

The phenomenology of the Shadow in history and literature*

Fear of 'the fall' into iniquity has been expressed throughout the history of Christendom as terror of being 'possessed' by the powers of darkness. Stories of possession have always compelled fascination and horror, Bram Stoker's *Count Dracula* being but a recent instance of this genre. Tales of vampires and werewolves have probably always been with us.

Perhaps the most famous example of possession is provided by the legend of Faust, who, bored with his virtuous academic existence, enters into a compact with the devil. Faust's problem would have been plain enough to a Jungian analyst, had the learned doctor been in a position to go to Zurich instead of consulting Mephistopheles. He was clearly suffering from a mid-life crisis. His single-minded pursuit of knowledge

* For a more detailed and challenging treatment of these themes, see *Total Man* by S. Gooch (Penguin, 1972), to which I am much indebted.

had led to a one-sided and over-intellectualized development of his personality, with far too much Self-potential unlived and 'locked away' in the unconscious. As usually happens in such cases, the repressed psychic energy demands attention. Unfortunately, Faust does not indulge in a patient self-analysis, holding dialogues with the figures arising from the unconscious in an effort to assimilate the Shadow, as any Jungian would advise; instead, he allows himself 'to fall into it' and be possessed.

The trouble is that like most patients in his situation (particularly thinking types) Faust believes that the answer to his problem must lie in more of the same thing, in a more determined perseveration of the old neurotic pattern (i.e. he must acquire still more *knowledge*). Like Dr Jekyll, another intellectual bachelor with a similar problem, he is intrigued by the numinosity of the Shadow when it 'personates' and, sacrificing his ego standpoint, he falls under its spell. As a result, it is all up with both of them and the outcome is the sort of thing that all analysts dread: Faust becomes a drunk and a libertine while Jekyll turns into the monstrous Mr Hyde.

Our fascination with Faust and Mephisto and Jekyll and Hyde derives from the archetypal nature of the problem they crystallize. In a sense, both Faust and Jekyll are heroes because they dare to do what most of us shirk: we prefer to behave like Dorian Gray, putting on an innocent face (Persona) for the world, keeping our evil qualities hidden in the hope that no one will discover their existence; we entertain thoughts of 'losing' the Shadow, renouncing our moral duality, atoning for the sin of Adam, and, once more At One with God, re-entering the Garden of Eden. We invent Utopia, El Dorado or Shangri-la, where evil is unknown, and we take comfort in Marxist or Rousseauesque phantasies that evil resides not in our nature but in the 'corrupt' society that everywhere holds us in chains. But change the nature of society and the evil will disappear never to return.

The stories of Jekyll and Faust, like the Biblical story of Adam's fall, are cautionary tales that bring us down to earth and back to the eternal reality of our own evil. All three are variations on the same archetypal theme: a man, bored with his circumstances, decides to ignore the prohibitions of the superego in order to liberate the Shadow, encounter the Anima, 'know her' and *live*. All go too far: they commit *hubris*. And *nemesis* is the inexorable result. 'The wages of sin is death.'

The anxiety which haunts all such stories is not so much a fear of being caught as fear that the evil side will get out of control. The plots of science fiction are designed to create the same unease, as indeed was Mary Shelley's *Frankenstein*, the prototype of them all. That this is a universal anxiety of mankind was understood by Freud, as may be gathered from his account of the phenomenon in *Civilization and Its Discontents*. Because of the time and circumstances in which he lived (middle-class Vienna at the end of the nineteenth century), Freud believed that the repressed evil that men and women feared was entirely sexual. His systematic investigation of this aspect of the Shadow, combined with the coincidental decline in the power of the Judeo-Christian superego, did much to purge our culture of its erotic demons, enabling many previously repressed components of the Shadow to be integrated within the total personality of individual men and women without forcing them to suffer the concomitant guilt which would certainly have afflicted earlier generations. This affords an impressive example on a collective scale of the therapeutic value attributed by Jung to the analytic process of recognizing and integrating components of the Shadow.

However, an aspect of the Shadow that still remains to be exorcised – as powerful as sexual lust but far more disastrous in its consequences – is the lust for power and destruction. That Freud should so long have ignored this component, in spite of witnessing the First World War and the subsequent rise of fascism, is, to say the least, surprising. One suspects that it had much to do with his determination to make his sexual theory the foundation of psychoanalysis. ('My dear Jung, promise me never to abandon the sexual theory. That is the most essential thing of all. You see, we must make a dogma of it an unshakable bulwark' (1963, p. 173)). Anthony Storr makes the interesting suggestion that it may also have been due to Freud's ill-feeling over the defection of Alfred Adler, who had pulled out of the psychoanalytic movement precisely because of his conviction that the drive for power played a more important role in human psychopathology than the desire for sex.

The task of confronting the brutal, destructive elements of the Shadow has become in the twentieth century the inescapable destiny of our species: if we fail, we cannot hope to survive. With good cause this has become our 'universal anxiety'. It is the Shadow problem of our time. 'We might just be in time to stop the apocalypse,' declares Konrad Lorenz. 'But it will be touch and go' (Nisbett, 1976. p. 90).

At this very moment in the history of mankind, evolution has put us on the spot. If we are not to annihilate ourselves and most other species on the face of the earth, then ontogeny must triumph over phylogeny. There is an urgent *biological* imperative to make the Shadow conscious. The moral burden of this immense task is greater than any previous generation could have even conceived: the destiny of the planet and our entire solar system (since we now know that we are the only sentient beings in it) is in our hands. Alone among the great psychologists of our epoch, Jung provided a conceptual model which might help to make this ontological triumph possible. In the Shadow concept he synthesized the work of Adler and Freud, and in his demonstration of the actualizing propensities of the Self he transcended them. Only by coming consciously to terms with our *nature* – and in particular with the nature of the Shadow – can we hope to avert total catastrophe.

The Shadow archetype

It would be misleading to conceive of the Shadow as a clearly defined archetype. In Jungian writings the concept is shrouded in confusion, and the more one reads about it, the more one is left with the impression that 'the Shadow' is a portmanteau term which has been used to accommodate all those aspects of the Self which are not evident in the conscious personality. Jung himself sometimes evinced exasperation with attempts to clarify the concept: 'This is all nonsense!' he once exclaimed after a long discussion on the subject. 'The Shadow is simply the whole unconscious' (von Franz, 1974). One cannot fail to be ambivalent about this part of the human psyche because, inevitably, it inheres all that is worst and best in mankind. It is usually the first complex to 'personate' in an analysis since it contains so much material relating to the patient's neurosis as well as much potential necessary for his cure.

In dreams the Shadow appears as a 'shady' character of dubious integrity, possessing the same sex as the dreamer and displaying characteristics customarily regarded by him as disreputable and 'inferior'. This figure may appear in different forms in different dreams, but common attributes are those of the burglar, pimp or con man. It is an almost universal finding amongst European patients, with sombre implications for harmonious race relations, that the Shadow often appears in their dreams in the form of a dark-skinned individual of a type which, whatever the liberal professions of the dreamer, is assumed by the collective to be of 'inferior' race. On the basis of this finding, it is possible to understand much racial prejudice in terms of Shadow-projection on to members of the group against which discrimination is displayed.

There are two relatively simple techniques which can be employed if one wishes to discover the main features of a person's Shadow complex. If he should happen to possess overt racial prejudices, it is sufficient to ask him what it is about the people of the race in question that he dislikes. Common responses are that they are untrustworthy, sexually promiscuous or perverse, morally delinquent, potentially criminal, dirty in their personal habits, violent, primitive, subversive, and so on. If he should deny all racial prejudice, then one may invite him, as Whitmont suggests, to participate in a 'parlour game' and discourse freely on the subject 'The Kind of Person that I Cannot Stand'. Within but a few minutes one has invariably elicited some revealing material.

The ease with which the Shadow can be unconsciously projected is the feature which makes its confrontation and assimilation most difficult: 'I didn't want to hit him, he *made* me do it.' Although, as Jung says, 'with insight and good will, the shadow can to some extent be assimilated into the conscious personality, experience shows that there are certain features which offer the most obstinate resistance to moral control.' These are the elements which have been projected: with these emotionally charged components

> both insight and good will are unavailing because the cause of the emotion appears to lie, beyond all possibility of doubt, in the *other person* [Jung's italics]. No matter how obvious it may be to the neutral observer that it is a matter of projections, there is little hope that the subject will perceive this himself. (*CW* 9, pt II, para. 16)

We much prefer to entertain idealized images of ourselves rather than acknowledge our personal weakness and guilt. It is much easier to blame others for our own shortcomings, particularly if we can persuade ourselves that the blame is deserved. But as Jung comments: 'One does not become enlightened by imagining figures of light, but by making the darkness conscious. The latter procedure, however, is disagreeable and therefore not popular.' (*CW* 13, para. 335). Shadow projection is an intractable vice of our species: it is at the bottom of all internecine strife and suspicion, all pogroms and wars.

However, inasmuch as the Shadow also incorporates aspects of the Self lying dormant and unused, it clearly has positive therapeutic implications. Moreover, much Self-potential that Judeo-Christian parents traditionally regarded as unacceptable is, from the biological standpoint, morally neutral, but has nevertheless been repressed into the Shadow through parental and pedagogic insistence. The repression of momentarily conscious and potentially positive aspects of the Self has, in fact, been symbolized in Christian mythology in the notion of the devil being a fallen angel.

In whichever culture a child grows up, it is usual, provided that he has been adequately parented, for him to identify his conscious personality with whatever his group holds to be 'Good' and for his Shadow complex to become the repository of all that is 'Bad'. Exceptions, however, do occur. A child whose parents are criminals, for example, will develop a superego possessing some characteristics which society regards as 'Bad' while his Shadow will incorporate unfulfilled capacities which society would deem 'Good'. As Edwin Muir says: 'The unfulfilled desires of the virtuous are evil; the unfulfilled desires of the vicious are good.' But it is never quite as simple as that. However criminal the parents are in legal terms, provided that they have been loving and present throughout the individual's childhood, they will succeed in actualizing much of the archetypal programme in the usual mannner, thus rendering him capable of affection and loyalty to people whom he recognizes as his own kind. Honour exists, after all, even among thieves.

But whether our parents were morally good, bad, or indifferent, the problem of dealing with the Shadow exists for each and every one of us – particularly if we care that our children should survive to bring up another generation. The only alternative to global catastrophe can be a collective refusal to project Shadow qualities on to social systems, political institutions and each other, and an acceptance of full moral responsibility for them in ourselves.

> Such an experience brings about an inner transformation, and this is infinitely more important than political and social reforms which are all valueless in the hands of people who are not at one with themselves. This is a truth which we are forever forgetting, because our eyes are fascinated by the conditions around us and riveted on them instead of examining our own heart and conscience. Every demagogue exploits this human weakness when he points with the greatest possible outcry to all the things that are wrong in the outside world. But the principle and indeed the only thing that is wrong with the world is man. (CW 10, para. 441)

Just as Jung regarded the Shadow complex as having an archetypal basis (the archetype of Evil, Satan, the Enemy, etc.), so he believed that the *moral complex* (the Freudian superego) was universally present and had certain features common to all members of the species. In this he was close to von Monakow's (1950) concept of a 'biological conscience' or *syneidesis* whose function is to secure optimal security and adaptation and to promote striving towards wholeness. Whether or not one accepts von Monakow's hypothesis, it seems extremely likely in such a highly sophisticated social animal as man, with such a long primate history, that the moral complex formed by each individual should have a phylogenetic basis. One would anticipate that an archetypal system of such evolutionary importance would find expression in moral attitudes which transcend culture, place and time. Anthropology has established that is indeed the case. The incest taboo, for example, is apparently a universal phenomenon in human communities, as are ideas that there is a fundamental distinction between murder and killing in warfare, that parents are obligated to their children, that it is wrong to seize your neighbour's property or his wife, and so on. Occasional communities may be found where some of the universal moral imperatives seem not to operate, but the existence of such aberrant groups affords no stronger argument against an archetypal foundation for the superego than does the existence of the Tchambuli refute the argument that sexual dimorphism is biologically based. It is probable that part of our innate equipment is a *moral tropism* – that just as we are programmed to approach familiar figures and objects and avoid strange ones, so are we also programmed to espouse 'Good' values and eschew 'Bad' ones. The very existence, not to say survival, of a human community demands that individuals coming into it be phylogenetically prepared to develop an appropriate moral sense and to experience guilt when that sense is offended. That the moral complex formed by members of different communities should show culture-related peculiarities is not surprising: the critical factor is the way in which members of all human communities learn rapidly to distinguish between 'right' and 'wrong' and display an impressive degree of agreement on the kinds of behaviour to be included in each category. The Ten Commandments not only describe the main features of the Judeo-Christian superego but are, when broadly interpreted, a pretty good approximation to the archetypal moral sensibility of mankind.

It is, of course, inevitable that the forms in which the moral sense is actualized will embody significant differences from culture to culture. Some will suppress adultery more severely than others; likewise homosexuality, incest and overt expressions of aggressive intent. The ecological circumstances of the culture, the relative preponderance of patrist or matrist influences, and so on, will clearly have their impact on the nature and severity of the moral complex formed. Thus the Arapesh superego tolerates sexuality but inhibits aggression, while the Dobuan superego inhibits sex but permits aggression. The Christian superego has traditionally been strict in its condemnation of both. But, whatever emphasis a culture may place on each of its repertory of moral prohibitions, it is a universal characteristic of human cultures that such prohibitions exist. It follows, therefore, that guilt, a subjective experience with immense collective implications, must have a long evolutionary history: for it has clearly played a vital role in the biological success of our species by acting as a powerful inducement to the maintenance of social cohesion. Moreover, by placing moral canons firmly in the realm of the sacred, pre-industrial societies ensured their sanctification, established their absolute authority and heightened the sense of remorse experienced by sinners so misguided as to break them.

Thus, religions are like other biological phenomena: they evolve in directions which enhance the welfare of those who have them. Elementary religions give way to more sophisticated ones through a sort of cultural Darwinism: those which promote survival gain adherents and grow; less successful religions lose adherents and disappear. The anthropologist Anthony Wallace has estimated that we have in the course of our evolution produced somewhere in the region of a hundred thousand religions of one sort or another.

In all cases their function has been broadly the same:

1 *Mythological-explanatory*: religion provides believers with an explanatory system which is both coherent and comprehensive: it explains how things began, how we came to assume our special place in the world. Usually the explanations given – simple or complex, according to the degree of sophistication attained by the culture and its people – are a set of variations on the archetypal theme of struggle between opposing forces: supernatural heroes or demi-gods war with one another for

dominion over the world and mankind and apportion the spoils between them. The struggle is often conceived as perpetual: it will go on till the end of time. But more advanced mythologies entertain the notion of the apocalypse and the millennium: they prophesy that one day the struggle will end, not in nothingness, but in the creation of a new order in which all opposites will be reconciled and all conflicts cease.

2 *Sanctification of the social and ethical code*: biologically, this is the most crucial function of religion. Not only does it ensure group cohesion but provides the justification, the means and the motive to induce individual members of the group to sacrifice their narrow self-interests to the wider interests of the community as a whole. Religion demands (and traditionally obtained) commitment and consecration to God, tribe and territory. This clearly does more than strengthen the cohesion of the group: it increases the resolve of its members to serve the group and, if called upon to do so, to die for it. As long as a religion is able to perform this function it will promote the survival of the group which adheres to it.

3 *Ritual*: ritual is the method by which sanctification is prescribed and maintained. Ritual, as Durkheim insisted, rejuvenates and reaffirms the morals and beliefs of the collective. It also provides reassurance and a sense of effectiveness in a capricious world through the use of sympathetic magic: ritual dances and ceremonies are ordained which, when properly performed, will guarantee fertility, success in the hunt, victory in battle, preservation from natural disasters and enemies, the regular recurrence of rain, and so on. Rain dances, anticipatory hunting and battle dances, etc., all in a sense resemble the famous 'waggle dance' of the honey bee (which actually mimes the distance and direction to be flown in order to reach a newly discovered source of food) – but with the added dimensions of belief and autosuggestion: the conviction that miming and wishing *combined* will make what is wanted come true. It is this aspect of religion which has most excited the condescension of rationalists, who have unconsciously replaced it with a mythology of their own – the myth of progress – the belief that the advance of science will bring nature so completely under our control that we shall no longer have to resort to religion, superstition or magic.

4 *Spiritual*: in the most advanced cultures, this has been regarded as the most exalted function of religion – the perception of a transcendent meaning, the sense of participating in a higher purpose soaring far above the mundane preoccupations of the purely personal ego, the experience of the numinosum, the feeling of awe, wonder and *participation mystique* in the order of nature and the Great Dance of the universe.

That religion should possess such critical importance for the survival of populations would indicate that it has an archetypal basis in the nature of our species. Of this Jung was in no doubt: 'The idea of the moral order and of God belong to the ineradicable substrate of the human soul' (*CW* 8, para. 528). Indeed, the very universality of religious phenomena, combined with the unquestioning way in which the great majority of individuals accept and retain the beliefs and mores of the culture into which they are born, suggests the existence of an innate mechanism far more extensive in its psychosocial implications than a mere imperative to distinguish between 'right' and 'wrong'.

Belief as an open-ended system

In all societies moral values are part of a much wider system of customs, beliefs and attitudes all of which, traditionally, have born the stamp of sacred authenticity. It is not just a moral sense that we are programmed to acquire, but a whole complex of religious, mythological, political and social *rules*. It may well be that the spur that encourages us to learn and conform to these rules is fear of rejection and abandonment, but such sanctions merely serve to confirm an imperative already present in the genome – a phylogenetic instruction *to learn the rules*.

This innately determined 'learning rule' functions as an open-ended system like Chomsky's language-acquisition device (p. 35): it is a neurophysiologically based complex primed to be programmed with the religious/mythological/moral 'vocabulary' of the culture. Thus, every child is born with the built-in assumption that his community will possess not only a language which he will quickly pick up, but also an inter-related system of beliefs and values which he must acquire and conform to. The survival value of such a 'rule-acquisition device' is evident. All societies codify themselves; and their success and continuity depends on the readiness of new members to learn the code. The alternative is social anarchy and a collective incapacity for competition or defence. If societies fail to codify themselves efficiently, therefore, or lose faith in their doctrines, they are gravely at risk. For in addition to the social tension that this lack of conviction creates, parents no longer know how to bring up their children, and their children, in turn, fail to actualize the religious and ethical potential of the Self.

History teaches that civilizations which lose faith in their gods normally crumble into barbarism and a protracted dark age, which endures until such time as a new culture arises or is imposed. It could be that a similar fate awaits us – or worse; for no previous period of decline and fall has had to contemplate the possibility of total extermination. The barbarism which succeeds cultural disintegration is not necessarily imposed from without: it arises from within, since the abandonment of civilized values exposes us collectively to possession by the worst elements of the Shadow. Liberated of all the cultural constraints which have evolved historically to contain him, the barbarian bursts out of his 'underground prison' like Jung's teutonic 'blond beast' (p. 122) and, ripping apart what remains of the ethical social fabric, 'takes over' in order to gratify his own ego-centred lusts and greed.

The barbarian is one whose ethical complex has failed to mature: he has not 'learned the rules' (because his 'culture', if he may be said to possess one, has few rules to learn) and, as a consequence, moral distinctions do not concern him. His personality remains unpolarized between Persona and Shadow. For such a man, integration of the Shadow – the beginning of true moral responsibility – is not possible because he *is* his Shadow and has no conscious standpoint from which to begin its integration. If one is to come to terms with the Shadow, a conscious orientation with a firm ethical foundation is indispensable; otherwise Dr Jekyll becomesMr Hyde. Those whose moral priorities are less than clear should not flirt with the Shadow, for 'possession' is the likely result, whence little can preserve them from the slide into barbarism.

During the long healthy phase in the life-cycle of cultures, however, barbarism is no problem, for the ethical code is both clear and sacred: the vast majority of human beings who have ever inhabited this planet have been blessed with the moral security which comes of absolute religious conviction. Barbarism is an aberration, an artefact of cultural decay, a regrettable by-product of the natural cycle governing the life of communities. For the greater part of their history all established societies meet the archetypal needs of the individuals born into them: they provide the explanatory system that the rule-learning device demands. When we learn about other societies, some of their customs – female circumcision, for example – may be objectionable to us because we have acquired different beliefs, but to the members of those societies which practise them they are natural and inevitable: they represent the way – the only conceivable way – that these things are done. They are as the gods have decreed. To label such practices as 'barbaric' is a misapplication of the term because they are the ritualized expression of an integrated culture: barbarism knows no ritual, its impulsive savagery acknowledges no rules.

The existence of an archetypal imperative to learn the rules would account for the ease with which human beings can be indoctrinated and for the readiness with which they accept – especially in childhood – the 'explanations' which they are given. The ready openness of the archetypal system determining the acquisition of belief has been recognized by educators in all ages who have insisted that indoctrination of the young should begin early: the Jesuits, for example, knew that provided they had sole charge of a child's education up to his seventh birthday it was enough to ensure his firm adherence to the Catholic Church for life.

Whether the explanatory system enshrined in a mythology has a theological basis or not matters little in the short term provided that it is *believed* by most adult members of the population and transmitted to the children, who then grow up believing it to be self-evidently true. In fact, the history of the twentieth century can be understood as a protracted conflict between rival mythologies. Hitler's bloody evocation of the Wotan myth results in mortal combat between National Socialism and the combined forces of Judeo-Christianity, Capitalism and Marxism; with the defeat of fascism, Marxism ranges itself against its former allies and the struggle resumes in the name of the Millennium and in the belief that the Class War (a secular version of the Holy War) between 'Good' workers and 'Bad' bourgeoisie will result in the apocalyptic triumph of the proletariat and the transformation of the cruel old order into the Utopian new, where all repression will cease, all conflict end, and every man, woman and child be free, happy and at peace. The uncomfortable fact that Marxism has indeed triumphed over half the globe and has nowhere fulfilled the prophesied bliss of the Millennium is no more of an embarrassment to true believing Marxists than is the failure of Jesus to achieve his second coming to Christians. One day it will happen. Two thousand years of waiting does not deter the devout.

> The perception of history as an inevitable class struggle proceeding to the emergence of a lightly governed egalitarian society with production in the hands of the workers is supposed to be based on an understanding of the subterranean forces of pure economic process. In fact, it is equally based on an inaccurate interpretation of human nature. Marx, Engels, and all the other disciples and deviationists after them, however sophisticated, have operated on a set of larger hidden premises about the deeper desires of human beings and the extent to which human behaviour can be molded by social environments. These premises have never been tested. To the extent that they can be made explicit, they are inadequate or simply wrong. They have become the hidden wards of the historicist dogma they were supposed to generate. (Wilson, 1978, pp. 190–1)

It is because of this fundamental flaw that Marxism is now on the defensive, much in the same way as Christianity has been on the defensive because of naive and out-of-date theological views on biology, geology and astronomy. Hence the passionate opposition to human ethology and sociobiology expressed by Marxist psychologists and sociologists who are mythologically committed to the belief that human nature is unstructured and that all human behaviour arises from conditioning by social agencies. Their 'explanatory system' will not permit them to accept that anything exists in the human psyche that cannot be harnessed to the service of the state. When confronted with evidence which suggests that archetypal structures function as the basis of human experience, they block up their ears and drum their heels, insisting that human nature cannot exist and that it is no fit subject for empirical inquiry. As Wilson himself has found to his cost, some academics argue that merely to discuss the subject is dangerous and firmly to be discouraged, while the more hot-headed of their students have branded all ethologists and sociobiologists as 'fascists' and passed motions with the aim of banning them from presenting their findings. Their behaviour puts one in mind of the medieval Church's attitude to Galileo and Copernicus.

However, Wilson, no less than the Marxists, is himself in the grip of a mythology: he is a committed reductionist and scientific materialist. Prophesying the death of theology, he argues that biology can 'explain' religion: 'sociobiology can account for the very origin of mythology by the principle of natural selection acting on the genetically evolving material structure of the human brain.' He goes on: 'If this interpretation is correct, the final decisive edge enjoyed by scientific materialism will come from its capacity to explain traditional religion, its chief competitor, as a wholly material phenomenon' (p. 192). But in comparison with religion, Wilson admits that scientific materialism is at a disadvantage: 'the spiritual weakness of scientific materialism,' he says, is that it can claim no 'primal source of power.'

This argument betrays not so much the spiritual weakness of scientific materialism as the psychic impoverishment of the purely mechanistic view; for Wilson fails to recognize that the 'primal source of power' lies not in religion, but in ourselves. However scientifically sophisticated they become, men will go on creating myths and religions because it is in the nature of their whole approach to reality to do so. There is no fundamental incompatibility between the religio-mythological approach and the scientific approach: both are means of apprehending the *Umwelt.* In the course of a lifetime, every individual accomplishes his own 'explanatory system', elaborates his own detailed variations on universal symbols and themes, makes his own commitment to the group which broadly shares his view of things, and accepts with his fellow members a mythologized interpretation of their *special* significance in comparison with other groups, as well as subscribing to those beliefs and values which the group consensus holds 'sacred'.

Science may continue to dismantle the ancient myths of our culture, but it can never entirely exorcise God from the story of creation. God as Will and First Cause, the Original Detonator of the Big Bang, He who set the whole universe in motion and is immanent in all its parts, the God of 'process theology', the God who as *imago Dei* is built into the Self.

Biology, morality and aggression

Morality, like religion, has an evolutionary history. If man is a moral creature, it is because all social mammals are moral creatures. This is not to say that they always behave morally, but that, by nature, they have the capacity to behave morally. The nineteenth-century philosopher, Herbert Spencer, believed that this moral propensity was expressed through two fundamentally different modes of functioning – that characterizing conduct with familiars (which he called 'the mode of amity') and that characterizing conduct with strangers (which he termed 'the code of enmity'). In his book *The Principles of Ethics*, he wrote:

> Rude tribes and civilized societies have had continually to carry on an external self-defence and internal co-operation, external antagonism and internal friendship. Hence their members have acquired two different sets of sentiments and ideas adjusted to those two kinds of activity. . . . As the ethics of enmity and the ethics of amity arise in connection with internal and external conditions respectively, and have to be simultaneously entertained, there is formed an assemblage of utterly inconsistent sentiments and ideas. (Quoted by Ardrey, 1961, p. 187)

The 'dual nature' of man, which has absorbed theologians no less than moral philosophers, is not, in fact, a peculiarly human phenomenon: all social animals distinguish between friend and foe, and modify their behaviour accordingly. Humans are not alone in displaying loyalty, love and altruism to their kith and kin and in being devious, hostile and destructive to those whom they perceive as potential enemies. Indeed, so universal is the tendency to discriminate against the 'out-group' in favour of the 'in-group' that Lorenz has argued that only animals capable of aggression towards their own kind are also capable of affection. It seems that making friends proceeds *pari passu* with making enemies. Both are opposite facets of the same innate capacity – the capacity for social behaviour. And both possess survival value for the species.

That aggression should be regarded as an essential part of our biological equipment – like pain, hunger, thirst or sex – is a view totally at odds with the influential behaviourist belief that aggressive behaviour is *acquired*, and occurs, when it does occur, purely as a response to frustration. Furthermore, if true, the view that aggression is innate, and therefore *ineradicable*, unfortunately cuts the ground from beneath the feet of social theorists who argue that violent crime, cruelty and war can be abolished from human affairs simply by changing the social system in such a way as to minimize frustration (e.g. by increasing national wealth, eliminating social inequality, etc.). Yet, the evidence that aggressive behaviour is an *a priori* characteristic in social mammals has been abundantly provided by ethology, and has been confirmed in man by all major schools of depth psychology. Paleo-anthropology and history both demonstrate the perennial ubiquitousness of armed conflict between human communities; and, in recent times, the spread of communism in the East and the growth of affluence in the West has been marked by no diminution of international tension or reduction in the statistics of crime; on the contrary, both have frighteningly increased. Moreover, clinical observations indicate that children reared by 'progressive' parents, using a permissive regime designed to eliminate frustration, are often more violently aggressive than their peers reared by more traditional means.

The Freudian view of aggression

Freud was largely ignorant of the rich diversity of instinctive patterns of behaviour occurring in nature because zoology in his time confined its observations to animals in captivity, where opportunities for actualizing instinctive potential were sadly lacking. That Freud considered sex to be the primary motive of living creatures was not so much because of the biological importance of procreation as because of the well-documented lasciviousness of animals in zoos: when territorial and dominance conflicts are ruled out by lack of space and competition, what else is there left for bored, well-nourished animals than copulation and self-abuse?

It was not until he was practically into his sixties that Freud conceded the existence of aggression as a primary instinct in its own right. Until then he had insisted that it was but a component of the sex instinct:

> The sexuality of most male human beings contains an element of *aggressiveness* – a desire to subjugate; the biological significance of it seems to lie in the need for overcoming the resistance of the sexual object by means other than the process of wooing. Thus sadism would correspond to an aggressive component of the sexual instinct which has become independent and exaggerated and, by displacement, has usurped the leading position. (1905, p. 71)

Having at last differentiated aggression from sex, Freud then proceeded to elaborate the distinction into his controversial dichotomy of a life instinct (Eros) opposed by a death instinct (Thanatos). This probably came about because he regarded aggression as a wholly destructive force without any positive use other than that of 'overcoming the resistance of the sexual object'. The death instinct, he argued, could either be directed outwards against others or inwards against the self.

This notion found wide currency but little acceptance. That an instinctive function could have self-annihilation as its primary goal was an idea quite contrary to the biological view of instincts as promoting behaviour to preserve life and encourage the reproduction of the species. Not being able to go all the way with the master, most Freudians compromised over the new position, preferring to speak of a 'destructive instinct' as opposing the sex instinct. But by adopting this compromise they confirmed the Freudian view of aggression as being essentially destructive in nature. Given Freud's intellectual influence on our culture, this partial view has served to strengthen superego disapproval of aggression and ensure its continued repression in the Shadow.

The ethological view

Ethology adopts a much broader approach to the matter, arguing that aggression, no less than sexuality, contributes to the survival of the species: it performs vital biological functions. These may be summarized as follows: (1) it promotes defence; (2) it permits access to valued resources (e.g. territory, food, water and females in oestrus); (3) it ensures good use of the available habitat by spreading the population out as widely as possible; (4) it affords an effective means of settling disputes within the group; (5) it provides leadership for the group – a factor which can prove critical for survival in times of danger; and (6) it promotes differential reproduction – i.e. the 'fittest' (more aggressive and dominant) males are more likely to sire the next generation and so pass on selectively advantageous genes.

In the great majority of species, including man, males are more aggressive than females, in the sense that males are more consistently and more predictably aggressive in a variety of circumstances (e.g. when territory or social position is threatened, or if one male attempts to seize another's food or mate). Females, on the other hand, tend to be aggressive mainly when the safety of their infants is at stake.

To argue that aggression actually promotes survival might seem paradoxical, but this is because of the dangerous age in which we live and because our Judeo-Christian cultural tradition encourages us to view aggressiveness as inherently evil and destructive. That aggression *can* be put to evil and destructive purposes by all animals is undoubtedly true, but such malevolent usage is exceptional because at all levels of the phylogenetic scale there are *rules* governing the circumstances in which aggression may be employed, how much of it can be appropriately expressed and when it should be inhibited. These biologically determined 'Articles of War' are related to the defence of territory, the maintenance of position in the dominance hierarchy and the right to mate; they also function like the Queensberry Rules in defining what forms of conflict are legitimate, and under what conditions a tournament may be said to have been won or lost.

Without such rules, social organization, depending as it does on the collaboration of aggregates of individually aggressive males, would be absolutely impossible. If aggression is to promote the welfare of the group, and not its destruction, there have to be collectively recognized constraints to its use. For this reason, the aggressive behaviour of a social mammal can be understood only in terms of the territorial behaviour, dominance behaviour, mating behaviour and hunting behaviour through which it is actualized. Because of the archetypal nature of all such patterns of aggressive behaviour, they are also to be understood in man in terms of their concomitant symbolic content, ideational forms, and related psychic-emotional states.

Thus, to summarize the ethological view, aggression is a fundamental and ineradicable characteristic of all social mammals including man: without aggression survival would be impossible; but survival also demands that aggression be constrained: 'And so has evolved throughout species that body of rules and regulations of infinite variety which, while encouraging the aggressive, discourages the violent. The problem of man is not that we are aggressive but that we break the rules' (Robert Ardrey, 1970, p. 259). In other words, in man aggression becomes a moral problem – the problem of dealing with the Shadow without becoming possessed by it.

Territory, dominance and strife

The relevance of the ethological evidence to our theme is that it throws light on the biological aspects of morality and the Shadow. By focusing attention on the biological nature of man's erotic experience, Freud enabled us to confront and integrate many sexual components that Victorian convention demanded should be kept unconscious. Ethology now makes it possible for us to acknowledge and accommodate Shadow elements related to aggression, sadism, and the desire for wealth, power and position. But just as Freud and Darwin had to bear the execration of the conservative Christian establishment of their world, so those of us who would wish to apply ethological concepts to the study of mankind must contend with the staunch disapproval of the liberal egalitarian consensus of the present time.

When, several million years ago, our ancestors abandoned the protection of the forests for the exposed African savannah, they found more sources of food, but they also became more vulnerable to predators and to each other. This was compensated for by the development of greater social cohesiveness as much as by greater intelligence, or the use of weapons or tools. Social regulation of masculine aggressiveness became essential not only in hunting and battle, but for the maintenance of law and order and the protection of the weak. The evolution of biologically sanctioned rules concerning the use, direction and intensity of aggressive behaviour was thus crucial to the social evolution of our species. Only through this strategem could the group be capable of sustaining itself, of protecting pregnant or lactating females and their slowly developing young, and of granting everyone a share in the assets that social co-operation can offer.

The great majority of mammalian societies are hierarchically organized and in many there is a territorial component. The biological advantage of a cohesive, hierarchically organized society is obvious. An oligarchy of dominant, aggressive males takes charge of the interests of the group, assuming full responsibility for its welfare, protecting its vulnerable members, defending its territory, and keeping its more unruly elements in order. In return, the members of the oligarchy, who have invariably had a struggle to get there, enjoy the perks of privilege – the pick of the sexually available females, more attention, food, respect, grooming, etc. – and their physical bearing and social conduct prove it. A dominant male can easily be picked out by his erect posture and direct, unabashed gaze, his tail and head held high. The arrogant swagger of dominant male baboons, for example, is most striking and has been compared, not inappropriately, to that of a Mafia boss or Western gun-slinger. Subdominant males, on the other hand, are prone to look down, to move about with lowered head, rounded shoulders and tail on the ground. Out of such beginnings came kings and nobles, peasants and serfs.

Ethological studies of social primates, like the macaques and savannah baboons, give us some idea of how early protohominids may have lived. An excellent description of a healthy primate community is given by Eaton (1976 pp. 97–106) who studied a troop of Japanese macaques living in a two-acre reserve at the Oregon Regional Primate Research Centre. The social order of the troop is determined by age, sex and dominance rank, and each class within the troop has its own specific roles. 'The most striking feature of social behaviour in the troop is the fact that a few males dominate all other animals.' The top position in the dominance hierarchy is held by the 'alpha' monkey, who seldom attains his exalted rank until he is eighteen or nineteen years old.

> Immediately below the alpha male are typically five or six 'subleader' males followed by most of the adult females, which . . . together with their infants and juvenile offspring form the middle of the hierarchy. The remainder of the adult males are at the bottom of the hierarchy, and in the wild they live on the periphery of the troop.

The 'aristocratic' principle is in evidence even in this society, since the dominance rank of an animal tends to be determined by the rank of its mother: 'only the sons of very high ranking females are allowed to stay in the centre of the troop; the other males are driven to the periphery when they are about five years old, about a year after they have reached puberty.'

Similar features are apparent in the social organization of savannah baboons. DeVore's picture of a baboon troop on the march has already been referred to: it shows dominant males in the centre of the troop together with their females and offspring, while the subdominant males keep to the periphery. In the customary social exchanges of daily life, a subdominant will show deference to a superior by presenting his buttocks to him – a form of 'saluting' which the superior may acknowledge by briefly 'mounting' the subdominant as if he were a female, or by condescendingly touching his rump. In this manner, each individual demonstrates that he 'knows his place' and status fighting, together with the social disruption it entails, is reduced to a minimum. Such primate behaviour has archetypal echoes in some human manifestations of deference, as well as in much overt and covert human sexual behaviour – e.g. in the modern homosexual inclination to differentiate 'butch' (dominant) from 'bitch' (subdominant) partners in the sexual act (which is usually performed from behind), in sado-masochistic master-slave rituals (where the dominant beats the subdominant on the buttocks, often as a preliminary to mounting him), and in the disciplinary practice still prevalent in many Anglo-Saxon schools, where a (dominant) master punishes a (subdominant) pupil by caning him on the ritually proffered buttocks.

These human aberrations aside, the main function of the dominance hierarchy is to control aggressive competition in the interests of social cohesion. That maintenance of the hierarchy is crucial for group survival may be judged from the mayhem that results when it is disturbed. 'The most potent cause of aggression is the threat of disruption of an established social organization' (Bernstein and Gordon, 1974).

An instructive, though appalling, instance of this occurred in the spring of 1925 when 100 adult male hamadryas baboons were released on to the small concrete island (measuring thirty metres by eighteen metres) at London Zoo known as Monkey Hill. By an act of inexplicable carelessness, six females were accidentally included in what was intended to be an all-male group. Vicious, long drawn-out battles for dominance ensued, and within eight months, twenty-seven members of the colony had died. Early in 1927 the number of dead reached forty-four, but by this time an uneasy dominance hierarchy had been established, and relative peace prevailed.

However, lamentable ignorance of the archetypal nature of hamadryas baboons and their social needs led to a fresh disaster when the zoo authorities put thirty more females on to the island: within a month half of these were literally torn to pieces by the resident males fighting for possession of them. By 1930, only thirty-nine males and nine females survived; and that year three males died and four more females were killed.

Such behaviour was grossly abnormal. Out of captivity these animals form a stable dominance hierarchy, respect each other's territories, and seldom challenge bonds between males and females once they have been formed. Yet, in this tragic zoo colony the 'rules' governing the use of aggression catastrophically failed to operate. Why?

Quite simply, the explanation is that Monkey Hill and its 'facilities' constituted a monstrous *frustration of archetypal intent.* Hamadryas baboons are so constituted as to need space (a troop of comparable size would need a range of about 60 square kilometres) in which to establish territory, win position in the social hierarchy, and, when successful in both these requirements, to collect a harem of females. Conditions on Monkey Hill rendered actualization of this archetypal programme impossible: the animals were grossly overcrowded and there were more males than females. With no chance of forming the stable units of one male with his attached harem, which is so characteristic of this species, an essential archetype of hamadryas social organization was violated and mayhem was the inevitable result.

Like most primates, baboons are extremely loyal to the group into which they were born and in which they normally live out their entire life-cycle. They are correspondingly hostile to strange baboons from other troops. That the animals on Monkey Hill fought with such psychopathic savagery was due, in no small measure, to the fact that they were all strangers, trapped and assembled from different troops, and crammed together in one small area where they could not possibly keep out of each other's way. The amity-enmity code was transgressed, no less than the 'rules' governing territorial, dominance and mating behaviour.

The lesson to be learned from this catastrophic experiment is a salutory one, for it demonstrates the dreadful consequences which can follow from the perversion of archetypal intent. Far from supporting environmentalist theories about the extreme plasticity of primate behaviour, such findings demonstrate the high degree to which primates are 'structured' and the extent to which they are dependent upon the existence of physical and social environments which respect that structure. That comparable disasters can occur in human communities has been well documented in cultures which have been overwhelmed by our own. One calamitous example is provided by a group of hunter-gatherers in Northern Uganda known as the Ik. Before they were excluded from their range of 40,000 square kilometres they were nomads like the !Kung Bushmen of Botswana. Forced to abandon their traditional way of life and turn to agriculture, they became hopelessly demoralized and their social organization disintegrated (Turnbull, 1972).

Whether man can be considered a territorial species has been the subject of much acrimonious debate, even among ethologists. DeVore and Konner are sceptical (1974) while Ardrey, Lorenz, Morris and Eibl-Eibesfeldt are in little doubt. In his *Love and Hate*, for example, Eibl-Eibesfeldt writes:

> As amongst animals, so amongst men, aggression leads to the territorial 'fencing-off' of groups and within groups to the formation of social hierarchies or ranking orders. Territorial aggression promoted the spread of human beings over the earth and has even resulted in the settlement of barren areas, in so far as the more aggressive peoples, or those with more sophisticated weapons technology have driven others into enclaves. And this has remained the case right into modern times: one has only to think of the settlement of North America or Australia by Europeans. By the moral standards of today such facts are painful to contemplate but the facts cannot be argued away – one need look no further than the Old Testament. (1971, p. 72)

A good case can be made for the argument that aggression performs the same functions in human communities as among other social animals. Certainly, wars between human armies have usually been over the same things that animals fight about: territory, resources and succession. There can be no doubt that men defend individual territories and group territories, and, as we have seen, xenophobia is an innate propensity that reveals itself at a very early age. As Eibl-Eibesfeldt points out, humans, like many other social species, scrupulously maintain *individual distance*, especially from strangers, and such behaviour is often unmistakably territorial. In libraries, for instance, strangers invariably sit at separate tables. When a person transgresses this rule and sits at a table which is already occupied when there are still other tables free, the original occupant will move away. Should there be nowhere left to move, then he will often erect symbolical barriers between himself and the newcomer by arranging a ruler or a pile of books as a kind of territorial boundary (Sommer, 1966).

As with most territorial species, the 'first come, first served' principle operates. A man seated in a train compartment has the right to stare at a newcomer without being thought impolite. The interloper recognizes the occupant's territorial rights by asking 'Is this seat taken?' or even formally requesting permission to enter and sit. Similar behaviour is to be observed in crowded restaurants. Apparently the territorial 'rules' decree that he who occupies a territory first possesses certain inalienable rights which must be uncritically accorded to him: this made possible the building of empires ('planting the flag') and the staking out of claims to land in the Far West.

As evidence for the existence of a human territorial heritage, Eibl-Eibesfeldt draws attention to the practice adopted by many human cultures of erecting phallic statues as boundary markers, and compares these with the 'phallic threat' observed in a number of primates (e.g. a baboon guarding his territory will display his erect penis at the approach of a stranger). This is an interesting example of sexual, aggressive and dominance behaviour all combined in the interests of territorial preservation.

Holding on to territory demands the use of aggression – but aggression applied within the context of the established social order and through adoption of the dual 'amity-enmity' code of aggressive behaviour. The enjoyment of proprietorial rights and of some share in the assets of the group depends on a willingness to know and accept one's place, to display 'amity' to one's partners and 'enmity' to potentially hostile neighbours.

The *dual nature* of man can be understood as a direct consequence of the evolution of territorial social groups, the survival of which has always depended on 'patriotism' – i.e. love of one's own land and people and hostility for 'the rest'. The existence of territorially linked social groups is thus the essential *condition* for warfare, if not its cause, and considerably antedates the emergence of our species: 'We have to recognize,' wrote Sir Arthur Keith, 'that the conditions that give rise to war – the separation of animals into social groups, the "right" of each group to its area, and the evolution of an enmity complex to defend such areas – were on earth long before man made his appearance' (1946).

Not that wars are always about territory or resources, they are often about ideas; but ideological warfare is not unrelated to territory or patriotism because through the psychic process of *reification* men readily become proprietorial about ideals. Such conflicts can be the most bitter and protracted of all: 'When truth kills truth, O devilish-holy fray!' Men will 'die like flies for theories and exterminate each other with every instrument of destruction for abstractions' (Durbin and Bowlby, 1938).

Readiness to do battle is one of the less appealing characteristics of our species, but it is unfortunately universal. Although some apparently peace-loving tribes have been described, they are invariably timid peoples who have been driven into inhospitable enclaves by their more aggressive neighbours where they have adapted to their circumstances by adopting a strategy of collective submissiveness. Reviewing the ethnographic evidence, Davie (1929) concluded that 'war plays a prominent part in the lives of most primitive peoples, and it is usually a sanguinary affair.' Andreski (1964) believes that warfare came into existence when hominid skill in the co-operative use of weapons had developed sufficiently for them to defend themselves effectively against beasts of prey. This evolutionary advance disturbed the ecological balance which had hitherto kept our numbers steady and as the population rose so competition for resources increased and the mutual killing began – an activity which our species has pursued with enthusiasm ever since.

The need for enemies

As social animals, we are programmed from a very early age to shrink from people whom we do not know and stick to people whom we do. This fundamental distinction between attachment and xenophobia is crucial not only for the preservation of the individual, but also for the survival of the group. Societies are closely integrated systems, each glued together by adherence to the familiar, all separated by hostility to the strange. The sinister truth is that for communities to thrive, enemies are as necessary as friends. External danger binds the group together, reduces personal animosity, enhances mutual trust, promotes altruism and self-sacrifice. A society surrounded by enemies is unified and strong, a society without enemies divided and lax. Men in groups are the same the whole world over: when there are no outsiders to fight, they turn on their compatriots. For a rush of adrenaline and a cure for boredom, for cameraderie and thrills, there is nothing like a good scrap.

The inverse relationship between military expansionism and internecine strife has been apparent throughout history. When the Roman Empire triumphed over its enemies Roman citizens began fighting amongst themselves. The Japanese, confined to their islands for centuries, indulged in an endless series of civil wars. For as long as Britain ruled a great empire and fought numerous colonial wars, her social institutions remained stable and intact; now that the empire has been dismantled, there are signs of increasing social conflict and industrial unrest. The countries most prone to revolutions are those least inclined to international adventures: examples are modern Spain, Portugal, and the countries of Latin America. It is clear, therefore, that neither the establishment of world government nor the creation of a powerful United Nations Organization would in themselves result in the abolition of armed conflict.

> The remedies of signing treaties of eternal peace, convening congresses and preaching condemnation of war, have been tried innumerable times and without much effect. They may be needed but in themselves are clearly insufficient. Given the propensities of human nature, the tendency of populations to grow beyond the resources

> they require has ensured the ubiquity of war, though not every single instance of war has had this factor as an immediate cause. (Andreski, 1964)

Andreski ends on a note of deep pessimism: 'Wars might cease to be a permanent feature of social life only after the restoration of the demographic balance whose disappearance at an early stage of cultural development made them inevitable.' In other words, the only possibility of abolishing war would be to abandon civilization altogether and return to the pre-Fall existence of the hunter-gatherers. There is, of course, no manner in which this could happen short of a global catastrophe.

On making the Shadow conscious

Aggression, like sexuality, is an ineradicable feature of human nature, and its manifestations in battle with outsiders for territory and resources and in struggle with insiders for power and prestige are everywhere characteristic of the life of mankind. Not even convocations of bishops, orders of monks, or associations of analytical psychologists are free of it. 'There are few fields in which internal conflicts are fought in a more unfair, unconscious and destructive manner than among analyzed . . . and allegedly "conscious" psychotherapists' (Guggenbuhl-Craig, 1971). Aggression is an unavoidable fact of human life.

> It is, therefore, as Freud says, an 'educational sin' if one does not prepare a person for the aggression with which he will sooner or later have to come to grips. All attempts to underrate aggression by referring to the alleged fact that it is learned – in the face of the available evidence to the contrary – are in the highest degree irresponsible. (Eibl-Eibesfeldt, 1971)

One aspect of this 'educational sin' is, as Freeman (1964) complains, that despite the ubiquity of human aggression, we lack anything resembling an adequate history of human cruelty and destructiveness. There is no compilation of the essential facts, nor has the phenomenology of the behaviour that occurs in the course of massacres and other outbreaks of violence been fully reported or analysed.

> The full realities are, indeed, of a kind that cannot be generally published, and those who observe them readily repress much of the horror they have experienced. . . . In my view, there is great need for dispassionate research into the phenomenology of the aggressive behaviour of the human animal, for until we have come to see its realities for what they are, we shall not achieve a scientific under-

standing of those realities nor be able to evolve ways of controlling them. (Freeman, 1964)

If we are to be absolved of the 'educational sin', therefore, it must be through understanding – both objective and subjective understanding – and this can only be achieved if we make the effort to overcome those *mechanisms of ego-defence* which human beings have evolved in the course of their cultural history and which perform so efficiently the function of keeping the Shadow unconscious. Ego-defence mechanisms have been clearly defined by psychoanalysis and the most important of them are projection, intellectualization, displacement, reaction-formation, repression and denial. Seeing through these defence mechanisms and perceiving how they work is more than half the battle in making the Shadow conscious. It is, therefore, essential that we look into them.

The first mechanism, *projection*, we have already encountered (pp. 215–16): it is that process by which we hive off on to others what we repress and deny in ourselves. Shadow projection is at the bottom of all racial and international prejudice and our facility for turning our opponents into devils'; it explains the readiness with which we can convince ourselves that our enemies are not men and women like 'us', but monsters unworthy of all humane consideration: there is only one thing to be done with such 'vermin' and that is exterminate them, etc. Hitler's speeches were full of such talk, and it is clear that he, and through him, the entire German nation collectively projected the Shadow on to the Slavs and the Jews, whom they significantly termed *Untermenschen* (subhumans). In his paper on 'Intergroup hostility and social cohesion', Murphy (1957) described how the Mundrucus of Brazil have traditionally divided the population of the world into themselves and the rest of mankind, whom they term 'Pariwat': Pariwat count as game and are spoken of in precisely the same manner as animals.

It is not just the personal Shadow that is projected on to the enemy, but the Archetype of Evil; and if the enemy should have a numinous leader (e.g. Hitler) then he becomes the living embodiment of that archetype.

Similarly, just as the archetypal Shadow is projected on to the enemy's leader, so the superego (or ego-ideal) is projected on to the leader of one's own side, with the result that whatever he decrees is by definition right and proper ('The Führer is always right'), and one can do in his name what one would be incapable of doing by oneself. Hitler clearly performed this function for the German people during the Third Reich. Moreover, through an extension of this process, the populations of warring nations manage to persuade themselves that God is on their side, even when (as during the two World Wars) He happens to be the same God.

It is this mechanism that makes war possible and, even, inevitable. The collective morality of each society ordains that while it is wicked to murder your own kind, it is good to kill strangers who threaten the group. Kerenyi's study of evil in mythology indicates that man considers everything which kills or destroys to be evil – unless it is done in the interests of the group. Once a band of strangers have been identified as threatening, the archetype of evil is automatically projected on to them and they become *Untermenschen* to be destroyed: the projection is the justification of the act. Righteous ends justify violent means and, hurriedly closing ranks in the 'divine thrill' of 'militant enthusiasm', we sink all rivalries, forget old scores, and become this happy band of brothers, we few, we happy few, marching forward to victory in what is unquestionably our finest hour. That Christ's injunction to love our enemies has met with so little success is because it would seek to override the archetypal programme ingrained in our genes – the programme which dictates that we beware of the stranger, clearly designate the common enemy, and find friends to fight him with.

But now that our planet has become both nuclear plant and global village, we can no longer afford this luxury. If we are to survive, we have not only to own consciously the personal Shadow, but we also have to assume both personal and collective responsibility for the Archetype of Evil. This is a moral task of such daunting stature as to be quite beyond the capacity of the great majority of mankind. Only if the leaders of the world attain such wisdom can there be hope of avoiding the infinite catastrophe of a third World War.

Rationalization, the inventing of bad 'reasons' to justify what we do and say on impulse, and *intellectualization*, by which we defuse emotionally explosive issues through the use of dry, abstract terminology, are two further techniques commonly employed to avoid becoming conscious of the Shadow. For example, those who advance arguments justifying the 'taking out' of Dresden, the dropping of atomic bombs on Japan, or napalm on the Vietnamese, make use of these mechanisms, which effectively reduce the speaker's feelings of guilt or emotional involvement in the horrifying events in question. Indeed, ego-defence mechanisms such as these invariably come into play during discussion of such loaded issues as war, violent crime, terrorism, etc., when it is assumed that such phenomena are consciously motivated and susceptible to rational explanation in terms of social or environmental variables: they are, in fact, unconsciously motivated, irrational, and due, ultimately, to the archetypal nature of man himself.

No less effective in avoiding confrontation with the Shadow are the mechanisms of *reaction-formation* (the outward display of the *opposite* of what is inwardly repressed and denied) and *displacement* (by which the feelings appropriate to a given situation are experienced by the ego as too dangerous and are consequently displaced on to less threatening situations). But all these techniques of defence are dependent for their success on the primary ego-defence mechanisms of *repression* and *denial.*

The repression concept was probably Freud's most important single contribution to depth psychology. Quite early in his development of psychoanalysis he realized that any mental content that is disturbing to the conscious mind can be repressed or 'pushed down' into the unconscious. Moreover, memory of the act of repression is itself repressed with the result that the whole incident is effectively forgotten. Unfortunately, this strategy brings only temporary respite to the ego, because, in the unconscious, the repressed content remains active and makes efforts to force its way back into consciousness. In order to keep it unconscious, therefore, repression is often backed up with *denial* – the flat refusal to accept the existence of ideas or events associated in any way with the content originally repressed.

An example will make all these mechanisms clear. Take, for instance, the case of a liberal penal reformer who writes a pamphlet attacking the inhumanity of prison officers, while secretly enjoying sexual phantasies in which he is the Commandant of a concentration camp. For most of his waking life his sadistic phantasies are kept out of consciousness (repression) and he only becomes aware of them when sexual urgency gives them enough force to make them conscious. Once orgasm is achieved they again become unconscious. Prisons fascinate him because they form the locus of his phantasy; and reading about them and visiting them affords some socially acceptable discharge of repressed energy (displacement). Secretly, he envies the prison officers because he would love to be in their position, but he cannot admit this because it would mean conscious acknowledgment and public revelation of his repressed sadistic longings. So he publicly castigates the officers for 'inhumanity' (projection) and writes a pamphlet about the subject (intellectualization), adopting an attitude of evident hostility towards the whole penal system (reaction-formation).

Next to projection, the defence mechanism with the most sinister social implications is displacement, for it leads to the obscene practice of *scapegoating*, by which the aggression that we dare not direct against someone stronger than ourselves is turned against someone weak and helpless. Alas, all creatures do this. In zoos, animals that cannot get at the targets of their fury will take it out on the weaker occupants of their cage. In the wild, an animal attacked by one of higher rank will not fight back but will pick on a third animal of lower rank to himself. So it is with men. In the absence of enemies at the gates, human aggression intended for the 'foreigner' is redirected against the 'enemy within'. Nazi persecution of the Jews began with passionate intensity when Germany, smarting under the Treaty of Versailles, still feared to challenge England

and France in open conflict: the dread machinery of the 'final solution' was already being constructed before the outbreak of war. Similarly, the persecution of witches was a particularly nasty example of religious scapegoating. The witch was much more than a personification of the Terrible Mother: she was a victim of displacement of the xenophobic reaction normally reserved for members of the out-group. As the 'enemy within' society, the Mistress of Satan came to afflict the Righteous; she was a cancer that had to be burnt out of the body politic if God's will was to prevail and all godly souls be preserved. As scapegoat, the witch carried the collective guilt of the population, and as a focus of group hatred she permitted all 'decent' people to remain peacefully unconscious of their own evil propensities. Her sacrifice at the stake promoted the cohesion of the Christian community by enabling its members (the godly in-group) to reaffirm their allegiance to the ordinances of God.

In modern secular society, minorities are scapegoated to similar ends – 'class enemies' in communist states, the Macarthy persecution of communists in the United States, the criminals, lunatics and sex deviants in all states. Ultimately, xenophobia is not just a fear of 'foreigners' but a fear of the *strange as such*: we are programmed not only to discriminate against strangers but strange behaviour in anyone, including familiars. This is true of many social animals. For instance, Niko Tinbergen has described how a herring gull caught in a net will struggle and get attacked by its fellows on account of its 'strange' behaviour. Collective security depends upon the predictability of familiars. For this reason all communities reward conformity to group norms and punish deviance. The degree to which deviance is tolerated varies from culture to culture (e.g. it is more tolerated in matrist cultures than in patrist ones), but all societies impose sanctions on members whose behaviour becomes unpredictable (i.e. 'strange'). Should these sanctions fail to 'normalize' him, then the offender is either removed or eliminated: hence the existence of the criminal law, prisons and lunatic asylums, the death penalty, exile and extradition. The combined forces of social conformity and xenophobia, therefore, perform the biological function of promoting survival through social cohesion by drawing familiars together, strengthening the bonds between them, reducing boredom and keeping them on their toes.

In the absence of pogroms and wars, the amity-enmity complex demands vicarious expression: hence the popularity of violent films and the universal masculine obsession with competitive sports – boxing, wrestling (where the protagonists are divided into goodies and baddies) and football (where the symbolic territorial conflict on the pitch is often not of sufficient intensity to gratify the militant enthusiasm of the spectators who prolong the conflict after the final whistle, using boots, bottles and bicycle chains, and redirect any residual aggression by smashing up the train that takes them home). Competitive athletics can also deputize for war. President Carter's refusal to allow American athletes to participate in the 1980 Olympic Games was a substitute for more direct action against the Soviet Union in response to its invasion of Afghanistan, but by denying the American and Russian people the opportunity to participate vicariously in the symbolic struggle between the two sides in the *temenos* of the Olympic stadium, he could have made the possibility of armed struggle on the battlefield more likely.

The unpalatable fact is that the propensity which men show in the first half of life to compete with one another, to dominate, fight, and, when 'necessary', kill one another, is a manifestation of the *individuation process* at work: it is, like altruism, love and intellectual achievement, an expression of the drive towards Self-fulfilment. It is hopeless to try and rationalize this fact away by subscribing to the romantic illusion that man is 'naturally good', that 'society' makes him bad, and that he destroys, pillages and slaughters only when frustrated or unfairly treated. All theoretical attempts to oppose society and man are meaningless. Vico's view of society as 'the work of man' makes little more sense than Marx's inversion of it. Human individuals and human society complement one another: they cannot exist independently because they evolved together. Our potential for culture resides in our biology as a species: we live in societies because we are social animals. As babies each one of us is born unfinished, with an evolutionary past and a social future: we need culture to complete us.

The Marxist myth denies biology in the same way as the Christian myth denied it. To insist that the condition of man can be explained purely in terms of his socio-economic history is as partial as explaining it in terms of his religious history, for it leaves out the most important fact of all: that man is an animal with a *natural* history; that the most essential features about him are *pre*-historic and recorded only in the fossils of his ancestors and, more significantly, in the DNA of his genes. As an explanatory model, social history is worthless if it takes economic theory and not natural history as its foundation: it becomes demonstrably bogus, it sinks to the level of all totalitarian propaganda, and if it survives it is as a rigid ideology based on the systematic distortion of questionable facts.

If the romantic view of man as a fundamentally good, peaceful creature were correct, we might flaunt the 'rules' of our culture with impunity, pull down the law courts and jails, fire the policemen and politicians, disband the armies and navies, share all our belongings equally with each other, and create Paradise on Earth. In fact, this wonderful dream is incapable of realization because the archetypes prevent it. The capacity of men to devise Utopian states in the imagination has never resulted in the creation of Utopia on earth: such phantasies have brought great benefits to mankind, it is true, but only when those responsible for the implementation of political ideals have respected the archetypal needs of those for whom they legislated. Too single-minded a pursuit of Utopia results in wholesale repression of the Self, and, ultimately, in triumph for the Shadow. The archetypes will not allow us to deny them for long. Socialist visionaries, for example, have consistently advocated, and attempted to impose, societies in which dominance hierarchies were to be abolished; invariably their efforts have resulted in the creation of a party-dominated bureaucracy as rigidly hierarchical and more brutally conservative than the social system that it replaced – and all in the name of an egalitarian ideology. In Russia, Eastern Europe, China, Vietnam, Cambodia, the story has been the same: societies cannot exist without a hierarchical structure; an archetypal need to organize ourselves collectively into a social pyramid is ingrained in our nature.

This is not a fashionable view to espouse; for the collective consensus would have us repress and deny our dominance, aggressive and proprietorial desires. Indeed, much contemporary reaction to discussion of the biology of territorial and hierarchical imperatives is reminiscent of how a Victorian hostess might have behaved had one dared to address her on the the subjects of masturbation or oral sex. The comparison is appropriate: if the Victorians were sexual prudes, many of our contemporaries are political prudes. Yet sociologists and political theorists of the future will have to take cognizance of the hierarchical archetype and acknowledge that complete social equality is a Utopian dream unsusceptible to realization. This is not to argue that we should revert to a social model based on the baboon troop. The whole point of civilization is, despite appearances to the contrary, to remove us from the lethal, unfettered competition of the jungle. But flatly to deny the operation of a hierarchical archetype in social organization is both dishonest and dangerous, since it can only promote those evils that it evolved to prevent – the evils of anarchy, disorder, and the ultimate disintegration of the group. What matters, after all, is not that we *are* aggressive, xenophobic, sexual, hierarchical and territorial but what *attitude* we adopt to these fundamental *a priori* aspects of our nature – how we live them, and how we mediate them to the group. It is the ethical orientation that counts.

However, in order to be ethical one must be conscious, and consciousness means awareness of things as they really are. We *have* to abandon the romantic dream that evil, conflict and aggression can be banished from human affairs, because it is when we *deny* our own capacity for evil that we project or displace it onto others. It is a blind abdication of the moral sense to conceive evil as always 'outside' (i.e. projected): the adversary is inside as well as outside – inside the individual as well as the group. We cannot hope to bring some resolution to the conflicts of our time by blaming them on to political opponents. If we would deal with collective evil we must acknowledge our own complicity, and if we bear our share of evil we cannot escape our share of collective guilt.

Guilt, and the fear that guilt induces, are at the root of the Shadow problem: that we go to such devious lengths as we do to keep the Shadow unconscious is because conscious acceptance of one's own evil entails suffering one's own guilt and, through that suffering, participating in the guilt of mankind. Yet, as the Second Christian Millennium draws to an end, we are left with little choice: *sine afflictione nulla salus* – without suffering there is no salvation. We too are responsible for the state of the world and its future – not the previous generation, not the political left or right, but us – you and me.

As opposite poles of the morality archetype, good and evil are ineradicable characteristics of the human condition. To pretend that we can embrace one and eliminate the other is to breed personal division and public disorder. Both individuation and planetary salvation demand that we be aware of our capacity for both good and evil and that we make ethical choices between the two. This moral responsibility is incumbent upon every one of us, but on none more than the political leaders of the world who, because of the technological ingenuity of our species, now hold the destiny of the solar system in their hands. Unfortunately, as a breed, politicians are not over-gifted with insight or humility: with few exceptions, individuation is not noticeably advanced in them.

Without some acknowledgment of the devil within us, individuation cannot proceed: coming to terms with one's own evil is the first and indispensable stage in conscious realization of the Self. True morality requires that the Shadow achieve consciousness, because on that condition alone can an individual become responsible for the events of his life and render himself accountable for what he has projected on to others. Inasmuch as it enhances social responsibility, consciousness of the Shadow benefits the group. And the more influential the individual, the greater the benefit – provided, of course, that he constellates a benevolent aspect of the moral archetype and does not, like Hitler, Stalin or Idi Amin, become a channel through which the Shadow can flow in blind destructiveness.

It was Jung's contention that the two moral poles were capable of reconciliation: awareness of the Shadow means suffering the tension between good and evil in full consciousness, and through that suffering they can be *transcended.* If one can bring oneself to bear the psychic tension that the opposites generate, the problem is raised to a higher plane, where the conflict is resolved: good is reconciled with evil, and a new synthesis follows between conscious and unconscious, between Persona and Shadow, between ego and Self. The reconciliation is attained neither rationally nor intellectually, but symbolically, and it was to this symbolic process that Jung gave the term *transcendent function.* Through the transcendent function the conscious personality and inner adversary are *both* transformed: as new symbols arise from the unconscious (e.g. mandala symbols like the Cross or the Golden Flower) the opposites are reconciled and transcended; the personality becomes better balanced, more integrated (Latin *integer* = whole, unimpaired, complete); the previously opposed *two* achieve *at-one-ment* in a balanced, integrated *Gestalt* which is greater than the sum of its contributing parts. Phenomenologically, the experience is one of liberation combined with an awareness of the inner strength that comes of reaching harmony (Greek *armonia* = a fitting or joining together) with something greater than mere ego. This is the essence of all 'religious experience' and corresponds to the Christian teaching that Crucifixion gives place to Resurrection, the will of the ego to the Will of God ('Not my will, but Thine').

The transcendent function cannot proceed through reason because reason acknowledges no ambiguity: truth is not falsehood, white is not black, everything is one thing or the other. But when permitted to do so, the psyche transcends reason and the rules of logic, no less than the opposites, for it sees no problem in the simultaneous perception of incompatibilities. As the great spiritual disciplines of the East affirm, wisdom lies in a profound awareness of the contradiction in all things. But the East has traditionally eschewed our deification of reason; and it has not shared our alienation from the psychic wealth contained in symbolic forms.

The etymology of the word *symbol* is itself illuminating. The Greek noun συμβολον referred to a token or tally which could be used as a verification of identity. An object, such as a bone, would be broken into two halves and each given separately to two people (e.g. members of the same sect or secret society) who could then identify each other by producing both halves and checking that they fitted together. Each tally-holder knew his own half to be genuine; when contact was made, 'goodness of fit' between the two halves of the συμβολον was the criterion which satisfied the other's *bona fides*. If perfect fit occurred a *Gestalt* was suddenly created out of the familiar (known) and the 'strange' (unknown) parts. The conjunction of συμ (=together) and βολον (from βαλλω = I throw) emphasizes the idea that contact or a connection must be made if meaning is to be perceived and genuine trust established: the strange must be 'thrown together' with the familiar to construct a bridge connecting the known with the unknown, ego-consciousness with the unconscious.

The statement that symbols possess a 'transcendent function' may sound both esoteric and disconcertingly 'Jungian'. Yet, strange to relate, neurological advances in the past decade have, quite independently, indicated that something closely akin to the transcendant function may be performed by a great bundle of nerve fibres called the *corpus cal-*

losum, or *cerebral commissure*, which, like the symbol, acts as a bridge – in this instance, a bridge connecting the two halves of the brain, the left and right *cerebral hemispheres*. Even more interestingly, a careful reading of the recent neurological literature reveals that the transcendent function is not the only Jungian concept to possess a possible neurophysiological equivalent. This fascinating parallelism will be discussed in the next chapter.

Part III

Synthesis and integration

· 13 ·

On being in two minds

Conflict is the product of duality. And since duality exists throughout nature, the opportunities for conflict are infinite – as are the opportunities for peace. For dissonance and harmony, opposition and concordance, balance and imbalance are conceivable only in the presence of polarity. Destruction, like creation, arises from the juxtaposition of opposing forces, and so basic are these contrapuntal oppositions to the fabric of our universe that consciousness and life itself would be inconceivable without them. Deprived of the co-ordinates – vertical and horizontal, North and South, East and West, above and below, left and right, back and forth, past and future – who could achieve orientation in space and time? And how could the Self, that dynamic mandala at the core of the human soul, ever become incarnate?

Since duality is indispensable to our world, it would be surprising were it not reflected in the structure and function of our bodies, and, not least, of our brains. If you take a human brain in your hands and examine it, the first thing that will strike you is that the greater portion of it is divided into two parts. These are the cerebral hemispheres, man's main claim to fame (Figure 13.1). For many centuries this arrangement stimulated curiosity and raised the question whether these two parts – so much larger in relation to body size in human beings than in other primates – perform different functions. The first indication that they do was noted by the ancient Egyptians, who observed that brain injury on one side can result in limb paralysis on the other. This intriguing 'cross over' of function was confirmed by neurologists in the nineteenth century both by clinical observation and by experiment: thus, Eduard Hitzig demonstrated that stimulation of cerebral hemispheric tissues just in front of the fissure of Rolando (Figure 13.2) caused patients to move muscles on the opposite side of the body. Similarly, stimulation of tissues just behind the fissure caused unanaesthetized patients (brain tissues feel no pain) to report sensory experiences in parts of the body opposite to the side of stimulation.

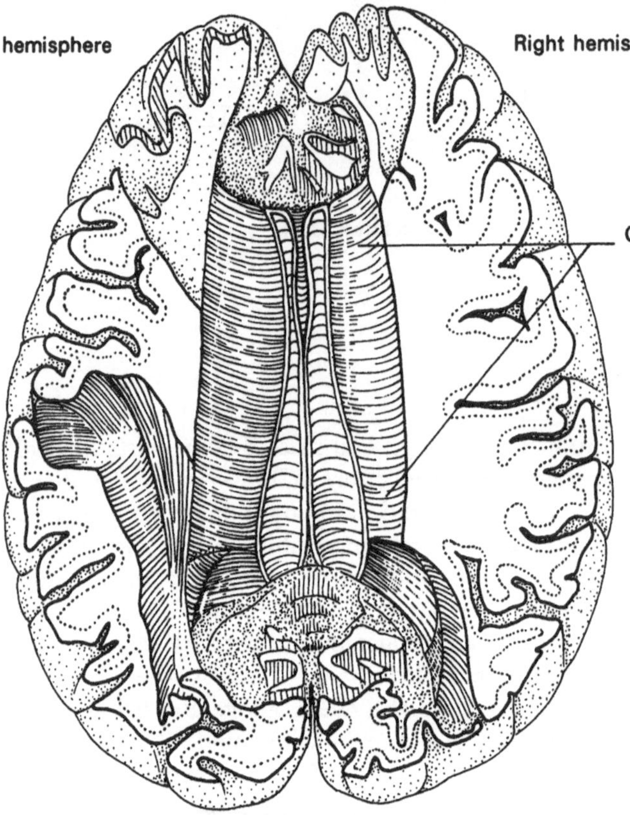

FIGURE 13.1 The corpus callosum seen from above after partial removal and dissection of both cerebral hemispheres

It is well established, therefore, that both cerebral hemispheres are concerned with contralateral movements and sensations. But what of psychic functions? Could there be any differences in mental functioning between the left and right sides of the brain?

Before examining the attempts of modern neurology to answer this question, it might be interesting to approach it from the cross-cultural standpoint and ask, as Jung might have done, what meanings human beings have universally attributed to the two sides: what is the *archetypal symbolism of left and right*? How do people, irrespective of culture, distinguish between the attributes of leftness and rightness, and are there any ubiquitous features in the distinctions which they make?

In fact, examination of the anthropological data reveals a remarkable degree of agreement (Russell, 1979). Indeed, the qualities attributed to left and right turn out to be so generally applicable as to warrant their summary in Table 13.1.

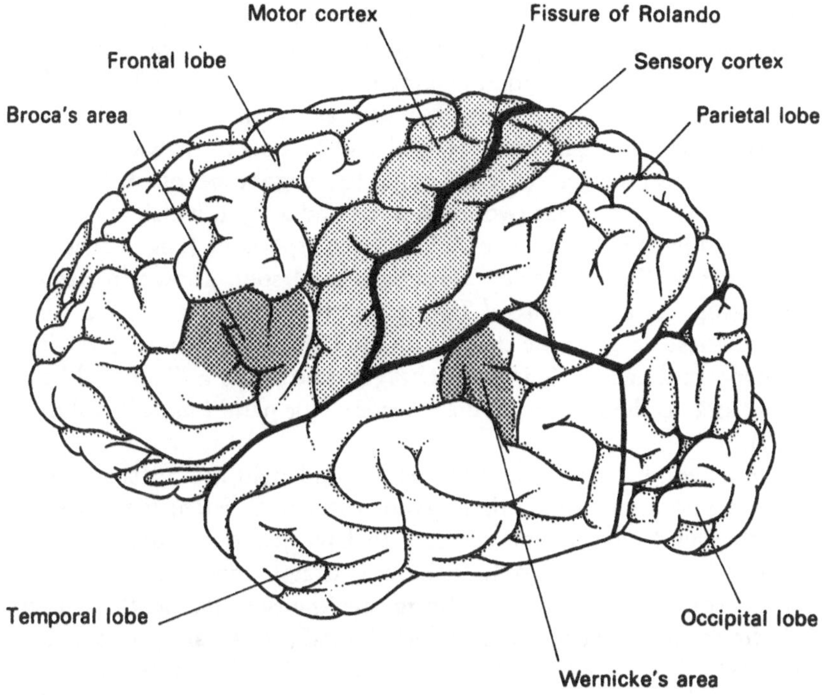

FIGURE 13.2 Lateral view of the brain: cortex of the left cerebral hemisphere showing the motor cortex and the sensory cortex (separated by the fissure of Rolando) and the speech areas of Broca and Wernicke

Table 13.1 The archetypal symbolism of right and left

Right	*Left*
Good, pure and sacred	Evil, impure and profane
Life, medicine and health	Death, poison and sickness
Heaven	Hell
Masculinity	Femininity
Activity	Passivity
The sun	The moon
Daylight	Darkness
Summer	Winter
Joy	Sorrow
Consciousness	Unconsciousness

It is apparent that many of these distinctions correspond to those of Taoist philosophy, where Yang, the creative and firm, is equated with the right and Yin, the receptive and yielding, with the left. Similarly, the

Alchemists associated the right with Mars and the King, the left with Venus and the Queen. In Islamic societies, and many others, the right hand is used for eating and in making religious offering while the left is reserved for cleaning the anus after defecation. In Christian theology, Christ sits on the right hand of God and at Calvary it was the good thief who was crucified on Jesus' right. The Bagobo people of Malaysia believe that everyone has two souls, a left and a right, which are subject to projection like the positive and negative aspects of Jung's 'Shadow'. According to Ruth Benedict: 'The right-hand soul, known in Bagobo terminology as the *Gimokud Takawanan* is the so-called "good soul" that manifests itself as the shadow on the right-hand of one's path. The left-hand soul called *Gimokud Tebang* is said to be a "bad soul" and shows itself as the shadow on the left side of the path' (quoted by Bogen, 1969).

The universal distinctions between left and right are further implicit in the connotations which these words carry in different languages. In English 'right' also means 'correct', to have justice on one's side. In French 'droit' means not only 'right' but 'straight' and 'untwisted'. The Italian word for right 'destro' also means 'the right moment'. 'Sinister' is Latin for left; it also means 'unlucky', 'bad', 'awkward', 'wrong' and 'perverse'. The Greek word for left, αριστερός, also means 'clumsy', 'erring' and 'crazy'; in classical times, to go mad was 'to turn off to the leftward of one's mind'. In Russian 'na levo', literally 'on the left', means 'on the side', 'under the counter', i.e. something obtained on the black market. The apparent universality of the meanings attached to left and right is remarkable. But it becomes even more impressive when considered in the light of modern discoveries about the activity of the two sides of the brain. For when one bears in mind the essential oppositeness of cerebral functioning, the correspondence between the cross-cultural and the neurological evidence is quite extraordinary. It is as if we as a species have collectively projected the functions of our two cerebral hemispheres out on to opposite sides of the *Umwelt*, the left cerebral functions on to the right and the right cerebral functions on to the left.

Neurophysiological understanding of the brain has advanced through the use of five principal techniques, the first two of which are the oldest and have already been mentioned. They are:

1 investigation of people who have suffered brain damage of various kinds;
2 electrical stimulation of specific areas of the brain;
3 investigation of patients who have had their corpus callosum (the bundle of fibres connecting both cerebral hemispheres) severed surgically as a treatment for severe epilepsy;
4 studies using the electroencephalogram (EEG);
5 investigation of the consequences of injecting anaesthetics into the left

or right carotid arteries which supply their respective cerebral hemispheres.

The first of these techniques yielded a wealth of information during and after the First World War, when tragically large numbers of soldiers on both sides sustained injuries of varying degrees of severity in different parts of the brain. When this evidence was collated it established beyond doubt that a number of functions were primarily represented on different sides of the brain: damage to the left side resulted in dysphasia (impairment of speech); dyslexia (difficulties with reading) and deterioration in the ability to do mental arithmetic and use logical thought, while damage to the right side caused a deficit in visuo-spatial capacities such as those required to dress oneself, find one's way round a hospital ward, and recognize patterns. On the whole, damage to the left cerebral hemisphere appeared to cause more serious incapacity than damage to the right, and this led to the conclusion that the left hemisphere is normally 'dominant' over the right 'subdominant' hemisphere. This assumption fitted well with the observation that the majority of people are right-handed (and probably have been since protohominid times) and the demonstration by Paul Broca and Carl Wernicke in the nineteenth century that the cortical areas concerned with the expression and comprehension of language are situated on the left.

Scientific interest in the bridge of nerve fibres connecting the two hemispheres – the so-called cerebral commissure or corpus callosum – remained dormant until comparatively recently. In the early 1940s it was found that surgical severance of these fibres (there are about two hundred million of them) dramatically reduced the incidence and severity of epileptic seizures in patients who were previously having intolerably frequent attacks, presumably because electrical activity generated in each hemisphere had been augmenting activity in the other via the cerebral commissure by some kind of 'positive feedback.' What surprised the surgeons who performed these early operations (known as commissurotomy) was that they appeared to result in no ill effects: this led to a decline in the reputation of the corpus callosum, some arguing that it had no function other than to hold the two sides of the brain together – a facile assumption that Warren McCulloch countered by observing that it was unlikely that such a large bundle of fibres had been brought into existence for the sole purpose of transmitting epileptic fits from one side of the body to the other! (Taylor, 1979).

The true importance of the corpus callosum did not begin to dawn on people until the 1950s and 1960s when Roger Sperry embarked on his classic studies of commissurotomized patients first at the University of Chicago and later at the California Institute of Technology. Sperry's work led him to the conclusion that in fact we possess 'two minds', one localized in the left hemisphere and the other in the right; cutting the communications between them prevents their normal integration into a phenomenological unity and makes possible the demonstration of their separate, though complementary, functions. Sperry was able to establish that the left hemisphere is indeed primarily concerned with the use of language and with abstract, analytic thought, while the right hemisphere is more involved in synthesizing sensory data into percepts. When, for example, a patient whose corpus callosum has been cut is blindfolded and given a glass tumbler to hold in his right hand (served by the left hemisphere) he is able to tell you exactly what it is; however, when the object is held in his left hand (served by the right hemisphere) he is quite unable to name it or describe it, but can nevertheless identify it if you show him a variety of objects – with a glass tumbler amongst them – to choose from. Moreover, such a patient can write with his right hand (which is only to be expected since the left hemisphere mediates the use of language) but he cannot draw with it; with his left hand, however, he can draw but he cannot write.

These and many other tests demonstrate that while the left hemisphere is better at using language and making logical deductions, the right hemisphere is superior at perceptual and construction tasks such as map-reading, block design and picture comprehension. In particular the right hemisphere appears to be accomplished at *Gestalt* or holistic perception of the kind which one uses in recognizing a face: it specializes in synthesizing fragments of sensory information into whole percepts. The left hemisphere, on the other hand, is more astute at analyzing and breaking down information into temporal sequences. This *sequential* processing of the left hemisphere has been contrasted by the Russian neurophysiologist, Luria, with the *simultaneous* perceptual processing of the right.

People seem to differ considerably as to the degree which the left 'mind' has come to dominate over the right, and this is reflected in the relative inclination of different individuals to use analytic as opposed to synthetic modes of thought: while some people tend to confine their attention to specific details, showing greater interest in how things differ from one another – like a botanist who specializes in classifying different varieties of grass, others prefer to seek universal characteristics, the common denominators underlying specific differences – like a Jungian collecting archetypal motifs from different mythologies and fairy tales. These two modes of approach are often referred to as 'convergent' and 'divergent' and may well depend on left and right hemispheric functioning respectively. Moreover, the 'obsessional' or 'compulsive' type of personality, with its meticulous attention to detail, could be associated with an exaggerated preponderance of left hemispheric activity.

Musical appreciation, which relies on Gestalt perception rather than logical analysis (unless one is a musicologist) is linked with the right hemisphere. Patients who have had their right hemispheres removed or who have suffered damage to the right temporal lobe show impaired musical abilities, while their use of language and reason remain intact. While they may be unable to recognize or recall tunes, however, they can nevertheless continue to *read* music when it is put in front of them.

The findings of Sperry's 'split brain' studies have been confirmed by workers using EEG and anaesthetic techniques. When a subject is relaxed and not making use of his cognitive or perceptual abilities, his EEG record shows an increase of alpha rhythm (brain waves of 8 to 10 cycles per second); when, on the other hand, he is asked to concentrate on a task his alpha rhythm is suppressed. A localized disappearance of alpha rhythm is, therefore, an index of activity in that part of the brain, and this provides researchers with a useful tool for studying the different functions of the two hemispheres. Using this technique, it has been demonstrated that subjects required to do mental arithmetic or serial or analytic tasks show suppression of alpha rhythm in the left hemisphere, while those asked to match coloured patterns, listen to music, or do synthetic tasks show alpha suppression on the right.

Similarly, the injection of anaesthetic into the carotid artery supplying the left hemisphere markedly impairs rational and linguistic abilities: subjects can still use language but their vocabulary and ability to construct grammatical, logical sentences is badly affected.

Fundamental distinctions between left and right hemispherical functioning have, therefore, been well defined and established. A number of workers have sought to establish generalizations defining the essential functions of the two sides. Thus, Arthur Deikman, of the Austen Riggs Medical Centre, characterizes the left and right hemispheres as 'active' and 'receptive' respectively. The left side is concerned with *doing*, with manipulating the environment and 'making a dent'. The 'receptive mode' characteristic of the right is concerned with monitoring events as they happen, with perceiving the world as it is rather than subjecting it to some purpose or design. While the left hemisphere commits itself to science, technology and exploitation of the world's diminishing resources, the right follows the *Wu-Wei* of the Taoists, flowing along with the rivers of change rather than struggling against them. The Californian psychologist Robert Ornstein makes a comparable distinction between the 'rational' functions of the left hemisphere and the 'intuitive' functions of the right, and argues that the thought processes characteristic of Western culture (i.e. logical, analytic, directed thinking) predominantly makes use of the left hemisphere while Eastern thought (which is more diffuse, synthetic and tolerant of paradoxes) is more dependent on the right.

Ornstein's suggestion is analogous to the belief advanced by other workers that human beings think simultaneously in two different ways, which can be described in computer terminology as *digital codification* (discursive, verbal and logical) and *analogic codification* (non-discursive, non-verbal and eidetic). Quoting this work with approval, Joseph Bogen (1969) writes: 'where *propositional* thought is typically lateralized to one hemisphere, the other hemisphere evidently specializes in a different mode of thought, which may be called *appositional*.' He is deliberately vague about what 'appositional' actually means, arguing that since the right hemisphere 'excells in capacities as yet unknown to us', the full meaning of 'appositional' will only emerge 'as these capacities are further studied and understood'. He equates this distinction to that traditionally made in everyday speech between 'reason' and 'emotion', the 'head' and the 'heart', evidently agreeing with Pascal's dictum that 'Le coeur a ses raisons que la raison ne connaît point.'

There are interesting parallels here with Freud's view that there are two modes of thought, which he termed 'primary process' and 'secondary process' thinking. Whereas secondary process thinking is logical and develops with the acquisition of language, primary process thinking is 'relatively unorganized, primitive, magical, undifferentiated, based on common motor reactions, ruled by emotions, full of wishful or fearful misconceptions, archaic, vague, regressive, primal' (Fenichel, 1946).

Moreover, most of Jung's work is compatible with the neurophysiological formulations which have achieved currency since his death. As we shall see, his therapeutic emphasis on the necessity for balance and integration between conscious and unconscious processes accords well with a theoretical neurophysiological 'mandala' of horizontal integration between left and right hemispheres and vertical integration between the phylogenetically old and recent brains. Throughout his life Jung stood as the champion of 'intuitive', 'receptive' modes of apprehension, insisting that they were no less valid than the rational and abstract. He maintained that the rationalism of modern life, with its depreciation of everything non-rational, had 'precipitated the function of the irrational into the unconscious' (CW, 7, para. 150). In his published works it is uncanny how often Jung uses the 'sided' concepts which have subsequently become common in modern neurophysiology: 'The same psychic system which, on one side, is based on the concupiscence of the instincts, rests on the other side on an opposing will which is at least as strong as the biological urge' (CW 5, para. 222). Again and again he returns to the theme of the opposites and the need for their reconciliation if the goal of individuation is to be approached: 'Conflict or comparison between incommensurables is impossible. The only possible attitude is one of mutual toleration, for neither can deprive the other of its validity' (CW 14, para. 150). 'Individuation means becoming a single homogeneous being' (CW 7, para. 266). 'The goal is only important as an idea; the essential thing is the opus which leads to the goal: that is the goal of a lifetime. In its attainment 'left and right' are united, and conscious and unconscious work in harmony' (*CW* 16, para. 400). Jung would have shared Bogen's respect for the 'appositional' and applauded his insistence that it be given equal weight with the 'propositional'. 'The two opposing "realities", the world of the conscious and the world of the unconscious, do not quarrel for supremacy, but each makes the other relative' (*CW* 7, para. 354).

The question arises as to why it is that the two hemispheres should have specialized in different, but complementary, functions in the course of evolution. There have been a number of suggestions. Washburn and Hamburg (1968), for example, argue that it reflects the novel demands made on a new right-handed, tool-making, weapon-using, talking animal – the left hemisphere evolving as the locus of the manipulatory, linguistic and logical skills necessary for survival, while the right hemisphere became the repository of visuo-spatial abilities. Jerre Levy (1974) sees the relationship between the two hemispheres as essentially *symbiotic*, each hemisphere performing functions that the other finds difficult, the symbiosis being consummated, as it were, across the corpus callosum. Bogen (1969) believes that the dual system increases the chances of finding an innovative solution to novel problems, but that it has the inherent drawback of increasing the likelihood of internal conflict. It is presumably in order to deal with this conflict that one hemisphere has come to dominate the other. Discipline is, after all, preferable to anarchy, not least among brain cells.

Cerebral imperialism: dominance and inhibition

Cerebral dominance, like all biologically determined human characteristics, is susceptible to environmental influences. It is probable that in all cultures the left hemisphere of individual men and women, with few exceptions, dominates over the right; but it is equally likely that in some cultures it is more dominant than in others. Our own culture is a case in point: ever since the Renaissance, stress has increasingly been laid on the need to develop left hemispheric functions at the expense of the right. Encouragement of the left hemisphere begins early in life with the emphasis placed in all Western primary schools on the need for proficiency in the three Rs (writing, reading and arithmetic). Although right hemispheric activities such as art, drama, dancing and music are given a place in the curriculum, fewer resources and fewer hours are allocated to them than to left-sided disciplines such as mathematics, languages, physics and chemistry; and at times of economic retrenchment it is invariably the right-sided activities which are pruned or curtailed.

Education reflects the ruling obsessions of society; and a culture such as ours which stresses the importance of rational, analytic processes rather than aesthetic, synthetic ones, and which places a higher value on material achievement than on symbolic expression, inevitably promotes a form of left hemispheric 'imperialism'. This intracranial imperialism proceeding within the microcosm of the skull has been mirrored by a macrocosmic imperialism on a global scale, where a right-wing, 'left hemispheric' oligarchy imposed its will on the increasingly left-wing 'subdominant' peoples of the world. Just as there has been bitter conflict between these opposing interests on the political level, so there is reason to believe that conflict occurs between the dominant and subdominant sides of the brain. As we noted in the last chapter, the psychodynamic techniques for dealing with inner conflicts have been elucidated by psychoanalysis. Recent advances in neurophysiology have tempted some workers to locate these 'ego-defence mechanisms' (e.g. repression, dissociation, denial, etc.) in the hemispheric nuclei linked by the tracts of the corpus callosum.

In the course of studying the relative responsiveness of the two hemispheres of commissurotomized patients, Gazzaniga (1973) tried presenting the picture of a nude woman first to the left hemisphere and then to the right:

> When the picture was flashed to the left hemisphere of a female patient, she laughed and verbally identified the picture as a nude. When it was later presented to the right hemisphere, she said in reply to a question that she saw nothing, but almost immediately a sly smile spread over her face and she began to chuckle. Asked what she was laughing at, she said: 'I don't know . . . nothing . . . oh that funny machine.'

This much-quoted example has been variously interpreted as illustrating the mechanisms of repression and denial. Moreover, dissociation has been noted by Sperry (1968): it seems that much of the time the left hemisphere is grandly indifferent to the activities of the right and is quite capable of disowning them. Thus, one of Sperry's commissurotomized patients, who had made an impulsive response with her left hand, exclaimed, 'Now I know it wasn't me who did that!'

Denial can be observed in patients who have suffered extensive lesions of the right hemisphere resulting in paralysis of the left side of the body: such patients tend to deny that there is anything wrong with them and seem to adopt an attitude of cold indifference to their often severe disabilities. (This corresponds to the 'belle indifférence' to their symptoms shown by neurotic patients who develop hysterical paralysis or hysterical blindness – when the condition has no organic basis but is psychically induced as a means of escaping conflict.) Patients who have suffered left cerebral lesions, on the other hand, are usually profoundly affected by them.

Dr David Galin of the Langley Porter Research Institute, San Francisco, suggests that the way in which the intact left hemisphere characteristically copes with a lesion in the right by denying its existence is due to 'an inhibition of information transfer across the corpus callosum for the damaged right side' (1974). Galin believes that such inhibition of neuronal transmission through the corpus callosum can occur in all people – not just those with right hemispheric lesions – and that it has the effect of functionally disconnecting ('dissociating') the right hemisphere from the left. If this is so, then it would mean that we are now in a position to investigate the neurophysiological mechanisms underlying the psychoanalytic phenomenon of repression. Galin argues that activity in the disconnected right hemisphere does not cease but persists, much in the same way as Freud maintained that repressed unconscious contents continue to be charged with energy and persist with a life of their own, their existence being betrayed by neurotic symptomatology or slips of the tongue. The personal unconscious, it seems, resides – if it can be said to reside anywhere – in the right cerebral hemisphere.

The location of the personal unconscious, visual imagery and primary process thinking in the right hemisphere would also indicate that this hemisphere should be predominant in the activities of dreaming, phantasizing and active imagination. Such indeed seems to be the case. Thus, EEG records have demonstrated greater activity in the right hemisphere than in the left both during dream sleep and during active sexual phantasy just prior to orgasm (Bakan, 1976). Wilder Penfield was able to induce dreams and visual hallucinations in patients having brain surgery under local anaesthetic by stimulating areas of the right cerebral cortex but not of the left. Moreover, several patients who had experienced frequent, vivid dreams before having their commissures cut reported that they no longer had dreams after the operation – presumably because the dream material was no longer available to the speech centres of the left hemisphere and hence could not be verbally formulated. (Bogen, 1969).

The intellectual bias of the left hemisphere and its somewhat condescending attitude to the activities of the right goes some way to explain the dismissive views commonly expressed in our culture concerning the value of dreams and phantasies; yet, as Dr Ernest Rossi, a Jungian analyst from Malibu, California, argued in a seminal paper ('The Cerebral hemispheres in analytic psychology'), 'since ancient times, dreams have been continually rediscovered as sources of higher, intuitive or more synthetic patterns of psychological growth and understanding.' He comments that the dichotomy between the synthetic approach of the right hemisphere and the analytic approach of the left directly reflects the psychotherapeutic distinction which emerged historically between the 'synthetic or constructive method' of Jung and the 'analytical (causal-reductive) method' of Freud. As Jung observed: 'The intellect has no objection to "analysing" the unconscious as a passive object; on the contrary such an activity would coincide with our rational expectations. But to let the unconscious go its own way and to experience it as a reality is something beyond the courage and capacity of the average European' (*CW* 12, para. 60). In contrast to the 'imperialist' attitude of Freud, Jung believed that the only way to approach the unconscious was 'to try to attain a conscious attitude which allows the unconscious to cooperate instead of being driven into opposition' (*CW* 16, para. 366).

> The conscious mind allows itself to be trained like a parrot, but the unconscious does not – which is why St. Augustine thanked God for not making him responsible for his dreams. The unconscious is a psychic fact; any efforts to drill it are only apparently successful, and moreover harmful to consciousness. It is and remains beyond the reach of subjective arbitrary control, in a realm where nature and her secrets can be neither improved nor perverted, where we can listen but may not meddle. (*CW* 14, para. 51)

Neurosis, Jung argued, was 'self-division' (*CW* 7, para. 428), the purpose of therapy was to heal the split. The 'merely conscious' ('left-dominant') man he saw as 'all ego', 'a mere fragment' inasmuch as he exists 'apart from the unconscious' (*CW* 12, para. 242). Healing is wholeness, and 'conscious wholeness consists in a successful union of ego and Self, so that both preserve their intrinsic qualities' (*CW* 8, para. 430n).

> Disalliance with the unconscious is synonymous with loss of instinct and rootlessness. If we can successfully develop that function which I have called transcendent, the disharmony ceases and we can then enjoy the favourable side of the unconscious. The unconscious then gives us all the encouragement and help that a bountiful nature can shower upon a man. (*CW* 7, paras. 195–6)

He implicitly warns against the dangers of left hemispheric imperialism: 'the unconscious has an inimical or inconsiderate bearing towards the conscious only when the latter adopts a false or pretentious attitude' (*CW* 7, para. 346). Unlike Freud, Jung conceived the essence of ego-consciousness as *limitation*:

> even though it reaches to the farthest nebulae among the stars. All consciousness separates; but in dreams we put on the likeness of that more universal, truer, more eternal man dwelling in the darkness or primordial night. There he is still whole, and the whole is in him, indistinguishable from nature and bare of all egohood. (*CW* 10, para. 304)

Having made his point about the creative potential of the right hemisphere and its importance in 'psychosynthesis' as opposed to the more 'left dominant' procedures of psychoanalysis, Rossi goes on to make some further suggestions as to how the metapsychology of Jung might relate to recent advances in neurology.

Possible neurological bases for Jung's concepts

Psychological types

Jung's classification of people into 'introverted' and 'extraverted' *attitude types* is too well known to require elucidation here, and his four *functional types* ('thinking', 'feeling', 'sensation' and 'intuition') have already been mentioned in chapter 5 (p. 68). In the light of the evidence already presented, it is hard to dissent from the suggestion made by Rossi that the extraverted and introverted attitude types could be related to left and right hemispheric functioning respectively. This attribution would accord with Deikman's distinction between the 'active mode' of the left hemisphere and the 'receptive mode' of the right.

When he comes to assign the functional types between the two hemispheres, however, Rossi is on less certain ground: he believes thinking and feeling to be associated with the left hemisphere and sensation and intuition with the right. Few, I imagine, would have difficulty in entertaining the notion that thinking is a left-sided activity, and intuition – which is concerned with building up an understanding of events from fragmentary information in the form of 'hunches' – a right-sided activity. As Rossi says, the ability 'to synthesize the whole from the part may well be the basic process underlying Jung's definition of intuition as one of the basic functions of the psyche, namely, perception of the possibilities inherent in a situation.' Rossi's suggestion is in complete agreement with Ornstein's view (reported on p. 253 above) that rational functions are performed by the left hemisphere and intuitive functions by the right.

Sensation, too, which is concerned with the perception of reality and with the processing of data about things and people *as they are*, may reasonably be seen as a right hemispheric function. It is when Rossi allocates feeling to the *left* hemisphere, however, that one has difficulty in going along with him. The reason he gives in justification of this attribution is Jung's insistence that feeling is a 'rational' function, since it is not just concerned with the conscious appreciation of emotion but with the evaluation of the significance and worth of whatever is perceived or experienced.

But as Rossi himself asserts, feeling is often experienced as an *affect*. To confine it, therefore, to the left hemisphere would seem mistaken.

Instead, it is more likely that it is a bilateral function, the affectual component being primarily localized in the right hemisphere and the evaluative or judgmental component in the left, their integration depending upon two-way traffic across the corpus callosum. This would appear to be reasonable speculation in view of Schwartz's (1975) demonstration of the importance of pathways between the limbic system of the midbrain (see Figure 13.3) and the cortex of the right hemisphere in the experience and expression of emotion. Moreover, there are few ideas which are not emotionally toned, and few emotions without ideational content. Yet with the exception of Jung, psychologists, no less than philosophers, have tended to discuss thoughts and feelings as if they were separate entities. We know from experience, however, that they are not. And the millions of connections which exist between the cerebral hemispheres and the emotional centres of the midbrain afford good neurological reasons why this should be so. Electrical stimulation of tiny areas of the hypothalamus (Figure 13.3) with micro-electrodes give rise to coarse emotions (anxiety, pleasure, fear, etc.) and not to fine or

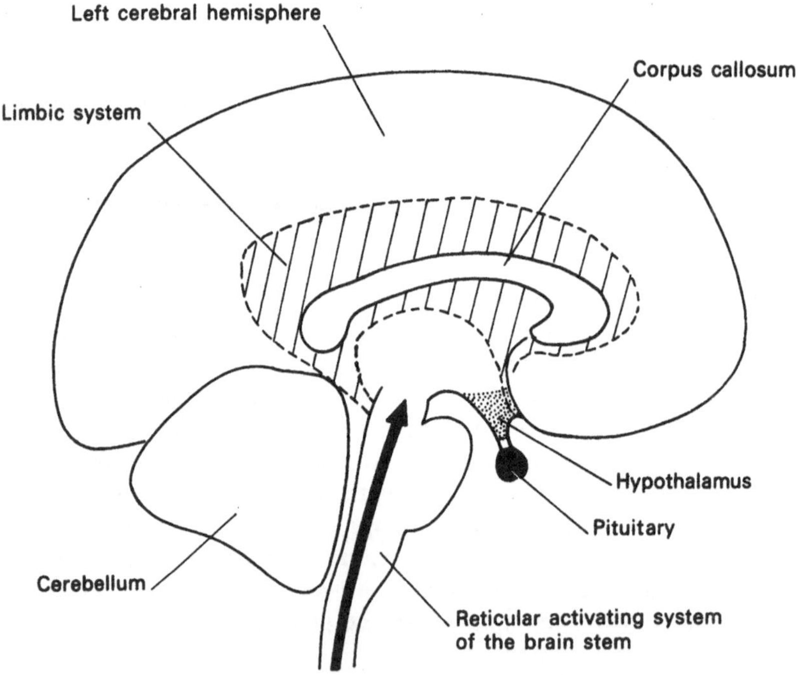

FIGURE 13.3 Diagrammatic representation of the left half of the brain, the cut surface being viewed from the right

complex feeling states, which are clearly dependent on elaboration in both cerebral cortices.

In summary, therefore, there is reason to suppose that the Jungian attitude and functional types may be subject to cerebral lateralization – the left hemisphere subserving the extraverted attitude and thinking function, the right contributing to the introverted attitude and intuitive and sensation functions, while the feeling function is mediated by both hemispheres acting in conjunction via the corpus callosum.

Ego and consciousness

Rossi follows Galin and others in locating ego-consciousness in the left hemisphere: 'whence comes our sense of self-awareness, identity, and control?' he asks. 'When we say "I know", "I can", "I will", from which side of the brain are we speaking? The very fact that we are speaking means it is coming from our left hemisphere because that is where the speech centres are located. When we say "I know", we usually mean that our left hemisphere knows. He quotes in his support the remark made by Sperry's commissurotomized patient when her right hemisphere acted impulsively through her left hand – 'Now I know it wasn't me that did that.' While acknowledging that each hemisphere has qualitatively different forms of consciousness, Rossi insists that 'we typically identify with the rational processes and verbal knowing of our left hemisphere.'

In linking the ego specifically to the left hemisphere Rossi may well be justified – especially in respect of members of our 'left-dominant' culture – but it would clearly be an error to confine to the left side of the brain consciousness as a whole. Consciousness is not a simple, unitary phenomenon which can be assumed to possess a discrete cerebral location, but a richly complex process dependent upon a vast network of neuronal structures which are probably hierarchically arranged. Thus cortical anaesthesia, ablation or auto-inhibition does not result in the abolition of consciousness, but only in an impairment of its finer, more differentiated functions: the lower levels of neuronal organization remain active together with the less discriminating consciousness associated with them.

Perception is largely a matter of selection and interpretation in the light of archetypal preparation and individual experience, as we argued in Chapter 4; it also depends on the integration of information coming from *all* sense modalities, with or without the intervention of consciousness. Percepts are assessed in the light of already existing knowledge, loaded with affect, and made potentially available to conscious experience: the perceptual-affectual activities of the right hemisphere and midbrain are combined, via the corpus callosum, with the abstract, analytical, verbal activities of the left. These cerebral processes, functioning as an enormously complex and integrated totality, are evidently the very stuff of consciousness, and are the consequence of brain functioning as a whole rather than of processes occurring in any specific group of neurones (apart from those of the *reticular activating system* of the brain stem, which seems to be the powerhouse driving the whole complex of systems subserving consciousness). In other words, consciousness consists of 'putting things together', and among other things, it depends on heavy traffic in both directions across the corpus callosum. According to Arthur Blumenthal (1977), consciousness is 'generated' by a complicated process of *transformation* through which *sequence* of events (left hemisphere) are turned into *simultaneous* perceptions (right hemisphere). Commissurotomy certainly does not abolish consciousness – only blocking the activity of the reticular activating system appears to do that – but it impairs consciousness qualitatively because it disrupts the transformation on which Blumenthal sets so much store. The corpus callosum thus contributes to the integration of hemispheric functions on which 'higher' consciousness depends, but like all other parts of the brain (except the reticular activating system), it is not indispensable. One cannot but agree with Roger Sperry that consciousness is a property of brain circuitry and brain chemistry working as a whole. And this squares with the Jungian view that individuation, personality development and greater consciousness are dependent upon the psyche functioning as a balanced totality.

To equate the conscious mind with one hemisphere and the unconscious with the other is a gross over-simplification: it savours too much of the 'geographical' view of the brain so beloved of the phrenologists. Consciousness and unconsciousness are not geological strata to be 'mapped', nor are they like citizens of two states whose political boundaries can be drawn; they are dynamic systems in perpetual flux, interacting with one another, as Jung thought, in a homeostatically controlled manner. 'Conscious' and 'unconscious' events occur in *both* hemispheres – though the essentially hierarchical organization of the brain means that the dominant hemisphere has the greater claim to be the seat of our conscious executive faculties.

Archetypes and the collective unconscious

Since archetypes typically express themselves in images and symbols, Rossi has no hesitation in locating them in the right hemisphere. This, too, is a misleading over-simplification. Dr J. P. Henry of Los Angeles is critical of Rossi's failure to take *subcortical structures* into account when discussing the possible neurological substrate of archetypal systems. Henry shares Rossi's view that ego-functions are represented predominantly in the left hemisphere and personal unconscious contents in the right; he also agrees that both systems are interlinked through the tracts of the corpus callosum, transmission along which can be inhibited ('repressed') in the manner suggested by Galin. Where Henry differs from Rossi – and one cannot but take Henry's side – is in placing the archetypal systems not in the right hemisphere but in the limbic system and the brain stem.

While the cerebral cortex is undoubtedly of the greatest significance for human psychology and neuro-physiology, containing as it does no less than 75 per cent of all the 10 or 12 thousand million neurones in the brain, it must not be forgotten that in all primates the phylogenetically much older parts of the brain still exist and still possess their full functional integrity. Yet for the greater part of this century psychologists have done their best to overlook this fact, devoting themselves tirelessly to the study of cognitive and perceptual processes while leaving emotion and instinct to the biologists. There are signs that this bias has begun to

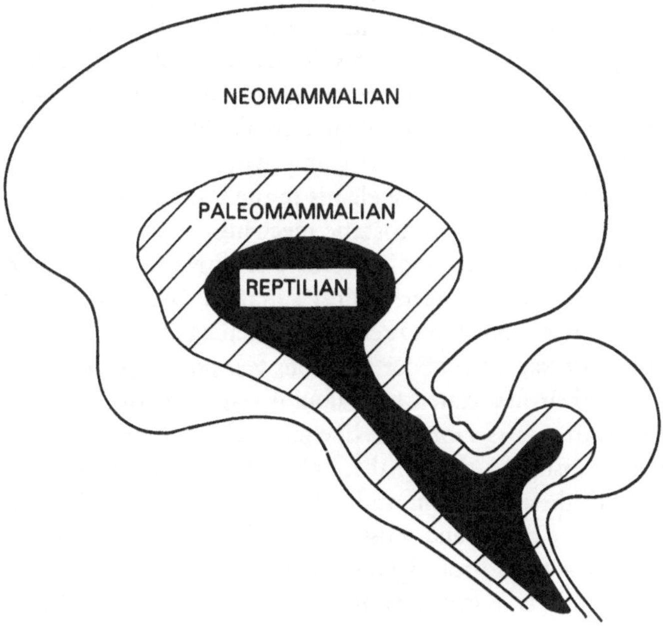

FIGURE 13.4 MacLean's three brains (from MacLean, 1973)

change – largely through the work of Paul MacLean, the American neuroscientist, who has conceived of the brain not as a unity, but as *three brains in one*, each with a different phylogenetic history, each differing in kind from the other despite the myriad interconnections linking them together, each with 'its own special intelligence, its own special memory, its own sense of time and space, and its own motor functions' (MacLean, 1976). Henry, and his colleague Stephens, argue that the dominant hemisphere represents a fourth and phylogenetically most recent system which is peculiar to our species.

In line with these suggestions, it is conceivable that the brain evolved in four stages:

1 *The reptilian brain*: this is the brain stem, an upward growth of the spinal cord and the most primitive part of the brain, which we share with all vertebrate creatures and which has remained remarkably unchanged by the march of evolution. It contains nuclei which control processes vital to the sustenance of life (i.e. the cardiovascular and respiratory systems) as well as the reticular activating system, which is responsible for alertness and the maintenance of consciousness. At this early evolutionary stage emotions had not emerged, nor had cognitive appreciation of future or past events. Behavioural responses at this level are largely governed by instinct and appear to be automatic.

2 *The paleo-mammalian brain*: this is made up of those subcortical structures collectively known as the midbrain, the most important components of which from our point of view are the limbic system, including the hypothalamus, and the pituitary gland (which controls and integrates the activities of all the endocrine glands in the body). The hypothalamic and pituitary systems are homeostatic mechanisms *par excellence*: they not only maintain a critical and supremely sensitive control of hormone levels but also balance hunger against satiation, sexual desire against gratification, thirst against fluid retention, sleep against wakefulness. By this evolutionary stage, the major emotions fear and anger have emerged together with their associated behavioural responses of flight or fight. Conscious awareness is more in evidence and behaviour is less rigidly determined by instincts, though these are still very apparent. The areas concerned with these emotions and behaviours lie in the limbic system, which includes the oldest and most primitive part of the newly evolving cerebral cortex – the so-called *paleocortex*. In all mammals, including man, the midbrain is a structure of the utmost complexity, controlling the psycho-physical economy and many basic responses and attitudes to the environment. An animal, deprived of its cerebral cortex, can still find its way about, feed itself, slake its thirst, and avoid painful stimuli, but it has difficulty in attributing function or 'meaning' to things: a natural predator will be noticed, for example, but not apparently per-

ceived as a threat. Thus, accurate perception and the attribution of meaning evidently requires the presence of the cerebral hemispheres.
3 *The neo-mammalian brain*: this is the *neocortex*, which is responsible for cognition and sophisticated perceptual processes as opposed to instinctive and affective behaviour.
4 *The human brain*: cerebral lateralization has occurred, with the development of the left dominant hemisphere responsible for rational, empirical thinking and the use of language and speech.

This evolutionary schema of brain functioning accords with the popular distinction made by James Olds between the 'hot' and 'cold' brains. The hot brain (the midbrain) may be readily identified with Freud's 'Id' which functions in accordance with the *pleasure principle*: it is impulsive, incautious and wanton – it demands its own way, and it wants it *now*. The cold brain (the neocortex) is more rational and it demonstrates a strong susceptibility to social conditioning: as custodian of the *reality principle* it is responsible for mediating the passions of the hot brain to the environment, causing them to heed the constraints and exigencies of outer necessity. This is but another example of how the brain works by achieving a balance between opposing systems.

Attempts to integrate the two disciplines of neurophysiology and ethology have led to a focusing of interest on the hot brain as a possible locus of neuronal systems subserving species-specific patterns of behaviour. MacLean (1975), in particular, suggests that phylogenetically determined patterns of behaviour, such as maternal attachment, courting and erotic behaviour, dominance and submission, and territorial defence, together with the emotions which accompany them, are dependent upon the activation of neuronal systems in the midbrain (especially the limbic system and the striatal complex).

MacLean's conclusions, largely derived from animal studies, are possibly no less applicable to man, as the work of Flor-Henry (1976) and Schwartz *et al.* (1975) would indicate. They have demonstrated that human emotional responses are dependent on neuronal pathways linking the limbic system of the midbrain with parietal and frontal areas of the right cerebral hemisphere. Moreover, Flor-Henry has made the truly fascinating discovery that this whole complicated right hemispheric/limbic affectional system is under the surveillance and control of the *left* frontal cortex – thus lending further weight to the conclusion that the left hemisphere can, via the corpus callosum, 'repress' or inhibit the activities, and especially the *emotionally toned* activities (which are the vital concern of psychiatrists), of the right.

While it may well be that psychic processes belonging to the personal Freudian' unconscious proceed in the right hemisphere, it seems probable that Jung was right when he guessed that the archetypal systems, if they could be given a local habitation and a name, must have their neuronal substrate located primarily in the phylogenetically much older parts of the brain. It is not, of course, possible to designate any precise neurological location for any of the archetypes. Inasmuch as one archetypal system can be differentiated from another, each must have an extremely complex and widely ramifying neurological substrate involving millions of neurones in the brain stem and limbic system (the instinctive or biological pole) and both cerebral hemispheres (the psychic or spiritual pole). When one considers which of the two hemispheres is more appropriate to the processing of archetypal components, one can agree with Rossi that it must be the right: 'Jung's concepts of archetype, collective unconscious and symbol are more closely associated with the use of the imagery, gestalt and visuospatial characteristics of right hemispheric functioning.' Rossi quotes a passage where Jung says,

> The archetype is essentially an unconscious content that is altered by becoming conscious and by being perceived, and it takes its colour from the individual consciousness in which it happens to appear. By a symbol I do not mean an allegory or a sign, but an *image* [Rossi's italics] that describes in the best possible way the dimly discerned nature of the spirit. A symbol does not define or explain; it points beyond itself to a meaning that is darkly divined yet still beyond our grasp, and cannot be adequately expressed in the familiar words of our language.

Rossi comments that although Jung makes it clear that the archetype is an imprint or pattern that exists independently of ego-consciousness, it can, nevertheless, achieve expression 'in the form of words, concepts and language of the ego's left hemispheric realm'; but once this happens 'they become only representations that take their "colour from the individual consciousness in which it happens to appear". It is precisely because the normal processes of the right hemisphere are not readily translated into the logical, verbal formulations of the left, that the ego perceives them on occasion as 'numinous': the *mysterium tremendum et fascinans* of archetypal symbols may be due to the left hemisphere's congenital inability fully to comprehend them. Many people, with an extraverted, convergent 'left hemispheric' attitude to life, seem reluctant to expose themselves to the symbolical aspects of experience, and it is probable that they count among their number a high proportion of those who are largely unaware of their dreams, and who have great difficulty in recalling dream events when asked to do so (Austin, 1971). Possibly, extraverts and convergent thinkers are more prone to inhibit information passing across the corpus callosum from the right.

However, Henry and Stephens (1977) believe that not only can the left hemisphere inhibit communication from the right, but that both hemispheres, in addition, may well be capable of suppressing communications from the limbic system. Moreover, they suggest that psychic health and personality integration depend as much on the maintenance of open communication between limbic system and cortex as on communication between the two hemispheres. Most interesting of all in the light of Jung's views on the function of dreams, is their suggestion that the neurophysiological purpose of dreaming is to promote integration of processes occurring in the limbic system with those of the cerebral hemispheres. Their hypothesis would square well not only with Jungian clinical experience but with Jouvet's finding that the low voltage, high frequency EEG waves characteristic of dreaming sleep originate in the brain stem and spread upwards through the midbrain to the cortex: 'It has been held that dreams represent information coming from the various "depths" of the unconscious. If Galin (1976) is correct, dreams might represent information coming from the limbic system by way of the right hemisphere during the special state of rapid-eye-movement (REM) sleep.' (Henry and Stephens, 1977, p. 111).

Concluding his persuasive and highly instructive review of the evidence, Henry declares that

> the metapsychological foundations built by Carl Jung are proving to be soundly conceived. There is a rapidly growing body of evidence linking our mammalian inheritance of basic brainstem functions with man's unique religious, social and cultural achievements. Society has scarcely begun to consider the implications of these discoveries.

The purpose of dreaming

Dreaming is a mammalian characteristic. No REM sleep has been detected in amphibians or reptiles, and only fractional amounts in birds. In mammals, on the other hand, REM sleep begins very early in life, being apparent not only immediately after birth, but in the uterus as well. It seems that REM sleep is necessary for normal activity in the central nervous system of all mammalian species. What can its biological purpose be?

One persuasive view of the phenomenon points out that in the course of development the young mammal has to adapt its old brain of reptilian inheritance to a much more recently acquired repertoire of behaviour patterns made possible by the evolution of the mammalian neocortex. The growth of neurones, and differentiation of the communications between them, continues for some considerable time after birth and Jouvet believes that it is during this crucial early period that dreaming plays an indispensable role in organizing the archetypal biogrammar into the complicated behavioural and psychic sequences involved in mating, hunting, dominance and the defence of territory. Jouvet suggests that the function of dreaming is essentially to activate neurones that are responsible for programming patterns of behaviour characteristic of the species. While these patterns are, of course, related to stimuli arising from the environment, the fundamental processes involved in integrating the archetypal biogrammar inherent in the genetic programme into the developing behavioural repertoire has to occur at night, in Jouvet's view, since it is only during sleep that the 'command neurones' are free from the need to meet the numerous demands of the environment normally encountered during wakefulness.

In line with Jouvet's hypothesis, some findings suggest that deprivation of REM sleep in rats may delay integration of the archetypal programmes for attachment and territorial behaviour with the higher cognitive processes of the cerebral hemispheres (e.g. Smith *et al.*, 1974). Moreover, Lucero (1970) has observed that after rats have been doing some hard learning they spend longer periods of the night in REM sleep. What is more, if they are prevented from experiencing REM sleep for two or three hours after they have been learning their learning proves to be less efficient.

Evidence that phylogenetically ancient structures play an important part in the nightly dreams of contemporary human beings can be found in studies which classify the content of dreams without going in any detail into their symbolism. In one statistical study, cited by Carl Sagan (1977), of the common dreams of college students, the following themes were reported in descending order of frequency:

1 falling
2 being pursued or attacked
3 repeated attempts at performing a task
4 experiences connected with academic work
5 sex.

It seems likely that all except the fourth category (which is clearly linked with the subjects' everyday preoccupations) are phylogenetically determined. Falling dreams are not surprising in a creature which, in the earlier stages of its evolution, spent its life in trees; nightmares of being attacked and pursued are only to be expected in a species whose primordial conflicts have involved hunting, fighting, and striving for dominance; repeated attempts to perform tasks would reflect our never-ending preoccupation with the need to master environmental vicissitudes, physical skills, religious rituals, social customs, etc., while the fifth category scarcely requires comment.

One interesting finding of this study was that half the subjects reported dreaming of snakes. While Freudians would doubtless see such dreams as evidence of phallic symbolism they can also be understood as a phylogenetic hangover, a vestigial warning system from our primate past. Freudians will counter that the essentially sexual content of dreams is borne out by sleep laboratory investigations which confirm that in men REM sleep is frequently associated with penile erection, but this is a piece of special pleading which fails to take into account the observation that a large number of physical changes characteristic of midbrain and brain stem activity occur during REM sleep in both sexes: e.g. changes in respiratory rate, pulse rate, body temperature and blood pressure. Dreams also frequently have a powerful affectual component – fear, anxiety, euphoria, despair – by no means obviously sexual. Moreover, anthropological and ethological evidence reveals that penile erection is often associated with archetypal functions other than sexual ones in both human and non-human primates: e.g. threat display, dominance and territorial behaviour. Jung's belief that snakes represent brain stem and spinal cord activities may well be nearer the mark, far-fetched though it sounds. For Jung anticipated by many years MacLean's hypothesis that the brain bears functional regions of ancient phylogeny in the midbrain and brain stem, and he made the surprising suggestion that animals in dreams represent activity in these regions, the 'lower' the animal on the phylogenetic scale the more primitive the region represented: 'with the snake the psychic rapport that can be established with practically all warm-blooded animals comes to an end. . . . As Hippolytus says, the Gnostics identified the serpent with the spinal cord and the medulla. These are synonymous with the reflex functions' (*CW* 9, pt ii, para. 396).

> The lower vertebrates have from earliest times been favourite symbols of the collective psychic substratum (higher vertebrates symbolize mainly affects), which is localized anatomically in the subcortical centres, the cerebellum and the spinal cord. These organs constitute the snake. Snake dreams usually occur, therefore, when the conscious mind is deviating from its instinctual basis. (*CW* 9, pt ii, para. 282)

Jung's approach to dreams was fundamentally biological. The study of dreams, he believed, 'opens the way to a general comparative psychology from which we may hope to gain the same understanding of the development and structure of the human psyche as comparative anatomy has given us concerning the human body' (*CW* 8, para. 476). 'A dream, like every element in the human structure, is a product of the total psyche. Hence we may expect to find in dreams everything that has ever been of significance in the life of humanity' (*CW* 8, para. 527). He rejected Freud's view of the 'dream work' whereby 'latent' wishes are fulfilled through transformation into the 'manifest content' of the dream. 'As against Freud's view that the dream is essentially a wish-fulfilment, I hold . . . that the dream is a *spontaneous self-portrayal, in symbolic form, of the actual situation in the unconscious*' (CW 8, para. 505, Jung's italics). '*I take the dream for what it is*. . . . The dream is a natural occurrence, and there is no earthly reason why we should assume that it is a crafty device to lead us astray. It occurs when consciousness and will are to a large extent extinguished' (CW 11, para. 41, Jung's italics). Dreams, Jung believed, are the means by which the psyche maintains its equilibrium.

> The psyche is a self-regulating system that maintains its equilibrium just as the body does. Every process that goes too far immediately and inevitably calls forth compensations, and without these there would be neither a normal metabolism nor a normal psyche. In this sense we can take the theory of compensation as a basic law of psychic behaviour. Too little on one side results in too much on the other. (CW 16, para. 330)

Writing dreams down and bringing them to analytic sessions for discussion and interpretation merely serves to enhance their compensatory effect. But

> lack of conscious understanding does not mean that the dream has no effect at all. Even civilized man can occasionally observe that a dream which he cannot remember can slightly alter his mood for better or worse. Dreams can be 'understood' to a certain extent in a subliminal way, and that is mostly how they work. (CW 18, para. 52)

Night after night dreams put us in touch with our phylogenetic past, with the 'unitary soul of humanity', and it is in this extraordinary achievement that their therapeutic importance lies.

> The evolutionary stratification of the psyche is more clearly discernible in the dream than in the conscious mind. In the dream, the psyche speaks in images, and gives expression to instincts, which derive from the most primitive levels of nature. Therefore, through the assimilation of unconscious contents, the momentary life of consciousness can once more be brought into harmony with the law of nature from which it all too easily departs, and the patient can be led back to the natural law of his own being. (CW 16, para. 351)

Jung saw his task as a psychotherapist as achieving a reconciliation between his patient and the '2 million year-old man that is in all of us'. Our difficulties, he argued, 'come from losing contact with our instincts, with the age-old unforgotten wisdom stored up in us. And where do we make contact with this old man in us? In our dreams' (1971, p. 76).

Dreams, therefore, are the language used in the life-long dialogue proceeding nightly between the ego and the Self: they are the means by which the individual becomes psychically related to the life-cycle of his species. Jung was the first psychologist to draw attention to the importance of *dream-series* in mediating and exemplifying this process. Taken singly, each dream compensation

> is a momentary adjustment of one-sidedness or an equalization of disturbed balance. But with deeper insight and experience, these apparently separate acts of compensation arrange themselves into a kind of plan. They seem to hang together and in the deepest sense to be subordinated to a common goal, so that a long dream-series no longer appears as a senseless string of incoherent and isolated happenings, but resembles the successive steps in a planned and orderly process of development. I have called this unconscious process spontaneously expressing itself in the symbolism of a long dream-series the individuation process. (*CW* 8, para. 550)

Jung's clinical observations are in agreement with the modern evidence that dreaming is associated with a preponderance of right hemispheric cerebral activity: 'It is characteristic that dreams never express themselves in a logical, abstract way but always in the language of parable or simile' (*CW* 8, para. 474). Written communications and inscriptions are not uncommon in dreams, but it is usually difficult to decipher their meaning, even in the dream; on waking it is often impossible to recall what was written in any detail. Dream time, dream arithmetic, and dream logic are also notoriously unreliable. As Robert Ornstein has suggested, it is as if the left and right hemispheres function like the sun and the stars. Although the stars keep their station in the heavens during the hours of daylight, we are unaware of them on account of the brilliance of the sun. But when the sun goes down and we are no longer dazzled by its radiance, the stars come into their own. So it is with dreaming. 'In sleep, fantasy takes the form of dreams. But in waking life, too, we continue to dream beneath the threshold of consciousness' (*CW* 16, para. 125). In the alert brain the rational, verbal brilliance of the left hemispheric system 'dazzles' (i.e. inhibits) our awareness of events occurring in the intuitive, symbol-producing right. It is when the sun sets in the left hemisphere that the stars come out in the right hemisphere and assume the form of dreams. Ornstein's metaphor is a pleasing one – not least because the equation of the sun with the 'light of consciousness' is very ancient, as is its setting with the 'night sea journey' of the hero. Every night, the extraordinary adventure is repeated: the onset of sleep heralds the death of one day's measure of the conscious life-span; the heroic ego consigns itself to the deep to hold communion with the ancestral spirits that reside there and, gathering their wisdom and their guidance, prepares for the miraculous birth of another day.

The transcendent function

The aim of Jungian psychotherapy is, in terms of the neurological model under discussion, to reduce the left hemisphere's inhibition of the right hemisphere and to promote increased communication in both directions across the corpus callosum. The therapeutic objective of achieving greater integration between the activities of both hemispheres would then correspond, as Rossi (1977) suggests, to what Jung called the *transcendent function*. The transcendent function resides in the mutual influence of conscious and unconscious, ego and Self, and Jung believed that there were two basic methods by which this mutuality could be brought about: 'the way of *creative formulation*' (e.g. active imagination, creative phantasy, dreams, symbols, art and aesthetics) and 'the way of *understanding*' (e.g. intellectual concepts, verbal formulations, conscious awareness and abstraction). Writing of these two approaches, Jung declared:

> One tendency seems to be the regulating principle of the other; both are bound together in a compensatory relationship . . . aesthetic formulation needs understanding of the meaning, and understanding needs aesthetic formulation. The two supplement each other to form the transcendent function. (*CW* 8, quoted by Rossi, 1977, p. 45)

The therapeutic measures advocated by Jung – dream amplification, active imagination, symbolic expression through painting, sculpture and music – all had the specific intention of promoting the integration of conscious and unconscious processes. In the light of modern neurophysiology we can now see them as a means of achieving interaction between both cerebral hemispheres and as an attempt to correct the culturally induced suppression of the right hemisphere by the left. Rossi speculates that the universal religious practices of mankind – prayer, ritual, the use of mantras and mandalas – possess the same purpose, the promotion of bilateral hemispheric integration. This suggestion is particularly persuasive in view of the finding by Dr Bernard Glueck (1975) and others that EEG records show greater synchrony between both sides of the brain in subjects practising transcendental meditation.

The notion of bringing both hemispheres into greater harmony offers a plausible neurological basis for the 'higher consciousness' which Jung described as the primary consequence of the transcendent function and 'the union of opposites':

> the union of opposites on a higher level of consciousness is not a rational thing, nor is it a matter of will; it is a psychic process of development which expresses itself in symbols. Historically, this process has always been represented in symbols, and today the development of individual personality still presents itself in symbolical figures.

Symbolism is the very essence of the transcendent function: 'since the symbol derives as much from the conscious as from the unconscious, it is able to unite them both, reconciling their conceptual polarity through its form and their emotional polarity through its numinosity' (*CW* 9, pt ii, para. 280)

> The unconscious can be reached and expressed only by symbols, which is the reason why the process of individuation can never do without the symbol. The symbol is the primitive expression of the unconscious, but at the same time it is also an idea corresponding to the highest intuition produced by consciousness. (Commentary on 'The Secret of The Golden Flower', p. 107.)

In order to facilitate the transcendent function, Jung encouraged his patients to indulge in spontaneous phantasies:

> you choose a *dream*, or some other *fantasy-image*, and *concentrate* on it by simply catching hold of it and looking at it. You can also use a *bad mood* as a starting point, and then try to find out what sort of fantasy-image it will produce, or what image expresses this mood. You then fix this image in the mind by *concentrating your attention*. Usually it will alter, as the mere fact of contemplating it animates it. The alterations must be carefully *noted down* all the time, for they reflect the psychic processes in the unconscious background, which appear in the form of *images* consisting of conscious memory material. In this way conscious and unconscious are united. (*CW* 14, para. 706, italics added)

Once again Jung's clinical intuition is in agreement with the neurological facts: dreams, phantasy-images, bad moods, are all right hemispheric functions; concentrating, attending, contemplating and writing down are all left hemispheric functions. 'In this way conscious and unconscious are united.' So are the left and right hemispheres.

Conclusions

When considered from the viewpoint of modern neurology, Jung's work stands as a brilliant vindication of his belief in the value of intuitive knowledge. For his theoretical formulations owed their origins to an intuitive genius powerful enough to prevail against the hostile intellectual currents of his time: the great originality, academic courage and moral determination which he displayed in propounding his ideas earned for him among his contemporaries a reputation for professional perversity, but in the two decades which have elapsed since his death his dogged affirmation of his own insight appears increasingly to have been justified.

In particular, his overriding conviction that the life-experience of individual men and women is profoundly influenced by phylogenetically acquired 'dominants' is more difficult to refute now than ever before, as is his view of the psyche as a homeostatic system which strives perpetually to achieve a balance between opposing propensities while at the same time actively seeking its own individuation. As a result, the hypotheses relating to the archetype, collective unconscious, symbol and transcendent function are beginning to receive more sympathetic consideration than Jung could ever have anticipated. Moreover, there is now good reason to suppose that the 'command neurones' subserving archetypal systems may be situated in the phylogenetically ancient cerebral regions of the midbrain and brain stem, and that dreams do indeed possess the crucial function that Jung ascribed to them of linking the inherent biogrammar of the species with the conscious awareness of the individual.

For all the importance of the older centres of the brain, however, the two cerebral hemispheres are the 'temenos' where the archetypal world and the contemporary world meet and where their manifold interactions are integrated. The folk wisdom distinguishing the attributes of left from right holds good in its contra-hemispheric mirror image – the left hemisphere mediating the yang of action, the right the yin of experience. The major distinctions between the two hemispheres are summarized in Table 13.2.

At the present stage of knowledge, it would be naive to attribute the transcendent function specifically to the corpus callosum, but the integrity of this bundle of fibres is probably indispensable to the individuation process. For although the old brain centres must profoundly influence events occuring in both cerebral hemispheres, they are in themselves probably inaccessible to consciousness and it is, consequently, at the inter-hemispheric level that psychoanalysis and psychosynthesis proceed.

Table 13.2 Summary of differences between left and right cerebral hemispheres

	Left hemisphere dominant	*Right hemisphere* subdominant
Awareness	more conscious	more unconscious
Mental institutions	ego/Persona/superego	Shadow/personal unconscious
Attitude type	extravert	introvert
Functional type	thinking	intuition

Table 13.2 Summary of differences between left and right cerebral hemispheres (continued)

	Left hemisphere dominant	*Right hemisphere* subdominant
	feeling (evaluative)	sensation
		feeling (affective)
Data processing	sequential	simultaneous
Mode of functioning	conceptual	perceptual
	'secondary process'	'primary process'
	propositional	appositional
	active	receptive
	convergent thinking	dreams, phantasies
	rational/abstract	visuo-spatial/concrete
	materialistic	aesthetic
	analytic	synthetic
	Logos principle	Eros principle
Typical symbols	words	images
Typical approach	orderliness	spontaneity
Attitude to own body	neglect	attention
Cultural contribution	mathematics	painting
	science	sculpture
	technology	music
	theology	mysticism

Finally, the usefulness of analytical psychology as a psychotherapeutic system has stood the test of time: not only does it provide a detailed description of the psychic consequences which may be presumed to follow from functional imbalance between the two hemispheres, but it has also developed effective techniques for redressing that imbalance by:

1 lessening the dissociation of one hemisphere from the other:

2 promoting functional development of the right hemisphere in compensation for the culturally induced 'hypertrophy' of the left; and

3 facilitating greater integration (the transcendent function) between both hemispheres.

Without knowing it, Jung advocated a therapeutic approach which was predominantly right hemispheric – it had to be in order to counter the left hemispheric biases of Western society. This does not mean that he saw wholeness as a goal to be reached purely by dedicating oneself to right hemispheric experience; on the contrary, wholeness entailed the 'union of opposites'. But such was the world in which he and his patients lived that he knew intuitively that individuation could only be advanced by giving weight to those 'irrational' propensities of the psyche that post-Newtonian science had taught us to repress. It was all a question of balance.

· 14 ·

A question of balance

On 18 December 1913, Jung, already embarked on his 'experiment with the unconscious' after his break with Freud, awoke from the following dream:

> I was with an unknown, brown-skinned man, a savage, in a lonely, rocky mountain landscape. It was before dawn; the eastern sky was already bright, and the stars fading. Then I heard Siegfried's horn sounding over the mountains and I knew that we had to kill him. We were armed with rifles and lay in wait for him on a narrow path over the rocks.
>
> Then Siegfried appeared high up on the crest of the mountain, in the first ray of the rising sun. On a chariot made of the bones of the dead he drove at furious speed down the precipitous slope. When he turned a corner, we shot at him, and he plunged down, struck dead.
>
> Filled with disgust and remorse for having destroyed something so great and beautiful, I turned to flee, impelled by the fear that the murder might be discovered. But a tremendous downfall of rain began, and I knew that it would wipe out all traces of the dead. I had escaped the danger of discovery; life could go on, but an unbearable feeling of guilt remained.
>
> When I awoke from the dream, I turned it over in my mind, but was unable to understand it. I tried therefore to fall asleep again, but a voice within me said, 'You *must* understand the dream, and must do so at once!' The inner urgency mounted until the terrible moment came when the voice said, 'If you do not understand the dream, you must shoot yourself!' In the drawer of my night table lay a loaded revolver, and I became frightened. Then I began pondering once again, and suddenly the meaning of the dream dawned on me. 'Why, that is the problem that is being played out in the world.' Siegfried, I thought, represents what the Germans want to

> achieve, heroically to impose their will, have their own way. 'Where there is a will there is a way!' I had wanted to do the same. But now that was no longer possible. The dream showed that the attitude embodied by Siegfried, the hero, no longer suited me. Therefore it had to be killed.
>
> After the deed I felt an overpowering compassion, as though I myself had been shot: a sign of my secret identity with Siegfried, as well as the grief a man feels when he is forced to sacrifice his ideal and his conscious attitudes. This identity and my heroic idealism had to be abandoned, for there are higher things than the ego's will, and to these one must bow.
>
> These thoughts sufficed for the present, and I fell asleep again.
>
> The small, brown-skinned savage who accompanied me and had actually taken the initiative in the killing was an embodiment of the primitive shadow. The rain showed that the tension between consciousness and the unconscious was being resolved. Although at the time I was not able to understand the meaning of the dream beyond these few hints, new forces were released in me which helped me to carry the experiment with the unconscious to a conclusion. (1963, pp. 173–4)

This was a prophetic dream with significance not just for Jung and the German people but for the whole of Western civilization. To the central European spirit, Siegfried, the blond god, the warrior hero, was the symbol of imperial aspiration; but Jung, far ahead of the prevailing *Zeitgeist*, knew that Siegfried must be sacrificed. The brown-skinned man, as symbol of the unconscious, was a recurrent figure in Jung's life, of equal importance with the 'dark' African continent itself in guiding him away from the Freudian Id to the archetypes of the collective unconscious. The imperial attitude to Africa as an 'interior' to be 'opened up' and exploited stands as a good metaphor for Freud's conception of the unconscious as something to be made known, put to the service of reason and, so to speak, 'colonized'. Before the Europeans embarked on their 'civilizing mission', Africa was an intact ecological system in which thousands of different tribes lived in a state of primordial homeostasis with each other and their 'environment of evolutionary adaptedness'.

> Into this rich, unconsciously integrated *matrix* had intruded the greedy, psychically-disintegrated, *ego*-driven white men, with their guns and their Mosaic-Evangelical version of Christianity, ruthlessly destroying the tribal infrastructure, imposing their alien culture and institutions, and in general smashing up beyond recall a harmony between man and nature, in order to exploit the earth of Africa for its metals, precious stones and other 'products' to gratify the ego-drives of a civilization now more than ever emerging in its true

> colours as the ultimate cuckoo in the nest of creation. (Booker, 1980)

When Jung visited Kenya and Uganda in the autumn of 1925, he came in a somewhat different spirit – to learn, before it was too late, something about the archetypal nature of mankind. Travelling with friends to Nairobi, he awoke as his train

> was just making a turn round a steep red cliff. On a jagged rock above us a slim, brownish-black figure stood motionless, leaning on a long spear, looking down at the train. Beside him towered a gigantic candelabrum cactus.
>
> I was enchanted by this sight – it was a picture of something utterly alien and outside my experience, but on the other hand a most intense *sentiment du déjà vu.* I had the feeling that I had already experienced this moment and had always known this world which was separated from me only by distance in time. It was as if I were this moment returning to the land of my youth, and as if I knew that dark-skinned man who had been waiting for me for five thousand years.
>
> The feeling-tone of this curious experience accompanied me throughout my whole journey through savage Africa. . . . I could not guess what string within myself was plucked at the sight of that solitary dark hunter. I knew only that his world had been mine for countless millennia. (1963, p. 239)

Jung's impulse to understand and relate to the denizens of the Dark Continent was indistinguishable from that which drove him to understand and relate to the contents of the collective unconscious. In order to make this possible, the 'imperial arrogance' of ego-consciousness (and the left hemisphere) had to be sacrificed: on the brown man's behalf, Siegfried had to be killed.

But to confine the implications of Jung's dream to his own life or to the imperial past would be to miss the point. In fact, the whole history of the world since the Renaissance can be summed up in the neurological allegory of the ascent and apotheosis of the dominant hemisphere. For it is this dissociated, left-sided intelligence that has enabled us to view nature as something to be 'mastered', social institutions as things to be 'engineered' and traditional values as constraints to be overthrown. It is this unprincipled visionary which has concocted the two great secular myths of our time – Marxism and what Eliade calls *le mythe du progrès infini* – and which has accomplished the total desacralization of both cosmos and society for the first time in human history. It is this unbalanced tyrant that has allowed us to commit monstrous crimes, equipped us to fight world wars and encouraged us to split atoms – that dread *hubris* for which the gods may surely make us pay the ultimate price.

As the current of history has accelerated to the Niagara of the present, it is as if Western culture has achieved a progressive subordination of the right hemisphere to the interests of the left. In a manner of speaking, the right hemisphere of modern man may be said to have suffered an 'atrophy of disuse' while the left hemisphere has become progressively 'hypertrophied' (I use these terms metaphorically and not in a neurological sense). The dominant hemisphere, as maker of plans and theoretical systems, has everywhere made free with the yang principle of right-handed activity so as to impose its will on reality, sustained in its course by an unquestioning acceptance of the myth of eternal progress – the trite belief that through ingenious application of the 'miracles of science' we are creating an ever better world, where suffering will be abolished and everyone made healthy, happy and free. In this spirit, Karl Marx put his left hemisphere to work in the Reading Room of the British Museum and as a direct consequence one-third of the world's population has now been offered the unappealing alternatives of slavery or genocide. (Is *slavery* too harsh a word? Not if one thinks about it. A slave is one who has no private property, is forced to spend his life in toil, and has a master/overseer whom he dare not defy and from whom he can never hope to escape. In comparison with slaves who are private property, slaves owned by the socialist state are better housed, clothed and fed, it is true, but, alas, they are slaves nevertheless.)

In the West, our technological triumphs, economic miracles, redistributed wealth, planned cities and welfare states have not noticeably coincided with greater personal happiness or any apparent flowering of the human spirit. Indeed, those indices of flourishing civilization, music, the arts, costume, philosophy, religion and architecture, all in their present forms would seem diagnostic of an imminent descent into barbarism. Delight in the glory of human existence is not what strikes one first on contemplating our materially pampered contemporaries; rather disenchantment, resentment, an obsession with material possessions, and an insatiable appetite for *more*.

The contemporary *Zeitgeist* has created on both sides of the iron curtain (itself a form of political commissurotomy) societies which are materially preoccupied, spiritually impoverished and technologically possessed; in a sense, the state socialism of the East and the consumer capitalism of the West are but opposite sides of the same coin – a purely materialistic conception of life. Where they still differ, fortunately, is in their attitude to personal freedom, the West having so far hung on to its humanist traditions, though there are signs that even this is changing as bureaucracies grow more powerful and the materialist compulsion pushes us further down the road towards the corporate state.

What, as everyone is asking nowadays, has gone wrong? If our neurological speculations are valid, how is it that the two sides of the brain have become so out of phase with one another, why have conscious and unconscious processes become so divorced? And what can be done, if it is not too late, to bring about a reconciliation?

The trouble began with The Fall. As hunter-gatherers, we obeyed nature, we adapted to our ecological niche, we accepted our lot as the innocent children of God, grateful for whatever it pleased Him to provide. Such was the primordial 'Paradise' in which our species lived out 99 per cent of its life. Then we sampled the forbidden fruit: we learned the secrets of agriculture and animal husbandry, relinquished our dependence on God, and started to bend nature to our will.

Societies before the Fall were societies without agriculture and without surpluses. They existed in a state of balance with all other species of flora and fauna, and the balance, which persisted for hundreds of millennia, was both outer and inner. Just as Man was homeostatically adapted to his environment, the ego was homeostatically adapted to the Self. Then, with increasing left hemispheric dominance, the masculine ego concerned itself with the discovery of ever more efficient ways of conceptualizing and exploiting what were later to be called 'the Laws of Nature'. But disaster did not threaten until the Renaissance and the birth of modern science:

> Nature and Nature's laws lay hid in night;
> God said: 'Let Newton be', and all was light.

The light was lit, but at a terrible price: by turning the intellect into an instrument dedicated to the discovery of objective truth we effectively divorced thinking from feeling; we made science amoral and in that moment ensured that its advances would lead to intemperate power rather than cautious wisdom. Detached from its archetypal roots, the technically accomplished ego began its rampage over the face of the earth, pillaging, polluting, exploiting, till the resources of the great globe itself have reached the point of bankruptcy.

We cannot say we were not warned. As we set out on the scientific adventure, Francis Bacon cautioned us that we could never hope to command nature unless we first learned to obey her. But no one heeded him: instead we learned to command nature by *defying* her. We were warned too by the medieval church: probing into the ways of God and putting His laws to our own selfish purposes would end in no good; it would provoke His wrath and result in our undoing. Was this superstitious timidity or true insight into where it would all lead?

'Newton's single vision' as Blake called it – the assumption that scientific method can provide the only means to knowledge – inevitably coincided with left-hemispheric hypertrophy and the inflation of ego-consciousness. (Ego-inflation, like economic inflation, is what happens when thinking is exalted above feeling and ideas are divorced from criteria of *value.*) The primordial sciences did not make this mistake. Before Alchemy became Chemistry all knowledge had a sacred dimension: unlike modern scientists, alchemists *revered* matter and expected to be spiritually transformed by their work. The post-Renaissance view of alchemical purpose is a travesty, a base projection of our own barren spirit: the alchemist's intention extended far beyond mere greed for gold: what he wanted was not so much to enrich his coffers as to transform his soul. The art required complete dedication of the whole man: *Ars requirit totum hominem.* In order to acquire the 'golden understanding one must keep the eyes of the mind and the soul well open, observing and contemplating by means of that inner light which God has lit in nature and in our hearts from the beginning' (*Musaeum Hermeticum*, 1678). As the same text put it, 'the mind must be in harmony with the work.' The modern scientific mind, by contrast, seems to lack harmony with itself, let alone 'the work'. (For a fuller comparison between modern and primordial scientific attitudes see Godwin in Waddington (1972), from which the above quotations were gleaned.)

In recognizing Paradise *Lost*, however, it is easy to lose sight of what we have gained. Pre-agricultural societies had no pollution, no overpopulation, no slums, no tanks, no cruise missiles, it is true, but they had no cathedrals, no libraries, no theatres, no anaesthetics either. And even if we wished to return to a pre-Fall existence, the dominant hemisphere would not allow it: we know far too much ever to revert to the simple homeostatically organized life of the hunter-gatherer. We have eaten of the fruit, and an angel with a flaming sword bars re-entry to Paradise. Even if we had the political will to abolish hydrogen bombs, we should continue to live under their threat. The left hemisphere of too many scientists knows how to organize their manufacture when 'the national interest' might render it 'imperative'.

So has Newton's light brought no advantages? Are not the majority of us – in the northern hemisphere at any rate – richer, better fed, more comfortable than ever before in the history of our kind? Undoubtedly. But again we forget the price. In counting our blessings we invariably overlook the shadow that they cast. Of course, antibiotics and perinatal care are good things in that they have spared us the anguish of infant mortality and greatly reduced the danger of losing prematurely the ones we love; but the Shadow side of medical progress has been a perilous increase in the size of the world's population. Technological innovation has, without question, produced wealth and comfort on an unprecedented scale and, through the peaceful use of nuclear energy, it could solve the world crisis in fuel supplies; but the shadow side of these developments is ugliness, noise, pollution, mineral exhaustion, the extinction of a growing multitude of animal species and the probability of nuclear catastrophe. Good and Evil behave as if they were opposite poles of a homeostatic system. What is happening on the global scale is an extension of what happens to an individual in a state of psychic imbalance, when ego has become dissociated from Self and is working *contra naturam*.

Possible remedies

How is the balance to be re-established? Jung's preliminary answer was the sacrifice of Siegfried. By this he did not imply a surgical need for collective left hemispherectomy, but a fundamental spiritual reorientation – an abandonment of left hemispheric imperialism and a subordination of the ego to the Self. That we should, in other words, give up seeking power and seek wisdom; and he conceived wisdom as lying in the attainment of a rich conscious relationship to all that is eternally valid (i.e. the realm of the archetypes).

This was a revolutionary position to adopt because it amounted to a total rejection of the 'colonial' view of the psyche, which has been with us long before Freud – for over two thousand years, in fact. It originated with Plato and was handed down to us through the Stoics, through Descartes, Spinoza and Kant. The notion of an Imperial Governor, called Reason, imposing his rule on rebellious tribes of Passions and Instincts, is also used by William Blake. It recurs, as we have seen, in Olds's conception of a 'hot' brain functioning under the restraint of a 'cold'. The revolutionary desire to overthrow the Governor also has a long history and it has resulted in a great variety of spiritual and political 'movements'. As would be expected in an extraverted, materialistic society like ours, the political movements have gained more attention and more adherents than the spiritual ones. But since political movements are about power and the possession and distribution of wealth, they have no remedy to offer for an imbalance which is inherently *psychic*.

While Jung was not hostile to politics – he was a firm upholder of the virtues of liberal democracy – he was completely out of sympathy with all forms of political extremism. Instead of projecting our neurotic problems out on to society and seeking political solutions for them there, he believed that we should assume full personal responsibility for them and seek psychological solutions within ourselves. As early as the 1920s he saw signs that this reorientation had started: 'The reaction which is now beginning in the West against the intellect in favour of feeling, or in favour of intuition, seems to me to mark a cultural advance, a widening of consciousness beyond the too narrow limits of a tyrannical intellect' (1962, p. 85). He applauded this trend because 'one-sidedness, though it lends momentum, is a mark of barbarism.' A high culture, on the other hand, is one in which the opposites balance one another. If Jung is right, then it could be that 'high' culture occurs at those times in history when *both* hemispheres are equally functional and their activities well-integrated.

Whatever reactions Jung may have detected 'against the intellect and in favour of feeling' during the 1920s, they would probably have been halted, or even thrown into reverse, by the impact of National Socialism and the Second World War. Only with the hippie generation of the 1960s did a popular movement against 'the Governor' adopt a specifically right hemispheric stance. Eastern philosophies and religious practices were taken up with great enthusiasm, as was the use of 'mind-expanding' drugs to make time stand still, heighten sensory perception and intensify inner experience, while the conventional values and competitive behaviour typical of consumer capitalism were vigorously rejected. Although the hippie phenomenon did not last, the growing contemporary interest in health foods, yoga exercises, jogging and physical sports reflects group right hemispheric activity, since it is the right hemisphere that concerns itself with the body in contrast to the left, which is relatively indifferent to the perception of somatic functions.

Despite these developments, however, our culture remains intractably 'left-sided'. A minority of people may be health-conscious, but the great majority display massive indifference to their physical well-being and, despite shrill warnings from the medical profession, continue to poison their bodies with a surfeit of animal fats, cigarettes and alcohol, take woefully insufficient exercise, and become flabby, sluggish and ill. Sport – a predominantly right-sided activity – has become more popular, it is true, but here too the left hemisphere shows every indication of remaining firmly in control as all sporting activities become increasingly 'organized', 'professional' and a source of 'big business'. Saddest symptom of all is the steady decay in the arts as they come increasingly under the dominance of the left hemisphere: mathematical sequences in music, incomprehensible abstractions in painting, elaborate gimmickry in sculpture – all needing books or words to 'explain' what they are about in *conceptual* terms instead of allowing them to speak directly in their own perceptual idiom to the right hemisphere where they belong. If a good wine needs no bush, neither does a good painting. When the hemispheres get out of balance we lose our sense of proportion; when the ego is detached from the Self all contact with the archetypal realm is lost, and art dies. 'The work of art,' wrote Ludwig Wittgenstein, the eminent Cambridge philosopher, 'is the object seen *sub specie aeternitatis*; and the good life is the world seen *sub specie aeternitatis*.' Our culture sees nothing *sub specie aeternitatis*; it despises the eternal and cares only for the here and now. Transhistoric and transcendental meaning are no longer considered. Inasmuch as we are interested in the past, it is a 'left-sided' interest, which seeks to pin man down to his place in that irreversible procession of events we call history: it goes no further than trying to explain how we came to be where we are. In this manner, we have *provincialized* time and completely overlooked the wonderful circumstance that we also live in *non*-historical time – in the archetypal experiences of life, love and death, in our imagination, and, above all, in our dreams. *Le régime nocturne de l'esprit* was rightly prized by the alchemists, for, as Gaston Bachelard maintained, the spirit's nocturnal life has a primordial value which transcends the diurnal life of the ego. Jung attributed so much importance to dreams for this reason, since they, more than any other psychic phenomenon, put us in touch with eternity and make individuation possible. 'Ultimately, every individual life is at the same time the eternal life of the species' (CW 11, para. 146).

This history of man's attempts to relate to the eternal is enshrined in his myths and religions. As was argued in chapter 12, religion evolved as a means of establishing absolute values in the interests of the stable continuity of the group. Each religion arises from the Self of gifted members of the group and is called out by the environmental and historical circumstances of the culture concerned. Thus, all religions are true expressions of the biological reality of the Self. This is not to say that they possess literal truth as judged by the logical criteria of the left hemisphere, but they do possess validity as experienced by the Self. Jung believed the God archetype – the archetype of the Sacred and Holy – to be a fundamental attribute of the Self, irrespective of whether God actually existed or not. For Jung, God was not so much a projection of the personal father, as Freud maintained, as a reflection of the Self. The eternal quality universally attributed to Him is an expression of the miraculous durability of the archetype of archetypes, the human genome. That the God archetype nowadays leaves so many of us untouched by its numinosity is because we have grown up in a culture whose 'God is dead' and whose religion has decayed, and the archetype has not been actualized in us. Yet it slumbers on in the deeper recesses of the Self.

> Our modern attitude looks back arrogantly upon the mists of superstition and of medieval or primitive credulity, entirely forgetting that we carry the whole living past in the lower storeys of the skyscraper of rational consciousness. Without the lower storeys our mind is suspended in mid air. No wonder it gets nervous. The true history of the mind is not preserved in learned volumes but in the living psychic organism of every individual. (CW 11, para. 56)

We shall never entirely escape from our need for mythology and religion: it is too fundamental a part of our nature, deeply irrational though it may seem.

> Everyone who has his eyes and wits about him can see that the world is dead, cold, and unending. Never yet has he beheld a God, or been compelled to require the existence of such a God from the evidence of his senses. On the contrary, it needed the strongest inner compulsion, which can only be explained by the irrational force of instinct, for man to invent those religious beliefs whose absurdity was long since pointed out by Tertullian. (*CW* 5, para. 30)

Religious belief is 'planned for' in the genome. People can no longer believe in God, yet they are programmed to believe in something. If God dies, they will find other vessels, however cracked, in which to pour their faith. Both Self and society need religion; without it both suffer and both ultimately perish. A secular religion, like communism or fascism, which is more acceptable to the left hemisphere, will flourish for a time, but precisely because its tenets are *man*made – and therefore profane – it cannot last for millennia or provide criteria of *absolute* value in the manner of a sacred religion: it will be abandoned when men tire of it or think they have found something better.

The trouble is that political programmes, like scientific ones, are predominantly the products of the left hemisphere and consequently tend to 'deny' and 'repress' their own Shadow. Prosperity, social justice, equality, the greatest good of the greatest number, all are high ideals, but their Shadow side is a vast bureaucracy, ubiquitous state ownership and intervention, statute books full of penal laws, more restrictions and less freedom. Moreover, to impose a Marxist paradise inevitably demands a ruthless Procrusteanism because it is an ideal which contravenes too many archetypes: it cannot be imposed and maintained save by the gun, backed up with officious censorship, an omniscient secret police force and a chain of concentration camps. Marxism without compulsion assumes that when men are made equal they will no longer wish to own personal property, acquire territory, compete for valued resources, or form groups to acquire power, pick quarrels and impose their will. But, in fact, these things are so deeply programmed in our nature that nothing short of tyranny will stop them.

'Man is not a machine that he can be remodelled for quite other purposes as occasion demands, in the hope that it will go on functioning as regularly as before but in a quite different way. He carries his whole history with him; in his very structure is written the history of mankind' (*CW* 6, para. 570). And that structure presupposes the sacred as well as the profane, the gods as well as Caesar.

> All ages before us have believed in gods in some form or other. Only an unparalleled impoverishment of symbolism could enable us to discover the gods as psychic factors, that is, as archetypes of the unconscious. Heaven has become for us the cosmic space of the

> physicist, and the divine empyrean a fair memory of things that once were. But 'the heart glows', and a secret unrest gnaws at the roots of our being. (*CW* 9, pt i, para. 50)

Observing the disintegration of Christianity, Jung predicted that the secret unrest gnawing at the roots of our being would cause many Westerners to turn for spiritual enlightenment to the East. He considered that this would occur as an enantiodromia, since he saw traditional philosophical and religious attitudes of the East as balancing and compensating those of the West and, had he been familiar with the modern neurological findings concerning the different functions of the left and right cerebral hemispheres, there can be little doubt that he would have linked Western attitudes with the left and Eastern with the right. 'While the Western mind carefully sifts, weighs, selects, classifies, isolates, the Chinese picture of the moment encompasses everything down to the minutest nonsensical detail, because all the ingredients make up the observed moment' (*CW* 11, para. 969).

> In general, meditation and contemplation have a bad reputation in the West. They are regarded as a particularly reprehensible form of idleness or as pathological narcissism. No one has time for self-knowledge or believes that it could serve any sensible purpose. . . . We believe exclusively in doing and do not ask about the doer, who is judged only by achievements that have collective value. (*CW* 14, para. 709)

Whereas the West approves of only one form of understanding – understanding through the intellect, 'the East teaches us another, broader, more profound, and higher understanding – understanding through life' (*CW* 13, para. 2).

Though deeply respectful of the East, however, Jung also predicted that few Westerners who attempted to adopt Eastern modes of thought would achieve much benefit thereby: 'Great as is the value of Zen Buddhism for understanding the religious transformation process, its use among Western people is very problematical. The mental education necessary for Zen is lacking in the West' (*CW* 11, para. 902).

> When faced with this problem of grasping the ideas of the East, the usual mistake of Western man is like that of the student in *Faust*. Misled by the devil, he contemptuously turns his back on science, and, carried away by Eastern occultism, takes over yoga practices quite literally and becomes a pitiable imitator. (Theosophy, [he commented, writing in 1929,] is our best example of this mistake). And so he abandons the one safe foundation of the Western mind and loses himself in a mist of words and ideas which never would

> have originated in European brains, and which can never be profitably grafted upon them. (1962, pp. 82–3)

He anticipated the fraudulent posturings of the 'trendy' devotees of the 1960s and 1970s, with their ill-digested scraps of 'Eastern wisdom', their flowing robes, joss sticks, mantras and imported gurus. He was fond of quoting the ancient Chinese warning, 'If the wrong man uses the right means, the right means work in the wrong way.' The path adopted by a man must be appropriate and true to his own nature and the history of his culture.

> If it ceases to be this, then the method is nothing more than an affectation, something artificially added, rootless and sapless, serving only the illegitimate goal of self-deception. It becomes a means of fooling oneself and of evading what may perhaps be the implacable law of one's being. This is far removed from the earth-born quality and sincerity of Chinese thought. On the contrary, it is the denial of one's own being, self-betrayal to strange and unclean gods, a cowardly trick for the purpose of usurping psychic superiority, everything in fact which is profoundly contrary to the meaning of the Chinese 'method'. For these insights result from a way of life that is complete, genuine, and true in the fullest sense; they are insights coming from that ancient, cultural life of China which has grown consistently and coherently from the deepest instincts, and which, for us, is forever remote and impossible to imitate. (1962, p. 83)

If we are to seek wisdom, therefore, and, as it were, bring the right cerebral hemisphere into more equal balance with the left, we must be true to our Western origins, and this includes giving due recognition to our Judeo-Christian heritage:

> Instead of learning the spiritual techniques of the East by heart and imitating them in a thoroughly Christian way – *imitatio Christi*! – with a correspondingly forced attitude, it would be far more to the point to find out whether there exists in the unconscious an introverted tendency similar to that which has become the guiding spiritual principle of the East. We should then be in a position to build on our own ground with our own methods. If we snatch these things directly from the East, we have merely indulged our Western acquisitiveness, confirming yet again that 'everything good is outside', whence it has to be fetched and pumped into our barren souls. It seems to me that we have really learned something from the East when we understand that the psyche contains riches enough without having to be primed from outside, and when we feel capable of

> evolving out of ourselves with or without divine grace. (CW 11, para. 773)

Discovering whether there exists in the Western psyche an introverted tendency similar to that which has been the guiding spiritual principle of the East is a labour synonymous with Jung's experiment with the unconscious, and it took him most of his life. As we have seen, it was the initial stage of the task which was for him the most stressful and the most dangerous, but he never regretted his decision to attempt it.

> Everything good is costly, and the development of the personality is one of the most costly of all things. It is a question of yea-saying to oneself, of taking one's self as the most serious of tasks, of being conscious of everything one does, and keeping it constantly before one's eyes in all its dubious aspects – truly a task that taxes us to the utmost. (1962, p. 95)

The Westerner who attempts it cannot, like the pre-revolutionary Asian, expect any support from his culture: indeed, as Jung knew all too well, the weight of Western culture would be against him. It therefore demanded ethical courage and great determination. 'The individual must give himself to the new way completely, for it is only by means of his integrity that he can go further, and only his integrity can guarantee that his way does not turn out to be an absurd adventure' (p. 95).

If, having taken serious note of these warnings, one nevertheless decides to undertake the experiment for oneself, how does one proceed? Jung's answer appears startlingly simple: one must learn *the art of letting things happen.*

> The art of letting things happen, action through non-action, letting go of oneself, as taught by Meister Eckhart, became for me the key opening the door to the way. We must be able to let things happen in the psyche. For us, this actually is an art of which few people know anything. Consciousness is forever interfering, helping, correcting, and negating, and never leaving the simple growth of the psychic process in peace. It would be simple enough, if only simplicity were not the most difficult of all things. To begin with, the task consists solely in objectively observing a fragment of fantasy in its development. Nothing could be simpler, and yet right here the difficulties begin. No fantasy-fragment seems to appear – or yes, one does – but it is too stupid – hundreds of good reasons inhibit it. One cannot concentrate on it – it is too boring – what would it amount to – it is 'nothing but', et cetera. The conscious mind raises prolific objections, in fact it often seems bent upon blotting out the spontaneous fantasy-activity in spite of real insight, even of firm determination on the part of the individual to allow the psychic

> process to go forward without interference. Often a veritable cramp of consciouness exists. (p. 93)

In other words, the left hemisphere persists in its customary work of domination and inhibition, and it requires patient practice to liberate the right hemisphere from its tyranny.

'If one is successful in overcoming the initial difficulties, criticism is still likely to start in afterwards and attempt to interpret the fantasy, to classify, to aestheticize, or to depreciate it. The temptation to do this is almost irresistible' (p. 93). But one must persevere. 'These exercises must be continued until the cramp in the conscious mind is released, or, in other words, until one can let things happen. . . . In this way a new attitude is created, an attitude which accepts the non-rational and the incomprehensible, simply because it is what is happening' (p. 94).

This activity, when persisted in, 'opens up' the lines of communication along the ego-Self axis, constellates the transcendent function, undoes the inhibition of traffic across the corpus callosum from right to left, and brings both hemispheres more into balance. The ego, it will be recalled, is an actualization of a deintegrate of the Self which, in the course of childhood development, becomes subject to the left hemispheric laws of time and causality. However, the residual Self remains unconscious and exempt from these laws, and when its symbols are encountered in dreams or by the use of active imagination (the art of letting things happen), they are experienced by the ego as irrational and strange. In a sense, we are, each and everyone of us, the two sons of Zeus – Castor, the mortal ego, and Pollux, the immortal Self. (Christ's injunction to 'rejoice because your names are written in heaven' is another expression of the dual nature of individuality, personal and suprapersonal.) Western life and Western education alienate the two, and favour Castor at the expense of Pollux; it is the aim of analytical psychology and the goal of the individuation process to bring about their reconciliation.

The records of his own active imagination and those of his patients provided Jung with a wealth of material which it became his life's work to decipher.

> The chaotic assortment of images that at first confronted me reduced itself in the course of the work to certain well-defined themes and formal elements, which repeated themselves in identical or analogous form with the most varied individuals. I mention, as the most salient characteristics, chaotic multiplicity and order; duality; the opposition of light and dark, upper and lower, right and left; the union of opposites in a third; the quaternity (square, cross); rotation (circle, sphere); and finally the centring process and a radical arrangement that usually followed some quaternary system. . . . The

> centring process is, in my experience, the never-to-be-surpassed climax of the whole development, and is characterized as such by the fact that it brings with it the greatest possible therapeutic effect. The typical features listed above go to the limits of abstraction, yet at the same time they are the simplest expressions of the formative principles here at work. In actual reality, the patterns are infinitely more variegated and far more concrete than this would suggest. Their variety defies description. I can only say that there is probably no motif in any known mythology that does not at some time appear in these configurations. . . . In general, my patients had only a minimal knowledge of mythology. (CW 8, para. 401)

When phantasies take the form of thoughts, 'intuitive formulations of dimly felt laws or principles emerge, which at first tend to be dramatized or personified' (e.g. they take the form of dialogues with the Anima/Animus or the Wise Old Man). When they are images which are drawn or painted, they are expressed in the *mandala* forms listed by Jung in the above passage.

> *Mandala* means 'circle', more especially a magic circle. Mandalas are found not only throughout the East but also among us. The early Middle Ages are especially rich in Christian mandalas; most of them show Christ in the centre, with the four evangelists, or their symbols, at the cardinal points. This conception must be a very ancient one, because Horus and his four sons were represented in the same way by the Egyptians. . . . An unmistakable and very interesting mandala can be found in Jacob Böhme's book XL *Questions concerning the Soule*. It is clear that this mandala represents a psychocosmic system strongly coloured by Christian ideas. Böhme calls it the 'Philosophical Eye' or the 'Mirror of Wisdom', by which is obviously meant a *summa* of secret knowledge. Most mandalas take the form of a flower, cross, or wheel, and show a distinct tendency towards a quaternary structure reminiscent of the Pythagorean *tetraktys*, the basic number. Mandalas of this sort also occur as sand paintings in the religious ceremonies of the Pueblo and Navaho Indians. But the most beautiful mandalas are, of course, those of the East, especially the ones found in Tibetan Buddhism. . . . Mandala drawings are often produced by the mentally ill, among them persons who certainly did not have the least idea of any of the connections we have discussed.' (CW 13, para. 31)

The mandala, therefore, is an ancient and ubiquitous expression of the Self, and in Europe it has tended to be linked with the figure of Christ, whom Edinger (1972) has described as 'a paradigm of the individuating ego'. As both man and God, Christ represents both ego and

Self, and bridges both personal and archetypal realms. That individuation requires sacrifice of ego-centred arrogance, an abandonment of left hemispheric imperialism, is implied by Christ again and again: 'If you would be perfect [*teleios* = complete, full grown],' he tells the rich youth, 'go, sell what you possess and give to the poor, and you will have treasure in heaven; it is easier for a camel to pass through the eye of a needle than for a rich (ego-inflated) man to enter the kingdom of heaven.' Moreover, Christ's instruction to pluck out your *right* eye or amputate your *right* hand if it causes you sin (i.e. if you become alienated from the Self), is a clear call to sacrifice left hemispheric dominance in the service of completeness.

For the European, to adopt the way to individuation is to follow symbolically in the path of Christ: it means sacrifice (of inflated ego-assertiveness) and crucifixion (between the opposites of reason and unreason); it requires wisdom, maturity, courage. It is far harder than the mere espousal of a determined rationalism which denies the unconscious, or a fanatical mysticism which denies reason, or a fugitive existentialism which denies man's archetypal nature. The solitary way taken by Jung is only to be followed by those whose ego-position is strong and who have adjusted well to the collective standards of their culture. Others, whose normal adjustment or personal development has been hindered by what I have termed a 'frustration of archetypal intent' occurring earlier in their lives, will require analytic help before they can set out on the individuation quest. 'Before individuation can be taken for a goal, the educational aim of adaptation to the necessary minimum of collective standards must first be attained' (*CW* 6, para. 590).

Not that the aim of Jungian psychotherapy is to 'normalize', in the sense of acting as an agent of the state, but rather to achieve a healthy balance between opposing systems and to enable the archetypal programme to be lived out to its fullest extent. Treatment consists, therefore, in facilitating the homeostatic propensities already at work within the patient. The Jungian approach to a neurosis is not to denigrate it or to attack it head on, for it too is a solution appropriate to the stage of development reached, an attempt, however imperfect, to achieve some kind of balance and to resolve the conflicts in the patient's life. It is not the neurosis which is the problem so much as the attitude of ego-consciousness to the neurosis and the extent to which this has prevented archetypal actualization from proceeding in the usual way.

In my own clinical experience I have found that the therapeutic activation of unactualized archetypal components depends on just two things: (1) the relationship which develops between patient and therapist (the so-called transference and counter-transference), and (2) the symbol-forming potential of the archeype. If one is to succeed, it is essential to abandon the Freudian view of the transference in favour of

Jung's. For Freud, the transference was a neurosis: the patient transferred on to the person of the therapist the neurotic feelings and distorted expectations he had developed while growing up in the care of his parents. This is all right as far as it goes, because something of the sort does indeed occur, but it leaves out an element of great therapeutic importance, namely, the archetypal dimension. What emerges in the transference is not just the personal parental complexes but the archetypal basis of the complexes as well. These aspects of the parental archetype which, for one reason or another, the personal parents *failed* to actualize, together with the unfulfilled longings to which these aspects give rise, are also constellated in the relationship with the therapist, and this provides him with his most potent therapeutic instrument. This crucial phenomenon occurs quite spontaneously as the transference develops and, properly understood and handled, enables the therapist to bring to birth in the psyche of his patient those aspects of the archetype that had previously existed only as potential. As a result, the patient can complete his business with the parents. Then, freed of what I have called the Flying Dutchman quest, he is able to proceed on the way of individuation.

In achieving this therapeutic goal, however, the symbol-producing capacity of the archetype is every bit as important as the archetypal aspect of the transference. Once activated, unlived archetypal potential begins to 'personate' in phantasies and dreams. If, at this stage, one encourages patients to practise active imagination, they become increasingly aware of these components appearing in the form of 'part personalities' or 'inner objects'. Many people can, with guidance, quickly acquire the knack of holding imaginary conversations with these characters – a practice which existentialist and gestalt therapists have made much of, without recognizing its archetypal origins and with little acknowledgment to Jung. The more attention given to these phantasy figures the more tangible they become, so that both patient and therapist can treat them as real people with a life, so to speak, of their own.

As time goes by, an interesting development occurs in the transference relationship: the patient becomes less dependent on the therapist as he gradually finds security in his inner relationship to the actualizing archetype and as he begins to recognize the tremendous potential of the Self. He is then, almost without realizing it, embarked on the individuation quest.

One does not have to be a doctor, let alone a 'Jungian', to learn the art of letting things happen. Nor is there any left hemispheric 'Do-It-Yourself' guide to The Way: 'A way is only *the* way when one finds it and follows it oneself' (1940). Ultimately, archetypes cannot be described or written about, only experienced in the ideas, images and feelings they give rise to, and there is no means of knowing for certain whether your experience of them is similar to mine.

> The needful thing is not to *know* the truth but to *experience* it. Not to have an intellectual conception of things, but to find our way to the inner, and perhaps wordless, irrational experience – that is the great problem. Nothing is more fruitless than talking of how things must or should be, and nothing is more important than finding the way to these far-off goals. (*CW* 18, para. 1292)

All that is required is the courage to become conscious of one's own individuality.

> Personality can never develop unless the individual chooses his own way, consciously and with moral deliberation. . . . The fact that the conventions always flourish in one form or another only proves that the vast majority of mankind do not choose their own way, but convention, and consequently develop not themselves but a method and a collective mode of life at the cost of their own wholeness. (*CW* 17, para. 296)

While one must be willing to sacrifice the arrogance of ego-consciousness and abandon the subjective attitudes characteristic of 'left hemispheric imperialism', consciousness, and the left hemisphere, nevertheless remain fundamental to the success of the whole venture. What one is seeking is no reversal of cerebral dominance, but a more equitable balance; not an abdication of ego-consciousness, but a widening and enriching of awareness. 'The more unconscious a man is, the more he will conform to the general canon of psychic behaviour. But the more conscious he becomes of his individuality, the more pronounced will be his difference from other subjects and the less he will come up to common expectations' (*CW* 8, para. 344). Individuation is 'the process of forming and specializing the individual nature', which already exists *a priori*; it means the development of the individual as a *personality*, i.e. 'as a differentiated being from the general, collective psychology. Individuation, therefore, is a process of differentiation, having for its goal the development of the individual personality' (*CW* 6, para. 757). But it has to occur in full conciousness, for 'life that just happens in and for itself is not real life; it is only real when it is *known*' (*CW* 12, para. 105).

The call to individuate is the call to become authentic – to live and affirm consciously one's own unique individuality. 'To the extent that a man is untrue to the law of his own being and does not rise to personality, he has failed to realize his life's meaning' (*CW* 17, para. 314). 'One cannot live from anything except what one is' (*CW* 14, para. 310).

It is apparent that the emphasis placed by Jung on the supreme importance of individual consciousness and personality development is completely opposed to the contemporary 'left hemispheric' notion that the ills afflicting Western civilization can be cured by 'political development', 'social engineering' and augmenting the powers of the state.

> The increasing dependence on the State is anything but a healthy symptom; it means that the whole nation is in a fair way to becoming a herd of sheep, constantly relying on a shepherd to drive them into good pastures. The shepherd's staff soon becomes a rod of iron, and the shepherds turn into wolves. (*CW*10, para. 413)

Though entirely accepting that the individual must do his duty by the collective and live up to his social, moral and familial responsibilities, Jung rejected the twentieth century deification of society and its obsession with the acquisition of wealth. ' "Society" is nothing more than a term, a concept for the symbiosis of a group of human beings. A concept is not a carrier of life. The sole and natural carrier of life is the individual, and that is so throughout nature' (*CW* 16, para. 224). And for him, the resources which really counted lay not outside in matter but inside the Self. In one of his most prophetic utterances he wrote:

> The man whose interests are all outside is never satisfied with what is necessary, but is perpetually hankering after something more and better which, true to his bias, he always seeks outside himself. He forgets completely that, for all his outward successes, he himself remains the same inwardly, and he therefore laments his poverty if he possesses only one automobile when the majority have two. Obviously the outward lives of men could do with a lot more bettering and beautifying, but these things lose their meaning when the inner man does not keep pace with them. To be satisfied with 'necessities' is no doubt an inestimable source of happiness, yet the inner man continues to raise his claim, and this can be satisfied by no outward possessions. And the less this voice is heard in the chase after the brilliant things of this world, the more the inner man becomes the source of inexplicable misfortune and uncomprehended unhappiness in the midst of living conditions whose outcome was expected to be entirely different. The externalization of life turns to incurable suffering, because no one can understand why he should suffer from himself. No one wonders at his insatiability, but regards it as his lawful right, never thinking that the one-sidedness of this psychic diet leads in the end to the gravest disturbances of equilibrium. That is the sickness of Western man, and he will not rest until he has infected the whole world with his own greedy restlessness. (*CW* 11, para. 962)

Jung wrote those words in 1944, and his prophecy is fulfilled. Western man *has* infected the world with his greed, and his restlessness continues. If our planet is to be saved for future generations of all species, not only our own, Nature must demand an enantiodromia – that we renounce the extraverted rape of the earth and, by mobilizing the transcendent function, turn inwards and invest in an introverted excavation of the Self. For anyone who believes that exponential growth can go on in a finite world is, as Kenneth Boulding has observed, either a madman or an economist. One can only pray that the enantiodromia will occur before the gods, sickened by our militant *hubris*, visit us with *nemesis*.

Glossary

Analysand: patient undergoing analysis.
Analyst: a therapist who belongs to one of the schools of *depth psychology*. Analysts of the Freudian school call themselves *psychoanalysts*, while analysts of the Jungian school call themselves *analytical psychologists*.
Analytical psychologist: an analyst who subscribes to the the theories and practises the therapeutic techniques devised by C. G. Jung.
Anima: the contrasexual complex in the male.
Animus: the contrasexual complex in the female.
Archetypes: innate neuropsychic centres possessing the capacity to initiate, control and mediate the common behavioural characteristics and typical experiences of all human beings irrespective of race, culture or creed.
Atrophy: wasting away.
Attachment: a tie of affection formed by one person or animal for another: in the sense used by Bowlby, the tie formed between an infant and his mother or mother-substitute. Hence *anxious attachment*: a term used by Bowlby to describe the state of those who suffer from the fear that their attachment figures may either be lost or prove inaccessible to them.
Autosome: a *chromosome* other than a sex chromosome.
Behaviourism: an approach to the study of psychology first proposed by J. B. Watson (1913) which rejected introspection, individual experience and mental events as the focus of investigation and insisted that psychology, like physics and chemistry, should be 'a purely objective, experimental branch of natural science', concerned with observable, measurable and replicable phenomena.
Cartesian dualism: the distinction made by René Descartes (1596–1650) between the body and the mind.
Chromosome: a complex, thread-like structure, numbers of which occur

in every cell of all animals and plants. Chromosomes carry the *genes*, which are the basic units of heredity.

Cognition: a general term covering all modes of conscious knowing.

Collective unconscious: term introduced by C. G. Jung to designate those aspects of the psyche which are common to all mankind. Throughout this book Jung's term is used synonymously with my term *phylogenetic psyche.*

Commissurotomy: the surgical operation of cutting the fibres of the cerebral commissure or *corpus callosum.*

Complex: a group of interconnected ideas and feelings which exert a dynamic effect on conscious experience and on behaviour. Complexes are to the *ontogenetic psyche* (or *personal unconscious*) what *archetypes* are to the *phylogenetic psyche* (or *collective unconscious*), the one being dependent on the other in the sense that complexes are 'personations' of archetypes.

Control theory: the study of the behaviour of systems through the formulation of quantitative models and the use of such concepts as positive and negative feedback.

Corpus Callosum: the bundle of nerve fibres connecting the brain cells of the left and right cerebral hemispheres; also known as the cerebral commissure.

Cybernetics: term introduced by Norbert Wiener (1948) for the theoretical study of control and communication in machines and physiological systems.

Depth psychologist: an *analyst*; especially used of Jungian analysts.

DNA: deoxyribonucleic acid; the basic hereditary material of all living organisms, making up the *genes* and located within the *chromosomes.*

Ecology: the branch of biology which studies animals in relation to their environment.

Ego: the part of the personality which one consciously recognizes as 'I' or 'me'.

Enantiodromia: the propensity of all polarized phenomena to go over to their opposite.

Environment of evolutionary adaptedness: the environmental circumstances in which a species originally evolved.

Epigenesis: biological theory of development proposed by Waddington (1957). It holds that the development of all biological characteristics, whether they be relatively sensitive or insensitive to environmental variation, is governed by the *genome.*

Epiphenomenalism: the view of mental phenomena which sees them as wholly dependent on neurophysiological processes occurring in the brain.

Eros principle: the principle of relationship presided over by the Greek God of Love. In addition to being the secret lover of Psyche, Eros was responsible for co-ordinating all the elements which make up the universe, for bringing harmony to chaos, and for permitting life to develop on earth.

Ethology: the study of the behaviour of organisms living in their natural habitats.

Gene: the basic unit of heredity, made up of *DNA*.

Genome: the complete genetic constitution of an organism, the entire genetic 'programme' characterizing the species.

Gestalt: an integrated whole, a complete entity more significant and organized than a mere summation of its constituent parts.

Homeorhesis: term used by Waddington (1957) to describe the tendency of growing organisms to persist in their course along specific pathways of development once they have started on them, despite environmental variations.

Homeostasis: maintenance of balance between opposing mechanisms or systems. A basic principle of physiology, Jung believed it also to be a basic law of psychic behaviour.

Hypertrophy: excessive growth or development; the opposite of *atrophy*.

Id: Latin word for 'it' used to translate Freud's original term '*das Es*'. 'It is the dark, inaccessible part of our personality; . . . it is filled with energy reaching it from the instincts, but it has no organization, produces no collective will, but only a striving to bring about the satisfaction of instinctual needs subject to the observance of the pleasure principle' Freud (1933).

Individuation: term used by Jung to designate the process of personality development which leads to the fullest possible actualization of the *Self*. 'Individuation means becoming a single, homogeneous being, and, in so far as "individuality" embraces our innermost, last, and incomparable uniqueness, it also implies becoming one's own self. We could therefore translate individuation as "coming to selfhood" or "self-realization" ' (*CW* 7, para. 266).

Inferior function: the one of Jung's four functions (thinking, sensation, feeling and intuition) which is most unconscious and thus least developed in a given individual.

Inflation: the state of ego-centric exhilaration which can follow the eruption into consciousness of highly charged unconscious (particularly archetypal) components.

Innate releasing mechanism: postulated neuronal centre responsible for the release and co-ordination of instinctively determined patterns of behaviour when appropriate *sign stimuli* are encountered by an organism in the environment.

Learning theory: that body of psychological theory which seeks to explain human and animal behaviour in terms of learned responses to environmental stimuli; in contrast to etholgical theory, which seeks to explain it in terms of instinctual developmental processes peculiar to the species in question.

Logos principle: finds expression in rational argument, logical deduction, and use of the word to further intellectual, social or spiritual ends.

Matrism: mother-orientated social structures occurring in cultures with mother-based theologies and reflecting characteristics of the mother archetype.

Monotropy: 'a tendency for instinctual responses to be directed towards a particular individual or group of individuals and not promiscuously towards many' (Bowlby, 1958).

Numenosum: experience of the Divine.

Ontogenetic psyche: those psychic structures and functions which are peculiar to individual members of the species.

Ontogeny: the development of an individual organism through the course of its life-cycle. Contrast with *phylogeny*.

Open programme: term introduced by Ernest Mayr to designate those forms of instinctive behaviour which permit an organism to adapt appropriately to environmental variations.

Operant conditioning: learning to perform certain acts which initially occur as random or spontaneous movements through rewards (e.g. food) or punishments (e.g. electric shock).

Patrism: father-orientated social structures occurring in cultures with father-based theologies and reflecting characteristics of the father archetype.

Persona: the mask used by an actor in classical times to represent his role; used by Jung to designate the characteristic roles we individually adopt in relating to others.

Personal unconscious: term used by Jung to designate the Freudian unconscious (i.e. the unconscious aspect of the *ontogenetic psyche)* and to distinguish it from his own concept of a *collective unconscious* (or *phylogenetic pysche*).

Phenomenology: school of philosophy inspired by the work of Edmund Husserl (1859–1938). It seeks to examine conscious events without any preconceptions about their causation in order to discover their essential structures and relationships.

Phrenology: the fallacious doctrine, advanced in the nineteenth century by Gall and Spurtzheim, that the mental abilities of an individual could be deduced by measuring the size of certain bumps on his skull. Originally known as craniology.

Phylogenetic psyche: those psychic structures and functions which are characteristic of all members of the human species; in this book the term is used synonymously with Jung's term *collective unconscious*.

Phylogeny: the evolutionary origin and development of a species.

Pleasure principle: according to Freudian theory, the propensity possessed by instincts to seek their gratification regardless of all other considerations. At first the infant is totally under its influence. Only later, as the ego develops, is the pleasure principle balanced by the *reality principle* so as to produce adaptive behaviour.

Psychiatrist: a medically qualified practitioner who specializes in the treatment of mental illness by physical, psychological and social techniques. He may or may not also be a *psychotherapist* or an *analyst.*

Psychoanalyst: an analyst who subscribes to the theories and who practices the therapeutic techniques devised by Sigmund Freud.

Psychologist (academic or experimental): a pure scientist who studies all behaviour, normal and abnormal, human and animal.

Psychotherapist: an eclectic therapist who uses his own mind to treat the minds of others with or without reference to unconscious processes or using the techniques of any particular school of analysis.

Reality principle: term used by Freud to designate the constraints imposed as a result of environmental circumstances on fulfillment of the *pleasure principle.* Freud believed that the reality principle developed in the course of *ontogeny*, whereas the pleasure principle was innate and present at birth.

Reification: the treatment of ideas as though they were tangible objects.

Self: the psychic aspect of the *genome*; the entire archetypal system of the unconscious; for Jung a dynamic concept at the heart of personality development and *individuation.* 'The *self* is not only the centre but also the whole circumference which embraces both conscious and unconscious; it is the centre of this totality, just as the ego is the centre of the conscious mind' (CW 12, para. 44).

Sex chromosomes: the pair of chromosomes which determine the sex of the individual.

Shadow: Jung's term for the aspect of the Self which remains unconscious because it is repressed by the *superego* or unactivated by the environment.

Sign stimulus: a specific perceptual stimulus possessing the capacity to trigger a specific *innate releasing mechanism.*

Superego: term introduced by Freud to designate the inner moral authority or ethical complex which monitors individual behaviour in such a way as to make it acceptable first to the parents and later to society.

Soteriology: the study of salvation.

Symbiosis: the union of two organisms, each of which depends for its existence on the other.

Syneidesis: term used by von Monakow (1950) to designate his concept of a 'biological conscience'. It is argued here that this is synonymous with the archetypal basis of Freud's *superego.*

Temenos: a sacred enclosure or precinct.

Testosterone: male hormone.

Transcendent function: Jung's term for the mutual influence which is exerted between the *ego* and the *self* in the course of personality development and *individuation*.
Tropism: 'the turning of an organism, or part of one, in a particular direction in response to some special external stimulus' (OED).
Umwelt: term introduced by von Uexküll to designate the perceptually selective and essentially subjective world in which each organism lives.
Uroborus: ancient symbol of a serpent bent in a circle and biting its own tail: considered by Erich Neumann (1954) to represent the primordial *Self* out of which ego-consciousness is born.
Weltanschauung: a philosophical view of the world as a whole.
Yang: the masculine principle of Taoist philosophy.
Yin: the feminine principle of Taoist philosophy.
Zeitgeist: spirit of the times, the consensus of thoughts, feelings and ideas prevailing at a given period.

Bibliography

AINSWORTH, M. D. (1963), 'The development of infant-mother interaction among the Ganda', in B. M. Foss, ed., *Determinants of Infant Behaviour*, vol. 2, Methuen, London.

ANDRESKI, S. (1964), 'The Origins of War', in J. D. Carthy and F. J. Ebling, eds, *The Natural History of Aggression*. Academic Press, London.

ARDREY, R. (1961), *African Genesis: A Personal Investigation into the Animal Origins and Nature of Man*, Collins, London.

ARDREY, R. (1967), *The Territorial Imperative: A Personal Inquiry into the Animal Origins of Property and Nations*, Collins, London.

ARDREY, R. (1970), *The Social Contract: A Personal Inquiry into the Evolutionary Sources of Order and Disorder*, Collins, London.

AUSTIN, M. D. (1971), 'Dream recall and the basis of intellectual ability', *Nature*, 231, p. 59–68.

BACHOFEN, J. J. (1967), *Myth, Religion, and Mother Right*, Routledge & Kegan Paul, London.

BAKAN, P. (1976), 'The Right Brain is the dreamer', *Psychology Today*, 10, pp. 66–8.

BAYNES, H. G. (1949), *Mythology of the Soul*, Methuen, London.

BENEDICT, R. (1934), *Patterns of Culture*, New American Library, Mentor, New York.

BERNSTEIN, I. S., GORDON, T. P., and ROSE, R. M. (1974), 'Factors influencing the expression of aggression during introductions to rhesus monkey groups', in R. L. Holloway, ed., *Primate Aggression, Territoriality and Xenophobia: A Comparative Perspective*, Academic Press, New York, pp. 211–40.

BETTELHEIM, B. (1955), *Symbolic Wounds*, Thames & Hudson, London.

BILLER, H. B. (1974), *Paternal Deprivation*, Lexington Books, Lexington, Mass.

BLUMENTHAL, A. L. (1977), *The Process of Cognition*, Prentice-Hall, Homewood, New Jersey.

BOGEN, J. E. (1969), 'The other side of the brain: an appositional mind', *Bulletin of the Los Angeles Neurological Societies*, 34, pp. 135–62.

BOOKER, C. (1980), *The Seventies: Portrait of a Decade*, Allen Lane, London.

BOWLBY, J. (1951), *Maternal Care and Mental Health*, WHO, Geneva; HMSO, London; Columbia University Press, New York.

BOWLBY, J. (1958), 'The nature of the child's tie to his mother', *International Journal of Psycho-Analysis*, 39, pp. 350–73.

BOWLBY, J. (1969), *Attachment and Loss. Volume 1: Attachment*, Hogarth Press and the Institute of Psycho-Analysis, London.

BOWLBY, J. (1973), *Attachment and Loss, Volume 2, Separation: Anxiety and Anger*, Hogarth Press and the Institute of Psycho-Analysis, London.

BOWLBY, J. (1979), *The Making and Breaking of Affectional Bonds*, Tavistock Publications, London.

BRONFENBRENNER, U. (1975), 'Who cares for America's children?', unpublished manuscript, Cornell University, cited by Lamb (1976).

BROWN, G. W., and HARRIS, T. (1978), *Social Origins of Depression*, Tavistock Publications, London.

BURTON, R. V. (1972), 'Cross-sex identity in Barbados', *Developmental Psychology*, 6, pp. 365–74.

CAMPBELL, J. (1949), *The Hero With A Thousand Faces*, Pantheon, New York.

DARWIN, C. (1859), *On the Origin of Species by means of Natural Selection*, John Murray, London.

DARWIN, C. (1871), *The Descent of Man and Selection in Relation to Sex*, John Murray, London.

DARWIN, C. (1872), *The Expression of the Emotions in Man and Animals*, John Murray, London.

DAVIE, M. R. (1929), *The Evolution of War*, Yale University Press, New Haven.

DAWKINS, R. (1976), *The Selfish Gene*, Paladin, London.

DEIKMAN, A. (1971), 'Bimodial consciousness', *Archives of General Psychiatry*, 125, pp. 481–9.

DEVORE, I., and KONNER, M. J. (1974), 'Infancy in hunter-gatherer life: an ethological perspective', in N. F. White, ed., *Ethology and Psychiatry*, University of Toronto Press, pp. 113–141.

DOLLARD, J., and MILLER, N. E. (1950), *Personality and Psychotherapy*, McGraw-Hill, New York.

DURBIN, E. F. M., and BOWLBY, J. (1938), 'Personal aggressiveness and war', in E. F. M. Durbin and G. Catlin, eds, *War and Democracy: Essays on the Causes and Prevention of War*, Kegan Paul, London.

DUVERGER, M. (1955), *The Political Role of Women*, UNESCO, Paris.

EATON, G. G. (1976), 'The social order of Japanese macaques'. *Scientific American*, 235, pp. 97–106.

EDINGER, E. F. (1972), *Ego and Archetype*, Putnam, New York.

EIBL-EIBESFELDT, I. (1971), *Love and Hate*, Methuen, London.

ELIADE, M. (1958), *Birth and Rebirth: The Religious Meanings of Initiation in Human Culture*, Harper, New York.

ELIADE, M. (1960), *Myths, Dreams and Mysteries*, Harvill Press, London.

ELIADE, M. (1980), 'A conversation with Mircea Eliade', *Encounter*, London, vol. LIV, no. 3, pp. 21–7.

ERIKSON, E. H. (1959), *Identity and the Life Cycle*, Psychological Issues, vol. I, no. 1, Monograph 1, International Universities Press, New York.

ERIKSON, E. H. (1962), *Young Man Luther: A Study in Psychoanalysis and History*, Norton, New York.

FENICHEL, O. (1946), *The Psychoanalytic Theory of Neurosis*, Routledge & Kegan Paul, London.
FLOR-HENRY, P. (1976), 'Lateralized temporal-limbic dysfunction and psychopathology', *Annals of the New York Academy of Sciences*, vol. 380, pp. 777–97.
FORDHAM, M. (1957), *New Developments in Analytical Psychology*, Routledge & Kegan Paul, London.
FORDHAM, M. (1964), 'The relation of the Ego to the Self', *British Journal of Medical Psychology*, vol. XXXVII, pp. 89–102.
FOX, R. (1967), *Kinship and Marriage*, Penguin, Harmondsworth.
FOX, R. (1975), *Encounter With Anthropology*, Peregrine, London.
FRANKL, V. E. (1965), *Man's Search for Meaning: An Introduction to Logotherapy*, Washington Square Press, New York.
FRAZER, SIR JAMES G. (1926), *The Worship of Nature* (The Gifford Lectures, University of Edinburgh, 1924–57), New York.
FREEMAN, D. (1964), 'Human aggression in anthropological perspective', in J. D. Carthy and F. J. Ebling, eds, *The Natural History of Aggression*, Academic Press, London.
FREUD, A. (1946), 'The psychoanalytic study of infantile feeding disturbances', *Psycho-Analytic Study of the Child*, 2, pp. 119–32.
FREUD, S. (1905), *Three Essays on the Theory of Sexuality, Standard Edition*, vol. 7, Hogarth, London.
FREUD, S. (1930), *Civilization and its Discontents, Standard Edition.* Vol. 21, Hogarth, London.
FREUD, S. (1933), *New Introductory Lectures on Psycho-Analysis, Standard Edition*, vol. 22, Hogarth Press, London.
FROMM, E. (1942), *The Fear of Freedom*, Routledge & Kegan Paul, London.
GALIN, D. (1974), 'Implications for psychiatry of left and right cerebral specialization', *Archives of General Psychiatry*, 32, pp. 572–83.
GAZZANIGA, M. S. (1973), 'The Split brain in man', in R. Ornstein, ed., *The Nature of Human Consciousness*, Freeman, New York.
GLUECK, B. C., and STROEBEL, C. F. (1975), 'Biofeedback and meditation in the treatment of psychiatric illness', *Comprehensive Psychiatry*, 16, pp. 303–21.
GODWIN, B. C. (1972), 'Biology and meaning', in C. H. Waddington ed., *Towards a Theoretical Biology*, vol. 4.
GOLDBERG, S. (1973), *The Inevitability of Patriarchy*, Maurice Temple Smith, London.
GORER, G. (1966), 'Psychoanalysis in the world', in C. Rycroft, ed., *Psychoanalysis Observed*, Constable, London.
GUGGENBUHL-CRAIG, A. (1971), *Power in the Helping Professions*, Spring Publications, New York.
GUGGENBUHL-CRAIG, A. (1977), *Marriage, Dead or Alive*, Spring Publications, Zurich.
HARDING, E. M. (1948), *Woman's Mysteries, Ancient and Modern*, Longmans, London.
HARLOW, H. F., and HARLOW, M. K. (1965), 'The Affectional systems', in A. M. Schrier, H. F. Harlow and F. Stollnitz, eds, *Behaviour of Nonhuman Primates*, Academic Press, London.

HENDERSON, J. L. (1967), *Thresholds of Initiation*, Wesleyan University Press, Middleton, Connecticut.
HENRY, J. P. (1977), 'Comment' (on 'The cerebral hemispheres in analytical psychology' by Rossi), *Journal of Analytical Psychology*, 22, pp. 52–7.
HENRY, J. P., and STEPHENS, P. M. (1977), *Stress, Health and the Social Environment: A Sociobiological Approach to Medicine*, Springer-Verlag, New York.
HERMANN, I. (1933), 'Zum Triebleben der Primaten', *Imago*, 19, p. 113.
HERZOG, E. and SUDIA, C. (1970), *Boys in Fatherless Families*, US Department of Health, Education and Welfare, Washington, D.C.
HINDUS, M. (1943), *Mother Russia*, Collins, London.
HOCHHEIMER, W. (1969), *The Psychotherapy of C. G. Jung*, Barrie & Rockliff, London.
HUTT, C. (1972), *Males and Females*, Penguin, Harmondsworth.
JACOBI, J. (1942) *The Psychology of C. G. Jung*, Routledge & Kegan Paul, London.
JACOBI, J. (1959), *Complex, Archetype, Symbol*, Routledge & Kegan Paul, London.
JAFFE A. (1970), *The Myth of Meaning in the Work of C. G. Jung*, Hodder & Stoughton, London.
JENSEN, G. D. and TOLMAN, C. W. (1962), 'Mother-infant relationship in the monkey, *Macaca nemestrina*: the effect of brief separation and mother-infant specificity'. *Journal of Comparative Physiology and Psychology*, 55, 131–6.
JOUVET, M. (1975), 'The function of dreaming: a neurophysiologist's point of view', in *Handbook of Psychobiology*, ed. M. S. Gazzaniga and C. Blakemore, Academic Press, New York.
JUNG, C. G. Most quotations in the text are taken from *The Collected Works of C. G. Jung*, edited by H. Read, M. Fordham, and G. Adler, and published in London by Routledge & Kegan Paul, 1953–78, in New York by Pantheon Books, 1953–60, and the Bollingen Foundation, 1961–7, and in Princeton, New Jersey, 1967–78. Quotation sources are indicated by the volume number followed by the number of the paragraph from which the quotation is taken (e.g. CW 11, para. 146). Sources other than *The Collected Works* are here listed chronologically:
JUNG, C. G. (1909), 'Die Bedeutung des Vaters fur das Schicksal des Einzelnen', *Jahrbuch fur psychoanalytische und psychopathologische Forschungen*, I, pp. 155–73. Subsequently translated as 'The significance of the father in the destiny of the individual', *CW* 4, paras 693–744.
JUNG, C. G. (1933), *Modern Man in Search of a Soul*, Kegan Paul, London.
JUNG, C. G. (1940), *The Integration of the Personality*, Kegan Paul, London.
JUNG, C. G. (1962), *Commentary on The Secret of the Golden Flower*, trans. Cary F. Baynes, Collins and Routledge & Kegan Paul, London.
JUNG, C. G. (1963), *Memories, Dreams, Reflections*, recorded and edited by Aniela Jaffe, Collins and Routledge & Kegan Paul, London.
JUNG, C. G. (1964), *Man and his Symbols*, Aldus Books, London.
JUNG, C. G. (1971), *Psychological Reflections, A New Anthology of His*

Writings, 1905–1961, selected and ed. Jolande Jacobi, Routledge & Kegan Paul, London.

JUNG, E. (1957), *Animus and Anima*, Spring Publications, New York.

KANT, I. (1848), *Critique of Pure Reason*, William Pickering, London.

KAUFMAN, I. C., and ROSENBLUM, L. A. (1967), 'Depression in infant monkeys separated from their mothers', *Science*, 155, pp. 1030–1.

KEITH, SIR ARTHUR. (1946), *Essays on Human Evolution*, Watts, London.

KELLOG, R. (1967), 'Understanding children's art', in *Readings in Psychology Today*, CRM Books, Del Mar, California. pp. 170–9.

KEPLER, J. (1619), *Harmonices mundi*, Book IV, Augsburg, quoted by Pauli (1955).

KERENYI, C. (1967), 'The problem of evil in mythology', in the Curatorium of the C. G. Jung Institute, ed., *Evil*, Zurich.

KLAUS, M. H., JERAULD, R., KREGER, N. C., MCALPINE, W., STEFFA, M., and KENNELL, J. H. (1972), 'Maternal attachment: importance of the first post-partum days', *New England Journal of Medicine*, 286, pp. 460–3.

LAMB, M. (1976), *The Role of the Father in Child Development*, John Wiley, New York.

LANGER, S. (1967), *Mind: An Essay on Human Feeling*, Johns Hopkins Press, Baltimore.

LEDERER, W. (1964), 'Dragons, delinquents, and destiny,' *Psychological Issues*, 4, Number 3.

LEICHTY, M. M. (1960), 'The effect of father-absence during early childhood upon the Oedipal situation as reflected in young adults'. *Merrill-Palmer Quarterly*, 6, 212–7.

LEVY, J. (1974), 'Cerebral asymmetries as manifested in split brain man', in *Hemispheric Disconnection and Cerebral Function*, eds. D. M. Kinsbourne and W. L. Smith, Thomas, Springfield, Illinois.

LORENZ, K. (1977), *Behind the Mirror: A Search for a Natural History of Human Knowledge*, Methuen, London.

LUCERO, M. A. (1970), 'Lengthening of REM sleep duration consecutive to learning in the rat', *Brain Research*, *20*, 319–22.

LURIA, A. R. (1973), *The Working Brain*, Basic Books, New York.

MACLEAN, P. D. (1973), *A Triune Concept of the Brain and Behaviour*, ed. T. J. Boag and D. Campbell, University of Toronto Press.

MACLEAN, P. D. (1975), 'Brain mechanisms of primal sexual functions and related behaviour,' in M. Sandler and G. L. Gessa, eds, *Sexual Behaviour, Pharmacology and Biochemistry*, Raven, New York, pp. 1–11.

MACLEAN, P. D. (1976), 'Sensory and perceptive factors in emotional functions of the triune brain', in R. G. Grenell and S. Gabay, eds, *Biological Foundations of Psychiatry*, Raven, New York, vol. 1, pp. 177–98.

MEAD, M. (1935), *Sex and Temperament in Three Primitive Societies*, William Morrow, New York.

MIDGLEY, M. (1979), *Beast and Man: The Roots of Human Nature*, Harvester Press, Hassocks, Sussex.

MITSCHERLICH, A. (1969), *Society Without the Father: A Contribution to Social Psychology*, Tavistock Publications, London.

MONAKOW, C. VON. (1950), *Gehirn und Gewissen, Brain and Conscience*, Morgarten, Zurich.

MONEY, J., and ERHARDT, A. (1972), *Man and Woman: Boy and Girl*, Johns Hopkins Press, Baltimore.

MORRIS, D. (1967), *The Naked Ape*, Jonathan Cape, London.

MORRIS, D. (1970), *The Human Zoo*, Jonathan Cape, London.

MORRIS, D. (1971), *Intimate Behaviour*, Jonathan Cape, London.

MOYNIHAN, D. P. (1965), *The Negro Family: The Case for National Action*, US Department of Labour, Washington, DC.

MURDOCK, G. P. (1945), 'The common denominator of culture', in *The Science of Man in the World Crisis*, ed. R. Linton, Columbia University Press, New York.

MURDOCK, G. P., and WHITE, D. R. (1969) Standard cross cultural sample, *Ethnology*, 8, pp. 329–69.

MURPHY, R. F. (1957), 'Intergroup hostility and social cohesion', *American Anthropology*, 59, p. 1028.

NEUMANN, E. (1954), *The Origins and History of Consciousness*, Pantheon, New York.

NEUMANN, E. (1955), *The Great Mother: An Analysis of the Archetype*, Routledge & Kegan Paul, London.

NEUMANN, E. (1973), *The Child: Structure and Dynamics of the Nascent Personality*, Hodder & Stoughton, London.

NISBET, A. N. (1974), *The Sociology of Emile Durkheim*, Oxford University Press, London and New York.

NISBETT, A. (1976), *Konrad Lorenz*, Dent, London.

OLDS, J. (1974), in W. R. Adey, ed., *Brain Mechanisms and the Control of Behaviour*, Heinemann Educational Books, London.

ORNSTEIN, R. E. (1972), *The Psychology of Consciousness*, Freeman, San Francisco.

PARKES, C. M. (1973), 'Factors determining the persistence of phantom pain in the amputee', *Journal of Psychosomatic Research*, 17, pp. 97–108.

PARSONS, T., and BALES, R. F. (1955), *Family, Socialization and Interaction Process*, Free Press, Chicago, Illinois.

PAULI, W. (1955), 'The influence of archetypal ideas on the scientific theories of Kepler', in C. G. Jung, and W. Pauli, *The Interpretation of Nature and the Psyche*, Routledge & Kegan Paul, London.

PLATO, *The Symposium*, Penguin, Harmondsworth.

RIESMAN, D. (1952), *The Lonely Crowd*, Yale University Press, New Haven.

ROBSON, K. S. (1967), 'The role of eye-to-eye contact in maternal-infant attachment', *Journal of Child Psychology and Psychiatry*, 8, pp. 13–25.

ROSSI, E. (1977), 'The cerebral hemispheres in analytical psychology', *Journal of Analytical Psychology*, 22, pp. 32–51.

RUSSELL, P. (1979), *The Brain Book*, Routledge & Kegan Paul, London.

SAGAN, C. (1977), *The Dragons of Eden*, Hodder & Stoughton, London.

SCHAFFER, H. R., and EMERSON, P. E. (1964), 'The development of social attachments in infancy', *Monographs of the Society for Research in Child Development*, vol. 29, no. 3, pp. 1–77.

SCHWARTZ, G. E., DAVIDSON, R. J., and MAER, F. (1975), 'Right hemisphere lateralization for emotion in the human brain: interactions with cognition', *Science*, 190, pp. 286–8.

SEXTON, P. C. (1969), *The Feminized Male*, Random House, New York.

SHELLEY, M. (1839), *Frankenstein*, Richard Bentley, London.

SINNOTT, E. W. (1955), *Biology of the Spirit*, Viking Press, New York.

SINNOTT, E. W. (1957), *Matter, Mind and Man*, vol. XI in the 'World Perspectives' series, Harper, New York.

SMITH, C. I., KITAHAMA, K., VALATX, J. L., and JOUVET, M. (1974), 'Increased paradoxical sleep in mice during acquisition of a shock avoidance task', *Brain Research*, 77, pp. 221–30.

SOMMER, R. (1966), 'Man's proximate environment', *Journal of Social Issues*, 22, pp. 59–70.

SPENCER, SIR HERBERT (1904), *The Principles of Ethics*, Williams & Norgate, London.

SPERRY, R. W. (1968), 'Hemisphere disconnection and unity in conscious awareness', *American Psychologist*, 23, pp. 723–33.

SPITZ, R. A. (1965), *The First Year of Life*, International Universities Press, New York.

SPITZ, R. A., and WOLF, K. M. (1946), 'The Smiling response: a contribution to the ontogenesis of social relations', *Genetic Psychology Monograph*, 34, pp. 57–125.

STOKER, B. (1904), *Dracula*, Constable, London.

STORR, A. (1968), *Human Aggression*, Allen Lane, London.

STORR, A. (1973), *Jung*, Fontana, London.

SUTTIE, I. D. (1935), *The Origins of Love and Hate*, Kegan Paul, London.

TAYLOR, G. R. (1972), *Rethink*, Secker & Warburg, London.

TAYLOR, G. R. (1979), *The Natural History of the Mind*, Secker & Warburg, London.

TEIT, J. A. (1900), *The Thompson Indians of British Columbia*, ed. F. Boas, The American Museum of Natural History Memoires vol. II, Jesup North Pacific Expedition Publications, New York.

TINBERGEN, N. (1951), *The Study of Instinct*, Oxford University Press, London.

TIGER, L. (1969), *Men in Groups*, Random House, New York.

TIGER, L., and FOX, R. (1972) *The Imperial Animal*, Secker & Warburg, London.

TURNBULL, C. M. (1972), *The Mountain People*, Simon & Schuster, New York.

TYLER, L. (1965), *The Psychology of Human Differences*, 3rd edn, New York, Appleton-Century-Crofts.

VAN GENNEP, A. (1960), *The Rites of Passage*, Routledge & Kegan Paul, London.

VON FRANZ, M.-L. (1970), *The Problem of the Puer Aeternus*, Spring Publications, Zurich.

VON FRANZ, M.-L. (1974), *Shadow and Evil in Fairytales*, Spring Publications, Zurich.

VON FRANZ, M.-L. (1975), *C. G. Jung: His Myth in our Time*, Hodder & Stoughton, London.

VON DER HEYDT, V. (1973), 'On the father in psychotherapy', in *Fathers and*

Mothers, Five Papers on the Archetypal Background of Family Psychology, ed. P. Berry, Spring Publications, Zurich.

WADDINGTON, C. H. (1957), *The Strategy of the Genes: A Discussion of Some Aspects of Theoretical Biology*, George Allen & Unwin, London.

WALLACE, A. F. C. (1966), *Religion: An Anthropological View*, Random House, New York.

WASHBURN, S. L., and HAMBURG, D. A. (1968), 'Aggressive behaviour in old world monkeys and apes', in P. Jay, ed., *Primates: Studies in Adaptation and Variability*, Holt, New York, pp. 458–68.

WATSON, J. D. (1968), *The Double Helix: A Personal Account of the Discovery of the Structure of DNA*, Weidenfeld & Nicolson, London.

WHITING, B. (ed.) (1963), *Six Cultures: Studies of Child Rearing*, Wiley.

WHITMONT, E. C. (1969), *The Symbolic Quest*, Barrie & Rockliff, London.

WILHELM, R. (trans.) (1951), *The I Ching or Book of Changes*, English translation by C. F. Baynes, Routledge & Kegan Paul, London.

WILHELM, R. (1962), *The Secret of the Golden Flower*, Collins and Routledge & Kegan Paul, London.

WILSON, E. O. (1975), *Sociobiology: The New Synthesis*, The Belknap Press of Harvard University Press, Cambridge Massachusetts, and London.

WILSON, E. O. (1978), *On Human Nature*, Harvard University Press, Cambridge, Massachusetts, and London.

WOLFF, A. (1956), *Structural Forms of the Feminine Psyche*, privately printed in Zurich, quoted by Whitmont (1969).

Index